The *Simple Art of*
Perfect Baking

By

Flo Braker

Photography by

Alan Richardson

Illustrations by

Kristee Rosendahl

CHAPTERS™

CHAPTERS PUBLISHING LTD., SHELBURNE, VERMONT 05482

Published by
Chapters Publishing Ltd.
2031 Shelburne Road
Shelburne, Vermont 05482

Library of Congress Cataloguing-in-Publication Data

Braker, Flo
        The simple art of perfect baking / by Flo Braker ;
    photography by Alan Richardson ; illustrations by Kristee Rosendahl.
        —Updated and rev.
            p.   cm.
        Includes bibliographical references and index.
        ISBN 0-9631591-3-5 : $24.95 — ISBN 0-9631591-2-7 (pbk.) : $19.95
        1. Baking.   2. Desserts.   I. Title.
    TX763.B76   1992
    641.8 ' 65—dc20   92-11095
                                                                            CIP

Trade distribution by
Firefly Books Ltd.
250 Sparks Avenue
Willowdale, Ontario
Canada M2H 2S4

Printed and bound in Canada by
Friesen Printers
Altona, Manitoba

Designed by Hans Teensma / Impress

Cover photograph by Alan Richardson: Charlotte Malakoff, page 182

To my honey

Acknowledgments

~

Writing a cookbook," says my friend Marion Cunningham, "is like cooking an elephant—an inch at a time." The writing of this book encompasses far more than the three years it took to produce a manuscript. Without my knowledge, it actually began thirty years ago. A large elephant, indeed.

The Simple Art of Perfect Baking is, more than anything, the result of my interaction with many wonderful people—whether in a book, a class or a chef's kitchen. Their knowledge, inspiration and support helped to evolve the ideas, techniques and recipes captured in the following pages. I take great pleasure in expressing my thanks and gratitude to some of the people who influenced my creativity, learning and growth. I also mention throughout the book other people whose insights on baking have had an influence for adaptation or inspiration. If I have overlooked anyone, I'm sincerely sorry.

In the early years when I baked alone in my kitchen for family, friends and a small baking business, books by Jim Beard, Julia Child, Craig Claiborne, John Clancy, Michael Field, Madeleine Kamman, Helen McCully and Paula Peck kept me company.

To my good fortune during this period of time, a loving friend, the late Ruth Lee Kolm, who shared my insatiable interest in baking, taught me all she knew about pie making.

A special thanks to Jack Lirio, with whom I shared three exciting years teaching pastry classes in San Francisco; this was an extremely influential period for my baking.

The challenge of teaching, answering baking queries and following recipes put me in contact with some of the most enthusiastic, intelligent people I have ever met: my students. Their feedback has spurred me to gather more baking information. Although I have supposedly been the teacher, I have actually been the beneficiary because I have learned so much from them.

Several other professionals gave me invaluable help.

At Jim Nassikas's Stanford Court Hotel in San Francisco, Jim Beard and his classes were challenging and brought me in contact with the superb pastry chefs Bruno Leutzinger and Jim Dodge; in Beard's beloved Seaside, Oregon, I baked cakes and pastries with some of the area's divine ingredients.

Jacques Pépin taught me more about baking while I learned French cooking.

Michael James's and Billy Cross's Great Chefs of France at the Mondavi Winery in Napa, California, provided an education from the French master chefs Jean Troisgros, Michel Guérard and Gaston Lenôtre.

The weeks I spent at École Lenôtre in Plaisir, France, and Richemont Professional School in Lucerne, Switzerland, were invaluable.

As I began to crystallize my baking experiences for this book, several talented people to whom I will always be grateful helped my dream come true.

Susan Lescher, my literary agent, who made my book possible and wisely suggested its direction.

Kristee Rosendahl, who transformed my desserts and techniques into magnificent illustrations and gave me a visual perspective.

Cindy Rink, my wordsmith, not only worked on my text but with her incredible intuition helped me understand what it was I wanted to say.

How lucky I was to have Shirley Rosenberg on the West Coast and Anne de Ravel on the East Coast tirelessly testing and retesting my recipes.

Debbie Peters, Karen Smythe, Doug Basegio and Gayle Ortiz, Alice Cox and Karen Ross made valuable contributions.

Jan Weimer, Barbara Tropp and Oona Aven have been a constant source of encouragement long before the first words of this book were on paper.

Gloria Adelson, with her unique taste and creativity, designed the jacket of the first edition.

From the beginning, the editor of the first edition of this book, Maria Guarnaschelli, an excellent teacher herself, understood and supported the teaching approach I wanted this book to have. With her interest in good writing and good food, she involved herself completely in molding my book with passionate enthusiasm and tireless attention to detail, for which I will be forever grateful.

My thanks to Kathy Jankowski and my other friends at William Morrow and Company for making the first edition of this book possible.

And through it all, Casey Carsten and Nancy Wiener were always there with incredible wisdom and humor.

Hazel Prince, with her special kindness, saw, tasted and heard it all.

To all my good friends who put up with my reclusive Rapunzel act in the kitchen tower, I couldn't have done it without you.

Updating and revising *The Simple Art of Perfect Baking* has been an absolute pleasure. Sincere gratitude to Barry Estabrook, editor-in-chief of Chapters Publishing, and to Barbara Kafka and Corby Kummer, who have championed the book since it first came out. Heartfelt thanks to fellow professionals Alan Richardson, Anne Disrude, Betty Alfenito, Evie Righter, Debbie Sachs, Michael Bauer and Adrienne Welch. Warm affection to Rux Martin, an ideal editor. I appreciate her hard work and innovative suggestions. It's through her eyes that I could see the book afresh.

I also wish to thank my mother and father, from whom I learned my love of food and an eye for detail, along with a philosophy that guided me through writing this book.

To my husband, Dave, who never doubted for one moment that I could do it, and our children Jeff and Julie, I can never say thank you enough.

And to all dedicated bakers, young and old, amateur and professional, from my heart, I salute you.

Flo Braker

Contents

~

Fillings, Frostings, Glazes, Toppings and Finishing Touches

Understanding Pastrymaking

Resources

Introduction

HAVE YOU ever had the same cake recipe produce different results? Have you thrown the cake away, blaming the recipe? My first years of cakemaking were filled with such events. I baked from recipes in every book available. Why did a recipe tell me to stir in the dry ingredients quickly with few strokes? Why did it tell me to pour the batter into the prepared baking pan, then let it sit for 20 minutes before baking? Why did I have to alternate the dry and liquid ingredients, beginning and ending with the dry? And if something went wrong, why?

How could I achieve a tender and flaky pie crust that no one would leave on the plate? I thought it wonderful that adding just a tablespoon of water could produce a cohesive pie dough, but why did it crumble and fall apart after it was baked?

I thought that because I was a conscientious baker, used the best ingredients and the proper utensils and followed the directions carefully, my results should have been perfect.

Now I know that the process involves more than magic. It really means attention to details such as precise measuring, correct oven temperatures and specific rack placement. It means polishing your skills, such as piping with a pastry bag. It also involves a bit of chemistry since each ingredient affects the results.

I wanted desperately to learn how the professionals made desserts and how they assembled and decorated them.

I tried to duplicate hundreds of glazes, textures and decorations in my own kitchen. Most of the time, the process was difficult because my first goal was that the dessert taste delicious, my second that it make a pretty presentation. I made mistakes, but my frustration became a challenge. I visited bakeries and quizzed bakers in the United States and in half a dozen European countries, took classes and did research into such ingredients as chocolate and sugar. The history associated with the world's most famous desserts was awe inspiring.

I brought home each country's sugar, flour and chocolate and experimented with them in both European and American recipes to test whether their ingredients were different from ours. When they differed, I learned how to adapt American ingredients in order to duplicate the textures and flavors I had tasted in Europe. I was not interested so much in reproducing specific recipes as in mastering European techniques to help in my baking. My own style has evolved into a blend of the traditional European approaches and American methods.

Since those early days of experimentation, baking has changed dramatically. The gap between the home baker and the professional has narrowed. Each has learned from the other. The home baker can now buy heavy-duty equipment and employ professional techniques. Professional bakers now use better ingredients, and although they still decorate ornately, the effect and taste are simpler and less rich than before. Often their best sellers are the cakes or pies we home cooks have been baking for years.

My book is designed to take the fear and unpredictability out of baking, to give you continually successful results in your own home. Appearance, though an important expression of pride in the desserts a home cook presents, is second to taste. Decorations can disguise an imperfectly shaped cake, but they won't change a bad texture or flavor.

For those of you who think assembling spectacular desserts cannot be part of modern life, I'll show you how easy it is to make them at different stages of time. The recipes that follow provide the kind of information you will need in order to learn how to judge for yourself the time required for each step and when you should move on to the next one. No one can tell you how long it will take you to stir in the flour or roll out the piecrust. But I can tell you what to look for when it is time to add the flour to the cake batter or the water to the piecrust or about how long a standard electric mixer will take to whip a precise number of large eggs to a specific consistency. I describe the consistency of the doughs and how to handle them. I give details for filling pans with batter and resting doughs. I tell you what to look for when you have to judge doneness. I give information on cooling, storing, when to frost, how to frost, how to finish. And always I try to provide the reasons why, so that when my instructions vary or are inconsistent with a similar recipe, you will have insight into the whole baking process.

The recipes in this book are for everyday as well as special occasions. Some require more time than others. I have provided all sorts of baking and pastry ideas, some classic, some modern. My hope is that you will feel free to interchange the cakes and frostings, pastries and fillings and decorations and finishing touches to create your own masterpieces or to make your family heirloom recipe the best it can be.

Perfectly Simple Favorites

Many cakes in this book are not difficult to prepare and are designated with the symbol ❆. These, however, are my favorites, the ones that I bake again and again, and the most requested by my friends and colleagues.

The "Secrets" of Perfect Baking

MEASURE ACCURATELY

WHEN PEOPLE ask me why their cake or pastry didn't turn out, I retrace all their steps and invariably discover they have measured inaccurately. If you want perfect results, you have to be meticulous about measuring. Although this point may seem obvious, many otherwise knowledgeable cooks do not know how to measure correctly. Often they do not realize, for instance, that there are two different types of measuring cups: one for liquid and one for dry ingredients. These two kinds of cups are not interchangeable. Many mistakes in baking result from the simple mistake of measuring dry ingredients in a Pyrex measuring cup (See page 15 for the correct use of measuring cups.)

Whatever method you choose to measure ingredients, be consistent. Either weigh all the ingredients on a scale or measure them all in measuring cups—don't do both.

Buy a Scale. Although precise measurement is possible with measuring cups, a scale makes measuring not only consistently accurate but also easier.

Measure Flour on a Scale. For years, the accepted procedure for precisely measuring flour for cakes meant sifting the flour first, then scooping it into a measuring cup and leveling it off with a knife. The next step required resifting the flour to remove lumps or to distribute it evenly with the baking powder and salt. Sifting 3 cups of flour twice is not fun.

When you weigh flour on a scale, you eliminate the first reason for sifting. Not only is measuring by weight fast and easy, but it leaves no room for error. I have seen people measure flour many ways: One cook dips the measuring cup directly into the bag of flour, then levels it off with a finger; another scoops up the flour and pours it into the measuring cup, taps it on the counter, then levels it off with a metal icing spatula. These are two different amounts of flour, even though the cup is the same.

When you use a scale, you are always certain you have exactly 1 cup of flour—no more, no less. For equivalent measures of flour in cups, ounces and grams, see page 389.

Measure Sugar on a Scale. Once you use a scale to measure brown sugar, you'll wonder why you haven't been weighing it all your life. Like flour, granulated sugar can pack unevenly in a measuring cup. Recipes demand that you "pack" brown sugar only to ensure accurate measurement. One cup of brown sugar weighs the same as 1 cup of granulated sugar, provided it is packed: 200 grams. Measure all sugars exactly as you would flour. With a scale, you can weigh 1 cup of powdered sugar, then sift it to break up lumps. Though 1 cup of powdered sugar weighs half the amount (100 grams) of 1 cup of granulated sugar, they are comparable in sweetness. (The recipes provide weight and volume measurement for sugar.) See Measure and Weight Equivalents, page 390.

Measure Eggs on a Scale. When I travel to different parts of the country to teach baking, I often discover differences from region to region in the size of "large" eggs.

When you make a pastry cream, the size of the egg can vary without causing great harm, but for some cakes, such as Classic American Spongecake (page 152), the size of the egg is crucial to success. "Large" eggs (the kind I call for in all the recipes), in the shell, should weigh 2 ounces apiece. By law, each dozen of "large" eggs must weigh at least 24 ounces. But their individual weights may vary; a dozen may include some eggs over 2 ounces, some under. If I am in doubt, I weigh them. If I find I need to compensate, I can mix 1 egg in a small bowl and use as much of it as I need to equal the amount needed for the recipe. If you usually buy "medium" or "small" eggs, a scale is worth its weight in gold. You can continue to buy the size you prefer, and when you bake, weigh your eggs until they are equivalent to the "large" variety (2 ounces each).

Weigh Every Ingredient You Can. Once you get into the habit of using a scale, as the professionals do, you'll find yourself using it for many other dessert ingredients, such as nuts, cocoa powder, butter, solid shortening, almond paste, chocolate, even apples and pears. Many of these items are labeled or sold by weight in the grocery store.

Furthermore, using a scale helps eliminate errors when dividing or doubling recipes. I also use my scale to weigh each filled cake pan to make sure the batter is equally distributed before I put it in the oven. Having become aware of the weight of ingredients, you then become sensitive to their proportions. Patterns, such as the balance of eggs to sugar, or sugar to nuts, begin to emerge.

Test Your Scale. I own several scales, but my favorite is the one whose platform is large enough to hold my mixing bowl. I just adjust the dial until 0 is even with the pointer and pour in the ingredient I need to weigh, such as flour or a specific amount of filling, glaze or cream. Testing your scale's accuracy is simple. One pint of water weighs a pound. Therefore, water weighing 8 ounces on your scale also measures 8 ounces by volume in a Pyrex measuring cup.

Use Measuring Cups Correctly. Precise measurement is possible with measuring cups, provided you use them properly. You must be certain your utensils and techniques for measuring are appropriate for what you are measuring. Dry and liquid measuring cups are different. Their cost is not an indicator of their accuracy. Stainless steel measuring cups with a flat lip, which come in graduated sizes, are for dry ingredients, and a Pyrex measuring cup is used for liquid ingredients.

I am often asked why a metal (dry-ingredient) measuring cup can't be used for liquids, since a cup is a cup. Using a metal measuring cup is fine if you're adding a cup of beef stock to Hungarian goulash; an ounce either way isn't going to make much difference. But liquids do not level off with the same degree of accuracy as dry ingredients, and the extra moisture can ruin your puff pastry.

Measuring dry ingredients in a liquid measuring cup is highly inaccurate. A woman hired me for a private lesson to help her with a cake recipe, which had repeatedly failed her. The problem was simple to diagnose: She measured the flour into a Pyrex measuring cup and tapped the container until the flour was level with the mark for a cup. When liquid measuring cups are used to measure flour, they can produce variations of as much as ¼ cup.

How do you accurately measure flour without a scale? When you bring flour home from the store, empty the entire bag into a large container, such as an apothecary jar or an airtight plastic box, making it accessible as well as insulating it from moisture. Your package of all-purpose flour probably says "presifted." Disregard that information, and consider it unsifted, since each package is stacked, packed and thrown around in being transported to your local grocery store. (The label "presifted" is misleading. I recently received a postcard from a puzzled cook asking where to buy unsifted flour for one of my recipes.)

To Sift Flour: You need to sift flour to remove lumps and to distribute evenly any other ingredients to be combined with it. When you are ready to measure, scoop some flour into a triple sifter. Now sift the flour onto a sheet of waxed paper. A triple sifter is imperative because the flour passes through three screens before reaching the waxed paper. If you use a single screen sifter, the flour may appear to have no lumps, but its granules have not been broken up finely. When you come to fold this flour into the batter for a génoise, it will not disperse as finely as it should. Tiny balls of flour, the size of miniature pearls, will then form during baking. Because the flour doesn't distribute properly, the cake's volume is affected. (If you don't own a triple sifter, sift the flour three times through a single-screen sifter.)

Scoop enough into your dry measuring cup until it mounds sightly over the top; then level it off with a flat metal spatula used for icing. This sifted flour is as precise a measurement as you can get without a scale. Scooping flour into a measuring cup and leveling it, without sifting first, will yield more flour than is called for in the recipes.

To Measure Sugar Accurately: Measuring powdered sugar calls for the same procedure as flour. When measuring granulated sugar, I pour the bag of sugar into a sturdy container. If I notice any lumps, I let the sugar flow through a sieve. I scoop it into the measuring cup as I do for flour and level it off with a metal icing spatula. I keep brown sugars in airtight plastic containers at room temperature to prevent their drying out and lumping too quickly. Brown sugar will also lump if it is stored in too cold a place.

To Measure Liquids Accurately: How do you measure liquids such as water, corn syrup, yogurt, even egg yolks and whites accurately? Pour the liquid ingredient into a Pyrex measuring cup; then determine by eye whether you have the exact amount. For instance, 5 large eggs equal 1 cup at eye level, 5 large egg yolks equal ⅓ cup, and 5 large egg whites equal ⅔ cup.

To Measure Fat Accurately Without a Scale: If the fat is butter, the sticks are usually marked in tablespoons and weights; there are 8 tablespoons per stick. To measure a few tablespoons accurately, I recommend marking the middle of the stick first, indicating 4 tablespoons on either side. Then, measuring 2, 3 or 6 tablespoons is easy.

I measure oils in a Pyrex liquid measuring cup.

Solid shortening must be packed into a dry measuring cup.

I do not recommend measuring butter or solid shortening using the water-displacement method, in which, for instance, if you need ¼ cup solid shortening, you fill a liquid measuring cup with water to the ¾-cup mark, then add the solid shortening until the water reaches the 1-cup line. Any moisture at this time on the fat is not welcome in the cake, pastry or chocolate recipes in this book.

For equivalent measures for butter, see page 390.

Set Aside Your Own Baking Center

To reduce frustration in baking, I have set aside part of my kitchen as a baking center. A baking center need not be an expansive, lavishly designed area; it only has to be a portion of counter space, which provides a comfortable work surface for you to roll doughs, whip cream, make cakes or decorate desserts. The other necessity is two drawers, either under the work surface or in close proximity to it.

In the drawers should be the small essential utensils—your toolbox— which you may need every time you bake. The tools are always there, in one place, ready for you to use. These little gadgets can even contribute to your ability to improvise in order to save a cake or pastry. If you forget to sift the powdered sugar and your 5-inch sieve is at hand, you can simply pour the sugar through and salvage the glaze while it is still the right temperature.

I recommend 30 essential things you should always have directly at hand when you bake.

One 18-inch ruler
3 sets of metal measuring spoons
1 pastry wheel
4 long, thin metal skewers
2 table forks
1 melon baller
One 2-inch paring knife
2 extra sets of beaters for electric hand mixer
One 5-inch sieve
1 small wooden spoon
2 sets of metal measuring cups
Paper labels
Aluminum foil
Plastic wrap
1 plastic bowl scraper (corne)

6 rubber spatulas
Three 8-inch flexible metal icing spatulas
Round wooden toothpicks
One 8-inch long metal whisk
1 vegetable peeler
Five 1/2-inch (#6) round decorating tips
1 portable timer
One 16-inch plastic pastry bag
1 small container of solid shortening
1 tape measure
Two 1-cup Pyrex measuring cups
1 permanent-ink marking pen
Waxed paper
2 oven mitts
1 pastry scraper

Follow Baking Times Carefully —But Use Other Indicators Too

Preheating the oven is essential because it creates a stable temperature. Have your oven calibrated regularly, as I do, because an accurate oven temperature is vital to perfect baking.

Follow the temperatures indicated in the recipes. Can you imagine what would happen if a cake batter were baked in a 425-degree oven instead of at 350 degrees, and a pie dough were baked at 350 degrees instead of at 425 degrees? The cake batter would form a crust prematurely before expansion and leavening, so its optimum volume would be sacrificed. The pie dough, baking in the cooler oven, would not form steam quickly for flaky expansion, and the proteins would not set soon enough, so its texture would not be at its best.

Though my baking times are based on precise measurement and match the pan size I specify, I know that ovens, even those that are perfectly calibrated, have their own eccentricities. Successful baking hinges on several factors:

- ☞ Use your senses and don't be a slave to my baking times. If you smell the cake or pastry or if it is browning sooner than expected, check to see if its baking is finished.

- ☞ When a recipe specifies a range for baking times, always check for doneness after the first time has elapsed.

- ☞ If you use a different size pan or its metal gauge is heavier or lighter, baking times can be longer or shorter.

- ☞ If you double the cake recipe, an adjustment of baking time is necessary.

- ☞ Extremes of weather conditions, hot or cold, can affect your ingredients, which in turn is a factor in speeding up or slowing down the baking.

- ☞ If you own more than one oven, write down how each one bakes (any hot spots, etc.) so you can refer to these notes in case you forget.

- ☞ The toothpick test is sometimes a useful indicator, but not for every cake. Overbaked cakes will always provide a clean toothpick free of any batter.

Therefore, remember that baking times are merely guidelines. You still must be attentive. Watch the color: Is it too brown; is it dull or still shiny? Press the top center surface of the cake to feel for springiness. Prick the pastry with a toothpick or skewer to feel for crispness.

STOCK YOUR OWN BAKER'S PANTRY

WHENEVER I use an item in my baker's pantry, I replace it, which helps to make dessert-making easier, faster and more spontaneous. My freezer holds cakes and doughs. I also keep unflavored buttercreams, chocolate shavings, flakes, cigarettes and curls, unbaked streusel and cake crumbs in it. I have 5 pounds of unsalted butter always on hand and a large variety of nuts. I toast 3 to 5 pounds of hazelnuts at a time, remove their skins, and then freeze them to save time when I am ready for baking.

In my refrigerator I store Classic Fondant (page 302) up to a year, Classic Marzipan (page 304) up to 2 months, Cocoa and Chocolate-Butter glazes (page 289) up to 2 weeks. Soaking or Stock Syrup (page 302) keeps indefinitely. Lemons are there at all times—2 or 3 of them.

In airtight metal containers at room temperature, I keep Decorator's Sliced Almonds (page 270) and Classic Praline (page 308). If the weather is humid and warm, they stay for 1 week, otherwise up to 10 days.

In a dry, cool room in my house I keep a variety of chocolate. An assortment of jams and liqueurs is always available.

LEARN FROM YOUR FAILURES

Mistakes in baking may even lead you to create a new dessert, a new trend or even a new category of dessert. Do you know the story of the baker who forgot to put the butter in the dough and then attempted to undo the mistake by rolling it in? This accidentally created puff pastry is now considered one of the most delicious forms of pastry.

Should you not like the results of your cake or pastry, don't throw the dessert away. You're lucky: You can eat your mistake. Some of my less-than-perfect desserts have been served in dimly lit rooms to family and friends. The ingredients you used taste superb, so if the cake or pastry is not perfect, be content that its flavor is better than what you can get at many bakeries, and people will not know there is a problem—unless you tell them!

Though I've made many mistakes and dimmed the lights more than a few times, I haven't yet invented anything as history-making as puff pastry, but I have learned a lot. When things didn't go well for me, it was most often because I didn't take the time to complete a specific process, because in doing it I didn't know what to expect or what to look for. The recipes that follow provide the kind of information you need in order to learn to judge for yourself the time required for each step and when you should move on to the next one.

More importantly, enjoy what you've made and give yourself a pat on the back. Your cake or pie should look handmade, not machine-made.

Equipment for Perfect Baking

A BAKING recipe can provide the clearest instructions and techniques, but you can be frustrated repeatedly if you don't use the proper equipment. The correct equipment, just like the proper techniques, can simplify and streamline your baking. Acquiring the right equipment need be neither an expensive nor an exhaustive process.

MEASURING EQUIPMENT

Scales: Scales use two fundamentally different methods to establish weight: balance and spring. The balance method is more accurate since it relies on the principle of gravity, measuring the object you are weighing against another object of preestablished weight. A spring scale registers the weight of an object by calibrating the degree to which a spring inside is compressed by the weight of the object.

Whether the scale uses the balance or spring action, I prefer one that can accommodate any size bowl or pan on top, with a dial you can adjust to 0 when you weigh an item, and markings that are in ounces, grams and pounds (preferably with ¼-ounce and 5-gram intervals). I check my scale's accuracy by weighing a pound of butter.

For Measuring Dry Ingredients (Volume Measurement): For measuring dry ingredients, I use lightweight, sturdy stainless steel cups that nest inside one another easily, each with a long handle. These can be found in ⅛-, ¼-, ⅓-, ½-, 1- and 2-cup sizes.

For measuring liquids, I use 1- and 2-cup Pyrex measuring cups, with ounce, cup and pint graduations on one side and milliliters on the other side. I have more confidence in the accuracy of aluminum measuring spoons than in plastic.

THERMOMETERS

Oven Thermometers: There are two types of oven thermometers: the spring type, which has two metals that expand to move the dial, and the more accurate mercury type. I prefer the mercury thermometer in a folding case, which stands open in the oven and can register temperatures to 600 degrees.

Expect the thermometer to indicate the proper temperature only after you have preheated the oven for at least 30 minutes. If the temperature is more than 25 degrees above or below the desired setting, it is time to have your oven calibrated (see page 17). If your oven does require calibration, in the meantime you can use the thermometer to know the oven's true temperature and adjust the controls to continue baking as the recipe directs.

Room Thermometer: I keep a thermometer in my kitchen year round so I have an indication of the change in temperatures from season to season. This takes some of the guesswork out of pastrymaking, such as knowing how long it will take butter to reach various room temperatures or giving an indication of how long fillings or such glazes as Chocolate-Butter Glaze will take to set up. It also tells me whether the room is too warm for chocolate work.

Refrigerator and Freezer Thermometers: I like to keep a thermometer in both the refrigerator and the freezer. The refrigerator thermometer is especially helpful when I make puff pastry. (The best temperature for pastrymaking and storing desserts is between 48 and 42 degrees.) If the refrigerator's temperature is 48 degrees, I know how long I should rest the puff pastry before I continue with the layering process. If the refrigerator is 45 degrees, I adjust the thermostat.

It's best that the freezer temperature be 0 degrees or less for storing butter, nuts, buttercream and cake crumbs.

Food Thermometers: Food thermometers are invaluable for cooking fillings and caramelizing sugar. Always buy a mercury rather than an alcohol thermometer for reliability. For a dependable temperature reading, it's best that the thermometer's stem be covered by at least 2 inches of the food, if at all possible.

To test a food thermometer, put it into boiling water. The needle should register 212 degrees. If it doesn't, then you have to compensate—or buy a new thermometer.

Mercury Thermometers: For crème anglaise, pastry cream, buttercreams and sugar, I use a thermometer that also doubles as a deep-frying thermometer. It is mounted on stainless steel and has the stages (such as "soft ball") clearly marked. You can clip it onto the side of the pan, but I don't recommend using this feature for fillings and sugar work. I put the thermometer in the cooking mixture and hold it in place with a mitt protecting my hand. There's no need to put it in when the mixture begins to cook, but do keep in mind that some time is required to get a reading, whether it's 160 or 310 degrees. If the thermometer is inserted too late, you could have passed the desired temperature.

When I want a less bulky mercury thermometer, I use one that looks as if it belongs in a laboratory—it's merely the unmounted thermometer stem. When I'm boiling small amounts of sugar syrup for Classic Buttercream or I want to test the temperature of the cooling sugar syrup for Classic Fondant, this thermometer is useful, though fragile. I own two of these thermometers; the one that ranges from −30 to 120 degrees Fahrenheit is useful for chocolate work; the other that ranges from 0 to 300 degrees Fahrenheit is useful for fillings and sugar syrups.

Instant Bi-therm Thermometer: I find this thermometer invaluable when I need an instant reading for temperatures of butter, water for melting chocolate, the melted chocolate itself or for any mixture you can place the stem into for just a few seconds. The instant thermometer with the dial the size of a half dollar is convenient and clear for quick readings.

TIMERS

I⊤ is equally important to measure time accurately. The timer on an oven is fine for timing baking if you're going to remain in the kitchen, but I recommend a portable timer to allow you to move about. The variety is endless: timers on cords worn like a necklace, clip-on magnet types and others. The features I prefer are (a) that its buzzer is easily heard, (b) that it dings for more than a brief second and (c) that it is digital, so seconds as well as minutes and hours can be set.

I use the same timer when cooking a filling or any recipe that gives times as indicators for different stages in its preparation. For example, in the recipe for Classic Butter Cake (page 47), you cream the butter for no more than 30 to 45 seconds. I set my timer for 30 seconds and press "start" when I begin. When the time is up, I will judge if my butter is at the stage the recipe describes or whether to proceed for a few more seconds. (It may be neither possible nor convenient to set the oven timer in this instance.) If your timer has a stopwatch feature, just press "start" and stop it after 30 seconds and check the butter's consistency.

If you have a timing device that keeps tabs on three separate activities, from personal experience I suggest that you label each timer channel or you're likely to end up with the bath tub overflowing, a raw cake and the company coming sooner than you anticipated.

RULERS

No BAKER should be without an 18-inch ruler, a tape measure and yardsticks. An 18-inch ruler is imperative. It reaches across everything, whereas a 12-inch may not. In fact, the 12-inch ruler may irritate you because it may constantly touch your beautiful glaze at the wrong moment.

WORK AREAS AND SURFACES

ROLLING DOUGH, making a cake, or glazing or assembling a dessert doesn't require a large area. But it does require one that is free of clutter and at a comfortable height. I work most efficiently with a work surface 3 feet long, 1½ feet deep and about 6 to 7 inches below my waist. Years ago I had a hinged table mounted on the side of a countertop to give me additional work space. I find this especially useful when I roll doughs since I have access to it from three sides.

I've worked on almost every conceivable work surface; what you choose is personal. I began rolling on a canvas pastry cloth in a frame because it required less flour for rolling and was easy to anchor to my counter. Soon I tried other surfaces, which were definitely easier to clean as well as level, smooth and without cracks.

Formica, granite and Corian are a joy since they are smooth and easy to clean and dry. Wood is fine, especially as a cutting surface for knives, and requires less flour for rolling doughs, but it is not as easy to clean.

Marble is about 11 degrees cooler than the room, and since it conducts heat well, it absorbs any warmth from the dough or your hands and keeps the dough cool. For hot days, I have a slab of marble that matches the dimensions of my refrigerator shelf. You can also put ice on jelly roll baking pans on top of the marble to chill it.

Stainless steel is smooth and easy to clean, but I find I use more flour on this type of surface when rolling doughs; this can be undesirable for certain pastries.

Plastic polyethylene boards are easy to sterilize and portable. Though you can use them for rolling doughs, I find them most valuable for cutting chocolate into matchstick-size pieces and for cutting individual portions, or for making imprints in foil.

Electric Mixers and Food Processors

I PREFER heavy-duty electric mixers with their 3 mixing attachments—the paddle or flat beater, the whisk and the dough hook—for many recipes. I use an electric hand mixer for whipping egg whites, whipping heavy cream or for mixing together small amounts of ingredients. When switching from a less powerful mixer to the heavy-duty type, you must reduce the machine's speed almost in half to accomplish the same job.

The food processor is ideal for preparing many doughs because it doesn't incorporate much air while accomplishing the task quickly. Some recipes blend together in the food processor perfectly, but for others, the speed is too fast and you lose control.

Mixing Bowls

YOU CAN'T be too rich, too thin or own too many mixing bowls. Over the years I've collected every size and shape imaginable—and sometimes the kitchen looks as if every bowl were in use.

I recommend stainless steel bowls because they react quickly to heat and cold. The shallow 1-, 1½-, 2- and 3-quart bowls that nest inside one another are invaluable for folding and mixing. For whipping egg whites or heavy cream, I use deep U-shaped bowls since their smaller surface area allows these ingredients to be whipped quickly and efficiently. For whipping a few egg whites or 1 cup of heavy cream, I use a 1½-quart size. A bowl with a 2½-cup capacity is great for placing in a saucepan of hot water for melting glazes and chocolate. (This is a pseudo double boiler.)

A copper bowl is a natural to use with egg whites, not just because the copper's chemical reaction with the egg whites facilitates whipping but also because of its shape, which is deep and round. If you own one, you might consider whipping cream or tempering chocolate in it too, since copper is very responsive to temperature. It heats up quickly and retains the temperature after you have removed it from the source, but should you plunge it into cold water, it responds quickly and cools down. Before using the bowl, clean its surface by pouring in 1 to 2 tablespoons of salt and vinegar; rub it briefly; then rinse it with cold water and wipe it dry.

Glass or ceramic bowls are heavy and trickier to use for chilling and heating but are easy to keep greasefree. I don't recommend plastic bowls since they can retain odors and aren't greaseproof.

Grinders and Graters

Nut Grinders: Finely ground nuts are vital to many batters, doughs and fillings. Your goal is to grind the nuts quickly and avoid crushing them, so that they retain rather than exude their natural oils. You have a variety of machines to choose from, some easier to operate than others. But since I used to pound blanched almonds between the folds of a kitchen towel with the end of a rolling pin to produce finely ground nuts, I will never complain about any of the following implements.

I prefer grinding nuts in equipment that provides a chute to push them down with a plunger of plastic or metal. It can be an electric grinder (Moulinex), with a small-hole drum attachment that can also grate cheese, or one of cast iron and enameled steel that clamps onto a countertop, or a rotary grater that you hold in your hand while you turn the handle. Each instrument produces some degree of powdery, flaky nuts.

An electric herb and spice mincer, which resembles a coffee-bean grinder, produces finely grated nuts too. Process 1 to 2 ounces of nuts (not more than ¼ cup) at a time.

A food processor can also be used, but I recommend the following technique: First grate the nuts, using the grater disk, pushing the nuts down the chute with the plastic plunger. Grate only 1 to 2 ounces of nuts at a time. Then replace the grater disk with the steel blade, and process with short on/off spurts, checking the nuts' consistency at all times. When the nuts are powdery with a cornmeal-like texture, pour out this amount and continue with another.

Graters: I use a stainless steel box-shaped grater to remove the zest (the colored portion) of citrus skin or to grate fresh ginger. I use the side with the fine-shredding perforated surface, the tiny slits of which are slightly scalloped.

Sifters and Strainers

Triple Sifter: I rely on a triple sifter, in which the flour passes through 3 mesh screens and 3 agitators, sifting 3 times with one action, to separate the granules of flour, particularly when I use cake flour. It is then easier to fold in the flour and to incorporate it better into the batter. Recipes that direct you to sift the flour 2 or 3 times assume you don't have a triple sifter.

Single-Screen Sifters: These are handy for sifting brown sugar, powdered sugar and cocoa powder.

Sieves: Have a wire sieve with fine (not extrafine) mesh conveniently located in your kitchen. It can make the difference between success or failure in your dessert making. Many times I have saved such mixtures as crème anglaise, glazes, fillings or frostings by pouring or pressing them through a sieve to remove bits of cooked egg or lumps.

You can also pour powdered sugar into the sieve, then tap it with the palm of your hand to dust over a pastry or cake. Using this technique, you can control the flow of powdered sugar over the dessert better than if you use a sifter.

Other Basic Baking Utensils

Pastry Blender: A pastry blender with 4 inflexible steel cutters is my preference for cutting or blending fat into flour for pastrymaking. It not only is more efficient than using a fork and knife or your fingertips but makes better pastry because you have more control over the blending of the fat into the flour and the metal doesn't warm the fat as you work.

Pastry Cutters: Cutting puff pastry, cookie dough, sour cream pastry or tart dough with the aid of a pizza cutter and a ruler is splendid. I recommend sharpening the cutter with a knife sharpener so doughs such as puff pastry are cut neatly and cleanly.

I classify lattice cutters, pastry wheels and square or round vol-au-vent cutters as specialty cutters. They are nice to own but not essential.

Rolling Pins: When I first changed from the ball-bearing type of rolling pin (with handles) to the French type (straight and smooth without handles), I found it strange. Now that I'm used to it, I find I have more control when I roll: I can apply the amount of pressure I want and easily direct its course. There are many other types of pins, some designed specifically for puff pastry and pie doughs. But for general purposes, I use the French rolling pin the most. Besides rolling pastry, it's great for lifting and transferring doughs, beating cold butter to soften it before rolling it into puff pastry, crushing stale cake crumbs for coating cakes or shaping tuiles (cookies) from the oven before they are crisp.

Pastry Brushes: Flat pastry brushes with ½-, 1- or 1½-inch natural bristles are great for glazing cookies, cakes and pastries with jams, egg wash, melted chocolate or Translucent Sugar Glaze. I reserve a flat brush that looks like a paintbrush for brushing off excess flour on puff pastry doughs during the layering process. I mark "glazing" on the wooden handles of others so they don't get used for cooking. A pastry brush can also be used to brush away unwanted powdered sugar or crumbs from your serving plate.

Wire Whisks: The whisk, with its many wires, multiplies a single stroke to blend ingredients quickly or to incorporate air. Whipping air into egg whites requires a balloon-type whisk with rounded, springy wires, whereas blending soft butter into a ganache requires more elongated, stiffer wires. A whisk is invaluable in emulsifying ingredients quickly with melted chocolate.

Dough Spacers: In order to roll your dough to a uniform thickness and level and even to a specific width, you can remove the guesswork by placing 2 dowels or 2 cardboard strips perpendicular to the rolling pin. Each stick borders a side of the dough so the rolling pin rolls over them as it extends the dough uniformly. (You can buy a set of 6 plastic rods with 3 different thicknesses, called paddywhacks.)

Pastry Scraper: A pastry scraper is usually metal with a wooden handle, but it can also be plastic. It can be used to lift flour or doughs easily and neatly off the work surface, similar to using a slice of bread to scoop the last bits of food from a dinner plate. Many pastry chefs use the scraper as a ruler, measuring and marking sections of pastry with it. However, it is unbeatable in its primary use—scraping a work surface clean.

Bowl Scraper: The bowl scraper, or corne, is one of my favorite utensils and probably the cheapest. It's a great aid in scraping a bowl since its shape is curved like the bowl's. Scooping airy mixtures, such as a ladyfinger batter, into a pastry bag is easily accomplished with a bowl scraper. Large amounts of airy mixtures can ride on this plastic scraper as you lift them out of the bowl into a pastry bag or prepared baking pan. For this purpose, it's superior to a rubber spatula, which cannot lift as much of the mixture and requires more manipulation, which can deflate a delicate batter.

Pastry Pricker: A pastry pricker, also known as a pastry docker, with ends of nails sticking out of a wooden rod, looks like an instrument for torture. It works well for pricking puff pastry before baking.

Two novel, quick methods for pricking pastry come from two masters. Michel Guérard holds a table fork, tines downward, in each hand and alternately taps one, then the other over the puff pastry as though playing drums. Gaston Lenôtre clips the thin wires from an old whisk just where they begin to curve so it looks like a wire broom. He taps these wires gently into the puff pastry to prick it.

Rubber Spatulas: Rubber spatulas, large and small, assist in folding, smoothing batters evenly and in stirring mixtures. At times I even use them for stirring such mixtures as Classic Crème Anglaise while it is cooking. I prefer the spatula over a wooden spoon for this purpose because it doesn't absorb other flavors as wood does. Be careful you don't leave the spatula in the saucepan while you are cooking.

Scissors: Two pairs of scissors should be on hand at all times. One that looks like sewing scissors cuts thin sponge cake layers, trims ladyfingers and cuts Paris-Brest (page 384) more efficiently, quickly and neatly than a knife. A heavy-duty pair of scissors is essential for less delicate matters, such as cutting tips from pastry bags or shapes from cardboard.

Saucepans: Small (2-cup) saucepans are ideal for melting small amounts of butter or heating glazes and jams.

It's best to use a stainless steel double boiler for stovetop cooking. But for melting chocolate or chocolate glazes, I improvise with a stainless steel mixing bowl that fits securely and snugly over another mixing bowl or saucepan.

Boiling sugar syrups requires a heavy-bottomed saucepan. If you caramelize sugar often (for nougatine and caramels, for example), I recommend you invest in a 3- or 5-cup copper sugar pot. These pots are not tin-lined since the high temperature required for boiling sugar would melt any tin. The straight sides make it easier to keep them free of sugar grains, thus avoiding unwanted crystallization.

Paper Products

Waxed Paper: Waxed paper is indispensable for sifting flour and powdered sugar and for grating zests, thereby eliminating another bowl to clean. It's also convenient to roll certain sweetened short doughs between two sheets before they are refrigerated.

Aluminum Foil: Aluminum foil's flexibility and strength make it easy to mold to a shallow baking sheet's form before it is greased and floured; then, after baking, cake removal is simple. If you are baking a crisp cookie, the cookie will be released without changing its shape when it is cool and firm. It's also good to use between layers of cookies in airtight metal tins because the aluminum foil won't absorb the butter from them as would an ink blotter. Foil is also useful for piping chocolate figures because the chocolate remains shiny when it is released from it.

Parchment Paper: Parchment paper (or baking parchment) is excellent for lining cake pans and baking sheets or for marking with pencil as a guide for piping specific shapes, such as Classic Meringue. You can also fashion paper cones from parchment.

Plastic Wrap: It's easier to remove dried royal icing figures or shapes from plastic wrap than from aluminum foil. Foil's strength keeps it from giving enough to avoid cracking the piped icing.

Cardboard: Send me something in a box, and you'll think I'm a preschooler! I immediately begin making stencils and templates to decorate desserts or cutting circles and rectangles from the cardboard to use as supports for the bottoms of cakes or desserts.

Doilies: Doilies are beautiful, their variety is endless, and I used them for years. But I now prefer just a tray or plate under cakes, pastries and desserts. If you choose to use a doily, a caution: Unless you put the dessert on it just before serving, the doily can absorb butter from the dessert and make the doily look as if it had been there since yesterday or had been used before.

Ovens

Electric and Gas Ovens: Baking in either electric or gas ovens can produce excellent results. But I'm convinced that individual ovens, like people, have their own personalities. For example, two of my ovens, exactly the same model and calibrated at the same time, bake differently. One bakes hotter toward the back of the oven; the other bakes more evenly. An oven with hot spots requires that pans be turned during the baking process to avoid uneven baking. (My test for indicating if and where there are hot spots is observing how a piecrust colors while baking.)

When possible, try to use only one oven rack at a time while baking; if not, be certain to space the racks to avoid overcrowding, which affects air circulation. Leaving at least a few inches' margin between the two baking pans and the oven's walls is best for even baking; otherwise, turn the cake or pie pans while baking to compensate for uneven heating.

Check the oven temperature for accuracy. I recommend having it calibrated by your serviceman every year. Calibrating the oven usually cures uneven baking problems, but electric or gas ovens cannot maintain one temperature setting at all times. The thermostat cycles off and on in its attempt to hold the temperature you set. If the oven is too hot or too cold, it may require replacement of its thermostat rather than calibrating. Any uneven or lengthy drift in the heating cycle while you bake meringues, cake batters, cream puff pastry or puff pastry can cause a permanent loss of steam, deflating it and affecting its volume. If you detect temperature drift, have your oven checked carefully. At the same time, check to see if the oven door closes tightly and if the vent filters require cleaning. A tight oven door maintains the interior temperature, while clean filters promote good air circulation.

Convection Ovens: Both home and professional convection ovens require that the baking temperature in a recipe be adjusted 50 degrees lower, and baking time usually reduced by a third. Pan placement in the convection oven is not a sensitive issue since the air flows constantly during baking.

Microwave: Though I own a microwave oven, I do not use it a lot for baking because I feel I don't have the same control over the baking process that I do with other ovens.

BAKEWARE

Baking Pans: Each of my recipes suggests which baking pan to use, and since I believe that variety is the spice of life, I've included many different shapes and sizes of desserts, cakes and pastries. I prefer baking in aluminum or tinned steel heavy-gauge pans, but if a pan's shape is unique and it is not made of a heavy material, I can't resist using it as long as its seams are well sealed. I almost always bake in the lower third of the oven rather than at the bottom, thus keeping the pan away from the heating element. This reduces the risk of burning the batter, even with a thin-gauge pan.

Identifying baking pans by measurement is a story in itself. Some manufacturers measure their pans rim to rim, some measure sloping side pans at the bottom, and still others use outside dimensions exclusively. This lack of a measuring standard is frustrating at times.

Straight-sided layer cake pans make finishing easier when you frost the cake. A 4-x-15½-x-4-inch-deep angel loaf pan is extremely useful for making one dessert to serve for a large group.

Baking Sheets: I keep a variety of baking sheets on hand for different purposes. My favorite all-purpose baking sheet is a 12-x-15½-inch sheet with a 45-degree-angle ½-inch rim on all four sides, open at the corners. The larger variety (17 x 14 x ½ inch) is also useful. A jelly-roll pan (10 x 15 x 1 inch) is a must for baking, and in addition, it is wonderful for catching drips while glazing cakes. A rimless baking sheet is useful in making chocolate curls, chocolate strips and chocolate cigarettes, as well as acting as a large spatula to help lift a dessert. For those who like to bake doughs using the double-pan method (by stacking two identical baking sheets together) to promote even baking, a commercially made insulated baking sheet is available.

Bakeware with Removable Bottoms: An angel food tube pan, 8- and 9-inch springform pans and 8- and 9-inch fluted tin quiche pans, all with bottoms that lift out, make it possible to unmold cakes without frustration.

Bottomless Bakeware: Some baking equipment comes without any bottoms. These are forms that are set on a parchment-lined baking sheet. Some of the shapes are rectangular; others are round, square or scalloped. In these forms you can bake tart doughs either with or without a filling. During baking, the pastry contracts just enough so that removal of the form after baking is easy.

I enjoy baking cakes in an expandable cake hoop. This is a strip of black steel or stainless steel about 2 inches high and up to 14 inches in diameter that is set on top of a baking sheet and filled with batter. After baking, the same hoop is used to assemble the cake with a filling, such as a Bavarian cream, and then refrigerated until set; it is then simply unmolded.

Piepans: Many different piepans are available, but I find a 9-inch Pyrex pie plate with sloping sides conducts the heat quickly and offers the advantage of letting me see the color of the bottom crust before I remove it from the oven. Although some cooks set the oven at a lower temperature when baking in Pyrex, I use the same temperature when baking in both metal and Pyrex pans.

EQUIPMENT USED AFTER BAKING

Cooling Racks: It's important to cool cakes, pies, tarts and cookies after baking. Cooling racks elevate the baked goods to allow air to circulate under them and cool them. Several designs are available. These include racks with wires that form a continuous circular coil; others crisscross close together. Some are rectangular and best for larger cakes, such as sheet cakes; others are best for supporting small baked items.

Storage Containers: Airtight metal containers help retain the freshness of many items such as Chocolate Meringue Mushrooms. To prevent baked goods sensitive to humidity, such as Classic Praline, from absorbing moisture at room temperature, I keep them in a canister called a Krispy Kan. The lid has a removable glass knob filled with blue nontoxic crystals that absorb moisture. When the crystals turn light lilac, it's time to place the knob in a hot oven to reactivate them. Many times I place this removable knob in another airtight metal container that has a more convenient shape for storing such small items as Macadamia Nut Brittle.

I freeze cake layers in airtight metal or plastic containers to protect their shape while they are stored. Ladyfingers freeze well in airtight plastic containers.

DECORATIVE EQUIPMENT

Flexible Metal Icing Spatulas: Flexible metal icing spatulas act as an extension of your hand when applying frosting, lifting flour to sprinkle over a batter or spreading a batter over a stencil. You need a more flexible spatula when frosting and finishing the contours of a cake than when lifting flour into a bowl of batter. Experiment to determine the type that works best for you; I use an 8-inch-long 1½-inch-wide thin-bladed stainless steel spatula most frequently, though I recommend an assortment of sizes and even offset types for occasions requiring small detail work, lifting desserts, etc.

Revolving Decorating Turntable: I prefer to frost cakes on a heavy cast-iron stand, topped with a thick 12-inch aluminum plate that revolves smoothly and steadily. This sturdy model works best and makes it easy to perfect your decorating and finishing techniques, but a lazy Susan or a rotating spice rack can be substituted.

Decorating Tips: There is a wide variety of decorating tips available, but only a few are really needed: ½-inch (#6), ⅜-inch (#4), ⁵⁄₁₆-inch (#3), and ¼-inch (#2) plain round tips and a (#4) open star.

Pastry Bags: Pastry bags come in different materials and sizes. I prefer the lightweight nylon kind because it's flexible and easy to control. For most mixtures, the 16-inch size pastry bag is best because it's large enough to fold a portion of the bag over your hand to form a cuff so the filling will not get on your hands. You can also make disposable pastry bags out of parchment paper (handmade paper cones), typing paper or waxed paper when piping only a small amount of chocolate, royal icing, buttercream, fondant or jam.

Decorating Comb and Pastry Tweezers: Both these tools make designs: The comb can make ridges, swirls and waves in chocolate and frostings; the pastry tweezers can make a pattern in pastry or marzipan.

SERVING EQUIPMENT

THE SERVING plate you choose for a dessert should complement the dessert's proportions and decoration. The plate can even set the mood, whether it be romantic, casual and rustic, fresh and springy, a holiday or a celebration.

A sharp or serrated knife can cut the dessert swiftly and neatly so the portions appear neat and attractive. Any handsome serving spatula can go in your other hand to help you guide the slice to the plate.

A Note About Eggs

WHEN THIS book was first published, the safety of eggs was not an issue. Since then, however, incidences of salmonella, or bacterial contamination, have been traced to raw or undercooked eggs, particularly on the East Coast, but also to a lesser degree in the South and West.

Scientists think that the contamination may originate in the ovaries of the hen, infecting the eggs before they are laid. This is not a problem when the eggs are fully cooked but can be dangerous if the eggs are not cooked to 160 degrees or cooked at 140 degrees for 3½ minutes, the point at which the bacteria are killed.

Until the problem has been eliminated, you may want to avoid recipes for mousses, some glazes and meringues that contain raw eggs (either yolks, whites or both), unless you are certain that your eggs come from an uncontaminated flock. (Recipes for cakes or other baked goods in which the eggs are cooked are, of course, perfectly safe.)

In addition, experts recommend the following safety procedures for handling eggs:

- Always buy eggs from refrigerated cases.

- Always store eggs on an inside shelf of the refrigerator, not in the door.

- Eggs should not remain out of the refrigerator for more than 1 hour.

- To bring eggs to room temperature, put them in a bowl of warm water for about 15 to 20 minutes.

- Discard any eggs that are unclean, cracked, broken or leaking.

- Always use clean work surfaces, utensils and storage containers.

I'm optimistic that this food-safety issue will soon be resolved. In the meantime, the potential of egg contamination differs from community to community, so my best suggestion is to pay close attention to what is being recommended locally. You may contact the food editor at your local newspaper, your state or local health department or the United States Department of Agriculture in Washington, D.C.

About the Organization of Recipes

THIS BOOK is organized according to the classic baking categories—butter cakes, sponge cakes and the various kinds of pastries—so as to give you an understanding of "the family tree" of cakes and pastries. From the "foundation" cakes and pastries, infinite variations can spring. After you have learned to make them, you can incorporate your own ideas or use your own fillings and frostings on them.

Understanding Cakemaking

Butter Cakes

Sponge (or Foam) Cakes

Butter Cakes

Recipes for Butter Cakes

Introduction

Tips for Perfect Butter Cakes

Recipes for Butter Cakes

INDICATES ❋ EASY RECIPE

Introduction

WHEN YOU are thinking of making a cake, it is usually a butter cake that comes first to mind. It's almost always butter cake recipes that have been passed down from generation to generation: American classics, such as the 1-2-3-4 Cake and Wellesley Chocolate Cake, as well as untitled splendors, such as yellow cake, gold cake, Bundt cake and pound cake. Butter cakes are what we eat in the afternoon with a cup of tea or after dinner with coffee or serve à la mode with our favorite flavor of ice cream for a special occasion.

Butter cakes offer the baker a dazzling array of possibilities. Not only do they combine beautifully with all kinds of fillings and frostings, but they can be made into almost any shape and eaten without adornment because of their moist textures.

When you need a cake that tastes like the ones your grandmother made, you'll go to the kitchen to make Buttermilk Cake (page 49). When you have to have a cake in a hurry, you'll dash off Butter Almond Cake (page 57), a rich creation that needs no frosting and tastes as if you spent all day in the kitchen. When you want a stunning cake to set before your family and guests, one that stays fresh without needing any refrigeration, you'll choose the sumptuous and extravagant Chocolate Gemini (page 94).

Even if you are a complete novice as a baker, you have probably made a pound cake or some kind of butter cake once or twice in your life. Making these cakes perfectly will fortify you with a large dose of confidence with which to climb upward to the more challenging heights of pastrymaking.

Making a perfect butter cake requires you to deal with the ingredient all the cakes of this type share in common: a large amount of fat in proportion to the eggs in the recipe. A successful butter cake also depends on how well you combine the liquids, such as the eggs, milk or other additions, with the fat to produce a smooth, creamy batter. And finally it also depends on how well you aerate the batter so it will rise to its fullest during baking.

Fat can absorb dry and liquid ingredients up to fairly large quantities. If your butter cake recipe calls for milk, you can easily replace it with yogurt, buttermilk, sour milk or even coffee, orange juice, applesauce, burnt sugar syrup or combinations of these. Each substitution will vary the taste and texture of the cake in a delicious and different way.

Three Ways of Making a Butter Cake

THE CREAMING METHOD

THE CREAMING method is one of the original methods for butter cakes. It always starts with creaming a solid fat, usually room-temperature butter, with sugar until they are light and fluffy. Then the rest of the ingredients are added, in a specific order, until the batter is formed. The entire process can be accomplished by hand, the way our mothers and grandmothers did it. Today this is more easily done by machine. I prefer the creaming method over all the others because if you do it properly, you will produce a perfect butter cake with a fine-grained texture and a velvety crumb *every single time.*

This process disperses millions of tiny, fat-covered air bubbles evenly throughout the sugar and requires from 4 to 7 minutes of whipping by machine. This may seem like a long time compared to other butter cakes you have made, but it is necessary in order to create the amount of volume you need to leaven the cake properly.

Then you add the eggs in a slow, steady stream to preserve the fluffy, creamy mixture you have created and also to build volume into it. (I don't usually separate the eggs in the creaming method. Whole eggs produce a finer, moister texture and the extra step produces no noticeable increase in volume.) You will continue to cream for 2 to 4 minutes, including the time it takes to add the eggs. More air bubbles are created in this period. The batter will appear very smooth but still light and fluffy (double to triple in volume).

Now you proceed to add the dry and liquid ingredients by hand rather than by machine, to give better control when you incorporate the ingredients. Adding these ingredients by hand is also the best way to make sure that you keep the batter creamy and smooth without disturbing its airy volume. In this process, the fat actually surrounds the flour, and the suspended air bubbles are held in place, resulting in maximum volume for the butter cake during baking.

The creaming method never fails to produce a butter cake with a superior texture—provided you are careful about the temperature of the fat, eggs and liquid as well as the sequence and timing with which you add all the ingredients.

The optimum temperature for butter that is to be creamed is 70 degrees (room temperature). If the butter is too cold or even too warm, it will not incorporate properly, nor will it be able to hold as many air bubbles as it should. Consequently, your butter cake will not rise to its potential volume when it bakes in the oven.

To test whether your butter is 70 degrees, you can insert an instant bi-therm thermometer (see Equipment for Perfect Baking, page 20) through its center. Or you can press your index finger in the middle of it to feel whether it is malleable but still cool.

For the creaming method, I look for unsalted butter that is waxy, smooth and pliable when at room temperature. This consistency is referred to as plastic. Solid shortening is also a plastic fat. These fats, when creamed, incorporate air, and the trapped air cells expand and produce volume during baking, giving your cake its texture. Plastic fats also tolerate the addition of liquids to the batter, helping to maintain a smooth emulsion.

Because solid vegetable shortening is 100 percent fat, it possesses good creaming properties. That means it is able to trap more air and produce a lighter texture than butter, which is composed of 80 to 85 percent milk fat, the rest being milk solids and water.

In order to determine which butter is best for my butter cakes, I compare brands. Besides tasting for a sweet flavor, I test to see which brand contains the most butterfat and the least amount of liquid and milk solids. The more butterfat present, the more capable the butter is of forming a good air bubble structure and the less chance there is of the batter's curdling when liquid is added.

I melt 4 ounces of each brand of butter, pour each into identical-size containers, then refrigerate all of them. As each chills, the butter separates, with the liquid and the milk solids sinking to the bottom and the butterfat rising to the top. When each has resolidified, I compare the amount of liquid in each. (The resolidified butter can't be used for creaming purposes. Not only is it grainy in texture, but it has lost plasticity and therefore its ability to cream and trap air .) There are many good butters; a national brand that works well for me is Land O' Lakes.

When the only butter available to me crumbles when I cut it cold, when it is granular or lumpy, or when tiny water droplets form around it, indicating high moisture content and poor plasticity, I blend half butter and half solid shortening. This way my butter cake has flavor and a good texture.

The eggs and any liquid you add to the butter cake must also be at 70 degrees. At this temperature—and only at this temperature—can these ingredients combine with and penetrate one another to give a smooth, homogeneous batter. If each of their temperatures is not 70 degrees, the batter will suddenly become wet and lumpy. An ingredient that is too cold, such as an egg refrigerated to 42 degrees, can solidify the finely dispersed butter (70 degrees) which is holding millions of minute air bubbles. The walls of these bubbles will then become rigid, pop open and collapse, allowing air to escape. (The same result occurs if a too-warm ingredient is added.) In essence, your emulsion breaks down, producing what is commonly called curdling of the batter. While curdling is not a complete disaster, it does affect the final texture and volume of your cake because there has been a reduction in the number of air bubbles so that the cake will neither rise as high as it should in the oven nor be as light and tender as it could be.

Although all butter cakes made with the creaming method depend upon air bubbles created during this process for their volume, some do include baking powder and/or baking soda for additional leavening.

THE COMBINATION METHOD

WHEN a butter cake recipe calls for liquid fat, such as melted butter or oil, I often employ the combination method. It is as old as the simple creaming method, and some schools of thought think it is just as good.

In this method, the dry ingredients are first combined with the liquid fat and eggs, and then whipped egg whites are carefully folded in to lighten the batter and help it rise during baking. Sometimes baking powder and/or baking soda are also added, but these leavenings are not needed when a denser, moister cake is desired, as in Tiffany's Heart (page 89). You can apply the combination method to the creaming method, but I usually find that the extra step of separating the eggs doesn't make the cake much lighter.

THE BLENDING METHOD

SOMETIMES, however, when a butter cake recipe calls for liquid fat, such as melted butter or oil, I employ the blending method. Cakes made with liquid fat tend to be denser and less high than others, and because liquid fat disperses completely through the batter during mixing, their texture is always moist and tender.

The blending method is the most modern and convenient for forming butter cake batters because it is almost always done in a single bowl. Because the fat is liquid, bringing all the ingredients together into a creamy mixture is an easy task. However, it is relatively more difficult to aerate the batter with this method. The solid fat used in the creaming method has more body, enabling it to create and trap air bubbles. Liquid fat lacks this quality of easy aeration. Therefore, baking powder and/or baking soda are called for to help provide the volume. Any butter cake recipe that qualifies for the blending method can be a candidate for the combination method. For example, in the recipe for Chocolate Cake Squares (page 87), a blending-method cake, you could separate the eggs and fold in whipped egg whites, thereby producing a drier, slightly higher cake.

WHY YOUR BUTTER CAKE RISES IN THE OVEN

NATURAL LEAVENINGS

THE FAT you used in your butter cake (butter or solid shortening) traps air bubbles, whether you have creamed it until light and fluffy (the creaming method) or stirred it with the other ingredients (the blending method) to form your batter. When you added eggs, you also created air bubbles. These two forms of leavening build natural aeration into your butter cake. Pound cakes, with their characteristically close, fine-grained, moist and dense textures, originated before chemical leavenings were heard of and rely exclusively on natural leavenings. In the oven, the liquid in the batter converts into steam through the air bubbles you have produced, expanding and leavening the cake.

By now you have seen that creaming the fat produces more air bubbles than stirring it does. But the amount of volume you get from creaming fat is dependent on a number of crucial details. Lard does not have as great a capacity to trap air as does butter or solid shortening; the type of fat you use influences how much volume you get. Furthermore, fat combines with liquid more easily when both are at room temperature.

CHEMICAL LEAVENINGS

LEAVENING butter cakes chemically has its place, too. Some bakers simply want their cakes to have that feathery-light quality baking powder and/or soda can impart. Some put in baking powder and/or soda as an extra assurance that the cake will rise, in the event that not enough aeration was built in when the batter was formed. Sometimes these leavenings are used for the sake of pure economics—you can use less butter with the addition of baking powder and/or soda and still get a light butter cake.

But besides adding to the volume and influencing the texture of a butter cake, chemical leavenings are chiefly used to lighten the grain as well as to make it more uniform.

The two chemical leavenings most commonly used in butter cakes, baking powder and baking soda, are classified as acid leavenings.

BAKING SODA

Baking soda is sodium bicarbonate. When it is moistened with an acidic ingredient in the batter, such as buttermilk, sour cream, nonalkalized cocoa powder, honey, molasses, chocolate, citrus juices, even cream of tartar, it releases carbon dioxide. Once you've prepared a batter containing baking soda, you should bake it immediately because carbon dioxide starts to release right after it is mixed.

For uniform distribution, sift the baking soda with the flour. It isn't necessary to dissolve it in water before you add it to a batter or dough since modern baking soda is a finer powder than that available in the past. Baking soda does not deteriorate with age as baking powder does. Some recipes call for adding baking soda with baking powder. Baking soda balances the acidic ingredient in the batter and provides additional leavening.

DOUBLE-ACTING BAKING POWDER

Baking powder is composed primarily of baking soda and an acid, phosphate salt (such as cream of tartar), with which it reacts to produce carbon dioxide. Carbon dioxide expands the batter.

Double-acting refers to a process that occurs in two stages. Some release of the carbon dioxide (gas) occurs when the powder is added to the cold batter. But most of its leavening power is released during baking. (When I began baking, single-acting baking powder was also available. Its full leavening power was released immediately.)

For best results, sift with other dry ingredients. If the baking powder is a few months old, test its effectiveness by mixing 1 teaspoon in ½ cup hot water; it should bubble enthusiastically.

Too much baking powder in a batter can result in a bitter-tasting cake and can also cause the cake to lose volume at the end of baking.

The Other Ingredients and Their Role

FAT

Butter cake recipes use butter, solid vegetable shortening or vegetable oil. Each one exerts its own particular influence on the cake's flavor and texture. The most flavorful fat is unsalted butter. I use it almost exclusively in my butter cakes precisely because of its superior taste.

No matter which method you use to incorporate the ingredients into the fat to make a butter cake, the fat always influences the cake's tenderness and its ability to stay fresh. Whether liquid or solid, fat particles disperse evenly throughout the other ingredients, and though fat may appear to dissolve into them, it really suspends itself among them. The result is a tender cake because the fat particles never cohere to one another tightly. Since the fat coats the other batter particles, it also retards the escape of moisture during baking and prolongs the cake's eating quality. That is why I usually advise against refrigerating butter cakes. When a cake is chilled, its high fat content tightens its texture, affecting its eating quality and taste so the cake doesn't seem to be tender or melt in your mouth at all. This is easy to understand when you consider the consistency of cold butter.

EGGS

Have you ever made a cake without eggs? It's difficult. Besides adding richness, flavor and color, eggs help build a homogeneous batter, binding the whole together. They are a basic ingredient of the liquid portion of your batter. Like fat, eggs incorporate air bubbles which contribute to the leavening. While baking, the protein in the eggs works with the flour to create the cake's structure.

The size and temperature of your eggs are, therefore, two of the most important aspects in making successful butter cakes. I always use large eggs, at room temperature. If you are in doubt about the size of your eggs, weigh them. Each of your large eggs should weigh 2 ounces in its shell. To bring eggs to room temperature, simply place the number you need in a mixing bowl and cover them with lukewarm water for 15 minutes. Then remove and dry them, and proceed with the recipe.

SUGAR

We usually think of sugar only as a sweetener, but it actually adds to the cake's volume, which affects its grain and texture. Creaming the sugar into the fat is not just a way to add this ingredient to the batter. Its granules rub against the fat, creating friction and helping trap air cells in the fat. During baking, sugar caramelizes, coloring the cake's crust. Since sugar traps moisture, it also contributes to the cake's freshness.

Granulated sugar is most commonly used in making butter cakes, but powdered sugar may be used to produce a denser, velvety texture, as in Cornmeal Pound Cake (page 60). Light or dark brown sugars and even molasses contribute flavor and additional moistness, as in Devil's Food Cake (page 53) and Fresh Ginger Cake (page 78).

FLOUR

Flour's protein content is not the most important factor in cakemaking, as it is in pastrymaking. All that is required is enough structure to help keep the batter intact because the egg protein in butter cakes contributes to both the form and the shape of the cake.

I prefer making my butter cakes with cake flour. It is high in starch and low in protein. It therefore blends easily into the batter and absorbs and retains moisture from it while baking. Butter cakes made with cake flour are also tender and have a fine grain and texture.

Sifting cake flour just prior to use is imperative since its fine texture lumps easily. After sifting, it blends and moistens more easily.

If only all-purpose flour is available to you, superb butter cakes are still possible. Just substitute all-purpose flour for the weight indicated in the recipe for cake flour. All-purpose flour is heavier than cake flour, so in terms of volume, there are more tablespoons of cake flour in 100 grams than in 100 grams of all-purpose flour. But the slight adjustment in volume is not a problem. The important consideration is the weight of the flour in proportion to the amount of liquid in the batter so that during mixing, the flour absorbs the amount of moisture, binds the ingredients and stabilizes the creamy emulsion.

You can also reduce the flour's protein content and raise the starch content by sifting 3 parts of all-purpose flour to 1 part cornstarch, thus making your own cake flour.

LIQUIDS

IN ADDITION to the liquids that instantly come to mind, such as water, milk, fruit juices and coffee, sometimes eggs, honey, molasses and melted butter can also be considered liquids. I agree with many professional bakers who prefer using a milk product as a liquid in their cakes because it contributes additional moistness, flavor, color and even sweetness.

Besides moistening the flour and dissolving the sugar and salt in your batter, liquids moisten baking soda or baking powder to begin the evolution of carbon dioxide, needed to produce volume in the cake.

SALT

WHEN unsalted butter was a gourmet item and difficult to find in a supermarket, I omitted the salt in my baking since there was enough in salted butter. Now that I use unsalted butter exclusively, I put in some salt when baking to emphasize the flavors of the ingredients. Salt combines with sugar to bring out its sweetness and balance with it.

FLAVORINGS

SPICES

I ENJOY using fresh spices sparingly in my cakes. They impart a hint of mystery to the cake's flavor rather than overpowering it. If you can identify the spice in the cake, you have usually used too much. When you buy spices, mark the date of purchase on the label. But the best test for freshness is to check for color and aroma. Ground spices will not keep as long as whole ones.

Spices that blend well with butter cakes are allspice, cinnamon, nutmeg (freshly grated is best), mace, cardamom and coriander.

EXTRACTS

PURE EXTRACTS are more expensive than imitation, but worth every penny. If you bake the same cake, one with the real and the other with the imitation flavor, a side-by-side tasting will always reveal a difference. Unfortunately some flavors, like coconut and pistachio, are available only in imitation form. Rather than use the imitation, I use the nuts to flavor buttercreams, pastry creams and Bavarian creams.

Vanilla flavoring blends perfectly with butter cakes, but I am skeptical about its effect in spice and chocolate butter cakes because those flavors tend to dominate. But I still add vanilla since I feel it marries well with almost every flavor, and studies show that only 10 percent of pure vanilla extract bakes out in the oven.

Choose your vanilla carefully. To determine which vanilla you prefer, let me suggest a method one clever vanilla company employed a few years ago. Although everyone is driven to taste vanilla since its smell is so divine, it doesn't taste good by itself. The vanilla company conducted the tasting by adding the flavoring to crème anglaise.

ZESTS

I F YOU don't have a fresh lemon, orange or lime, don't use a dried variety as a substitute for its flavor. Use another flavor like vanilla instead. People are sometimes confused when I say lemon zest. The zest is just the yellow portion of the rind. The white portion under it is bitter.

COCOA POWDER AND CHOCOLATES

T HERE ARE two types of unsweetened cocoa powder. Nonalkalized or "natural," such as Hershey's, is simply chocolate liquor (nonalcoholic) with most of the cocoa butter (fat) removed after hydraulic pressure. Alkalized cocoa, such as Van Houten, Droste and Bensdorp, is often called Dutch-processed (the formula was created by a Dutchman in the 1800s). Alkalized cocoa powder has a milder taste and is darker and sometimes redder than nonalkalized.

Since most recipes merely call for "cocoa powder," and since the type of cocoa powder you use does make a difference in the resulting cake's texture, it is helpful to understand when it is best to use each of them.

Because cocoa is an acid ingredient, it takes part in the leavening process of brownies, cookies and cakes by reacting with an alkaline ingredient, such as baking soda, and producing carbon dioxide. However, alkalized (Dutch-processed) cocoa powder contains its own alkali, so when it is combined with baking soda, there is an alkaline overload and the dessert can come out unleavened with a heavy texture. To create the correct pH balance when baking with Dutch-processed cocoa, reduce the amount of baking soda and add some baking powder, itself a mixture of acid and alkaline ingredients.

There is no set formula for adjusting the baking soda and baking powder in these types of recipes. When a recipe using unsweetened cocoa powder calls for baking soda only, or more baking soda than baking powder, use nonalkalized cocoa. If baking powder is the only leavening, or if there is more baking powder than baking soda called for, use alkalized (Dutch-processed) cocoa.

Generally, I choose a semisweet chocolate that tastes good to me to flavor my butter cakes. I use Ghiradelli or Guittard (French Vanilla), and sometimes Baker's or Hershey's. I save the more expensive, specialty brands like Cocoa Barry, Lindt, Tobler, Callebaut and Valrhona for fillings, frostings, piping designs and buttercreams. But an exception is when chocolate is a predominant ingredient in the batter, such as in Tiffany's Heart (page 89). Then I use a quality-brand chocolate.

TIPS FOR PERFECT BUTTER CAKES

☞ Measure all ingredients accurately.

☞ Grease and flour your pans carefully to guarantee successful removal of your butter cake. My experience based on tests with several methods of pan preparation has convinced me that solid shortening, rather than oil or clarified, melted or soft butter, is the best fat for coating cake pans. Besides being easy to use, practical, tasteless, free of moisture and capable of withstanding the baking temperature without burning, solid shortening has the consistency that is perfect for filming. It attracts just the right amount of flour in an even layer to ensure ease of removal and also a perfectly shaped baked cake. (This is especially true when the pan has an unusual decorative shape.) All-purpose flour coats the pan more evenly than cake flour, which has a tendency to lump.

☞ Have all measured ingredients at hand before making the batter.

☞ Move from one step to the other without delay.

☞ When you alternate the liquid with the dry ingredients, your goal is to mix the ingredients smoothly, without overworking the batter and losing the air bubble structure. Begin stirring in the middle of the mixture and form a widening spiral as you incorporate the dry or liquid ingredients. When you reach the sides of the bowl, scrape them clean and integrate what you gather into the rest of the batter. If more stirring or blending is necessary, move in the same direction and retrace the imaginary spiral formation back to the center, where you begin. The speed with which you stir or blend at first need not be too fast, but after most of the ingredient has been incorporated, you can stir faster to bring everything together smoothly.

☞ If you are using a pan you have not used before, fill it only ⅔ full. After baking, you will know for the next time how high the batter rises in your new pan.

☞ The key to which method you use to make your butter cake is the fat, which determines the cake's volume and, ultimately, its texture. If the fat is solid such as butter, the creaming method will give you the finest, most velvety texture. If the fat is liquid, use the blending or combination method.

Classic Butter Cake

S IMPLE, fresh ingredients harmonize, with no one flavor overwhelming the other, in this all-American yellow cake. You'll enjoy it for its obvious homemade taste and its ability to blend perfectly with other flavors, fillings and frostings.

Frost with Bittersweet Chocolate Frosting (page 286) or Chocolate Sabayon Buttercream (page 287).

This cake is the base for Lemon Parfait Cake (page 83). Don't hesitate to use it for other desserts such as Victorian Maple Cake (page 82).

MAKES TWO 8-X-1 ½-INCH ROUND LAYERS

Baking Equipment: Two heavy-gauge straight-sided 8-inch cake pans

2 ½	cups (250 grams) sifted cake flour
2	teaspoons baking powder
¼	teaspoon salt
3	large eggs, room temperature
1	cup (8 ounces) milk, room temperature
1	teaspoon vanilla
6	ounces (1 ½ sticks) unsalted butter, room temperature
1 ½	cups (300 grams) granulated sugar

Baking preparations: Position the rack in the lower third of the oven, 5 to 6 inches from the bottom; preheat oven to 350 degrees.

Using a paper towel, grease the bottom and sides of the pans with solid shortening. Dust generously with all-purpose flour, shake to distribute, tap out excess and insert 8-inch rounds of parchment or waxed paper.

Ingredient preparations: Pour the flour, baking powder and salt in that order into a triple sifter. Sift onto a sheet of waxed paper to distribute ingredients evenly and to remove any lumps in the cake flour; set aside.

Crack the eggs into a small bowl, and whisk together just to combine the yolks and whites. (This guarantees even dispersion in the batter.)

Pour the milk into a liquid measuring cup, add the vanilla and stir to combine.

Place the butter in a bowl of a heavy-duty mixer.

Making the cake: With the flat beater (paddle), cream the butter on medium speed (#5) until it is lighter in color, clings to the sides of the bowl and has a satiny appearance. (This should take no more than 30 to 45 seconds.)

Maintaining the same speed, add the sugar in a steady stream. When all the sugar is added, stop the machine and scrape the gritty, sandy mixture clinging to the sides into the center of the bowl. Continue to cream at the same speed for 4 to 5 minutes, or until the mixture is very light in color and fluffy in appearance.

With the mixer still on medium speed, pour in the eggs, very cautiously at first, tablespoon by tablespoon, as if you were adding oil when making mayonnaise. If at any time

Baker's Notes

☞ For a special treat, substitute eggnog for the milk and add ⅛ teaspoon fresh-grated nutmeg. The cake is rich and moist enough to eat alone, adorned with only a sprinkling of powdered sugar.

☞ Like all butter cakes, this batter is adaptable to an endless variety of sizes and shapes of baking pans. You can use: Two 9-inch round baking pans; bake 25 to 30 minutes. One 9-x-13-x-2¼-inch pan; bake about 35 to 37 minutes. One 10-inch tube pan; bake 55 to 60 minutes.

Understanding Cakemaking

the mixture appears watery or shiny, stop the flow of eggs and increase the mixer's speed until a smooth, silken appearance returns. Then return to medium speed and resume adding the eggs.

Continue to cream, stopping the mixer and scraping the sides of the bowl at least once. When the mixture appears fluffy, white and increased in volume (it almost resembles whipped cream cheese and any grainy appearance has disappeared), detach the flat beater (paddle) and bowl from the mixer. (The total process of adding the eggs and incorporating them into the mixture takes 3 to 4 minutes.) Tap the paddle against the edge of the bowl to free excess creamed mixture.

With the aid of a metal icing spatula, lift one-fourth of the flour mixture and sprinkle it over the creamed mixture. Stir it in with a rubber spatula. Then pour in one-third of the vanilla-flavored milk, stirring to blend together. Repeat this procedure, alternating dry and liquid ingredients, ending with the flour. With each addition, scrape the sides of the bowl, and continue mixing until smooth. (Stirring the flour in last rather than the liquid binds the batter together to form the desirable consistency. Doing this by hand rather than by machine gives more control in incorporating the ingredients and reduces the risk of over-mixing.)

Baking the cake: Spoon equal amounts of batter into each pan, using a large kitchen serving spoon. (When all the batter has been divided, you may weigh each pan to check for equal distribution, which is required for a perfectly symmetrical cake.) With a rubber spatula, spread the batter, working from the center outward, creating a slightly raised ridge around the outside rim. (Since heat is conducted faster near the metal rim, mounding the batter around the edges assures more even, level baked layers. Batters containing chemical leavenings also have a tendency to bake higher in the middle, forming domelike shapes; the outer ridge compensates for this.)

Bake for 30 to 35 minutes, or until the baked surface springs back slightly when touched lightly in the center and the sides begin to contract from the pan.

Cooling the cake: Place cake pans on racks and let them cool for 5 to 10 minutes. With mitts, tilt and rotate each pan, gently tapping on the counter to see if each layer is being released from the metal sides. If not, or if in doubt, run a small metal spatula or the thin blade of a table knife between the layer's outer edge and the metal rim, freeing the sides and allowing air to get under each layer as it is rotated.

Cover one of the layer pans with a cooling rack, invert it onto the rack and carefully lift pan to remove. Slowly peel off the parchment liner, turn the paper over so that the sticky top side faces up, and reposition it on top of the layer. Cover with another rack, invert the layer right side up and remove the original rack. (Reusing the liner in this way prevents the layer from sticking to the rack while it cools and also provides a temporary base for lifting and storing.) Repeat with the other layer. Then allow both to cool completely.

Storing the cake: If you plan to use the cake within 24 hours, wrap the layers individually in plastic wrap and store them at room temperature. To freeze, cover the plastic-wrapped layers with foil. Label each package, indicating contents and date. Freeze for no longer than 2 weeks.

Buttermilk Cake

ONE BITE of this cake, and you know without a doubt it is homemade. Its tender crumb and old-fashioned flavor will make it a standard in your baking repertoire.

This cake provides the basis for Victorian Maple Cake (page 82), Lemon Parfait Cake (page 83) and Fraisia (page 84).

MAKES TWO 8-X-1 ½-INCH ROUND LAYERS

Baking Equipment: Two heavy-gauge straight-sided 8-inch round cake pans

2 ½	cups (250 grams) sifted cake flour
1 ½	teaspoons baking powder
½	teaspoon baking soda
¼	teaspoon salt
3	large eggs, room temperature
1	cup (8 ounces) buttermilk, room temperature
1	teaspoon vanilla
6	ounces (1 ½ sticks) unsalted butter, room temperature
1 ½	cups (300 grams) granulated sugar

Prepare this cake following each step in Classic Butter Cake (page 47), with the following differences:

Sift baking soda with the dry ingredients.

Substitute buttermilk for milk.

White Butter Cake

THIS CAKE, frosted with Maple Italian Meringue (page 266), makes a magnificent wedding cake.

Its buttery flavor and velvety texture combine well with any type of frosting or buttercream. Chocolate is an especially good match here. For example, fill the cake with strawberry jam and frost the top and sides with Chocolate Sabayon Buttercream (page 287). The only hint that you are eating a butter cake made completely with egg whites rather than whole eggs or egg yolks is its snowy white color. The batter is thick enough to have glazed or dried fruits folded into it; or even chopped nuts or tiny chunks of chocolate.

MAKES TWO 8-X-1 ½-INCH ROUND CAKES

Baking Equipment: Two heavy-gauge straight-sided 8-inch cake pans

2 ½	cups (250 grams) sifted cake flour
2 ½	teaspoons baking powder
¼	teaspoon salt
2	egg whites, room temperature, *plus* 3 egg whites, room temperature

(continued)

☞ To make a Lemon Meringue Cake, split each layer in half horizontally and spread Classic Lemon Curd (page 258) equally between 3 of the layers. Frost the top and sides with Classic Italian Meringue (page 265).

☞ Buttermilk produces a light, rich flavor with a tender crumb. The buttermilk's lactic acid reacts with the baking soda to produce carbon dioxide and aids in leavening the cake.

☞ If you can, seek out a buttermilk with a higher content of butterfat for a more buttery flavor.

☞ You may substitute sour milk or crème fraîche for buttermilk. To make sour milk, stir 1 teaspoon fresh lemon juice or vinegar into 1 cup of milk.

☞ I sometimes like to add ¼ teaspoon each of almond and lemon extract with the vanilla.

1	teaspoon granulated sugar
1	cup (8 ounces) milk, room temperature
1	teaspoon vanilla
8	ounces (2 sticks) unsalted butter, room temperature
1 ½	cups (300 grams) granulated sugar

Baker's Notes

☞ This cake may be substituted for Buttermilk Cake (page 49) or Classic Butter Cake (page 47) anytime.

☞ The egg whites are added in two different forms in this recipe. The first addition of egg whites, unbeaten, contributes to the batter's liquid. The second addition of whites, whipped, performs the function of lightening the batter. These techniques are what produce a moist white butter cake with a fine texture. (For more on egg whites, see Egg-White Foams, page 149.)

Baking preparations: Position rack in lower third of oven; preheat oven to 350 degrees.

Using a paper towel, grease the bottom and sides of the pans with solid shortening. Dust generously with all-purpose flour, shake to distribute, tap out excess and place 8-inch rounds of parchment or waxed paper on the bottom of the pans.

Ingredient preparations: Pour the flour, baking powder and salt in that order into a triple sifter. Sift onto waxed paper and set aside.

Place 2 egg whites in a small mixing bowl, and whisk briefly, just enough to break up their structure so they will pour easily.

Place the remaining 3 egg whites in a 1½-quart mixing bowl. Set the 1 teaspoon sugar for whipping the whites nearby.

Pour the milk into a liquid cup measure, add the vanilla and stir just to combine.

Place the butter in the bowl of a heavy-duty mixer.

Making the cake: With the flat beater (paddle), cream the butter on medium speed (#5) until it is lighter in both color and texture (about 30 seconds).

Maintaining the same speed, add the 1½ cups sugar in a steady stream. When all the sugar is added, stop the machine and scrape the mixture clinging to the sides into the center of the bowl. Continue to cream at the same speed until the mixture is almost white and appears fluffy (about 4 to 5 minutes).

With the mixer still on medium speed, pour in the 2 egg whites, very cautiously at first, tablespoon by tablespoon, as if you were adding oil when making mayonnaise.

If at any time the mixture appears watery or shiny, stop the flow of whites and increase the speed until a smooth, silken appearance returns. Then decrease the speed to medium again and resume adding the whites.

Continue to cream, for about 3 more minutes, scraping the sides of the bowl at least once. When the mixture resembles whipped cream cheese and has increased in volume, detach the beater and bowl. Tap the beater against the edge of the bowl to free the excess.

Using a rubber spatula, stir in one-fourth of the flour mixture. Then add one-third of the vanilla-flavored milk, stirring to blend together. Repeat the procedure, alternating dry and liquid ingredients, ending with the flour. With each addition, scrape the sides of the bowl, and continue mixing until smooth.

Whip the remaining 3 whites with an electric hand mixer on low speed until small bubbles appear (about 30 to 45 seconds). Then increase the speed (#10), and add the 1 teaspoon of sugar. Whip until stiffer, shiny white peaks form (about 45 to 60 seconds more). When you judge whether you have finished the whipping process, keep in mind that the whites are going to be folded into the batter. It is therefore better to underwhip than to overwhip. If the whites are too stiff, folding them in becomes much more difficult and in the process you may overwork the batter, deflating some of the volume that is so essential to the cake's tender texture.

Using a rubber spatula, fold half the whipped whites into the batter. With a wire whisk, whisk the remaining whites in the bowl just to unite them again and tighten them. Fold into batter just until incorporated.

Baking the cake: Using a large kitchen serving spoon, spoon equal amounts of batter into each pan. (If you want to make sure you have equal layers after all the batter has been divided, weigh each pan on your scale to check for equal distribution.) Then, with a rubber spatula, working from the center, spread the batter outward, creating a slightly raised ridge around the outside rim.

Bake for 30 to 35 minutes, or until the surface springs back slightly when it is touched lightly in the center and the sides begin to contract from the pan.

Cooling the cake: Place the pans on racks to cool for 5 to 10 minutes. With mitts, tilt and rotate each pan, gently tapping it on the counter to see if each layer is released from the sides. If not, or if in doubt, run a small metal spatula or the thin blade of a table knife between the layer's outer edge and the metal rim, freeing the sides and allowing air to get under the layer as it is rotated.

Cover a layer with a cooling rack, invert it onto the rack and carefully lift pan to remove. Slowly peel off the parchment liner; turn the paper over so that the sticky top side faces up; then reposition it on top of the layer. Cover with another rack, invert the layer right side up and remove the original rack. Repeat with the other layer. Then allow both to cool completely.

Storing the cake: If you don't plan to use the cake within 24 hours, wrap each layer individually in plastic wrap and store at room temperature.

To freeze, cover the plastic-wrapped layers with foil. Label each package, indicating the contents and date. Freeze for no more than 2 weeks.

Banana Sheet Cake

SINCE THIS is my favorite banana cake, I make it a lot. For a simple dessert, make this cake in an 8-inch round pan and serve it with strawberries and lightly whipped cream. The subtle tang of the strawberries offsets the natural sweetness of the banana.

A lemon buttercream (or any other made with a citrus fruit) also complements the banana cake's flavor and texture nicely.

Banana Sheet Cake is the foundation for Americana Banana Roll (page 80).

MAKES ONE 12-X-15 ½-INCH CAKE

Baking Equipment: One 12-x-15½-x-½-inch baking sheet

1	cup (100 grams) sifted cake flour
½	teaspoon baking soda
⅛	teaspoon baking powder
⅛	teaspoon salt

(continued)

Baker's Notes

☞ One 8-inch round cake layer may be made with this batter. Prepare as directed below. Bake in a 350-degree oven for 30 to 35 minutes.

☞ I like to mash the banana with a pastry blender. It's not important to puree the banana completely; some very small lumps are fine.

1	large egg, room temperature
½	cup (1 large) mashed ripe banana
1	tablespoon sour cream
1	teaspoon lemon zest
5 ½	tablespoons (2 ½ ounces) unsalted butter, room temperature
½	cup (100 grams) granulated sugar

Baking preparations: Position rack in lower third of oven; preheat oven to 375 degrees.

Using a paper towel, lightly grease a small area in the center of the baking sheet with solid shortening and line the pan with foil, leaving a 2-inch overhang at each short end (the dab of shortening holds the foil in place). Lightly grease the foil with shortening and sprinkle with all-purpose flour. Shake the pan to distribute flour and tap out excess.

Ingredient preparations: Pour the flour, baking soda, baking powder and salt in that order into a triple sifter. Sift onto a sheet of waxed paper to distribute the ingredients; set aside.

Crack the egg into a small bowl, and whisk briefly just to combine the yolk and white. Combine the mashed banana, sour cream and lemon zest in a small bowl; set aside.

Place the butter in the bowl of a heavy-duty mixer.

Making the cake: With the flat beater (paddle), cream the butter on medium speed (#5) for 30 to 45 seconds, or until it is smooth and lighter in color. (This is a small amount in a large bowl, but you can adjust most heavy-duty machines so the attachment reaches lower in the bowl.)

Maintaining the same speed, add the sugar in a steady stream. Then stop the mixer, and scrape the mixture clinging to the sides into the center of the bowl. Continue to cream at the same speed until the mixture is light in color and fluffy in appearance (about 3 to 4 minutes).

With the mixer still on medium speed, pour in the egg, very cautiously at first, as if you were adding oil when making mayonnaise. Continue to cream for 1 to 2 more minutes, scraping the sides of the bowl at least once. When the mixture is quite fluffy and has increased in volume, detach the beater and bowl. Tap the beater against the edge of the bowl to free the excess.

With the aid of a metal spatula, lift half the flour mixture and sprinkle it over the creamed mixture. Stir it in with a rubber spatula. Then add the mashed banana mixture, stirring to blend. Scrape the sides of the bowl with each addition. Add the remaining flour mixture and stir until smooth.

Baking the cake: Scoop the thick batter onto five different areas over two-thirds of the prepared baking sheet. With a metal spatula, spread and coax the batter to cover the two-thirds of the sheet. Now extend it to the rest of the sheet in as even a layer as possible. (At first you will not believe it will cover the entire sheet, but it will. Don't rush. The layer will be very thin, but that is just the way it should be. It will increase in volume in the oven.)

Bake for 8 to 10 minutes, or until the cake is light golden brown, the sides are beginning to contract from the metal, and the cake springs back when lightly touched in the center.

Cooling the cake: Remove the pan from the oven. Using a thin-bladed knife, gently release any portion of the cake sticking to the long sides of the pan. Pull up on the foil overhangs, one at a time, to release foil from the pan's edges. Finally, loosen foil from the bottom of the pan by gently lifting up on the flaps, and transfer it to a large rack to cool.

Place a sheet of foil over the cake and manipulate the foil in a tent fashion (this holds in the moisture as it cools, but prevents sticking to the cake). Cool for 30 minutes. Then proceed to assemble it into a dessert, such as Americana Banana Roll (page 80).

Devil's Food Cake

THIS LIGHT, moist, flavorful classic American chocolate cake will be welcome at any dessert table. Though the cake is not as sweet or dense as other varieties of chocolate cakes, the brown sugar blends with the cocoa powder to provide a rich dimension.

This has been a favorite of mine since childhood. Serve it plain with whipped cream and fresh raspberries or with your favorite ice cream, or frost it with Bittersweet Chocolate Frosting (page 286) and coat it with chopped walnuts.

Devil's Food Cake is the foundation for Chocolate Gemini (page 94).

MAKES ONE 9-X-13-INCH CAKE

Baking Equipment: One 9-x-13-x-2¼-inch cake pan

2	cups (200 grams) sifted cake flour
1	teaspoon baking soda
¼	teaspoon salt
½	cup (50 grams) unsifted cocoa powder
½	cup (4 ounces) lukewarm water
½	cup (4 ounces) buttermilk, room temperature
½	cup (4 ounces) water
2	teaspoons vanilla
2	large eggs, room temperature
4	ounces (1 stick) unsalted butter, room temperature
1	cup (200 grams) granulated sugar
1	cup (200 grams) light brown sugar, packed

Baking preparations: Position rack in lower third of oven; preheat oven to 350 degrees. Using a paper towel, grease the bottom and sides of the pan with solid shortening. Dust generously with all-purpose flour, shake to distribute, tap out excess and insert parchment paper or waxed paper to line the bottom.

Ingredient preparations: Pour the flour, baking soda and salt in that order into a triple sifter. Sift onto a sheet of waxed paper to distribute the ingredients; set aside.

Place the cocoa in a 1-quart mixing bowl. Add the ½ cup of lukewarm water and whisk

Baker's Notes

☞ You can also bake two 8-inch round cake layers for 22 to 25 minutes at the same oven temperature.

☞ Light brown sugar is milder in flavor than dark brown sugar, but either is fine.

☞ This recipe has a high proportion of sugar to fat, so be patient when creaming the two together. When you begin to cream them, it's hard to believe the mixture will become light and fluffy.

to combine; set aside to cool.

Pour the buttermilk, the ½ cup water and the vanilla into a liquid cup measure.

Crack the eggs into a small bowl, and whisk together just to combine the yolks and whites.

Place the butter in the bowl of a heavy-duty mixer.

Making the cake: With the flat beater (paddle), cream the butter on medium speed (#5) for 30 to 45 seconds, or until it is smooth and lighter in color.

Reduce the speed to low (#3), add the sugars (first the granulated, then the brown) in a steady stream. If the machine's speed is too high, the sugars will dance in the bowl and jump out.

When all the sugar is added, stop the machine and scrape the mixture clinging to the sides of the bowl into the center. The mixture will appear sandy. Increase the speed to medium again and cream until the mixture is light in color, fluffy in texture and appears as one mass instead of as several pieces of sugar (this will take 6 to 7 minutes).

With the mixer still on medium speed, pour in the eggs, cautiously at first, tablespoon by tablespoon, as if you were adding oil when making mayonnaise.

If at any time the mixture appears watery or shiny, stop the flow of eggs, and increase the speed until a smooth, silken appearance returns. Then decrease the speed to medium and resume adding eggs.

Continue to cream, scraping the sides of the bowl at least once, until the mixture appears fluffy and velvety and has increased in volume. (This process, including the addition of eggs, takes about 1 minute. If you take longer, you risk losing the smooth emulsion and therefore lose some volume in the oven.) Stop the machine and spoon in the cooled cocoa mixture, resume at medium speed (#5) and mix just until incorporated. Detach the beater and bowl; tap the beater against the edge of bowl to free the excess.

Using a rubber spatula, stir in one-fourth of the flour mixture. Then add one-third of the buttermilk mixture, stirring to blend together. Repeat this procedure, alternating dry and liquid ingredients, ending with the flour. With each addition, scrape the sides of the bowl and continue mixing until smooth, never adding liquid if any flour is visible.

Baking the cake: Pour the batter into the pan. With a rubber spatula, spread the batter, working from the center outward and creating a slightly raised ridge around the outer rim.

Bake for 40 to 42 minutes, or until the baked surface springs back slightly when touched lightly in the center, the sides contract from the pan, and a toothpick removed from the center is free of cake.

Cooling the cake: Place the cake on a rack to cool for 5 to 10 minutes. With mitts, tilt and rotate pan, gently tapping it on the counter to see if the cake releases from the sides.

If not, or if in doubt, run a small metal spatula or the thin blade of a table knife between the outer cake edge and the metal rim, freeing the sides and allowing air to get under the cake as it is rotated.

Place a cooling rack over the baking pan, invert it onto the rack and carefully lift the pan to remove. Slowly peel off parchment liner, turn it over so that the sticky top side faces up and reposition it on top of the cake. Cover with another rack, invert the layer right side up and remove the original rack. Cool completely.

Storing the cake: If you plan to use the cake within 24 hours, wrap it in plastic wrap and store it at room temperature.

To freeze, cover the plastic-wrapped package with foil, labeling the contents and date. Freeze for no longer than 2 weeks.

Dark Chocolate Cake

THE UNSWEETENED chocolate flavors the cake with the deep, rich taste of chocolate. I enjoy filling and frosting this cake with Classic Italian Meringue (page 265).
MAKES TWO 8-X-1 ¾-INCH ROUND LAYERS

Baking Equipment: Two heavy-gauge straight-sided 8-inch round cake pans

3	squares unsweetened chocolate
2 ½	cups sifted cake flour
1 ½	teaspoons baking powder
½	teaspoon baking soda
¼	teaspoon salt
3	large eggs, room temperature
1	cup milk, room temperature
1	teaspoon vanilla
8	ounces (2 sticks) unsalted butter, room temperature
1 ½	cups granulated sugar

Ingredient preparations: Melt the chocolate in a small bowl set over a saucepan of hot water (no hotter than 120 degrees).

Pour the flour, baking powder, baking soda and salt in that order into a triple sifter. Sift onto a sheet of waxed paper to distribute ingredients evenly and to remove any lumps in the cake flour; set aside.

Crack the eggs into a small bowl and whisk together just to combine the yolks and whites. (This guarantees even dispersion in the batter.)

Pour the milk into a liquid measuring cup, add the vanilla, and stir to combine.

Baking preparations: Position the rack in the lower third of the oven, 5 to 6 inches from the bottom; preheat oven to 350 degrees.

Using a paper towel, grease the bottom and sides of the pans with solid shortening. Dust generously with all-purpose flour, shake to distribute, tap out excess and insert 8-inch rounds of parchment or waxed paper.

Making the cake: Place the butter in a bowl of a heavy-duty mixer. With the flat beater (paddle), cream the butter on medium speed (#5) until it is lighter in color, clings to the sides of the bowl and has a satiny appearance. (This should take no more than 30 to 45 seconds.)

Maintaining the same speed, add the sugar in a steady stream. When all the sugar is added,

Baker's Note

☞ Optional Garnish: Finish the cake with any chocolate shape, such as Chocolate Flakes (page 282).

stop the machine and scrape the gritty, sandy mixture clinging to the sides into the center of the bowl. Continue to cream at the same speed for 4 to 5 minutes, or until the mixture is very light in color and fluffy in appearance.

With the mixer still on medium speed, pour in the eggs, very cautiously at first, tablespoon by tablespoon, as if you were adding oil when making mayonnaise. If at any time the mixture appears watery or shiny, stop the flow of eggs and increase the mixer's speed until a smooth, silken appearance returns. Then return to medium speed and resume adding the eggs.

Continue to cream, stopping the mixer and scraping the sides of the bowl at least once. When the mixture appears fluffy, white and increased in volume, detach the flat beater (paddle) and bowl from the mixer. (The total process of adding the eggs and incorporating them into the mixture takes 3 to 4 minutes.) Add the cooled, melted chocolate to the batter. Tap the paddle against the edge of the bowl to free excess creamed mixture.

With the aid of a metal icing spatula, lift one-fourth of the flour mixture and sprinkle it over the creamed mixture. Stir it in with a rubber spatula. Repeat this procedure, alternating dry and liquid ingredients, ending with the flour. With each addition scrape the sides of the bowl, and continue mixing until smooth.

Baking the cake: Spoon equal amounts of batter into each pan, using a large kitchen serving spoon. With a rubber spatula, spread the batter, working from the center outward, creating a slightly raised ridge around the outside rim.

Bake for about 35 minutes, or until the surface springs back slightly when touched lightly in the center. Do not overbake: Chocolate firms as it cools.

Cooling the cake: Place cake pans on racks and let them cool for 5 to 10 minutes. With mitts, tilt and rotate each pan, gently tapping on the counter to see if each layer is being released from the metal sides. If not, or if in doubt, run a small metal spatula or the thin blade of a table knife between the layer's outer edge and the metal rim, freeing the sides and allowing air to get under each layer as it is rotated.

Cover one of the layer pans with a cooling rack, invert it onto the rack and carefully lift pan to remove. Slowly peel off the parchment liner, turn the paper over so that the sticky top side faces up and reposition it on top of the layer. Cover with another rack, invert the layer right side up and remove the original rack. Repeat with the other layer. Then allow both to cool completely.

Storing the cake: If you plan to assemble the cake within 24 hours, wrap the layers individually in plastic wrap and store them at room temperature. To freeze, cover the plastic-wrapped layers with foil. Label each package, indicating contents and date. Freeze for no longer than 2 weeks.

Butter Almond Cake

THIS IS a moist butter cake with a subtle almond flavor. When small strawberries or fresh raspberries are available, I substitute them for the jam and nuts and arrange the berries on top of the cake as though it were a tart.

MAKES 8 TO 12 SERVINGS

Baking Equipment: 5½-cup shallow fluted tube pan

⅔	cup (70 grams) sifted cake flour
¼	teaspoon baking powder
⅛	teaspoon salt
4	large eggs, room temperature
8	ounces (1 scant cup) almond paste, room temperature
1	cup (200 grams) granulated sugar
5	ounces (11 tablespoons) unsalted butter, room temperature
1	teaspoon orange zest
¼	cup raspberry jam
3 ½	ounces (¾ cup) toasted sliced almonds

Baking preparations: Position rack in lower third of oven; preheat to 350 degrees.

Using a paper towel, grease the bottom and sides of the pan with solid shortening. Dust generously with all-purpose flour, shake to distribute and tap out excess.

Ingredient preparations: Pour the flour, baking powder and salt into a triple sifter. Sift onto a sheet of waxed paper and set aside.

Crack the eggs into a small mixing bowl; whisk together just to combine yolks and whites. Place the almond paste in the bowl of a heavy-duty mixer.

Baker's Notes

☞ You can also bake this batter in a 9-inch square pan, greased, floured and lined with baking parchment.

☞ If you are using a fluted mold, as I suggest, grease, then flour it carefully; lining with baking parchment is not necessary.

Understanding Cakemaking

Making the cake: With the flat beater (paddle), beat the almond paste on low speed (#3) for 30 seconds. Maintaining the same speed, add the sugar in a steady stream, and beat until incorporated (about 1 minute).

Continue on low speed while adding the butter, tablespoon by tablespoon. Stop the machine after all the butter has been added, and scrape the mixture clinging to the sides down into the center of bowl. Increase the speed to medium (#5) and cream until mixture is smooth, lighter in color and fluffy in texture (about 3 to 4 minutes). No lumps of almond paste should be visible.

With the mixer still on medium speed, pour in the eggs, cautiously at first, tablespoon by tablespoon, as if you were adding oil when making mayonnaise. Each time the egg is absorbed, add a little more. If at any time the mixture appears watery or shiny, stop the flow of egg and increase the speed until a smooth, silken appearance returns. Then decrease the speed to medium and resume adding the eggs.

Continue to cream, scraping the sides of bowl at least once, until the mixture appears light in color and fluffy in texture (about 2 to 3 minutes). Detach the beater and bowl, and tap the beater against the side of the bowl to free the excess. Stir in the orange zest with a rubber spatula.

With the same rubber spatula, stir in the flour mixture, scraping the sides of the bowl often and mixing until smooth.

Baking the cake: Pour the batter into the prepared pan, spreading it level with the rubber spatula.

Bake for 35 to 40 minutes, or until the top is golden brown and a toothpick inserted near the center is removed free of cake. (It is perfectly natural for this cake to shrink slightly toward the end of baking.)

Cooling the cake: Place the cake on a rack to cool for about 5 minutes. With mitts, tilt and rotate the pan and gently tip it to see if the cake releases from the sides. If not, or if in doubt, run a small metal spatula or thin table knife between the cake edge and metal rim, freeing the sides and allowing air to get under the cake as it is rotated.

Turn the cake out onto a rack, remove the pan and invert the cake right side up to cool completely.

Finishing the cake: On the day of serving, spread the raspberry jam over the entire surface of the cake, using the back of a spoon (if necessary, warm jam slightly to make spreading easier). Top with the toasted almonds. Serve at room temperature.

Storing the cake: Store at room temperature, or freeze before decorating.

Crystal Almond Pound Cake

IF YOU LIKE almond paste, you'll love this moist, rich pound cake with sparkling citrus glaze. This delightful cake, which melts in your mouth, is welcome at brunch as well as after dinner. (See photograph, page 72.)

MAKES 8 TO 10 SERVINGS

Baking Equipment: One 8½-inch tube pan or other 7- to 8-cup decorative baking pan

¾	cup (75 grams) sifted cake flour
½	teaspoon baking powder
⅛	teaspoon salt
1	teaspoon lemon zest (1 lemon)
1	teaspoon orange zest (1 orange)
5	large eggs, room temperature
1	teaspoon vanilla
7	ounces (¾ cup) almond paste, room temperature
1	cup (200 grams) granulated sugar
8	ounces (2 sticks) unsalted butter, room temperature

Citrus Glaze

3	tablespoons lemon juice
3	tablespoons orange juice
¾	cup (150 grams) granulated sugar

Baking preparations: Position rack in lower third of oven; preheat oven to 350 degrees.

Using paper towel, generously grease the bottom and sides of the pan with solid shortening. Dust generously with all-purpose flour, tilt to coat evenly and tap out the excess.

Ingredient preparations: Pour the flour, baking powder and salt in that order into a triple sifter. Sift onto a sheet of waxed paper to distribute the ingredients evenly; set aside.

Grate only the colored portion of the lemon and orange rind for their zests; set aside.

Crack eggs into a small bowl. Add the vanilla and whisk together briefly just to combine yolks and whites. Place the almond paste in the bowl of a heavy-duty mixer.

Making the cake: With the flat beater (paddle) and using low speed (#2), break up the almond paste (about 30 seconds). Maintaining the same speed, slowly add the 1 cup of sugar in a steady stream, and beat until incorporated. (If you add the sugar too quickly, the almond paste jumps out of the mixing bowl.)

Continue on low speed while adding the butter, tablespoon by tablespoon, taking about 1 minute. Stop the machine after all the butter has been added, and scrape the mixture clinging to the sides into the center of the bowl. Increase the speed to medium (#5), and cream until the mixture is lighter in color and fluffy in appearance (about 3 to 4 minutes).

☞ As in other pound cakes, the eggs are the only source of liquid. But the combination of the almond paste and the eggs and other ingredients produces a very moist cake.

☞ Make the glaze just before you are ready to brush it over the warm cake. I love applying this glaze to other cakes as a special decorative addition. After the cake has cooled, a thin, sparkling finish appears.

☞ If your brand of almond paste is not malleable at room temperature, you can process it for a few seconds in your food processor bowl fitted with the plastic blade.

☞ This recipe demonstrates the most effective way to incorporate almond paste into a cake batter smoothly.

Understanding Cakemaking

With the mixer still on medium speed, pour in the eggs, cautiously at first, tablespoon by tablespoon. After each portion of the eggs has been absorbed into the mixture, add more. If at any time the mixture appears watery or shiny, stop the flow of eggs and increase the speed until a smooth, silken appearance returns. Then decrease the speed to medium, and resume adding the eggs.

Continue to cream, stopping the mixer and scraping the sides of the bowl at least once. When the mixture appears fluffy, velvety and white, and has increased in volume (including the time to add the eggs, about 2 to 3 minutes), detach the beater and bowl. Tap the beater against the edge of the bowl with enough force to free the excess.

Using a rubber spatula, stir in the lemon and orange zests. Then stir in the flour mixture, about one-half at a time, scraping the sides of the bowl often and mixing until smooth after each addition.

Baking the cake: Spoon the batter into the pan, and spread it level. Bake for about 45 to 50 minutes, or until the sides begin to contract from the pan, the cake springs back when lightly touched and a wooden toothpick inserted comes out free of cake.

Finishing the cake: Place the cake on a rack to cool for 5 to 7 minutes while preparing the glaze.

Pour the lemon juice, orange juice and the ¾ cup of sugar into a small bowl; stir with a pastry brush to blend.

With mitts, tilt and rotate the pan, and gently tap it to see if the cake is releasing from the metal sides. If not, or if in doubt, run a small metal spatula or the thin blade of a table knife between the outer cake edge and the metal rim, freeing the sides and allowing air to get under the cake as it is rotated.

Turn the cake out onto a cooling rack and position it over a sheet of foil or waxed paper (it will catch any drippings when the glaze is applied). Brush the entire surface of the warm cake with all of the glaze.

Cooling the cake: Allow the glazed cake to stand for at least 4 hours, or until it is completely cool and the glaze has set like a sheet of crystals, before you remove it from the rack to a serving dish. Lift it by crisscrossing two large metal icing spatulas under the cake. Serve at room temperature.

Storing the cake: This dessert can't be frozen because the glaze breaks down and becomes watery when defrosted.

Cornmeal Pound Cake

ADDING cornmeal to this pound cake provides a delicate crunch to its satiny texture.

MAKES 12 TO 14 SERVINGS, WITH 2 TO 3 THIN SLICES PER SERVING

Baking Equipment: One 10-inch tube pan or other 12-cup decorative Bundt-type pan

2 ½	cups (250 grams) sifted cake flour
1 ½	teaspoons baking powder
¼	teaspoon salt
3 ¾	cups (1 pound) unsifted powdered sugar
4	large eggs, room temperature
1	cup milk, room temperature
8	ounces (2 sticks) unsalted butter, room temperature
¾	cup (4 ounces) yellow cornmeal
¼	cup (25 grams) unsifted powdered sugar

Baker's Notes

☞ The best way to test if this cake has finished baking is with a toothpick since the texture is dense.

☞ A pound of powdered sugar is equivalent in sweetness to ½ pound of granulated sugar.

☞ This cake's flavor improves after one day's aging.

Baking preparations: Position rack in lower third of oven; preheat oven to 350 degrees.

Using a paper towel, grease the bottom and sides of the pan with solid shortening. Dust generously with all-purpose flour, shake to distribute, and tap out the excess.

Ingredient preparations: Pour the flour, baking powder and salt in that order into a triple sifter. Sift onto a sheet of waxed paper, and set aside.

Sift the 3¾ cups of powdered sugar to remove lumps onto another sheet of waxed paper.

Crack the eggs into a small bowl, and whisk just to combine yolks and whites.

Pour the milk into a liquid cup measure.

Place the butter in the bowl of a heavy-duty mixer.

Making the cake: With the flat beater (paddle), cream the butter on medium speed (#5) until smooth (about 30 seconds).

Reduce the speed to low (#3), and slowly add the sifted sugar (if the speed is any higher, your face will be covered with flying powdered sugar). When all the sugar is added (about 1 minute), stop the machine and scrape the mixture clinging to the sides into the center of the bowl. Continue to cream on medium speed (#5) until the mixture is light in color and fluffy in texture (3 to 4 minutes).

With the mixer still on medium speed, pour in the eggs, cautiously at first, tablespoon by tablespoon, as if you were adding oil when making mayonnaise. If at any time the mixture appears watery or shiny, stop the flow of eggs, and increase the speed until a smooth, silken appearance returns. Then decrease the speed and resume adding eggs.

Continue to cream, scraping the sides of the bowl at least once, or until the mixture appears fluffy white, velvety and increased in volume (about 2 to 3 minutes). Detach the beater and bowl from the mixer, and tap the beater against the side of the bowl to free the excess.

Using a rubber spatula, stir in one-fourth of the flour mixture. Then add one-third of the milk, stirring until blended. Repeat the procedure, alternating dry and liquid ingredients, ending with the final addition of flour. Scrape the sides of the bowl often and mix until smooth after each addition. Stir in the cornmeal just until blended.

Baking the cake: Spoon the batter into the prepared pan, and spread it evenly with the rubber spatula.

Bake for 62 to 67 minutes, or until a toothpick inserted near the center of the cake comes out clean.

Understanding Cakemaking

Cooling the cake: Place the cake on a rack to cool for 10 minutes. With mitts, tilt and rotate the pan, and gently tap it to see if the cake releases from the sides. If not, or if in doubt, run the blade of a small metal spatula along the cake's edge and the metal rim of the pan, freeing the sides and allowing air to get under the cake as it is rotated. Place the rack on top of the cake and invert. Cool completely.

Storing the cake: If you plan to serve the cake within 24 hours, wrap it in plastic wrap and store it at room temperature. This cake's flavor improves after one day's aging.

To freeze, cover the plastic-wrapped package with foil, labeling the contents and date. Freeze for no longer than 2 weeks.

Finishing the cake: Pour the ¼ cup powdered sugar into a sieve, and tap to coat cake's surface lightly. Cut the cake into thin slices with a sharp or serrated knife, using a sawing motion.

Apricot Pound Cake

THIS LUSCIOUS, buttery-flavored pound cake tastes even better with its tangy apricot filling. Its rectangular shape makes it possible to use an easy cutting technique before you apply the filling.

MAKES 8 TO 10 SERVINGS

Baking Equipment: 9-x-5-x-3-inch loaf pan

2	cups (200 grams) sifted cake flour
¼	teaspoon salt
5	large eggs, room temperature

1	teaspoon vanilla
½	teaspoon almond extract
1	teaspoon lemon zest (1 lemon)
1	teaspoon orange zest (1 orange)
8	ounces (2 sticks) unsalted butter, room temperature
1 ⅓	cups (265 grams) granulated sugar

Dried Apricot Filling, optional

| 3 | ounces (⅓ cup) dried apricots |
| ⅓ | cup water |

Baking preparations: Position rack in lower third of the oven; preheat oven to 350 degrees.

Using a paper towel, lightly grease the bottom and sides of the loaf pan with solid shortening. Dust generously with all-purpose flour, shake to distribute and tap out the excess.

Ingredient preparations: Pour the flour and salt into a triple sifter. Sift onto a sheet of waxed paper to distribute the salt evenly and to remove any lumps in the flour.

Crack the eggs into a small bowl and whisk together just enough to combine yolks and whites. Add the vanilla and almond extracts and stir to combine.

Grate only the colored portion from the lemon and orange for best flavor.

Place the butter in the bowl of a heavy-duty mixer.

Making the cake: With the flat beater (paddle), cream the butter on medium speed (#5) until it is lighter in color, clings to the sides of the mixing bowl and has a satiny appearance (this should take 30 to 45 seconds).

Maintaining the same speed, add the sugar in a steady stream. When all the sugar is added, stop the machine and scrape the mixture clinging to the sides into the center of the bowl. Continue to cream at the same speed for 3 to 4 minutes, or until the mixture is very light in color and fluffy in appearance.

With the mixer still on medium speed, pour in eggs, cautiously at first, tablespoon by tablespoon, as if you were adding oil when making mayonnaise. If at any time the mixture appears watery or shiny, stop the flow of eggs, and increase the speed until a smooth, silken appearance returns. Then decrease the speed to medium, and resume adding eggs.

Continue to cream, stopping the mixer and scraping the sides of the bowl at least once. When the mixture appears almost white and fluffy and has increased in volume (about 2 to 2½ minutes), detach the beater and bowl. Tap the beater against the edge of the bowl to free the excess. Stir in the lemon and orange zests with a rubber spatula.

Stir in about one-third of the flour at a time. Scrape the sides of the bowl often and mix until smooth after each addition.

Baking the cake: Spoon the batter into the prepared pan. With a rubber spatula, spread the batter, working from the center outward and creating a slightly raised ridge around the outside rim of the pan. (Even though the batter is manipulated so it is higher around the edges and lower in the center, this cake will still peak and crack in the center as it bakes as a result of aeration. This is characteristic of a heavy batter.)

Baker's Notes

☞ For a simpler version, you can omit the filling and serve the cake plain.

☞ Since a pound cake's texture is dense, I recommend using a wooden toothpick to test if baking is completed rather than relying on touching the top of the cake for springiness.

☞ Choose dried apricots for your filling that are bright orange and meaty.

Understanding Cakemaking

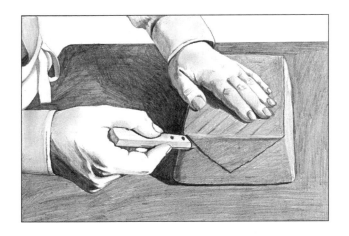

Clockwise from top left:
Making shallow V-shaped cuts on the ends of the cake. Slicing V-shaped section out of cake, using cut ends as a guide. Applying filling.

Bake for 50 to 55 minutes, or until a wooden toothpick inserted in the center comes out free of cake. The cake, with its crust golden, should begin to contract from the pan sides.

Cooling the cake: Place the cake on a rack to cool for 5 to 10 minutes. With mitts, tilt and rotate pan, and gently tap it on the counter to see if the cake is releasing from the metal sides. If not, or if in doubt, run a small metal spatula or the thin blade of a table knife between the outer cake edge and the metal rim, freeing the sides and allowing air to get under the cake as it is rotated.

Cover the cake with a cooling rack, invert it onto the rack and carefully lift pan to remove it. Cover with another rack, invert the cake, right side up, and remove the original rack. Cool completely.

Making the filling: No more than 30 minutes before filling the cake, begin the apricot filling, if desired. Proceed to cut the pound cake as directed below.

Place the apricots in a 1-quart heavy-bottomed saucepan. Pour the water over them and allow to soak for 5 minutes. Then, over medium heat, bring the mixture to a boil. Reduce the heat to medium-low and simmer until almost all the water is evaporated (about 5 to 7 minutes). While the mixture is warm, spoon it into a food processor fitted with the metal blade, and process until it has a sticky paste consistency.

Filling the cake: Once the cake has completely cooled, place it on the counter. With

(recipe continued on page 73)

Tiffany's Heart
SEE PAGE 89 FOR RECIPE

65

Duchess Cake
SEE PAGE 203 FOR RECIPE

Chocolate Rhapsody
SEE PAGE 124 FOR RECIPE

Juliet Cake
SEE PAGE 130 FOR RECIPE

Lemon Tart With Blueberries
SEE PAGE 347 FOR RECIPE

Gardenia Cake
SEE PAGE 127 FOR RECIPE

Victorian Maple Cake
SEE PAGE 82 FOR RECIPE

71

Crystal Almond Pound Cake
SEE PAGE 59 FOR RECIPE

a 12-inch serrated knife, trim the top of the cake to make it level. Then turn it upside down, making the top of the cake the base.

With the tip of a small paring knife, lightly trace a V on one short end of the cake, beginning at the corners of the seam (that is, where the sides meet the top) and ending just below the middle of the cake (see illustration, page 64). Each side or leg of the V should be about 2½ inches long (depending on the size of your cake, of course). Turn the cake around, and do the same to the other end of the loaf.

Insert the paring knife into the lines you have traced to the depth of about ½ inch. Do this to every corner of the cake. These notches will serve as a guide for cutting a deep V-shaped piece that will be lifted out of the pound cake.

Position the cake directly in front of you, with one of its short ends parallel to the edge of the counter. Taking the right side first, insert a 12-inch serrated knife into both notches, and slowly saw diagonally down that side of the V. Check often to ensure that the knife is staying in the notch and following the correct angle. Turn the cake around, and repeat the procedure on the other side. Carefully lift the triangular portion from the body of the cake, and set aside.

Using a metal spatula, spread a thin, even film of the dried apricot filling into the valley you have created in the cake. Then replace the triangular-shaped piece, pressing down gently to fit it into place. The filling should not be too apparent, and the cake should look almost as it did before being cut.

Storing the cake: If you plan to serve the cake within 24 hours, wrap it in plastic wrap and store at room temperature. To freeze, cover the plastic-wrapped package in foil. Label, indicating the contents and date. Freeze for no longer than 2 weeks.

Yogurt Bundt Cake

IF YOU'RE not already a yogurt lover, you will be instantly converted after tasting this adaptation of Bert Greene's cake. The yogurt is a refreshing alternative to the usual addition of sour cream or buttermilk.

MAKES 8 TO 10 SERVINGS

Baking Equipment: 10-inch tube pan or other 12-cup decorative tube pan

2 ½	cups (250 grams) sifted cake flour
1 ½	teaspoons baking powder
1	teaspoon baking soda
¼	teaspoon salt
2	ounces (⅓ cup) unblanched almonds
4	large eggs, room temperature
8	ounces (¾ cup) unflavored yogurt, room temperature
2	teaspoons lemon zest (1 lemon)
8	ounces (2 sticks) unsalted butter, room temperature
1 ½	cups (300 grams) granulated sugar

(continued)

Glaze, optional

½   cup (50 grams) unsifted powdered sugar

1   tablespoon water

1   tablespoon seedless raspberry jam

8   whole blanched almonds

Baker's Notes

☞ If you prefer, substitute crème fraîche for the yogurt.

☞ Grind the nuts in such a way to keep them powdery rather than oily, and you will be rewarded with a great cake. (See grinders in the equipment section, page 23.)

☞ For this recipe, you need an 8-ounce container of yogurt, which, because yogurt is thicker than water, measures ¾ cup.

Baking preparations: Position rack in lower third of oven; preheat oven to 350 degrees.

Using a paper towel, generously grease the bottom and sides of the pan with solid shortening. Dust generously with all-purpose flour, shake to coat, and tap out the excess.

Ingredient preparations: Pour the flour, baking powder, baking soda and salt in that order into a triple sifter. Sift onto a sheet of waxed paper to distribute the ingredients evenly; set aside.

Process the unblanched almonds in a nut grinder such as a Mouli or other rotary-type grater until the mixture has the consistency of cornmeal; you need ¾ cup ground.

Crack the eggs into a small bowl, and whisk just to combine the yolks and the whites.

Pour yogurt into a liquid cup measure.

Grate only the yellow part of the lemon for the zest.

Place the butter in the bowl of a heavy-duty mixer.

Making the cake: With the flat beater (paddle), cream the butter on medium speed (#5) until it is lighter in color, clings to the sides of the mixing bowl, and has a satiny appearance (about 30 to 45 seconds).

Maintaining the same speed, slowly add the granulated sugar. When all the sugar is added, stop the machine, and scrape the mixture clinging to the sides down into the center of the bowl. Continue to cream at the same speed or until the mixture is very light in color and fluffy in appearance for 4 to 5 minutes.

With the mixer at medium speed (#5), pour in the eggs, cautiously at first, tablespoon

by tablespoon, as if you were adding oil when making mayonnaise. If at any time the mixture appears watery or shiny, stop the flow of eggs, and increase the speed until a smooth, silken appearance returns. Then decrease the speed to medium, and resume adding eggs.

Continue to cream, stopping the mixer and scraping the sides of the bowl at least once. When the mixture appears fluffy, light in color and velvety and has increased in volume (about 2 to 3 minutes total from the time you began adding the eggs), detach the beater and bowl. Tap the beater against the edge of the bowl to free the excess. Then stir in the almonds and lemon zest with a rubber spatula.

Using the rubber spatula, stir in one-third of the flour mixture. Then add one-half of the yogurt, stirring to blend together. Repeat, alternating dry and liquid ingredients, ending with a final addition of flour. Scrape the side of the bowl often, and mix until smooth after each addition.

Baking the cake: Spoon the batter into the pan, and spread it level with the rubber spatula. Bake for 45 to 50 minutes, or until the cake springs back slightly when touched lightly in the center, the sides begin to contract from the pan and a wooden toothpick inserted in the center comes out free of cake.

Cooling the cake: Place the cake on a rack to cool for 5 to 10 minutes. With mitts, tilt and rotate the pan, and gently tap it on the counter to see if the cake is releasing from the sides. If not, or if in doubt, run a small metal spatula or the thin blade of a table knife between the outer cake's edge and the metal rim, freeing the sides and allowing air to get under the cake as it is rotated.

Cover the cake with a cooling rack, invert it onto the rack, and carefully lift the pan to remove. Cool completely.

Storing the cake: If you plan to use this cake within 24 hours, wrap it in plastic wrap and store at room temperature.

If you are freezing it, cover the plastic-wrapped package with foil. Label the package, indicating the contents and date. Freeze for no longer than 2 weeks.

Finishing the cake: Measure the powdered sugar, and sift it into a 1-quart mixing bowl to remove any lumps. Add the water and raspberry jam and stir with a rubber spatula. Coat the entire surface of the cooled cake with a pastry brush, if desired.

Toss the whole almonds with the remaining glaze, and place each one strategically on the cake to decorate it.

Sour Cream Cake With Cocoa Filling

Baker's Notes

☞ Baking in a decorative tube pan causes the cocoa filling to create a pleasing swirling design on the cake's exterior.

☞ It is important to have the glaze ready when the cake is finished baking because the glistening effect is made by the heat of the cake as it cools.

☞ Incidentally, an 8-ounce container of sour cream is ¾ cup.

THE DOUBLE glaze on this cake adds a complexity of flavors and shows off its contours. For years I wondered how pastry shops produced such a shiny, translucent finish. The technique I finally learned from a Swiss baker is included in this recipe, but you can use it on any cake you wish to glaze.

MAKES 12 TO 14 SERVINGS

Baking Equipment: One 10-inch Bundt pan or other 12-cup decorative tube pan

Cocoa Filling
¼	cup (50 grams) brown sugar, packed
1	tablespoon granulated sugar
1	tablespoon cocoa powder
½	teaspoon ground cinnamon

Cake
2 ¾	cups (275 grams) sifted cake flour
2	teaspoons baking powder
½	teaspoon baking soda
¼	teaspoon salt
3	large eggs, room temperature
1	teaspoon vanilla
6	ounces (1 ½ sticks) unsalted butter, room temperature
1 ½	cups (300 grams) granulated sugar
8	ounces (¾ cup) sour cream, room temperature

Glazes
½	cup strained apricot jam
1	recipe Translucent Sugar Glaze (page 268)

Baking preparations: Position rack in lower third of oven; preheat oven to 350 degrees.

Using a paper towel, generously grease the bottom and sides of a decorative tube pan with solid shortening. Dust generously with all-purpose flour, shake to distribute and tap out excess.

Making the filling: Pour the brown sugar, 1 tablespoon granulated sugar, cocoa and cinnamon in that order into a sieve over a 1-quart mixing bowl. Press through the sieve with the back of a spoon and set aside.

Ingredient preparations: Pour the flour, baking powder, baking soda and salt in that order into a triple sifter. Sift onto a sheet of waxed paper to distribute the ingredients evenly and to remove any lumps in the flour; set aside.

Crack the eggs into a small bowl, and whisk just to combine yolks and whites. Add the vanilla; stir to blend.

Place the butter in the bowl of a heavy-duty mixer.

Making the cake: With the flat beater (paddle), cream the butter on medium speed (#5) until it is lighter in color, clings to the sides of the mixing bowl and has a satiny appearance (about 30 to 45 seconds).

Maintaining the same speed, add the 1½ cups sugar in a steady stream. When all the sugar is added, stop the machine and scrape the mixture clinging to the sides into the center of the bowl. Continue to cream at the same speed, or until the mixture is very light in color and fluffy in appearance (about 4 to 5 minutes).

With the mixer still on medium speed, pour in the egg mixture, cautiously at first, tablespoon by tablespoon, as if you were adding oil when making mayonnaise. If at any time the mixture appears watery or shiny, stop the flow of eggs and increase the speed until a smooth, silken appearance returns. Then decrease to medium speed again, and resume adding eggs.

Continue to cream, stopping the mixer and scraping the sides of the bowl at least once. When the mixture appears fluffy white and velvety and has increased in volume (2 to 3 minutes total from the time you began adding the eggs), detach the beater and bowl. Tap the beater against the edge of the bowl to free the excess.

Using a rubber spatula, stir in one-third of the flour mixture. Then add one-half of the sour cream, stirring to blend together. Repeat this procedure, alternating dry and liquid ingredients, ending with the flour. With each addition scrape the sides of the bowl often, and mix until smooth.

Baking the cake: Spoon one-third of the thick batter into the decorative tube pan. Using a rubber spatula, distribute the batter evenly around the bottom. Sprinkle one-half of the cocoa filling over the top, shaking the pan lightly to distribute the mixture evenly. (Do not be concerned if some of the filling clings to the outside rim of the pan.) Repeat with another third of the batter, distributing it evenly and smoothly. Sprinkle on the last half of the filling and add the final third of the batter. Spread the batter evenly and level it again.

Bake for 55 to 60 minutes, or until the top springs back slightly when lightly touched, the sides begin to contract from the pan and a wooden toothpick inserted in the center comes out free of cake.

Making the glazes: Fifteen minutes before the cake is finished baking, begin glaze preparation. Spoon the strained apricot jam into a 1-quart saucepan. Measure the sugar for Translucent Sugar Glaze, and sift into a 1-quart mixing bowl to remove any lumps.

Finishing the cake: Place the cake on a rack to cool for 5 to 7 minutes. While it is cooling, heat the jam just to simmering, and cook to evaporate some of its liquid and thicken it (about 2 to 3 minutes). Do not overcook. When cool, the consistency should not be as chewy as caramel candy. To test, put a drop of jam, which has been simmering a minute, on an ice cube. Then rub the jam between your thumb and forefinger to feel its consistency. (Different brands of jam produce different results, and you should retest if you use a different brand.)

With mitts, tilt and rotate the pan, and gently tap it on the counter to see if the cake is releasing from the metal sides. If not, or if in doubt, run a small metal spatula or the thin blade of a table knife between the outer cake edge and the metal rim, freeing the sides and allowing air to get under the cake as it is rotated.

Place a rack over the cake pan, invert it onto the rack, and carefully lift the pan to remove. Place the cake on its rack over a sheet of foil or waxed paper to catch the glaze's drippings. Coat the cake's surface with the hot apricot glaze, using a pastry brush. Wait for 5 minutes, so the glaze will adhere to the hot cake, before you apply the next glaze; otherwise, the two merely mix together.

Now make Translucent Sugar Glaze. Using another pastry brush, cover the apricot-glazed cake with it. If the coating is too thick, appearing opaque rather than translucent, stir in a few drops of water at a time until it reaches the desired consistency. Use all the glaze and cover the entire cake. As the cake cools, the glaze will dry.

Cooling the cake: For prettiest results, do not move the glazed cake to a serving plate for several hours. Giving it time to cool completely allows the glazes to dry and prevents cracking.

To move the cake from its rack to a serving plate, slip two long metal icing spatulas under it, crisscross them and lift.

Storing the cake: Serve at room temperature (no refrigeration is necessary). The cake freezes well, but unfortunately, the glaze does not.

Fresh Ginger Cake

ONCE YOU make this cake, you'll agree that there is no substitute for fresh ginger. It is adapted from a recipe by Sylvia Vaughn Thompson. Enjoy it plain, sprinkled with powdered sugar.

MAKES 8 TO 10 SERVINGS

Baking Equipment: One 6-cup ring mold, about 9½ inches in diameter

1 ½	cups (150 grams) sifted cake flour
1	teaspoon baking soda
¼	teaspoon salt
1	large egg, room temperature
¼	cup light molasses
¼	cup dark corn syrup
½	cup (4 ounces) water
4	ounces (1 stick) unsalted butter, room temperature
½	cup (100 grams) light brown sugar, packed
2	teaspoons lemon zest (1 lemon)
2	teaspoons grated fresh ginger
¼	cup (25 grams) unsifted powdered sugar

Baker's Notes

☞ You may bake the batter in a 9-inch cake pan, too.

☞ Either light or dark brown sugar is fine.

☞ To grate fresh ginger, peel the paperlike skin of the ginger with a small paring knife, exposing about 1½ inches of the ginger.

☞ Buttermilk may be substituted for the water.

Baking preparations: Position rack in lower third of oven; preheat oven to 350 degrees.

Using a paper towel, generously grease the bottom and sides of the ring mold with solid shortening. Dust generously with all-purpose flour, tilt to cover and tap out excess.

Ingredient preparations: Pour the flour, baking soda and salt in that order into a triple sifter. Sift onto a sheet of waxed paper and set aside.

Crack the egg into a small bowl, and whisk just to combine the yolk and white.

Pour the molasses, corn syrup and water into a liquid cup measure; stir to combine.

Place the butter in the bowl of a heavy-duty mixer.

Making the cake: With the flat beater (paddle), cream the butter on medium speed (#5) until it clings to the sides of the mixing bowl and has a satiny appearance (about 30 seconds).

Maintaining the same speed, add the sugar. Then stop the machine, and scrape the mixture clinging to the sides down into the center of the bowl. Continue to cream at the same

Understanding Cakemaking

speed for 2 to 3 minutes, or until the mixture is lighter in color and fluffy in appearance.

With the mixer still on medium speed, pour in the egg, cautiously at first, tablespoon by tablespoon, as if you were adding oil when making mayonnaise. If at any time the mixture appears watery or shiny, stop the flow of egg and increase the speed until a smooth, silken appearance returns. Then decrease the speed to medium, and resume adding egg.

Continue to cream, stopping the mixer and scraping the sides of the bowl at least once. When the mixture appears fluffy and velvety and has increased in volume (about 1 to 2 minutes), detach the beater and bowl. Tap the beater against the edge of the bowl to free the excess. Stir in the lemon zest and ginger.

Using a rubber spatula, stir in one-fourth of the flour mixture. Then add one-third of the molasses mixture, stirring to blend together. Repeat, alternating dry and liquid ingredients, ending with the flour. Scrape the sides of the bowl often, and mix until smooth after each addition.

Baking the cake: Pour the batter into the ring mold and spread it slightly higher toward the outer edge so it will bake more evenly. Bake for about 35 to 37 minutes, or until the sides begin to contract from the mold, the surface springs back slightly when lightly touched in the center and a wooden toothpick inserted comes out free of cake.

Cooling the cake: Place the cake on a rack to cool for 5 to 10 minutes. With mitts, tilt and rotate the mold, and gently tap it on the counter to see if the cake is releasing from the sides. If not, or if in doubt, run a small metal spatula or the thin blade of a table knife between the outer cake edge and the metal rim, freeing the sides and allowing air to get under the cake as it is rotated. Place an 8-inch-wide strip of parchment paper, then a rack on the top of the cake, invert and carefully remove the ring mold. Cool completely.

Storing the cake: The cake may be baked up to 24 hours ahead, wrapped in plastic wrap and stored at room temperature. To freeze, cover the plastic-wrapped package with foil. Label it, indicating the contents and date. Freeze for no longer than 2 weeks.

Finishing the cake: Place a cooling rack on top of the cake (it will make a pattern for decorating the cake). Pour powdered sugar into a sieve. Using the palm of your hand to control the flow of the sugar, gently tap the sieve, sprinkling the sugar evenly over the cake.

To transfer the ring-shaped cake, slide two 8-inch or longer metal spatulas under it, crisscross the spatulas; then carefully lift the cake onto a serving plate.

Americana Banana Roll

A LIGHT sour cream-flavored filling is the perfect complement to the sweetness of the tender, moist banana cake. Don't wait for an excuse to make this dessert. It doesn't take long to prepare, and assembling it into a dessert can come very soon after baking because the thin cake cools quickly.

MAKES 8 TO 10 SERVINGS

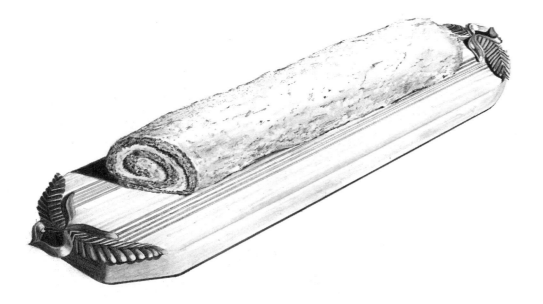

Decorating Equipment: Two 12-x-15½-x-½-inch baking sheets

One Banana Sheet Cake (page 51)
1   **tablespoon granulated sugar**

Filling
¾   **cup (6 ounces) heavy cream**
2   **tablespoons sour cream**
1   **tablespoon granulated sugar**
1   **teaspoon vanilla**

3   **tablespoons unsifted powdered sugar**

Advance preparations: Prepare Banana Sheet Cake as directed on page 51. Cool it no more than 30 to 60 minutes under the foil tent. Then prepare to roll the cake.

Slip a 12-x-15½-x-½-inch baking sheet under the foil-lined cake. Sprinkle 1 tablespoon granulated sugar over the cake's surface. Place two 18-inch strips of foil lengthwise on top of the sugared cake, one overlapping the other; then place the second baking sheet on top of the foil. Invert the cake on it, and carefully peel the baking foil from the cake to avoid tearing the thin layer. (The sugar crystals prevent the cake from sticking to the foil strips while it is inverted.)

Making the filling: Combine the filling ingredients in a 1½-quart mixing bowl, and whip them until some cream dropped from the beater or whisk does not disappear on the surface of the mixture in the bowl. Another test is to draw the beater or whisk through the center of the cream in the bowl; if the track stays in place, you are ready to spread the filling on the cake. The cream will appear soft, shiny and smooth but stiffer than for most desserts. It will coat the cake layer, sticking to it and staying in place when rolled.

Baker's Note

☞ I prefer rolling the cake on foil rather than on plastic wrap or parchment paper because of the foil's strength and flexibility.

Understanding Cakemaking

Rolling the cake: Lift the cake on the two overlapping sheets of foil off the baking sheet so that one of its long sides is parallel to the edge of your counter. (The cake will be rolled lengthwise.)

Spread the cream evenly over the cake with a rubber spatula, up to 1 inch before reaching the long end farthest from you. (Some of the filling will move to that end as you roll.)

Begin rolling by flipping the edge of cake nearest you over onto itself. Then, with the aid of the foil that extends on either side of the cake, roll the cake lengthwise until you reach the other end. With your hands, wrap some of the foil around the roll to assist you in rounding the shape as you work toward the other end of the cake (otherwise, the cake will stick to your hands).

Serving the cake: Cut each end of the roll on the diagonal for eye appeal, and sprinkle a light coating of powdered sugar over it to disguise any cracks in the cake. Lift it onto a serving plate with the aid of a long, wide spatula or a baking sheet without sides.

Victorian Maple Cake

T̲reat yourself to an old-fashioned combination. You'll love the blend of the butter cake with the refined flavor of pure maple syrup in a fluffy, light frosting. (See photograph, page 71.)

M̲akes 8 to 10 servings

Decorating Equipment: 8-inch cardboard round, cake decorating turntable, metal skewer

Two 8-inch layers Buttermilk Cake (page 49)
1   recipe Maple Italian Meringue (page 266)
1   ounce pecans, chopped fine

Advance preparations: Prepare two layers of Buttermilk Cake as directed on page 49.
Split each layer in half to create four ¾-inch-thick layers.
Prepare Maple Italian Meringue as directed on page 266.

Assembling the cake: Place one of the ¾-inch layers on the cardboard round and then on the cake decorating turntable. Spread Maple Italian Meringue about ¼ inch thick over the layer. Top with another layer, gently pressing it to level the cake. Spread with more meringue. Repeat the procedure with the third layer, leveling it, then spreading with the meringue. Top with the last layer, again pressing it carefully to level.

With the cake on the turntable, spread a thin film of the meringue along the sides and top of the cake to set any loose crumbs to the cake. (The height of the cake makes it difficult to hold it in your hand while you coat the sides with the frosting.) Remove all crumbs from the metal icing spatula before applying more meringue to the cake. (Since this frosting tends to be very sticky, it's a good idea to dip the spatula into a tall glass of warm water, then to dry it before making another application.)

To finish the cake, spread another thin layer of the frosting around the sides and on top. Then smooth the sides and top with the aid of your turntable and metal spatula.

☞ This dessert may be prepared over a 2-day period.
First day: Bake cake layers.
Second day: Frost and decorate.

Optional decorating technique: After you have applied the frosting, place a metal skewer on a stove burner. Heat it over a medium-high heat for about 3 to 5 minutes. Transfer the cake to a nearby surface. Score the cake, making lines that form the letter M. (The hot metal caramelizes the sugar in the frosting, crystallizing an impression on the surface of the cake. If this does not happen, the skewer isn't hot enough.) Each time you lightly touch the top of the frosting to make a line, return the skewer to the burner to reheat.

Hold the cake in one hand, and press the finely chopped pecans around its base with your other hand.

Storing the cake: Do not refrigerate, but serve the cake at room temperature on the day it is assembled. This way the flavors and textures are at their peak.

Lemon Parfait Cake

THE REFRESHING lemon flavor and subtle mingling of butter, almond and coconut make this cake as appealing inside as out.
MAKES 8 TO 10 SERVINGS

Decorating Equipment: 8-inch cardboard round, cake decorating turntable, 1½-inch flower-shaped cutter

	One 8-inch layer Classic Butter Cake (page 47) or Buttermilk Cake (page 49)
1 ½	cups freshly grated coconut (page 271)
2	ounces (3 tablespoons) Classic Marzipan, optional (page 304), room temperature
1	recipe Lemon Almond Cream (page 259)
¼	cup (25 grams) unsifted powdered sugar
	Candied lilacs or candles, optional

Baker's Notes

☞ This dessert may be prepared over a 2-day period.
First day: Bake cake layer; prepare freshly grated coconut; prepare and tint Classic Marzipan.
Second day: Prepare Lemon-Almond Cream; assemble and decorate dessert.

☞ I prefer to make my own marzipan because it's better tasting, less sweet and easier to handle than the store-bought variety. Surprisingly, the recipe is not difficult, and it remains fresh for several weeks if it is carefully wrapped and refrigerated.

Understanding Cakemaking

Advance preparations: Prepare Classic Butter Cake or Buttermilk Cake as directed on page 47 or 49. (When the layers are cool, wrap and freeze one layer; use the other for this dessert.)

Prepare freshly grated coconut as directed on page 271. Place 1½ cups on a baking sheet, such as a 12-x-15½-inch sheet.

If desired, prepare the Classic Marzipan on page 304 and tint the 2 ounces with 1 drop yellow food coloring as directed.

Prepare Lemon Almond Cream as directed on page 259; refrigerate until ready to use.

Assembling the cake: Place the cake on a flat surface, and split it into two ¾-inch-thick layers (review, if necessary, the techniques for splitting a cake on page 234).

Turn the top layer upside down so the cut side is up, and center it on the cardboard round on the turntable. Spread about ⅓ of the lemon-almond cream evenly over this layer; then top it with the other layer. Spread the sides and top with the remaining cream.

Hold the cake in one hand directly over the baking sheet covered with the grated coconut, and tilt the cake slightly. With the other hand, pick up some of the coconut and press it into the filling along the sides. Rotate the cake as you apply the coconut until the sides are completely covered. Sprinkle the remaining coconut on top. Press the coconut lightly into the filling with the flat side of a clean metal spatula to ensure that it adheres.

Pour the powdered sugar into a sieve, and tap its edge to sprinkle the sugar evenly over the cake.

Optional decorations: Roll the marzipan paper-thin, about 1/16 inch thick (see rolling marzipan on page 86). Cut out about 20 flowers; then place them near the edge of the cake, overlapping slightly. Pierce each flower's center with a candied lilac or a candle, if desired.

Fraisia

FRAISIA is synonymous with strawberries. This European-style strawberry shortcake combines a filling of freshly whipped cream, white chocolate and juicy, sweet strawberries with a buttery, tender cake. It is topped with the almond-flavored marzipan.
MAKES 10 SERVINGS

Decorating Equipment: 8-inch stiff cardboard round, cake decorating turntable, small paper cone

       One 8-inch layer Buttermilk Cake (page 49)
7   **ounces (¾ cup) Classic Marzipan, optional (page 304), room temperature**
       Green food coloring
Filling
   ¼   **cup strawberry preserves**
1 ¼   **cups (10 ounces) heavy cream**
   1   **tablespoon granulated sugar**
   1   **teaspoon vanilla**

2 ounces white chocolate, finely grated

2 ½ cups (25 to 30) fresh strawberries, hulled

Cornstarch

1 recipe Classic Royal Icing, optional (page 269)

Advance preparations: Prepare Buttermilk Cake as directed on page 49. When the layers are cool, freeze one layer for another time.

If desired, prepare the Classic Marzipan as directed on page 304, and wrap it tightly in plastic wrap to prevent drying. Refrigerate it if it is made ahead, and bring it to room temperature when you are ready to use it. Then tint with 2 drops of green food coloring as directed on page 305, and wrap it in plastic until time to decorate the dessert.

Assembling the cake: Split the layer in half so each is about ¾ inch thick. Center one layer, cut side up, on a cardboard round of the same size and place it on the decorating turntable. With an 8-inch flexible metal icing spatula, spread a thin layer of strawberry preserves evenly over the layer, being certain to reach completely to the edge. Center the top layer over this.

Now you are ready to layer the whipped cream and strawberries on top of the cake. Whip the cream with the sugar and vanilla until soft peaks form. Fold in the white chocolate. Spread about one-third evenly over the top of the cake with a rubber spatula. Arrange some of the strawberries, points up, close together in the cream, stopping 1 inch short of the edge. (The fruit is likely to have a variety of sizes; use the largest on the bottom layer.)

Whip the remaining cream with a whisk until stiffer, firmer peaks form; this consistency is essential to support the marzipan covering. Spread a few more tablespoons of whipped cream over the fruit, holding them in place as though they were bricks with mortar. Continue arranging more strawberries, stacking another layer on the first. Spread another couple of tablespoons of whipped cream onto this layer; then arrange the remaining strawberries on top. After three layers of fruit, the center will be higher than the edges, forming a dome.

Baker's Notes

☞ This dessert may be prepared over a 2-day period.
First day: Bake Buttermilk Cake layer and prepare Classic Marzipan.
Second day: Prepare the filling, and assemble the dessert.

☞ I prefer to make my own marzipan because it's better-tasting, less sweet, and easier to handle than the purchased variety. Surprisingly, the recipe is not difficult to make, and it remains fresh for several weeks, if it is carefully wrapped and refrigerated.

☞ This dessert can be simplified by splitting the cake layer in half horizontally and filling it with small fresh strawberries and a layer of sweetened whipped cream. Sprinkle the top of the cake with powdered sugar.

☞ Alternatively, to cover the cake layer with Marzipan, spread ¼ cup strawberry preserves over the cake's surface. Roll out the marzipan as directed. Using an 8-inch cake pan, trace around it with a small paring knife. Gently lift the marzipan circle and place it on the cake layer.

Understanding Cakemaking

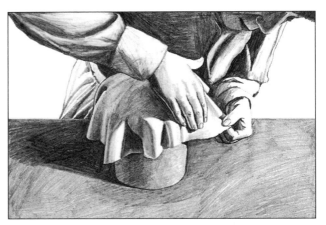
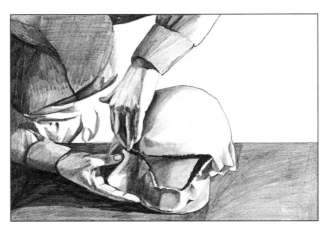

Clockwise from top left:
Draping the marzipan circle over the dessert. Stretching the marzipan to elongate it to eliminate pleats at the base of the dessert. Pressing the marzipan against the cardboard's edge to remove excess neatly.

Place the cream around and on top of the strawberries. With the metal icing spatula, push the cream into the crevices and along the cake sides, at the same time smoothing the edges and top and shaping the dessert into a perfectly formed dome. The cake edges require only a thin film of cream to allow the marzipan to adhere, if you are using it.

Rolling the marzipan: The method for rolling marzipan is similar to rolling short dough for a pie crust. Shape the marzipan into a flat disk 4 inches in diameter, and place it on a surface very lightly dusted with cornstarch. Position the rolling pin in the center, and roll away from yourself in a steady, even stroke. Take care not to roll off the edge, or the marzipan will become too thin, making it difficult to handle. Lift the marzipan, and turn it a couple of inches to the right; if it sticks to the surface, dust it lightly with cornstarch. Again center the rolling pin and continue to roll until you have formed a circle 14 inches in diameter and less than ⅛ inch thick. (If the marzipan should tear at any time, overlap the two torn areas, and roll to seal them together.) Brush off excess cornstarch with a pastry brush.

Applying the marzipan: To achieve a smooth finish without a crease, place the dome-shaped dessert with its cardboard bottom on a stand that is smaller in diameter than the cake itself (you may use a smaller cake pan or a large can).
Wind the marzipan circle loosely onto the rolling pin, lifting it to cover and decorate the dessert. This reduces the risk of tearing the marzipan and at the same time helps maintain its shape. Place the rolling pin across the circle of marzipan, one-third from the top edge. Lift the top section of marzipan over the pin, toward you.

Hold the rolling pin with the marzipan about 3 inches above the far end of the dessert; begin to unroll it carefully, allowing for a 1-inch overhang. Work across the top and down the other side, unrolling as you go, until the entire dessert is draped in marzipan, leaving at least a 1-inch overhang all around. Now fit the marzipan to the contour of the dessert, gently smoothing it down and over the edge of the cardboard as though you were working with fabric for a garment.

To ensure a neat, unwrinkled finish, begin smoothing again at the top with the palm of your hand, following the curvature of the dome. Each time pleats form near the cardboard base, stretch the marzipan gently (with one hand) to elongate it and eliminate the pleats. Press the marzipan against the cardboard to maintain the smooth finish. Continue working down and around the cake until you have a completely smooth surface. With all the folds eliminated, press the marzipan firmly against the cardboard's edge to release the excess.

Finishing the cake: If desired, prepare Classic Royal Icing as directed on page 269 and a paper cone as illustrated on page 244.

Form leftover marzipan scraps into a ball. Divide in two, and roll each half into a thin 15-inch cord. Drape one of the cords over the top of the dome. Overlap with the remaining cord, creating an x pattern. Press against the overhang and the cardboard to remove the excess. Form the leftover into a ball, and roll it out until it is ⅛ inch thick. With a small knife, cut out a rectangle approximately 2½ x 1½ inches. Fill a paper cone with the icing, and pipe "FRAISIA" in script on the rectangle. Place it in front of the dessert.

Storing the cake: This dessert should be served the day it is assembled. Refrigerate it uncovered. Remove it from the refrigerator 2 hours before serving, and allow it to reach room temperature.

Chocolate Cake Squares

OCCASIONALLY at the end of my baking classes, after I have demonstrated several recipes and their techniques in detail, I love to bring this cake out as a sharp contrast. It is a snap to make. Its light, moist texture and its sinfully rich chocolate flavor make it impossible for anyone to eat just one square.

MAKES THIRTY-FIVE 1 ½-INCH SQUARE CAKES

Baking Equipment: 10-x-15-x-1-inch jelly roll pan

4	ounces (1 stick) unsalted butter
1	cup (8 ounces) cold water
½	cup unflavored vegetable oil
2	eggs, room temperature
½	cup (4 ounces) buttermilk, room temperature
1	teaspoon vanilla
2	cups (280 grams) unsifted all-purpose flour
2	cups (400 grams) granulated sugar

(continued)

¼ cup (25 grams) unsifted cocoa powder
1 teaspoon baking soda
¼ teaspoon salt

Glaze
3 ¾ cups (1 pound) unsifted powdered sugar
¼ cup (25 grams) unsifted cocoa powder
6 tablespoons milk
4 ounces (1 stick) unsalted butter
1 teaspoon vanilla

Baker's Notes

☞ I like to cut the cake into squares and, depending on the event we're celebrating, decorate them accordingly. I enjoy placing a candied violet on each square with buttercream leaves, tinting marzipan and cutting out different shapes, or perhaps piping designs with royal icing. When I had my baking business, these small cakes were a best seller.

☞ The technique for cutting glazed cake into perfect squares is useful in other recipes, too.

Baking preparations: Position the rack in the lower third of the oven; preheat oven to 350 degrees.

Using a paper towel, grease the bottom and sides of the pan with solid shortening. Dust generously with all-purpose flour, shake to distribute, and tap out the excess.

Place a cooling rack on a counter that is not likely to be in the way. The chocolate cake will be removed to this rack after baking, then glazed immediately and left to sit.

Ingredient preparations: Melt the 4 ounces of butter in a small saucepan. Remove from heat; cool for 5 minutes; then add the water and oil.

Break the eggs into a bowl; whisk to combine. Add the buttermilk and vanilla and stir to combine.

Pour the flour, granulated sugar, cocoa, baking soda and salt in that order into a triple sifter over the bowl of a heavy-duty mixer. Sift into the bowl.

Attach the bowl to the mixer and add the butter and water mixture.

Making the cake: With the flat beater (paddle), blend the ingredients on medium-low speed (#3) for about 30 to 45 seconds. Add the buttermilk mixture; resume the same speed and blend just until smooth (about 30 to 45 seconds). Remove the flat beater and bowl from the mixer. Tap the beater against the edge of the bowl to remove excess.

Baking the cake: Pour the batter into the prepared pan, beginning around the edge of the pan and then into the center. With the rubber spatula, manipulate the batter from the center so the batter is higher along the sides (this assures a more level surface after baking). Bake for 20 to 22 minutes, or until the cake springs back slightly when lightly touched in the center and the sides begin to contract from the pan.

Making the glaze: While the cake is baking, begin the glaze preparation. Place a sieve over a 1½-quart mixing bowl; set nearby.

Pour the powered sugar and cocoa in that order into a triple sifter, and sift into a 3-quart mixing bowl.

Pour the milk into a small saucepan, add the 4 ounces of butter and melt over low heat.

Pour the hot milk mixture into the powdered sugar mixture and stir to combine. Add the vanilla and blend. Pour the mixture through the sieve over the bowl, and push it through with the aid of a rubber spatula.

Finishing the cake: When the cake has finished baking, remove it to the cooling rack. Immediately pour the glaze (its consistency is thicker than heavy cream, but runny) over the hot cake from the top of the pan's short side down almost to its other short end. Spread the glaze with the spatula over the surface. Do not worry if some glaze touches the pan's rim; this will be removed later. Spread the glaze just to cover; then stop. (The heat from the cake will keep the glaze liquid enough to spread, but too much manipulation of the glaze will dull its finish.)

Cooling and cutting the cake: Do not touch or move the cake for at least 4 hours or the glaze will crack. (Waiting overnight is fine. Don't cover or refrigerate it.) The glaze's surface will set as the cake cools.

To cut the cake into neat individual squares, you need a sharp small paring knife, a small glass of hot water, a paper towel and an 18-inch ruler.

First, free the glaze sticking to the rim of the pan. Dip the blade of the knife into the hot water, wipe it with the paper towel, and then trace the perimeter of one side of the pan to release just the glaze, not the cake. Repeat this procedure along the sides. (Now the baking pan may be picked up without the glaze's cracking.) Remove the cooling rack from under the pan so it does not tilt when you cut the squares.

Place the ruler next to one of the longest sides (15 inches). With the tip of the knife blade mark 1/16-inch-long notches in the glaze every 1½ inches along the entire length. Repeat on the opposite side, so that the notches line up directly across from each other. Repeat this procedure on the short sides of the pan, too.

With the paring knife, dipped into hot water and wiped, score just the glaze (not cutting through the cake) in a straight line from one notch to the other, using the ruler as a guide. When you are finished, the pattern for the squares has been formed.

Now cut through the scored lines, heating and cleaning the paring knife each time. Decorate each square, if desired.

Storing the cake: The cake is so moist that it may remain in the baking pan for several hours after being cut with no fear of its getting stale. (Covering its surface is not recommended since it mars the glaze.) You can also wrap the unglazed cake in the pan with foil, freeze it, then glaze it as described above at a later date after completely defrosting it.

Remove each square with a small metal spatula onto a paper case for serving. Any leftover glazed squares may be placed in a sturdy container and frozen for up to 1 week.

Tiffany's Heart

T HIS IS a stunning, simple cake for the incurable romantic who adores chocolate and raspberries together. It's the freshest box of candy you'll ever eat.
(See photograph, page 65.)
MAKES 8 TO 12 SERVINGS

Baking and Decorating Equipment: One 8-inch heart-shaped pan, stiff cardboard

☞ If fresh raspberries
are not in season, try
fresh small strawberries.
Or just pipe a design on
the cake with any left-
over glaze.

☞ The fruit for the
glaze must be at room
temperature or the glaze
will solidify the moment
it touches the fruit.

☞ You can also use an
8-inch straight-sided pan
for this cake.

2	ounces (½ cup) pecans
⅓	cup (45 grams) unsifted all-purpose flour
⅓	cup (65 grams) granulated sugar
⅓	cup (65 grams) light brown sugar, packed
3	eggs, room temperature
1	teaspoon granulated sugar
3	ounces (6 tablespoons) unsalted butter
6	ounces semisweet chocolate
2	tablespoons water
1	tablespoon rum
1	recipe Chocolate-Butter Glaze (page 289)
1	cup fresh raspberries, room temperature

Baking preparations: Position the rack in the lower third of the oven; preheat oven to 350 degrees.

Using a paper towel, grease the bottom and sides of the pan with solid shortening. Dust generously with all-purpose flour, shake to distribute, tap out the excess and insert parchment liner.

Trace the shape of the pan on the cardboard. Cut the heart shape from the cardboard; set aside until the baked cake is unmolded from the pan.

Ingredient preparations: Grind the pecans until they have the consistency of cornmeal; you need ¾ cup ground. Add the flour to the nuts.

Measure granulated and brown sugars; set aside.

Separate the eggs, placing the whites in a deep 1½-quart mixing bowl and the yolks in a small bowl. Place 1 teaspoon granulated sugar near the whites for whipping time.

Melt the butter and chocolate in a small heavy-bottomed saucepan over very low heat. Stir in the water and blend until smooth.

Making the cake: Transfer the warm chocolate mixture to a 3-quart mixing bowl, and while it is still warm, stir in the granulated and brown sugars. Cool for 5 minutes. Then stir in the egg yolks until incorporated. Add the rum and blend. Pour in the nuts and flour mixture and mix together.

With an electric hand mixer, whip the egg whites on medium-low speed until small bubbles appear and the surface is frothy (about 30 seconds). Increase the speed to high (#10), add the 1 teaspoon sugar and whip until soft, white peaks form (about 1 minute).

Scoop a third of the whites into the chocolate mixture and stir-fold with a rubber spatula to lighten it. Then fold in the remainder.

Baking the cake: Scoop the batter into the prepared pan, and smooth evenly with the rubber spatula. Bake for 25 minutes, or until it feels soft but not liquid in the center. Do not overbake; chocolate firms as it cools.

Cooling the cake: Remove the pan from the oven to a cooling rack for 15 to 20 minutes. Then tilt and rotate the pan, and gently tap it on the counter to see if the cake is

Pouring chocolate glaze onto center of cake.

Spreading glaze with flexible metal icing spatula.

being released cleanly from the metal. If not, or if in doubt, run a small metal spatula between the cake's edge and the metal rim, freeing the sides and allowing air to get under the layer as it is rotated.

Cover the pan with the cardboard, invert the cake onto it and carefully lift the pan to remove. Peel off and discard the parchment liner.

Storing the cake: Store and serve the cake at room temperature (refrigeration changes its flavor and texture).

The cake may be baked ahead, cooled, wrapped in plastic wrap, then wrapped again in foil and frozen for up to 2 weeks. After it is defrosted, apply the glaze.

Glazing the cake and berries: Prepare Chocolate-Butter Glaze as directed on page 289. Place 3 tablespoons of the glaze in a 3-quart mixing bowl and set aside.

Place the cake on its cardboard on a cooling rack over a jelly roll pan. Glaze the cake as suggested in glazing techniques on page 241.

If necessary, place the bowl with the reserved glaze over warm water just to liquefy it and until it's no warmer than body temperature.

Pour the raspberries on top. Gently slide a rubber spatula under the berries, and fold the two together. Repeat this 3 more times. The object is partially to coat some of the raspberries, not all of them.

Carefully scoop the raspberries on top of the cake. Or lift the chocolate-covered berries gently with your fingertips and place them individually on top of the cake.

Rehrücken

THIS VIENNESE favorite is a wonderful cake that does not bake all the way through so that it has a deliciously creamy inside. Traditionally, its shape and decoration were intended to resemble a saddle of venison prepared for roasting.

The following is an adaptation of my favorite version of rehrücken, which I had at Schloss Rabenstein, an incredible medieval castle near Graz, Austria.

MAKES 10 TO 12 SERVINGS

Baking Equipment: 12½-x-4¼-inch rehrücken pan

> **Double recipe Chocolate-Butter Glaze (page 289)**
>
> 3 ounces (½ cup) unblanched almonds
> ¾ cup (90 grams) unsifted all-purpose flour
> 6 large eggs, room temperature
> 1 teaspoon granulated sugar
> 8 ounces semisweet chocolate
> 8 ounces (2 sticks) unsalted butter
> 1 cup (200 grams) granulated sugar
> 1 teaspoon vanilla
> 2 ounces (½ cup) slivered almonds

Advance preparation: At least 1 hour before you glaze the cake, prepare Chocolate-Butter Glaze as directed on page 289.

Baking preparations: Position rack in lower third of oven; preheat oven to 350 degrees.

Using a paper towel, grease the bottom and sides of the pan with solid shortening. Sprinkle with granulated sugar, tapping out the excess. (Use sugar instead of flour for the rehrücken pan because it maintains the pan's distinctive definition during the baking and because the cake releases from the pan more successfully than if the pan is dusted with flour.)

Ingredient preparations: Process the almonds in a nut grinder (or other rotary-type grater) until they have the consistency of cornmeal; you need 1 cup ground. Combine with the flour in a small bowl and set aside.

Crack 3 eggs into a 1-quart mixing bowl. Separate the remaining 3 eggs, placing the whites in a deep 1½-quart mixing bowl and adding the yolks to the whole eggs. Place the 1 teaspoon sugar near the bowl of egg whites.

Cut the chocolate into matchstick-size pieces and combine them with the butter in a small heavy-bottomed saucepan. Place over very low heat and stir occasionally until the mixture is liquid and smooth.

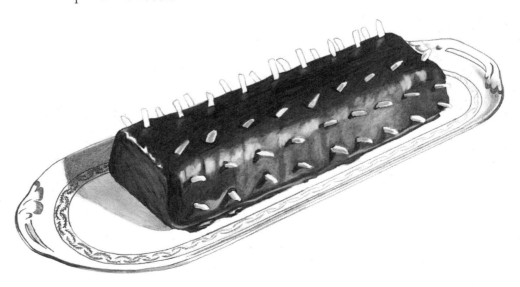

Making the cake: Pour the melted chocolate and butter into a 3-quart mixing bowl, and while it is still warm, stir in the 1 cup sugar. Cool for 5 minutes. Then stir in the egg mixture until well blended. Add the vanilla and blend.

Pour in the flour and nut mixture and mix together.

With an electric hand mixer, whip the egg whites on low speed until frothy, then raise speed to high (#10), add the teaspoon of sugar, and whip until soft, white peaks form (about 1 minute). Peaks should remain smooth and elastic enough to be folded into the thick chocolate mixture properly.

Then stir and fold one-third of the egg-white mixture into the chocolate mixture with a rubber spatula to lighten it; fold in the remainder.

Baking the cake: Pour the batter into the pan, filling it no more than ¼ inch below the top rim of the pan or it will overflow during baking (you may have ⅓ cup batter left over). Smooth the batter level with the rubber spatula.

Bake for about 35 to 38 minutes. The cake will rise above the pan about an inch and crack down the center a bit. The outer edges of the cake will be firm; the interior in the center of the cake will still appear fudgy or puddinglike. This is fine, and your cake is done. (Inserting a toothpick into this cake will not give you an accurate indication.)

Cooling the cake: Place on cooling rack for 15 to 20 minutes. As the cake cools, the chocolate sets, making removal easier. Insert a thin-bladed knife around the edges, freeing them and allowing air to get under the cake. Cover with a rectangular strip of stiff cardboard, then a cooling rack; invert and allow the cake to cool for 5 more minutes. Now carefully lift the baking pan from the cake. Allow the cake to cool completely before freezing or glazing it.

Finishing the cake: Place the cake with its cardboard on a cooling rack over a baking pan with sides, such as a jelly roll pan. The ends of the cake are uneven after cooling. Simply trim them even with the center of the cake, using a serrated knife and a steady sawing motion. You may use these small pieces of cake to patch the center of the cake to make it level; merely press the pieces into place.

Before glazing the cake, you may want to refer to glazing techniques on page 241.

Apply a thin coat of Chocolate-Butter Glaze to give a smooth appearance to your patched cake area, but don't apply so much that you lose the ribbing effect of the cake.

Place the glaze over a hot-water bath to reliquefy it for the next step in glazing the cake. When the glaze is thinner (body temperature), remove it from the water; wipe the bottom of the container dry; then pour the glaze over the cake. Pour from one end to the other, down the center. Apply the glaze with a small flexible icing spatula to any spots you missed while pouring. Then run the spatula under the cake and its cardboard to remove any chocolate drips.

When the glaze has set (at least 1 hour), space six rows of the slivered almonds along the length of the cake.

Storing and serving the cake: Store at room temperature. Serve each slice with lightly whipped cream, if desired.

Baker's Notes

☞ The cake freezes perfectly; glaze it after defrosting.

☞ I like to work with more glaze than I actually need to cover the cake. This affords me the best finish possible. Any leftover glaze keeps in a covered container in the refrigerator for up to 1 week or freezes for up to 3 weeks.

☞ A rectangular, ridged metal pan shaped like a saddle of venison, the Rehrüchen pan is inexpensive and available from kitchen stores or mail-order specialty shops.

Chocolate Gemini

SPLIT into halves and decorated, this cake is as elegant a devil's food cake as you could wish. Without the chocolate curls, it is unpretentious enough to share a plate with a scoop of your favorite vanilla ice cream. **(See photograph, page 158.)**

MAKES TWO 4-X-13-INCH CAKES, 8 SERVINGS EACH

Baker's Note

☞ You may freeze one half of this cake for another time.

Decorating Equipment: 2 rectangles of stiff cardboard, cake decorating turntable

> **One 9-x-13-inch Devil's Food Cake (page 53)**
> **Chocolate Cigarettes, optional (page 283)**
> **Double recipe Bittersweet Chocolate Frosting (page 286)**

Advance preparations: Prepare Devil's Food Cake. Cool it as directed on page 54.

If desired, prepare 40 to 50 Chocolate Cigarettes, each 5 to 6 inches long, as directed on page 283. If they are not to be used the same day, store them in a sturdy container in a cool room. When the cake is cool, split it in half lengthwise, forming two 4-x-13-inch cakes. With the aid of a long, wide metal spatula or a straight-sided baking sheet, lift each cake onto a cardboard strip to fit.

Split each rectangular cake in half horizontally, referring to the suggested techniques on page 234, if necessary.

Prepare Bittersweet Chocolate Frosting as directed on page 286.

Assembling the cake: Carefully lift off the top layer of the cake, and set it nearby. (Remember, butter cakes are not flexible the way sponge cakes are, so the entire layer will need support from a long, wide spatula or a straight-sided baking sheet. Should the layer break into two pieces, no one will ever know. Just put it together on the cake and proceed.)

Place the bottom layer with its cardboard on the turntable. Spread some of the frosting (about 8 to 10 tablespoons) on the layer. Top it with the other layer. Frost the sides and top (review the techniques, if necessary, on page 235). You need half the frosting (one recipe of Bittersweet Chocolate Frosting) to fill and frost this rectangular cake.

Repeat this process for filling and frosting the second cake.

Optional decorations: Place Chocolate Cigarettes on top of each cake on an angle.

Storing the cake: Store and serve at room temperature.

Sponge (or Foam) Cakes

Introduction

WHEN YOU think of a cake to serve for a very special event, such as a formal dinner party, a reception or perhaps an anniversary, you're likely to imagine desserts with glistening glazes, fillings of silky, smooth buttercreams and elegant finishing touches like chocolate curls. The cakes inside these handsomely tailored desserts are usually sponge cakes.

Though not always as lusciously mouth-watering to eat just by themselves as butter cakes, sponge cakes marry brilliantly with all different flavors of buttercream, pastry cream, fondant and with innumerable fillings and frostings, giving you the basis for making a dazzling array of elegant desserts for all occasions in your own kitchen.

Lots of eggs, sugar and little or no fat form the basic composition of every type of cake in the sponge category: spongecakes, génoises, angel foods and chiffons, as well as meringues and dacquoises, except the latter two usually have no flour or fat folded in. *(I refer to all the cakes in this family as sponge cakes, and to one of the members of this family as a spongecake.)* The methods for making these cakes are unlike those used to make butter cakes. The egg is to the sponge cake what butter is to the butter cake, and making a perfect sponge cake depends on how well you whip the eggs to create what is known as a foam. That is why this group is also known as foam cakes among bakers. And finally, how well the cake turns out also depends on how deftly you combine this foam with the other ingredients, such as sugar, flour and sometimes a little butter, to preserve its foamy, smooth structure so it will rise to its fullest during baking.

The lack of fat and the delicate structure created by foaming large amounts of eggs normally produce a leaner, lighter, sometimes drier cake than a butter cake. The sponge batter's consistency adapts beautifully to being piped through a pastry bag to yield the different shapes of some of the world's classic sponge cake favorites, among them ladyfingers and meringue disks. Unlike the butter cake, a sponge cake cannot be baked in a fancy-shaped cake pan like a Bundt pan because once it has been baked, its structure is too delicate for it to be removed from the pan in one piece. But the sponge cake's consistency lends itself to an endless variety of other desserts.

Sponge cakes rely almost exclusively for their volume on two natural leavenings: aeration and steam. The aeration is produced by the whipped egg foams, which foam and trap air. The air whipped into the batter produces a foamy mass containing minute air bubbles; these expand in the oven, their walls stretching and thinning until maximum volume is attained. Then the heat changes the protein in the eggs from their liquid state to solid so they coagulate or set, thereby shaping the cake's final structure. The evaporation of the moisture in the batter transforms into steam during the baking process and escapes through these air bubbles, providing another major source of leavening to the cake.

THE INGREDIENTS AND THEIR ROLE

EGGS

FRESH EGGS are crucial for optimum aeration. They have the greatest capacity to hold in air bubbles and in the process build the cake's structure (grain and texture) and flavor. You can tell a fresh egg by its appearance once cracked because it has a yolk that domes up, rather than lies flat, and a thick, translucent white that has body and is not runny.

CREAM OF TARTAR

MANY sponge cake recipes call for cream of tartar whenever egg whites are whipped. Cream of tartar makes the whites smooth and stable for easy folding into the batter without causing the egg-white foam to deflate too much. However, when folding an egg-white foam into a mixture, I find whipping a small portion of sugar into the whites works just as well as cream of tartar. Substituting a small portion of the recipe's sugar for the cream of tartar is not only just as effective in stabilizing the whites and making them smooth but also simplifies the process since the sugar is already in the recipe. The addition of cream of tartar or a small amount of sugar softens an egg-white foam so that it requires more whipping time to reach the proper consistency. Adding cream of tartar to egg-white foams can also stabilize the millions of tiny air bubbles, thus preventing their collapse in the oven during the cake's baking and giving the structure the time it needs to set its shape. In some of my sponge cake recipes, such as Classic American Spongecake (page 152), cream of tartar is indispensable.

SUGAR

CERTAIN moist spongecake recipes, such as Classic American Spongecake (page 152) and Hazelnut Sponge With Raspberry Whipped Cream (page 172), contain a large amount of sugar, which is the chief reason for their exceptionally moist and tender texture.

Sugar interrupts the gluten development and slows the coagulation or setting of the flour and egg proteins in the oven. During the time it takes for the cake to bake, the sugar retains some of the cake's moisture. Though sponge cakes made with a lot of sugar blend perfectly with any number of fillings and frostings, they are also delicious without them.

Spongecake recipes that are low in sugar, such as Classic European Spongecake (page 162) and Sponge Ladyfingers (page 169), are somewhat dry and have a fine grain. Because their sugar content is not exceedingly high, their baking time is shorter than that for Classic American Spongecake. These kinds of spongecakes function best when they are combined with sumptuous fillings, even thin meringue layers, to create some of the world's most spectacular dessert creations.

FLAVORINGS

IN MAKING sponge cakes, I don't add any liquid flavoring or citrus zest to the eggs before whipping them because I find the natural oils of these additions retard the full development of foaming and aeration. I add the flavoring either toward the end of whipping the egg foam or into the melted butter, if that is used. Best of all, I like to crush anise or caraway seeds to a fine powder or grate either fresh nutmeg, fresh ginger, or even chocolate and add them to my sponge recipes.

Another essential flavoring, the soaking syrup, is brushed on the cake after it has been baked and just before it is assembled. This is a sugar syrup combined with liquor, liqueur, coffee, tea or fruit juices. It keeps the cake moist for at least a week as well as imparting another dimension of flavor. Some of the cakes in the sponge cake section are so moist and full of flavor that you may feel it is gilding the lily to moisten them any further with dessert syrup.

BUTTER

EVEN THOUGH butter adds richness and prolongs the life of the cake, its primary use in sponge cakes is as flavoring. In order to keep the foamy batter smooth, the only way to add butter is in liquid form. It is gently folded in after being melted but not when it is too hot lest it deflate the foamy mixture in any way. You may also use hazelnut, almond or walnut oils if you want to perfume the cake with their unique flavors.

FLOUR

SOME OF the sponge cake recipes call for sifting sugar with a portion of the recipe's flour. This technique reduces the flour's natural tendency to lump, making the folding process easier and faster, an important factor in guaranteeing maximum aeration and hence a more tender cake.

NUTS

FINELY GROUND nuts act as part of the flour, adding flavor and contributing bulk. But ground nuts cannot build the same structure as flour. Depending upon the amount of ground nuts in the recipe, a cake's volume can be slightly less and its texture coarser. Grinding the nuts finely is very important in these cakes. (See nut grinders on page 23.)

TIPS FOR PERFECT SPONGE CAKES

☞ Always sift flour after measuring to prevent lumping and to ensure a smooth, homogeneous batter.

☞ Sift a portion of the granulated sugar with the cake flour after you have measured the cake flour to keep the flour from lumping, making folding easier.

☞ Use cake flour in making sponge cakes. It is easy to fold into foamy batters and contributes to the cake's delicate structure. If only all-purpose flour is available to you, sift together 3 cups all-purpose flour with 1 cup cornstarch or potato starch to reduce the protein content. Set this aside in a closed container to use when you need a substitute for cake flour for your sponge cakes.

☞ Use fresh eggs; they make a cake rise higher than do older eggs.

☞ Bowls and utensils must be fat-free when you whip any part of the egg, especially the white, or it will not whip properly.

☞ Avoid under- or overwhipping egg foams. A foam cake's volume and texture depends upon whipping eggs, whole or separated, to the proper consistency. Follow each recipe carefully.

☞ Fold in ingredients carefully, or you will deflate the mixture too much and affect the cake's leavening. Practice your technique with Classic American Spongecake (page 152). The next easiest cake for practicing your folding technique is Classic Génoise (page 104).

☞ All sponge batters are delicate, so gently spoon the batter without delay into the prepared pan. Bake it immediately in a preheated oven. Don't bang the baking pans on the counter before baking; this could rupture the air cells.

☞ The most reliable test for doneness is to insert a round wooden toothpick into the cake's center and remove it. If it contains no traces of cake, the cake is done. (A flat toothpick is unreliable because it can slip through the foamy texture too easily.)

☞ If you need several thin layers of sponge cake, bake a thick layer in one pan and slice it into separate layers. Using this method will guarantee moister layers than baking several separate cakes. Slicing a sponge cake horizontally is not difficult because its porous and springy texture makes it flexible.

☞ Sponge cakes can tolerate refrigeration without suffering changes in their textures because of their low fat content. As with other desserts, however, their flavors are at their full-bodied best when the chill is removed.

Recipes for Génoise Cakes

INDICATES ❀ EASY RECIPE

Génoise Cakes

A GÉNOISE is high in eggs and sugar and contains little or no fat. What distinguishes a génoise from other cakes in the sponge category is the technique of whipping a foam from whole eggs, sometimes in combination with egg yolks. Egg white meringue is never incorporated into a génoise.

A génoise that contains whole eggs as well as egg yolks, such as Honey Génoise (page 107), Brown Sugar Génoise (page 105) or Génoise Sheet (page 117), is moister, denser and less spongy than one made without egg yolks. These génoise cakes may not need to be soaked with a dessert syrup if you are assembling thin layers with other fillings and frostings.

THE WARM-METHOD SPONGE TECHNIQUE

TO PREPARE the eggs for optimum foaming capacity when making all kinds of génoise, I use a bain-marie, or water bath—a technique of first warming the eggs and sugar to a temperature no higher than 100 degrees, then whipping them. This technique is called the warm-method sponge.

Though you can whip your eggs and sugar to the desired volume without using the warm method, my recipes are designed for this technique because it ensures that every time you make a génoise you will have begun with eggs at their proper temperature. Everything else will fall into place: Your sugar will dissolve, thereby uniting it with the eggs into a solution. Then the eggs will whip to their maximum volume faster, and their warmth will soften the natural fat (lecithin) in the yolk, surrounding the air cells and stabilizing the volume.

THE INGREDIENTS AND THEIR ROLE

EGGS

Whole eggs can never be whipped as stiff as egg whites, but you want to whip them until they are thick enough to be folded into other ingredients without deflating the egg foam more than is absolutely necessary. (Remember, it is the air you whip into the eggs that creates the cake's "sponginess.")

The whipped whole eggs' foam is ready to have the other ingredients folded into it when the mixture ribbons out from the lifted electric mixer's whisk attachment and remains slightly suspended on the surface of the foam. I call this a whole-egg meringue.

Since the composition of the egg yolk is half fat, not as much air can be incorporated into it as into a whole egg; therefore, adding one yolk to a mixture does not produce as many air bubbles as a whole egg. But additional egg yolks stabilize the whipped foam and produce a richer, moister, more tender génoise.

SUGAR

G RANULATED sugar is customary for the génoise. But I like using other sugars to vary the taste and texture. Honey and molasses, in small quantities, add flavor, moisture and color. Their thick consistency also increases the mixture's viscosity, making it easier to incorporate and retain air cells.

BUTTER

I F I USE butter, I always put the unsalted kind in my génoise. It must be melted and still liquid, but it cannot be bubbling hot when it is incorporated into the batter or it will rupture the air bubbles.

Folding flour into the batter, if done gently, will not cause much loss of air, but folding fat into the batter can deflate the airy mixture even when it is done gently. Pour the melted butter into a small mixing bowl. When it is time to fold it in, pour about 1 cup of the batter on top, and fold the two together until combined; then incorporate the mixture into the larger portion of batter. This prevents overfolding and too much loss of volume.

The amount of butter for a génoise recipe is arbitrary. The more you use, the moister the cake and the longer it will remain fresh.

Classic Génoise

I CANNOT think of a filling, frosting or even a flavor that you can't pair with Classic Génoise successfully, thereby making it the most versatile in the cake repertoire.

This is used in Gâteau Rouge (page 139), Lucerne Cheese Torte (page 134) and Lemon Mist Torte (page 142).

MAKES ONE 8-X-1 ¾-INCH ROUND LAYER

Baking Equipment: One heavy-gauge straight-sided 8-inch round cake pan

1	cup (100 grams) sifted cake flour
1	tablespoon granulated sugar
⅛	teaspoon salt
1	ounce (2 tablespoons) unsalted butter
4	large eggs, room temperature
½	cup (100 grams) granulated sugar
1	teaspoon vanilla

Baking preparations: Position rack in lower third of oven; preheat oven to 350 degrees.

Using a paper towel, grease the bottom and sides of the pan with solid shortening. Dust generously with all-purpose flour, tilt to distribute; then tap out excess and insert a parchment or waxed paper liner.

Ingredient preparations: Pour the flour, 1 tablespoon sugar and salt in that order into a triple sifter. Sift onto a sheet of waxed paper to distribute the sugar evenly and to remove any lumps in the flour; set aside.

Melt the butter in a small saucepan over low heat. Pour into a 1-quart mixing bowl and set aside.

Crack the eggs into the bowl of a heavy-duty mixer. Add the ½ cup sugar and whisk by hand to combine. Rest the bowl in a shallow pan, such as a 10-inch skillet, filled with 1 inch of water that feels hot to the touch (120 degrees). To prevent the eggs from setting, whisk them continuously for about 30 seconds.

Now test if the mixture has warmed to body temperature, taking care that it doesn't exceed 110 degrees. Rub a little of the mixture between your thumb and forefinger; it should feel smooth, not granular.

Making the cake: Attach the bowl to the mixer, and with the whisk attachment, whip on medium speed (#5) until the mixture has cooled and increased considerably in volume (tripled or more), appears light in texture and almost white in color and has thickened to the consistency of a whole-egg meringue (about 3 to 4 minutes). Pour in the vanilla during the final moments of whipping.

Test if it's time to fold in the flour by lifting the whisk. If some of the mixture falls back into the bowl in ribbons and remains on the surface, proceed. But if it sinks back into the batter right away, continue whipping for a few more minutes, or until the desired consis-

Baker's Notes

☞ A génoise batter is assembled quickly, so have all your ingredients, utensils and equipment ready.

☞ Sift the flour and sugar immediately prior to making the cake. If you sift them too far ahead, the flour will become compact from sitting and may pick up moisture. The addition of sugar to the flour helps disperse the flour particles so that when you fold these dry ingredients into the batter, the process is more efficient. Less folding is required, and the chance of the flour's lumping during its incorporation is decreased.

☞ This batter may be baked in a 9-inch springform or 9-inch round cake pan for 20 to 22 minutes, to produce a 9-x-1 ¼-inch layer.

☞ If I use the cake when it is fresh, I seldom use a dessert syrup. But if the cake is left out overnight or is stale, then a dessert syrup is helpful. The syrup makes it possible to keep the dessert longer, and it adds to the complexity of flavors.

tency is achieved. Then remove the bowl and its whisk from the mixer.

With the aid of a flexible metal icing spatula, scoop up one-third of the flour mixture and sprinkle it over the top. Using a rubber spatula, fold the mixture into the batter just until incorporated. Repeat the procedure two more times, folding just until all the flour has been absorbed.

Gently pour about 1 cup of the batter into the melted butter, and with the rubber spatula, fold until combined. Return the butter mixture to the reserved batter and again fold to combine.

Baking the cake: Gently pour the mixture into the pan, taking care not to deflate the foam structure. With a rubber spatula, smooth the top of the batter, working from the center outward, until a slightly raised ridge forms around the outside rim. (Since the cake bakes faster near the metal rim, mounding the batter around the edges assures a more evenly baked layer.)

Bake for 25 to 27 minutes, or until the top springs back slightly when lightly touched, sounding spongy when tapped, and the sides begin to contract from the pan. An aroma similar to that of freshly scrambled eggs will pervade your kitchen, indicating the cake is done.

Cooling the cake: Place the cake on a rack to cool for 5 to 10 minutes. With mitts, tilt and rotate the pan and gently tap it on the counter to see if the cake is releasing from the metal sides. If not, or if in doubt, run a small metal spatula or the thin blade of a table knife between the outside cake edge and the metal rim, freeing the sides and allowing air to get under the layer as it is rotated.

Cover the pan with another cooling rack, invert it onto that rack and carefully lift the pan from the cake to remove. Slowly peel off the parchment liner, turn it over so that the sticky side faces up, and reposition it on top of the cake. Cover with the first rack, invert the layer right side up and remove the top rack. Allow cake to cool completely.

Storing the cake: If you plan to use the génoise later in the day or the next day, leave it out, uncovered, on a rack to air-dry. (Most génoises benefit from slight staling since they will absorb the dessert syrup more easily.)

To use within 2 days, wrap the génoise in plastic wrap.

To freeze, cover the plastic-wrapped package in foil. To protect the cake's delicate structure, place the foil-wrapped package in a sturdy container, such as a metal tin, before freezing. Add a label, indicating the contents and date. Freeze for no longer than 10 days.

Brown Sugar Génoise

THIS fragrant and mildly spicy génoise is a complete contrast to the plain Classic Génoise.

This is the foundation for St. Lily Peach Cake (page 128).

MAKES ONE 8-X-1 ¼-INCH ROUND LAYER

Baking Equipment: One heavy-gauge straight-sided 8-inch round cake pan

¾	cup (75 grams) sifted cake flour
1	tablespoon granulated sugar
½	teaspoon ground cinnamon
⅛	teaspoon salt
3	tablespoons heavy cream
2	large eggs, room temperature
2	egg yolks, room temperature
¼	cup (50 grams) light brown sugar, packed
¼	cup (50 grams) granulated sugar

Baker's Notes

☞ Heavy cream adds richness in this recipe, taking the place of butter. Lightly whipping the cream makes it easier to fold it into the batter, keeping the batter smooth without deflating its volume.

☞ Brown sugar adds its own interesting flavor. If you have only dark brown sugar available, use it; light brown sugar's flavor is milder.

Baking preparations: Position rack in lower third of oven; preheat oven to 350 degrees.

Using a paper towel, grease the bottom and sides of the pan with solid shortening. Dust generously with all-purpose flour, tilt to coat, tap out the excess and insert a parchment or waxed paper liner.

Ingredient preparations: Pour the flour, 1 tablespoon granulated sugar, cinnamon and salt in that order into a triple sifter and sift onto waxed paper to distribute the ingredients evenly; set aside.

Pour the heavy cream into a 1½-quart bowl and whisk it briefly by hand just until some thickening occurs but before any peaks form (about 30 to 45 seconds).

Crack the whole eggs into the bowl of a heavy-duty mixer. Add the egg yolks and sugars and whisk ingredients to combine. Rest the bowl in a shallow pan, such as a 10-inch skillet, filled with an inch of hot tap water (120 degrees). To prevent the eggs from setting, whisk them continuously for 30 seconds, or until the mixture has warmed to body temperature. Rub a little of the mixture between your thumb and forefinger; it should feel smooth not granular.

Making the cake: Attach the bowl to the mixer and with the whisk attachment, whip the mixture on medium speed (#5) until it has cooled and increased considerably in volume (tripled or more), appears light in texture and pale in color and has thickened to the consistency of a whole-egg meringue (about 3 to 4 minutes).

Test if it's time to fold in the flour by lifting the whisk. If some of the mixture falls back into the bowl in ribbons and remains on the surface, proceed. But if it sinks back into the batter right away, continue whipping for a few more minutes, or until the desired consistency is achieved.

Scoop one-third of the flour mixture onto a flexible metal icing spatula, and sprinkle it over the egg mixture. Fold it in until incorporated. Repeat two more times, folding until all the flour has been absorbed.

Pour about 1 cup of the mixture into the bowl of lightly whipped cream. With a rubber spatula, fold until combined. Then return the cream mixture to the larger bowl, and fold the two together to combine.

Baking the cake: Gently pour the mixture into the pan, taking care not to deflate the foam structure. With a rubber spatula, spread the batter, working from the center outward, until a slightly raised edge forms around the outside rim.

Bake for 20 to 22 minutes, or until the center springs back slightly when lightly touched, sounding spongy when tapped, and the sides contract from the pan.

Cooling the cake: Place the cake on a rack to cool for 5 to 10 minutes. With mitts, tilt the pan and gently tap it to see if it releases from the sides. If not, or if in doubt, run a small metal spatula or a thin table knife between the outside cake edge and the metal rim, freeing the sides and allowing air to get under the layer as it is rotated.

Turn the cake out onto the rack and remove the pan. Peel off the parchment liner, turn it over so that the sticky side faces up and reposition it on top of the cake. Cover with another rack, invert the layer right side up and remove the top rack. Allow the cake to cool completely.

Storing the cake: If you plan to use the génoise within 24 hours, leave it uncovered, on a rack to air-dry.

To use within 2 days, wrap it in plastic wrap.

To freeze, cover the plastic-wrapped package with foil. To protect the cake's delicate structure, place the foil-wrapped package in a sturdy container, such as a metal tin, before freezing. Label the package, indicating the contents and date. Freeze for no longer than 10 days.

Honey Génoise

THE SMALL amount of honey adds flavor, sweetens, moistens and helps smooth the mixture.

This is the foundation for La Fleur (page 132).

MAKES ONE 8-X-1 ¾-INCH ROUND LAYER

Baking Equipment: One heavy-gauge straight-sided 8-inch round cake pan

1	cup (100 grams) sifted cake flour
1	tablespoon granulated sugar
⅛	teaspoon salt
1	ounce (2 tablespoons) unsalted butter
1	teaspoon lemon zest
3	large eggs, room temperature
2	egg yolks, room temperature
½	cup (100 grams) granulated sugar
1	tablespoon honey

Baking preparations: Position rack in lower third of oven; preheat oven to 350 degrees.

Using a paper towel, grease the bottom and sides of the pan with solid shortening. Dust generously with all-purpose flour, tilting it to coat. Tap out the excess and insert a parchment liner.

Baker's Notes

☞ I prefer to use a mild-flavored honey.

☞ You can substitute maple syrup for honey—delicious.

Ingredient preparations: Pour the flour, 1 tablespoon sugar and salt into a triple sifter. Sift onto a sheet of waxed paper; set aside.

Melt the butter in a small saucepan over low heat. Pour into a 1½-quart mixing bowl; add the lemon zest; set aside.

Crack the eggs into the bowl of a heavy-duty mixer. Add the egg yolks, the ½ cup sugar and honey; whisk by hand to combine the ingredients. Rest the bowl in a shallow pan, such as a 10-inch skillet, filled with 1 inch of water that feels hot (120 degrees). To prevent the eggs from setting, whisk them continuously for about 30 seconds.

To test if the mixture has warmed to body temperature, taking care that it doesn't exceed 110 degrees, rub a little of the mixture between your forefinger and thumb; it should feel smooth, not granular.

Making the cake: Place the bowl on the mixer, and with the whisk attachment, whip the mixture on medium speed (#5) until it has cooled and increased considerably in volume (tripled or more), appears light in texture and pale in color and has thickened to the consistency of a whole-egg meringue (about 3 to 4 minutes).

Test if it's time to fold in the flour by lifting the whisk. If some of the mixture falls back into the bowl in ribbons and remains on the surface, proceed. But if it sinks back into the batter right away, continue whipping for a few more minutes, or until the desired consistency is achieved.

Scoop one-third of the flour on a flexible metal icing spatula and sprinkle it over the batter. Using a rubber spatula, fold it into the batter just until incorporated. Repeat one or two more times, folding until all the flour is incorporated.

Gently pour about 1 cup of the batter into the lemon-flavored melted butter, and with a rubber spatula, fold until combined. Then return butter mixture to reserved batter and again fold to combine.

Baking the cake: Gently pour the mixture into the pan, taking care not to deflate the foam structure. With a rubber spatula, smooth the batter, working from the center outward, until a slightly raised ridge forms around the outside rim.

Bake for 25 to 27 minutes, or until it springs back slightly when lightly touched, sounding spongy when tapped, the sides begin to contract from the pan and the top is golden brown.

Cooling the cake: Place the cake on a rack to cool for 5 to 10 minutes. With mitts, tilt and rotate the pan, and gently tap it on the counter to see if it is releasing from the metal sides. If not, or if in doubt, run a small metal spatula or the thin blade of a table knife between the outside cake edge and the metal rim, freeing the sides and allowing air to get under the layer as it is rotated.

Cover the pan with a cooling rack, invert it onto the rack and carefully lift the pan to remove. Slowly peel off the parchment liner, turn it over so that the sticky side faces up and reposition it on top of the cake. Cover with another rack, invert the layer right side up and remove the original rack. Allow the cake to cool completely.

Storing the cake: To use the génoise later in the day or the next day, leave it out, uncovered, on a rack to air-dry.

To use within 2 days, wrap it in plastic wrap.

To freeze, cover the plastic-wrapped package in foil. To protect the cake's delicate structure, place the foil-wrapped package in a sturdy container, such as a metal tin, before freezing. Label, indicating the contents and date. Freeze for no longer than 10 days.

Nut Génoise

THIS GÉNOISE is coarser in texture than other génoises because of the finely ground nuts, which are added to the batter as part of the flour. Select your favorite kind of nuts for this cake.

This is the foundation for Mocha Imperiale (page 137).

MAKES ONE 9-X-1 ½-INCH ROUND LAYER

Baker's Notes

☞ The success of your cake hinges on whipping your egg foams as in Classic Génoise (page 104).

☞ This cake's flavor benefits from the addition of a nut oil, such as almond or hazelnut. You can, however, substitute an unflavored vegetable oil.

Baking Equipment: One heavy-gauge straight-sided 9-inch round cake pan

1 ¼	cups (125 grams) sifted cake flour
⅛	teaspoon salt
1 ½	ounces (¼ cup) unblanched almonds
¼	cup almond oil
4	large eggs, room temperature
1	egg yolk, room temperature
¾	cup (150 grams) granulated sugar

Baking preparations: Position rack in lower third of oven; preheat oven to 350 degrees.

Using a paper towel, grease the bottom and sides of the pan with solid shortening. Dust generously with all-purpose flour, tilt to coat, tap out the excess and insert a parchment or waxed paper liner.

Ingredient preparations: Pour the flour and salt into a triple sifter and sift into a small mixing bowl.

Using a nut grinder or rotary-type grater, process the nuts until they have the consistency of cornmeal; you need ½ cup ground. Combine with the flour and set aside.

Pour the oil into a 1-quart mixing bowl; set aside.

Crack the eggs into the bowl of a heavy-duty mixer. Add the egg yolk and sugar and whisk the ingredients by hand to combine. Rest the bowl in a shallow pan, such as a 10-inch skillet, filled with an inch of water that feels hot (120 degrees). To prevent the eggs from setting, whisk them continuously for 30 seconds.

Now test if the mixture has warmed to body temperature, taking care that it doesn't exceed 110 degrees. Rub a little of the mixture between your thumb and fingers; it should feel smooth, not granular.

Making the cake: Place the bowl on the mixer, and with the whisk attachment, whip the mixture on medium speed (#5) until it has cooled and increased considerably in volume (tripled or more), appears light in texture and pale in color and has thickened to the consistency of a whole-egg meringue (about 4 to 5 minutes).

Test if it's time to fold in the flour mixture by lifting the whisk. If some of the mixture falls back into the bowl in ribbons and remains on the surface, proceed. But if it sinks back into the batter right away, continue whipping for a few more minutes, or until the desired consistency is achieved.

Scoop one-third of the flour-nut mixture on a flexible metal icing spatula and sprinkle it over the top of the batter. Using a rubber spatula, fold it into the batter, just until incorporated. Repeat procedure two more times, folding until all the flour-nut mixture is incorporated.

Gently pour about 1 cup of the batter into the oil, and with a rubber spatula, fold until combined. Then return mixture to reserved batter, and again fold to combine.

Baking the cake: Gently pour the mixture into the pan, taking care not to deflate the foam structure. With a rubber spatula, smooth the batter, working from the center outward, until a slightly raised ridge forms around the outside rim. (Since the cake bakes faster near the metal rim because metal attracts heat first, mounding the batter around the edges assures a more evenly baked layer.) Bake for 25 to 30 minutes, or until the top springs back slightly when lightly touched and the sides begin to contract from the pan.

Cooling the cake: Place the cake on a rack to cool for 5 to 10 minutes. With mitts, tilt and rotate pan, and gently tap it on the counter to see if the cake is being released from the sides. If not, or if in doubt, run a small metal spatula or the thin blade of a table knife between the outside cake edge and the metal rim, freeing the sides and allowing air to get under the layer as it is rotated.

Cover the pan with a cooling rack, invert it onto the rack and carefully lift the pan to remove. Slowly peel off the parchment liner, turn it over so that the sticky side faces up and position it on top of the cake. Cover with another rack, invert the layer right side up and remove the original rack. Allow the cake to cool completely.

Storing the cake: If you plan to use the génoise later in the day or the next, leave it out, uncovered, on a rack to air-dry.

To use within 2 days, wrap in plastic wrap.

To freeze, cover the plastic-wrapped package in foil. To protect the cake's delicate structure, place the foil-wrapped package in a sturdy container, such as a metal tin, before freezing. Label the container, indicating the contents and date. Freeze for no longer than 10 days.

Almond Paste Génoise

ALMOND PASTE, vanilla, lemon zest and butter blend together to form a génoise you'll make again and again. This cake's charm is that it may be served simply with fresh fruit and whipped cream or given a more elaborate treatment with a dessert syrup and a buttercream, then coated with Decorator's Sliced Almonds (page 270).

This is the foundation for Gardenia Cake (page 127).

MAKES ONE 9-X-1 ¾-INCH ROUND LAYER CAKE

Baking Equipment: One heavy-gauge straight-sided 9-inch round cake pan

1	cup (100 grams) sifted cake flour
1	tablespoon granulated sugar
⅛	teaspoon salt
2	ounces (4 tablespoons) unsalted butter
2 ½	ounces (¼ cup) almond paste, room temperature
¾	cup (150 grams) granulated sugar
3	large eggs, room temperature
2	egg yolks, room temperature
1	teaspoon vanilla
1	teaspoon lemon zest

Baker's Note

☞ Adding the sugar to the almond paste early creates enough friction to break it up, preventing lumpiness and providing its even distribution in the batter later.

Baking preparations: Position rack in lower third of oven; preheat oven to 350 degrees.

Using a paper towel, grease the bottom and sides of the pan with solid shortening. Dust generously with all-purpose flour, tilt it to distribute, tap out the excess and insert a parchment or waxed paper liner.

Ingredient preparations: Pour the flour, 1 tablespoon sugar and salt in that order into a triple sifter. Sift onto a sheet of waxed paper; set aside.

Melt the butter in a small saucepan over low heat. Pour into a small mixing bowl; set aside.

Place the almond paste in the bowl of a heavy-duty mixer. With the flat beater (paddle), break up the almond paste on medium speed (#4) for 10 to 15 seconds. Maintaining the same speed, add the ¾ cup of sugar in a steady stream until the almond paste is in pieces the size of small peas. Remove the bowl and detach the beater.

Crack the eggs into the bowl of almond paste and sugar, add the egg yolks and whisk to combine the mixture. Rest the bowl in a shallow pan, such as a 10-inch skillet, filled with 1 inch of hot tap water (120 degrees). To prevent the eggs from setting, whisk them continuously for 30 seconds, or until the mixture warms to body temperature. Some small lumps of almond paste will remain.

Making the cake: Position the bowl back on the mixer, and with the whisk attachment, whip until the mixture cools and increases in volume (triples or more), appears light in texture and almost white in color and thickens to a consistency resembling a whole-egg meringue (about 2 to 4 minutes). Add the vanilla and lemon zest during the final moments of whipping.

Test if it's time to fold in the flour by lifting the whisk. If some of the mixture falls back into the bowl in ribbons and remains on the surface, proceed. If it sinks right away, continue whipping until desired consistency is reached. Then remove the bowl and its attachment from the mixer.

With the aid of a flexible metal icing spatula, scoop up one-third of the flour mixture and sprinkle it over the egg mixture. Using a rubber spatula, fold it into the batter until incorporated. Repeat the procedure two more times, folding until the flour has been absorbed.

*Understanding
Cakemaking*

Pour about 1 cup batter into the melted butter, and with a rubber spatula, fold until combined. Now pour this butter mixture into the reserved batter, folding again to combine.

Baking the cake: Gently pour the mixture into the prepared pan. With a rubber spatula, smooth the batter level.

Bake for 30 to 36 minutes, or until the center springs back slightly when touched and sounds spongy when tapped.

Cooling the cake: Place the cake on a rack to cool for 5 to 10 minutes. With mitts, tilt pan, gently rotating and tapping to see if it releases from the sides. If not, or if in doubt, run a small metal spatula or a thin table knife between the outside cake edge and the metal rim, freeing the sides and allowing air to get under the layer.

Place the rack on top of the pan, invert onto a counter and lift the pan. Peel off the parchment liner, turn it over so that the sticky side faces up, and reposition it on top of the cake. Cover with another rack, invert the layer right side up and remove the top rack. Allow the cake to cool completely.

Storing the cake: If serving the génoise within 24 hours, leave uncovered on a rack to air-dry.

If using within 2 days, wrap in plastic wrap.

To freeze, cover the plastic-wrapped package with foil. Label the package, indicating the contents and date. Freeze for no longer than 10 days.

Orange Génoise

THIS GÉNOISE, with its fresh taste of orange, is unusually large, resembling an American-style spongecake. It is delicious on its own with fresh strawberries.

This is the foundation for Juliet Cake (page 130).

MAKES ONE 10-X-3-INCH ROUND TUBE CAKE

Baking Equipment: One 10-inch tube pan, with removable bottom

1 ½	cups (150 grams) sifted cake flour
1	teaspoon baking powder
12	egg yolks (¾ cup), room temperature
1	cup (200 grams) granulated sugar
⅔	cup (6 ounces) orange juice, room temperature

Baking preparations: Position rack in lower third of oven; preheat oven to 325 degrees.

A dry (ungreased) tube pan allows this batter to climb and cling to the sides and rise to its full height.

Ingredient preparations: Pour the flour and baking powder in that order into a triple sifter. Sift onto a sheet of waxed paper; set aside.

Place the egg yolks in the bowl of a heavy-duty mixer and whisk by hand to combine. Then add the sugar and juice and whisk briefly to blend. Rest the bowl in a shallow pan, such as a 10-inch skillet, filled with an inch of water that feels hot to the touch (120 degrees). To prevent the eggs from setting, whisk them continuously for about 30 seconds.

Making the cake: Attach the bowl to the mixer and whip the mixture with the whisk attachment on medium speed (#5), until it has cooled and increased considerably in volume (tripled or more), appears light in texture and pale in color and has thickened to the consistency of a whole-egg meringue (about 5 to 6 minutes).

Test if it's time to fold in the flour by lifting the whisk. If the mixture flows back into the bowl in ribbons and remains on the surface, it's time to fold; if the mixture sinks into the batter right away, continue whipping until the desired consistency is reached.

Scoop one-third of the flour mixture on a flexible metal icing spatula and sprinkle it over the yolk mixture. Using a rubber spatula, fold into the batter until incorporated. Repeat two more times, folding until all the flour is incorporated.

Baking the cake: Gently pour the mixture into the pan, taking care not to deflate the foam structure. With a rubber spatula, level the surface.

Bake for 45 to 50 minutes, or until the top springs back slightly when lightly touched and sounds spongy when tapped.

Cooling the cake: Remove the cake from the oven and immediately invert it over a long-necked bottle to cool for about 2 hours. To remove the génoise from the pan, slip a flexible metal spatula carefully down one side of the pan and slowly trace around the perimeter to release the cake. Keep the spatula up against the pan to ensure as smooth-sided a cake as possible.

When the sides are free, push up on the removable bottom to release the cake completely. Tilt the cake, with the removable bottom still attached, and gently tap the bottom against the counter to loosen the cake. Rotate the cake, tapping a few more times, until it appears free. Cover the cake with a rack and invert; remove the bottom of the pan.

Storing the cake: If you plan to use the génoise up to 2 days after baking, wrap it in plastic wrap.

To freeze, cover the plastic-wrapped package with foil. To protect the cake's delicate structure, place the foil-wrapped package in a sturdy container, such as a metal tin, before freezing. Label the container, indicating the contents and date. Freeze for no longer than 10 days.

Chocolate Génoise

Tᴴɪꜱ ᴍᴏɪꜱᴛ génoise, made with semisweet chocolate, has a richer chocolate flavor than Cocoa Génoise (page 115).

This is the foundation for Pistachio Cake (page 131).

Mᴀᴋᴇꜱ ᴏɴᴇ 8-x-1-ɪɴᴄʜ ʀᴏᴜɴᴅ ʟᴀʏᴇʀ

Baking Equipment: One 8-inch springform pan

Baker's Notes

☞ I vary the cake's flavor by substituting other fruit juices, such as pineapple juice, for the orange juice.

☞ The baking powder ensures the leavening for this amount of batter and replaces some of the foaminess resulting from the absence of egg whites. If this were not a tall cake, there would be no need for baking powder.

☞ Inverting large, deep foam types of cakes while they cool is important in maintaining the structure and texture developed during baking.

3	ounces semisweet chocolate
1 ½	ounces (3 tablespoons) unsalted butter
⅓	cup (35 grams) unsifted cake flour
1	tablespoon granulated sugar
¼	teaspoon baking powder
2	large eggs, room temperature
2	egg yolks, room temperature
¼	cup (50 grams) granulated sugar
1	teaspoon vanilla

Baker's Notes

↪The technique for folding in the melted chocolate reduces the risk that the génoise batter will lose volume.

↪ Using melted chocolate rather than cocoa to flavor the génoise creates a heavier batter. To prevent a heavy, dense cake, a small amount of baking powder is added.

↪ To prevent a dry texture, underbaking is better than overbaking. The foam from the eggs combines with the chocolate, and a crust forms during baking, making it trickier to detect doneness. When chocolate is warm, it is liquid; the same is true in a cake. As the cake cools, the chocolate will solidify.

Baking preparations: Position rack in lower third of oven; preheat oven to 350 degrees.

Using a paper towel, grease the bottom and sides of the springform pan with solid shortening. Dust generously with all-purpose flour, tilt to coat, tap out the excess and insert a parchment or waxed paper liner.

Ingredient preparations: Chop the chocolate into matchstick-size pieces and place them with the butter in a 1½-quart mixing bowl that fits snugly over another bowl half-filled with hot (140-degree) water. (The water temperature can be this high because the addition of butter reduces the risk that the chocolate will scorch.) Stir occasionally until the mixture is melted and smooth; remove from the water; set aside to cool slightly.

Pour the flour, 1 tablespoon sugar and baking powder in that order into a triple sifter. Sift onto a sheet of waxed paper to distribute the ingredients evenly; set aside.

Place the eggs and egg yolks in the bowl of a heavy-duty mixer. Add the ¼ cup sugar and whisk ingredients by hand to combine. Rest the bowl in a shallow pan, such as a 10-inch skillet, filled with 1 inch of hot tap water (120 degrees). To prevent the eggs from setting, whisk them continuously for about 30 seconds, or until the mixture has warmed to body temperature, taking care that the temperature doesn't exceed 110 degrees. Rub a little of the mixture between your thumb and finger; it should feel smooth, not granular.

Making the cake: Place the bowl on the mixer, and with the whisk attachment, whip the mixture on medium speed (#5) until it has cooled and thickened, appears paler in color and resembles a whole-egg meringue and has increased in volume and tripled or more (about 3 minutes). Add the vanilla toward the end of whipping.

Test if it's time to fold in the flour by lifting the whisk. If some of the mixture falls back into the bowl in ribbons and remains on the surface, proceed. But if it sinks back into the batter right away, continue whipping for a few more minutes, or until the desired consistency is achieved. Remove the whisk and bowl from the mixer.

With the aid of a flexible metal icing spatula, scoop one-third of the flour mixture and sprinkle it over the top. Using a rubber spatula, fold into the batter just until incorporated. Fold in the remaining flour in two more additions.

With the aid of a rubber spatula, gently pour one-third of the batter onto the chocolate mixture, and fold until combined. Now pour the rest of the batter onto the chocolate mixture and fold together until combined.

Baking the cake: Gently pour the batter into the prepared pan, taking care not to deflate the foam structure you've created. With the rubber spatula, level and smooth the surface.

Bake for 20 to 23 minutes, or until the top springs back slightly when lightly touched and the sides begin to contract from the pan. Do not overbake.

Cooling the cake: Place the cake on a rack to cool for 5 to 10 minutes. With mitts, tilt the pan, and gently tap it to see that it has contracted from the sides. If not, or if in doubt, run a small metal spatula or the thin blade of a table knife between the outside cake edge and the metal rim, freeing the sides and allowing air to get under the layer as it is rotated. Then release and remove the outside of the springform pan. Allow to cool completely on rack.

When the cake is cool, cover it with another cooling rack, invert it onto the rack and carefully remove the springform bottom from the cake. Slowly peel off parchment liner, turn it over so that the sticky side faces up and reposition it on top of the cake. Cover with the first rack, invert the layer right side up and remove the top rack.

Storing the cake: If you plan to use the génoise the same day, leave it on the rack, uncovered, until ready.

To use within 2 days, wrap in plastic wrap and store it at room temperature.

To freeze, cover the plastic-wrapped package with foil. Label the package, indicating the contents and date. Freeze for no longer than 10 days.

Cocoa Génoise

COCOA POWDER substitutes for part of the flour to make this moist génoise taste of rich chocolate.

This is the foundation for Chocolate Rhapsody (page 124).

MAKES ONE 9-X-1 ¼-INCH ROUND LAYER

Baking Equipment: One 9-inch springform pan

⅓	cup (35 grams) unsifted cake flour
⅓	cup (35 grams) unsifted cocoa powder
1	tablespoon granulated sugar
2	ounces (4 tablespoons) unsalted butter
3	large eggs, room temperature
2	egg yolks, room temperature
⅔	cup (130 grams) granulated sugar
1	teaspoon vanilla

Baking preparations: Position rack in lower third of oven; preheat oven to 350 degrees.

Using a paper towel, grease the bottom and sides of the pan with solid shortening. Dust generously with all-purpose flour, tilt it to distribute, tap out the excess and insert a parchment liner.

☞ You can also bake one 9-x-1¼-inch square layer (bake it for 22 to 25 minutes).

☞ Additional egg yolks in the recipe offset the chance that the cocoa powder might produce a dry cake.

☞ This cake settles slightly when removed from oven because of the small amount of flour. This is OK. If you used more flour, the appearance, but not the flavor, would be perfect.

Ingredient preparations: Pour the flour, cocoa and 1 tablespoon sugar in that order into a triple sifter. Sift onto a sheet of waxed paper to distribute the ingredients evenly; set aside.

Melt the butter in a 1-quart saucepan over low heat. Pour into a 1- to 1½-quart mixing bowl; set aside.

Place the eggs and egg yolks in the bowl of a heavy-duty mixer. Add the ⅔ cup sugar and whisk ingredients by hand to combine. Rest the bowl in a shallow pan, such as a 10-inch skillet, filled with 1 inch of hot tap water (120 degrees). To prevent the eggs from setting, whisk them continuously for about 30 seconds, or until the mixture has warmed to body temperature, taking care that it doesn't exceed 110 degrees. Rub a little between your thumb and forefinger; it should feel smooth, not granular.

Making the cake: Attach the bowl on the mixer, and with the whisk attachment, whip the mixture on medium speed (#5) until it cools and thickens, appears paler in color and resembles a whole-egg meringue and increases (triples or more) in volume (about 3 to 4 minutes). Pour in the vanilla during the final moments of whipping.

Test if it's time to fold in the cocoa-flour mixture by lifting the whisk. If some of the mixture falls back into the bowl in ribbons and remains on the surface, proceed. But if it sinks back into the batter right away, continue whipping for a few more minutes, or until the desired consistency is achieved.

Scoop one-half of the flour mixture on a flexible metal icing spatula, and sprinkle it over the top. Using a rubber spatula, fold it into the batter just until incorporated. Repeat again, folding until the flour has been absorbed.

Gently pour about 1 cup of the batter into the melted butter, and with the rubber spatula, fold until combined. Return the butter mixture to the reserved batter, and again fold to combine.

Baking the cake: Gently pour the batter into the pan, taking care not to deflate the foam structure. With a rubber spatula, smooth the surface.

Bake for 25 to 27 minutes, or until the top springs back slightly when touched, the sides begin to contract from the pan and the cake sounds spongy when tapped.

Cooling the cake: Place the cake on a rack to cool for 5 to 10 minutes. With mitts, tilt the pan and gently tap it to see that it releases from the sides. If not, or if in doubt, run a small metal spatula or the thin blade of a table knife between the outside cake edge and the metal rim, freeing the sides and allowing air to get under the layer as it is rotated. Then release the sides of the springform. Allow the cake to cool on the rack completely.

When it is cool, cover with another cooling rack, invert it onto the rack and carefully remove the springform bottom. Slowly peel off the parchment liner, turn it over so that the sticky side faces up and reposition it on top of the cake. Cover with the first rack, invert the layer right side up and remove the top rack.

Storing the cake: If you plan to use this génoise the same day, leave it on the rack until ready.

To use within 2 days, wrap in plastic wrap.

To freeze, cover the plastic-wrapped package with foil. Label the package, indicating the contents and date. Freeze for no longer than 10 days.

Génoise Sheet

Avery thin and pliable layer, a génoise sheet can be cut into strips to form a multi-layered cake. A sheet can also be filled and rolled. This cake is endlessly adaptable. This is the foundation for Gift Box Gâteau (page 229).

MAKES ONE 12-x-15 ½-INCH CAKE

Baking Equipment: One 12-x-15½- x-½-inch baking sheet

⅔	cup (70 grams) sifted cake flour
1	tablespoon granulated sugar
⅛	teaspoon salt
2	ounces (4 tablespoons) unsalted butter
3	eggs, room temperature
2	egg yolks, room temperature
½	cup (100 grams) granulated sugar
1	teaspoon vanilla

Baking preparations: Position rack in lower third of oven and preheat oven to 450 degrees.

Using a paper towel, lightly grease a small area in the center of the baking sheet with solid shortening and line the pan with foil, leaving a 2-inch overhang at each short end. Lightly grease the foil with shortening and sprinkle it with all-purpose flour. Shake the baking sheet to distribute the flour and tap out excess.

Ingredient preparations: Pour the flour, 1 tablespoon sugar and salt in that order into a triple sifter. Sift onto a sheet of waxed paper; set aside.

Melt the butter in a 1-quart saucepan over low heat. Pour into a 1-quart mixing bowl; set aside.

Crack the eggs into the bowl of a heavy-duty mixer. Add the egg yolks and ½ cup sugar and whisk the ingredients by hand to combine. Rest the bowl in a shallow pan, such as a 10-inch skillet, filled with 1 inch of water that feels hot to the touch (120 degrees). To prevent the eggs from setting, whisk them continuously for about 30 seconds.

Now test if the mixture has warmed to body temperature by sticking your forefinger in it. Rub the mixture between your thumb and finger; it should feel smooth, not granular.

Making the cake: Attach the bowl on the mixer, and with the whisk attachment, whip the eggs and sugar mixture on medium speed (#5) until it has cooled and increased considerably in volume (tripled or more), appears light in texture and pale in color and has thickened to the consistency of a whole-egg meringue (about 3 to 5 minutes). Add the vanilla in the final moments of whipping.

Baker's Notes

☞ This glorious cake is delicate and quite moist. The most important thing to remember is not to overbake it. Overbaking will give you a drier cake that will split when you roll it.

☞ A génoise has less foam structure than a spongecake and hence a shorter baking time.

☞ The oven is deliberately set at 450 degrees. At this temperature the cake will bake quickly without drying out. Do not bake it past an ivory color!

With the aid of a flexible metal icing spatula, scoop half the flour and sprinkle it over the top. Using a rubber spatula, fold it into the batter just until incorporated. Repeat again, folding just until all the flour is absorbed.

Gently pour about 1 cup of the batter into the butter, and with the rubber spatula, fold until combined. Return the butter mixture to the reserved batter and again fold to combine.

Baking the cake: With the aid of the rubber spatula, pour the batter from the bowl down the center of the prepared pan in a strip 5 to 6 inches wide. Spread the batter as evenly as possible with an 8-inch flexible metal icing spatula. Spread from the center to the sides and corners. Use the sides as a guide. The batter should be level with them.

Bake for 5 minutes. Then check to see if the baking is finished. The surface should be ivory-colored. Press lightly near the center with your fingertips; if it springs back, it is done. The short sides of the cake will begin to contract from the foil, too. If the cake is not finished, return it to the oven for 1 to 3 more minutes, watching it carefully.

Cooling the cake: Remove the pan from the oven and place it on a large rack. Using a thin-bladed knife, gently release any portion of the cake sticking to the long sides of the pan. Pull up on the foil overhangs, one at a time, to release the foil from the pan's edges. Finally, loosen the foil from the bottom of the pan by gently lifting the foil flaps.

Cover the baked génoise sheet with another baking sheet and invert. Remove the original baking sheet, peel off the foil carefully to avoid tearing the cake; then turn it over so that the sticky side faces up, and reposition it back on the cake. Cover with a large cooling rack and invert right side up. Allow the cake to cool on the rack for at least 30 to 60 minutes.

Storing the cake: If you plan to use the génoise later in the day, leave it uncovered on the rack.

To use within 2 days, slip a baking sheet under the foil and cake. Cover with foil and freeze.

Génoise Ladyfingers

Tʜᴇsᴇ ladyfingers are richer and more tender than the spongy variety on page 169. They are excellent served with sorbet or leftover buttercream.

They are used in Susie Gumberts' Pièce de Résistance (page 120).

Mᴀᴋᴇs sɪx ᴅᴏᴢᴇɴ 3-ɪɴᴄʜ ʟᴀᴅʏғɪɴɢᴇʀs

Baking Equipment: Two 12-x-15½-x-½-inch baking sheets, 16-inch pastry bag, ½-inch (#6) round decorating tip

1 ¼	cups (125 grams) sifted cake flour
1	tablespoon granulated sugar
2	ounces (4 tablespoons) unsalted butter

2	large eggs, room temperature
4	egg yolks, room temperature
½	cup (100 grams) granulated sugar
1	teaspoon vanilla
1	cup (100 grams) unsifted powdered sugar

Baking preparations: Position one rack in lower third and the other rack in the upper third of the oven; preheat oven to 425 degrees.

Line each baking sheet with baking parchment to fit. Using a pencil and ruler, draw parallel lines on the paper 3 inches apart, across the 12-inch (short) side of each sheet in rows ½ to 1 inch apart; these lines are guides for piping the ladyfinger batter. (Each baking sheet with 3 rows each yields 3 dozen ladyfingers.)

Fit the pastry bag with the decorating tip and place it near the baking sheets.

Ingredient preparations: Pour the flour and the 1 tablespoon granulated sugar in that order into a triple sifter. Sift onto a sheet of waxed paper; set aside.

Melt the butter in a 1-quart saucepan over low heat. Pour into a 1-quart mixing bowl; set aside.

Place the eggs and egg yolks in the bowl of a heavy-duty mixer. Add the ½ cup granulated sugar and whisk by hand to combine. Rest the bowl in a shallow pan, such as a 10-inch skillet, filled with 1 inch of hot tap water (120 degrees). To prevent the eggs from setting, whisk them continuously until the mixture has warmed to body temperature, taking care that it doesn't exceed 110 degrees (about 30 seconds). Rub a little of the mixture between your thumb and forefinger; it should feel smooth, not grainy.

Making the cake: Place the bowl on the mixer, and with the whisk attachment, whip the mixture on medium speed (#5) until it has cooled and increased considerably in volume (tripled or more), appears light in texture and pale yellow in color and has thickened to the consistency of a whole-egg meringue (about 4 to 5 minutes). Pour in the vanilla during the final moments of whipping.

Test if it's time to fold in the flour by lifting the whisk. If some of the mixture falls back into the bowl in ribbons and remains on the surface, proceed. But if it sinks back into the batter right away, continue whipping for a few more minutes, or until the desired consistency is achieved.

With the aid of a flexible metal icing spatula, scoop a third of the flour mixture and sprinkle it over the surface. Using a rubber spatula, fold it until incorporated, scraping the sides of the bowl when necessary. Repeat procedure two more times, each time folding until the flour has been absorbed.

Gently pour about 1 cup of the batter into the butter, and with the rubber spatula, fold until combined. Return the butter mixture to the rest of the batter and again fold to combine.

Forming the ladyfingers: Without delay, scoop the batter into the pastry bag. With one hand guiding the tip and the other hand pressing against the batter-filled bag, pipe ½-inch-wide fingers, 3 inches in length (½ to ¾ inch apart, giving room to spread),

Baker's Notes

☞ All the batter should go into the pastry bag when you're ready to pipe. If no one can hold the bag while you're filling it, place the bag in a large glass to steady it.

☞ If you're lucky enough to have two ovens, position the racks in the lower third of each since the ladyfingers cook best that way.

☞ This batter makes wonderful madeleines, too. Pipe the batter, half fill molds and bake in a preheated 350-degree oven for 15 minutes.

between the marked lines as your guide. Keep the tip at a 45-degree angle, lifting it slightly to cut off the flow of batter as each ladyfinger is formed. Each ladyfinger will spread a bit as you pipe the others.

Baking the ladyfingers: Pour the powdered sugar into a sieve. With the palm of your hand, tap the side of the sieve to sprinkle the sugar over the ladyfingers.

Bake for 5 to 6 minutes, or until the ladyfingers are firm but spongy when pressed lightly with your finger and are barely colored.

Cooling the ladyfingers: Remove the baking sheets from the oven and transfer the parchment paper with the ladyfingers on it to a cooling rack. When the ladyfingers are cool, slide a pancake-type spatula under each side to release each ladyfinger from the paper. (If you lift from either end, the ladyfingers might break or tear.)

Storing the ladyfingers: If using ladyfingers the next day, freeze them when they are cool. (Ladyfingers get stale quickly unless soaked with dessert syrup.) Place them in a plastic container with waxed paper between the layers. Freeze for no more than 10 days.

Susie Gumberts' Pièce de Résistance

I THINK this is the best chocolate dessert in the world. Susie Gumberts, my mother, began this family classic, and I was raised on it, as were my children. It is made by layering and surrounding a light chocolate mousse with homemade lady fingers. We usually think of soaking ladyfingers with a dessert syrup, but while chilling, the ladyfingers soak up all the mousse and become wonderfully moist.

You can enjoy this charming dessert alone with coffee or even after a filling meal.

Equipment: 9-inch springform pan

1   recipe Génoise Ladyfingers (page 118)
    Chocolate Curls (page 283)

Chocolate Filling

8   large eggs, room temperature
1   teaspoon granulated sugar
12   ounces Baker's German sweet chocolate
6   tablespoons granulated sugar
¼   cup (2 ounces) hot tap water
1   teaspoon vanilla

½   cup (4 ounces) heavy cream
1   tablespoon granulated sugar
1   teaspoon vanilla

Advance preparations: Prepare Génoise Ladyfingers as directed on page 118.

Prepare Chocolate Curls as directed on page 283. Store in a sturdy container in the freezer until you are ready to decorate. Freezing keeps these flakes dry and fresh indefinitely, and any heat from your fingertips will not melt them when you handle and arrange them on cakes.

Baking preparations: Lightly butter the springform pan sides only, dust with granulated sugar and tap out the excess. This will prevent the ladyfingers from sticking to the pan, facilitating the molded dessert's release. Insert a circle of parchment or waxed paper.

Line the sides of the pan with about 22 ladyfingers; then line the bottom. You may have to tear some to patch the spaces between the ladyfingers. Do not worry if every crevice is not filled; just fill the spaces that are ¼ inch wide or wider.

Making the filling: Separate the eggs, placing the whites in the bowl of a heavy-duty mixer and the yolks in a small bowl. Set the 1 teaspoon sugar near the egg whites.

Pour the hot water (120 degrees) into the bottom of a 1½-quart double boiler. Place over very low heat to maintain the water's temperature at 120 degrees but no higher.

Chop the chocolate into 1-inch pieces and place in the top of the double boiler. Pour the 6 tablespoons of sugar on top of the chocolate, then the ¼ cup hot tap water (120 degrees). Pouring the water in after the sugar aids in dissolving the sugar. The hot water also hastens in melting the chocolate. (The primary function of this water, though, is to make the chocolate a smoother, creamier mixture for combining later with the whipped whites.)

Place the mixture in the top of a double boiler, the water temperature of which should remain just under a simmer. Allow the heat to penetrate the mixture for a couple of minutes before you stir it with a rubber spatula. Then stir occasionally until the mixture is smooth and shiny. Add the egg yolks and stir briskly to combine until smooth and shiny. Remove from the double boiler. Transfer the chocolate mixture to a 3-quart mixing bowl and stir in the 1 teaspoon vanilla.

Attach the bowl to the mixer, and with the whisk attachment, whip the whites on low speed (#2) until small bubbles appear and the surface is frothy (about 30 to 45 seconds).

Baker's Notes

☞ This dessert may be prepared over a 2-day period.
First day: Prepare Génoise Ladyfingers.
Second day: Make Chocolate Filling and assemble the dessert.
It is best if assembled the day before serving.

☞ For a note on uncooked egg whites, see page 31.

Understanding Cakemaking

Increase the speed to medium (#5), add the reserved 1 teaspoon sugar and whip until soft white peaks form (about 1 minute). Detach the bowl and attachment from the mixer and whisk by hand with the attachment to combine the whipped mass.

Stir and fold about ½ cup of the whipped egg whites into the chocolate mixture to lighten it. Then fold in the remaining whites.

Assembling the dessert: Pour a third of the chocolate mixture over the ladyfingers and spread it level. Layer with ladyfingers again as you did for the bottom of the springform. Pour another third of the chocolate mixture over this layer of ladyfingers. Repeat with the ladyfingers again, ending with the last of the chocolate mixture.

Cover the top with foil and refrigerate for several hours before decorating.

To decorate: Whip the cream with the 1 tablespoon sugar and 1 teaspoon vanilla until soft peaks form. Spread on top of the dessert and top with Chocolate Curls. Before serving, carefully remove the springform rim. Then slip a wide metal spatula under the parchment liner and transfer the dessert to a serving plate.

Zebra Torte

SIMPLE INGREDIENTS—chocolate, heavy cream and hazelnuts—combine in this dessert. The ground hazelnuts take the place of flour in this chocolate-nut génoise, and the result is a dark, rich cake studded with fragments of chewy nuts.

MAKES ONE 8-INCH ROUND CHOCOLATE NUT GÉNOISE, 8 TO 10 SERVINGS

Baking and Decorating Equipment: One 8-inch springform pan, small paper cone

3	ounces (½ cup plus) hazelnuts
3	ounces (6 tablespoons) unsalted butter
4	ounces semisweet chocolate
4	large eggs, room temperature
½	cup (100 grams) granulated sugar
2	ounces (⅓ cup) hazelnuts
2⅓	cups heavy cream
2	tablespoons (25 grams) granulated sugar
1	teaspoon vanilla
3	ounces semisweet chocolate

Baking preparations: Position rack in lower third of oven; preheat oven to 350 degrees.

Using a paper towel, grease the sides of the springform pan with solid shortening. Dust generously with all-purpose flour, tilt to coat, tap out the excess and insert a parchment or waxed paper liner.

Ingredient preparations: Using a nut grinder or rotary-type grater, grind the 3 ounces of hazelnuts for the batter until the mixture has the consistency of cornmeal; you need 1 cup minus 2 tablespoons ground.

Place the butter in a 1-quart heavy-bottomed saucepan. Chop the 4 ounces of chocolate into small pieces and add to the butter. Then, over very low heat, melt the two, whisking occasionally to prevent scorching. When the mixture is almost melted, remove it from the heat and blend until smooth (the heat will eventually melt the remaining chocolate and butter). Pour into a 2½- to 3-quart mixing bowl to cool slightly.

Crack the eggs into the bowl of a heavy-duty mixer. Add the ½ cup sugar and whisk the ingredients by hand to combine. Rest the bowl in a shallow pan, such as a 10-inch skillet, filled with an inch of water that feels hot to the touch (120 degrees). To prevent the eggs from setting, whisk them continuously for 30 seconds, or until the mixture has warmed to body temperature.

Making the cake: Attach the bowl to the mixer, and with the whisk attachment, whip the mixture on medium speed (#5) until it cools and thickens, appears paler in color and resembles a whole-egg meringue, and increases (triples or more) in volume (3 to 5 minutes).

Test if it's time to fold in the ground nuts by lifting the whisk. If some of the mixture falls back into the bowl in ribbons and remains on the surface, proceed. But if it sinks back into the batter right away, continue whipping for a few more minutes, or until the desired consistency is achieved.

Sprinkle the nuts over the batter. Using a rubber spatula, fold just until incorporated.

Carefully pour the whipped egg mixture into the cooled chocolate and butter. Fold until the chocolate mixture is incorporated uniformly.

Baking the cake: Gently pour the mixture into the pan. With a rubber spatula, smooth the top slightly. (The batter near the metal rim of the pan will set first and remain slightly higher after baking.)

Bake for 35 to 37 minutes, or until the center springs back slightly when lightly touched and sounds spongy when tapped. The crusty top makes the toothpick test unreliable.

Cooling the cake: Place the cake on a rack to cool for 45 minutes to 1 hour. The top will crack, and the cake will appear to fall. After it has cooled, remove any loose crust. Run a knife blade around the sides of the cake; then release the sides of the pan.

Cover the génoise with another cooling rack, invert it onto the rack and carefully remove the springform bottom from the cake. Slowly peel off the parchment liner, turn it over so that the sticky side faces up and reposition it on top of the cake. Cover with the first rack, invert the layer right side up, and remove the top rack.

Storing the cake: If you plan to use the génoise the same day, leave it on the rack until ready.

To use within 2 days, wrap in plastic wrap.

To freeze, cover the plastic-wrapped package with foil. Label the package, indicating the contents and date. Freeze for no longer than 10 days.

Baker's Notes

☞ This dessert must be made ahead and frozen for at least 4 hours before serving. When I am having a lot of company and must prepare the food in advance, it is a perfect choice.

☞ If I want to use less heavy cream when I assemble the dessert but still create the same finished effect, I stack several 8-inch cardboard circles (about 4 or 5) under the baked cake. Then I slip the spring-form rim around this structure and close it. This elevates the cake so that less cream is needed to cover it. (You might want to trim the cardboards' diameters just a little so the fit is not so tight that you spring the mechanism on the pan.)

Assembling the cake: Grind the 2 ounces of hazelnuts until they have the consistency of cornmeal, using a nut grinder or rotary-type grater; you need ⅔ cup ground. Set aside.

Lift the cake onto a clean 8-inch springform pan base, lined with a circle of parchment or waxed paper (so removal to a serving plate will be easy); then lock the sides into position. Using your fingertips, press the outer edges of the cake level with the center of the cake. (This doesn't harm the cake's texture. It also re-forms it to an 8-inch cake because it contracts a bit during baking.) Fit the springform rim around the cake-lined pan and lock it into place. (See the Baker's Note on page 123 for an alternate plan.)

Whip the cream with the sugar and vanilla until soft peaks form and the beaters make tracks that slowly close. Fold in the ground nuts; then spoon the whipped cream into the pan on top of the cake. Tap lightly on the counter to ensure the cream packs evenly around the edges of the pan. Using a 12-inch flexible metal icing spatula or one long enough to reach across the 8-inch-wide pan, smooth the cream's surface even with the top edge of the metal rim. Wipe the rim with paper toweling to clean off any excess whipped cream.

Place the dessert in the freezer for at least 4 hours, or until the cream is completely frozen. (The purpose of freezing the torte is to aid in removing the springform rim so that it leaves a perfect finish of smooth, molded whipped cream on top.)

Decorating the cake: While the dessert is in the freezer, chop the 3 ounces of chocolate into small pieces and place them in a small bowl that fits snugly in another one partially filled with 120-degree water. When the chocolate is liquid and smooth, fill the paper cone with it. Cut the tip to provide a thin flow of chocolate. Remove the dessert from the freezer and place it on a strip of waxed paper. Pipe thin lines of chocolate back and forth over the dessert's surface. Exert light pressure on the paper cone, never easing your pressure on the cone or on your back-and-forth movement. Also deliberately extend the chocolate lines over the edge of the springform rim to make straight, continuous lines, not interrupted ones. When you have piped enough lines, carefully clean the springform rim of any chocolate with a paper towel. This provides a neat finish when the springform rim is removed. (It is best to decorate before the rim is too frozen so the chocolate will not be too difficult to remove.) Return the dessert to the freezer.

Serving the cake: When the cream is firm, remove the springform rim. Since the dessert is frozen, you need to moisten the sides with a sponge full of cold water (not warm, or you melt the cream) to loosen the cake. After unmolding, smooth the sides with a metal icing spatula if necessary. Refrigerate for at least 4 hours to defrost.

Chocolate Rhapsody

Inspired by two famous chocolate desserts, Germany's Black Forest torte and Hungary's Rigo Jancsi, I like trimming the round cake into an octagon for a dramatic finishing touch. The chocolate mousse is smooth and silky with the divine taste of chocolate, not butter or egg whites. **(See photograph, page 67.)**
Makes 8 to 10 servings

Decorating Equipment: 9-inch springform pan, small paper cone, octagonal cardboard stencil, optional

> **One 9-inch layer Cocoa Génoise (page 115)**
> ½ cup Soaking Syrup, optional (page 302)
> ½ cup framboise or maraschino liqueur

Dark Chocolate Mousse
> 3 eggs, separated, room temperature
> 4 ounces semisweet chocolate
> 6 ounces (1 ½ sticks) unsalted butter, room temperature
> 2 tablespoons (25 grams) unsifted cocoa powder
> ½ cup (100 grams) granulated sugar
> 1 recipe Regal Chocolate Glaze (page 290)
> Cocoa Piping Syrup, optional (page 291)

Advance preparations: If desired, make an octagonal-shaped stencil for a finishing touch: Mark a 9-inch stiff cardboard round with eight 1¾-inch lines with the aid of a ruler. Each line should be the same length and should not cross the other. Cut along each line to form the stencil.

Place a 9-inch round of baking parchment or waxed paper in the bottom of a clean springform pan for convenient removal of dessert later; set aside.

Prepare Cocoa Génoise in a 9-inch springform pan as directed on page 115.

Prepare Soaking Syrup as directed on page 302.

Combine Soaking Syrup and framboise in a liquid cup measure; set aside.

Making the mousse: Place the whites in the bowl of a heavy-duty mixer and the yolks in a small bowl. Place plastic wrap on the surface of the bowl over the yolks to prevent their drying. Set aside.

Cut the chocolate into matchstick-size pieces, and place them in a 1-quart mixing bowl that fits snugly over another bowl half-filled with hot water (120 degrees). When the chocolate is smooth and liquid, remove the bowl, and set it aside to cool.

In a 3-quart mixing bowl, work the butter with a rubber spatula until it is soft, malleable and close to the consistency of mayonnaise. (The butter will easily mix with the other ingredients but still give body to the mixture. Melted butter would give a completely different texture.) Stir in the cooled but still liquid chocolate with a rubber spatula until blended. Next stir in the egg yolks, one by one, and then the 2 tablespoons cocoa until smooth and blended. Set aside.

You may want to review Warm-Method Meringue on page 212 before proceeding.

Add the sugar to the egg whites and whisk the ingredients by hand to combine. Rest the bowl in a shallow pan, such as a 10-inch skillet, filled with 1 inch of hot tap water (120 degrees). Whisk the mixture until it is body temperature (about 30 to 45 seconds).

Place the bowl on the mixer, and with the whisk attachment, whip it on medium speed (#5) until it is cool and white, stiff but still shiny, and elastic peaks form (about 3 to 4 minutes).

Scoop one-third of the meringue into the bowl with the chocolate mixture and fold to lighten it. Then fold in the remaining meringue until blended. Refrigerate for 4 hours.

Baker's Notes

☞ This dessert may be prepared over a 2-day period.
First day: Bake cake; prepare Soaking Syrup and octagonal stencil.
Second day: Prepare Chocolate Mousse; assemble and decorate. After the cake is filled with the mousse, it needs 2 to 3 hours in the refrigerator to firm.

☞ Use the dessert syrup if you wish. I use it only if the cake is not fresh.

☞ The flavor and texture of your mousse are greatly influenced by the quality of the chocolate you choose. I use a dark chocolate that tastes rich and silky and leaves a wonderful aftertaste. What is a wonderful aftertaste? One that makes you say, "I must have more!" (See page 278 for a discussion of chocolate.)

☞ If time is short, glaze the dessert on top and omit the steps for cutting it into an octagon and decorating it with Cocoa Piping Syrup.

☞ See page 31 for a note on recipes containing uncooked eggs.

Assembling the cake: Cut Cocoa Génoise horizontally into two equal layers, each about ⅝ inch thick. When lifting each layer, use the removable bottom from a quiche pan to prevent tearing.

Place the bottom génoise layer, cut side up, on the bottom of the springform pan. If the dessert syrup is being used, brush half over the top, using a pastry brush. Spoon the mousse on this layer.

Place the other cake layer on top of the mousse and gently press to level and distribute filling evenly. Brush with syrup. Cover the container with foil or plastic wrap and refrigerate to firm the mousse. (The springform pan gives form to the dessert and makes it easy to cover to keep moisture in before finishing and serving.)

Finishing the cake: As soon as the mousse is firm, the cake may be glazed and trimmed (if you are in a hurry, freeze it for 1 hour). A cold, firm filling facilitates trimming the dessert to make a neater, cleaner cut.

Prepare Regal Chocolate Glaze as directed on page 290.

Carefully remove the springform rim. With a flexible metal icing spatula, spread the liquid glaze over the surface of cold dessert until smooth and even.

Slide a wide metal spatula between the parchment and the metal springform bottom, and lift the dessert onto a baking sheet or cutting board.

Optional decorations: To trim, pour hot tap water into a tall glass and dip a long (12-inch) serrated knife into the water. Place the cardboard octagonal stencil close to or on the top of the dessert and cut, tracing the edge. Repeat, dipping and wiping the knife each time you cut another edge.

If desired, prepare Cocoa Piping Syrup as directed on page 291. When the syrup is at the proper consistency for piping, fill the paper cone half full and decorate the dessert's surface. Return the dessert to the refrigerator until serving time.

Serving the cake: Remove from the refrigerator just 30 minutes before serving. For neat slices, cut with a sharp, thin-bladed knife, straight down. Wipe the blade clean for each cut.

Trimming the cake into an octagonal shape using a cardboard stencil as a guide.

Gardenia Cake

THIS SIMPLE, tailored dessert combines almond, apricot and chocolate. Almond Paste Génoise is soaked with amaretto-flavored syrup and glazed with apricot jam, then with chocolate butter glaze. The gardenia blossom's pristine whiteness contrasts dramatically with the gleaming chocolate glaze. (**See photograph, page 70.**)
MAKES 10 SERVINGS

Decorating Equipment: 9-inch stiff cardboard round, small paper cone

One 9-inch Almond Paste Génoise layer (page 110)
- ½ cup Soaking Syrup (page 302)
- 1 recipe Chocolate-Butter Glaze (page 289)
- ¼ cup amaretto liqueur
- ¼ cup (3 ounces) strained apricot jam
- 1 teaspoon orange zest
- ½ cup (6 ounces) strained apricot jam

- 1 gardenia blossom, fresh or made of marzipan

Advance preparations: Prepare Almond Paste Génoise as directed on page 110.
Prepare Soaking Syrup as directed on page 302.
Prepare Chocolate-Butter Glaze as directed on page 289.
Combine Soaking Syrup and amaretto in a liquid measuring cup.
Place the ¼ strained apricot jam and the orange zest in a small saucepan over low heat to melt and combine flavors.
Measure the strained apricot jam mixture for the glaze.

Assembling the cake: Place the génoise on a flat surface and split it into two layers, each about ⅞ inch thick. Lift the top layer and set aside.
Place the bottom layer, cut side up, on the cardboard round for easier handling. Brush with half the dessert syrup, using a pastry brush. Then, with an 8-inch flexible metal icing spatula, spread with ¼ cup of the strained apricot jam to produce a thin film, extending to the edge of the cake.
Center the other layer over the strained apricot jam, brush it with the remaining dessert syrup and then spread the ½ cup apricot jam to coat the entire cake. Allow this glaze to set until it no longer feels too sticky to the touch (about 1 to 2 hours).
To hasten the drying process of the glaze, place it in front of a small electric fan for 35 to 45 minutes, rotating it occasionally to dry evenly. Place cake as close to the fan as possible, elevating the dessert on a few books, if necessary.

Making the chocolate glaze: While the apricot glaze is drying, fill the bottom of a 1½-quart double boiler with hot tap water (120 degrees). Place Chocolate-Butter Glaze in the top container over the water. Stir occasionally until smooth. Remove from heat to cool until close to 80 degrees, when it will be thicker and ready to glaze the cake.

Baker's Notes

☞ This dessert may be prepared over a 2-day period.
First day: Bake Almond Paste Génoise; prepare Soaking Syrup.
Second day: Prepare filling and glazes and assemble dessert.

☞ The gardenia should be pesticide-free and is only for garnish.

Understanding Cakemaking

Glazing and decorating the cake: You may want to refer to glazing techniques (page 240). Place the dessert on a cooling rack over a dry baking sheet to catch the excess Chocolate-Butter Glaze since the glaze is reusable. After coating the cake with the glaze, scrape any remaining from the baking sheet into a small bowl. When it is cooler (approximately 15 to 20 minutes), it will become thick enough to pipe onto the cake. When the glaze is ready, fill the paper cone half full, and pipe two lines in each direction so they intersect on top of the cake. Set aside at room temperature until serving.

At serving time, wrap a small piece of plastic wrap around the stem of the fresh gardenia before inserting it into the cake at the point where the piped chocolate lines intersect.

Storing and serving the cake: Store and serve at room temperature.

St. Lily Peach Cake

A WONDERFUL choice for a summer meal, this dessert blends the taste and textures of fresh, silky peaches and softly whipped cream with cake richly flavored with brown sugar.

MAKES 8 TO 10 SERVINGS

Decorating Equipment: 8-inch stiff cardboard round, cake decorating turntable, 14-inch pastry bag, #70 decorating tip

One 8-inch round layer Brown Sugar Génoise (page 105)

Filling and Frosting
1	small (7-ounce) fresh peach
1 ¼	cups (10 ounces) heavy cream
2	tablespoons (25 grams) granulated sugar
1	teaspoon vanilla

Baker's Notes

☞ You may want to review decorating with whipped cream techniques on page 239.

☞ The beveling technique is an interesting way of giving dimension and drama to your decorating.

Beveling the dessert.

Advance preparations: Prepare Brown Sugar Génoise as directed on page 105.

Blanch the peach by placing it in a 1½-quart saucepan filled with boiling water to cover. Turn off heat and let sit for 15 to 30 seconds. Remove the peach and run it under cold water to stop any cooking. Set aside to cool completely. (This can be done several hours before assembling. If so, refrigerate the blanched peach.)

Assembling the cake: Split the cake in half (review methods on page 234, if necessary).

Turn the top layer of the cake upside down, center it on the cardboard round and transfer to the turntable.

Whip the heavy cream with the sugar and vanilla until soft peaks form.

Spread the equivalent of 3 tablespoons cream over the cake layer. Peel the blanched peach and cut thin slices (about ¼ inch) to cover the cream-topped layer. Spread with another thin layer of the whipped cream (about 3 tablespoons) to cover.

Center the second layer on top. Slip the cleaned spatula under the cardboard to aid in lifting the cake. Hold in one hand while frosting with the other hand to coat the sides with a thin film as smoothly and evenly as possible. Then return to the turntable to frost over this initial coating and finish the top and sides.

Decorating the cake: To create a beveled edge, hold the flexible metal icing spatula blade in a slanted position on the seam where the sides and top meet. Pressing the blade lightly but holding it steady, rotate the turntable. Now the top and sides are smooth, and a slight ledge has been formed on the cake.

Mark a lattice pattern on top of the cake with the clean edge of the spatula. Mark the lines, in each direction, close together.

Fit the pastry bag with the decorating tip and fill it with the remaining whipped cream; pipe a leaf design on the beveled edge.

Storing the cake: Refrigerate until 1 hour before serving.

Serve the day assembled since whipped cream tastes and looks best when fresh.

Juliet Cake

Tʜɪs ᴄᴀᴋᴇ is as memorable for its delicate and airy texture as for its fresh orange blossom flavor. Covered with a supple, satiny buttercream and decorated with flowers made from Royal Icing, this is a romantic dessert. **(See photograph, page 68.)**

Mᴀᴋᴇs 12 ᴛᴏ 14 sᴇʀᴠɪɴɢs

Baker's Notes

☞ Review techniques of frosting with buttercream (page 238).

☞ Prepare the Royal Icing Flowers, if using, at least 2 hours before serving and Italian Meringue Buttercream 1 to 2 hours before serving.

☞ Pesticide-free pansies or the tiny florets of lilac blossoms may be used in place of the Royal Icing Flowers.

Decorating Equipment: 10-inch stiff cardboard round, cake decorating turntable, 14-inch pastry bag, ¼-inch (#2) round decorating tip

One 10-inch Orange Génoise (page 112)

Frosting

1 recipe Italian Meringue Buttercream (page 267)
3 tablespoons orange juice
1 tablespoon orange zest (1 orange)

Decorations, optional:

1 recipe Classic Royal Icing (page 269)
50 nontoxic silver dragées (for decoration only)

Advance preparations: Prepare Orange Génoise as directed on page 112.

Prepare the Italian Meringue Buttercream as directed on page 267 at least 1 to 2 hours before serving the dessert.

If decorating with Royal Icing Flowers, prepare them at least 2 hours before decorating: Prepare a small handmade paper cone as directed on page 244, and Classic Royal Icing as directed on page 269. Fill the cone and cut the end to create a small opening. Pipe out five small dots to form a ⅜-inch circle (the size of a small button) on a strip of waxed paper and place a silver dragée in the center of each. Pipe at least 50 flowers. Allow to dry; store them in a metal container at room temperature.

Making the frosting: Flavor Italian Meringue Buttercream with orange juice and zest.

Assembling the cake: Place the cake on the cardboard round, then on the turntable. Cover the sides and top with a thin coat of the buttercream. Finish the sides and top with the buttercream.

Optional decorations: Mark crisscrosses all around the sides of the cake with the clean edge of the icing spatula, so that it resembles the side of a drum. (Leave the top's smooth surface plain.) Spoon the remaining buttercream into the pastry bag, fitted with the ¼-inch tip, and trace these marked lines.

Pipe dots of buttercream where the lines intersect and place a royal icing flower on top of each, including along the top edge of the cake.

Storing the cake: Don't freeze this cake once it is frosted; the frosting will crack.

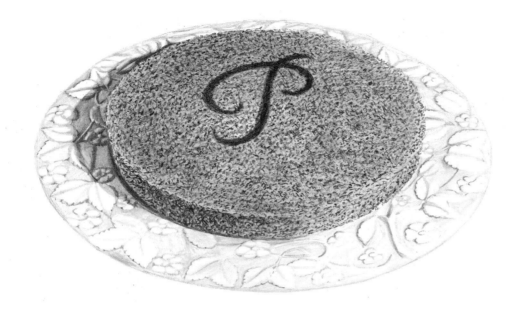

Pistachio Cake

THIS IS the quintessential dessert to show off a distinctive pistachio flavor. The technique in this dessert provides a surprise when sliced, as each serving reveals a layer of chocolate génoise buried in its blanket of gossamer-smooth Bavarian cream.

MAKES 10 TO 12 SERVINGS

Decorating Equipment: 8-inch springform pan, 8-inch stiff cardboard round, P template (optional)

       One 8-inch layer Chocolate Génoise (page 113)

4   **ounces (¾ cup) whole raw pistachio nuts, shelled**

1   **recipe Pistachio Bavarian Cream (page 252)**

1   **tablespoon cocoa powder**

Advance preparations: If desired, make a template for a finishing touch: Buy acetate from an art supply store. (The joy of an acetate template is that it is reusable. To clean, run under water and pat dry.) Trace the letter P from an art book, newspaper, etc., with a pencil or felt pen. Cut it out, using a utility knife. (The thinner the acetate, the easier it is to cut. The thicker it is, the easier it is to lift it from the cake after using.)

Lightly oil the inside rim of the springform pan to facilitate the dessert's removal. Trim ½ inch from the cake's edge, using a small paring knife. Place a round of parchment or waxed paper inside the pan and center the génoise on it (this will make it possible to remove the dessert from the metal disk to a serving plate later).

Prepare Chocolate Génoise as directed on page 113.

Bring 1½ cups water to a boil, pour in 8 ounces of pistachio nuts (4 ounces from the recipe for Bavarian cream on page 252 and 4 ounces from the above ingredients for the decoration) and bring just to the boil. Immediately pour the nuts into a sieve and shake to remove as much moisture as possible. The skins slip off easily while the nuts are moist and warm. Set aside half the nuts.

Place half the blanched nuts on a baking sheet and allow them to air-dry for 3 hours or as long as overnight. Then place in a preheated 300-degree oven to roast them slightly, enhancing their flavor but without coloring them (about 5 to 10 minutes). Remove from oven. When the nuts are cool, grind them to the consistency of cornmeal. Set aside until time to decorate the dessert.

The springform pan may leak, so place it on a baking sheet. (Once assembled, the dessert will go into the freezer for a short time to hasten the setting of the cream, so be certain the baking sheet fits in your freezer.)

Prepare Pistachio Bavarian Cream as directed on page 252.

Assembling the cake: Pour Pistachio Bavarian Cream into the springform pan, being certain that the gap between the trimmed cake and pan is filled, thus completely covering the génoise. The filling will come 1 inch below the springform's top rim.

Place the dessert in the freezer for 30 minutes to hasten the chilling and setting of the Bavarian cream. Cover the top of pan with foil. Then refrigerate for at least 6 hours or preferably overnight.

Serving the cake: Up to 6 hours before serving, remove the dessert from the refrigerator and pat a damp sponge all around the outside of the pan. The moisture from the sponge will begin to loosen the Bavarian cream from the inside of the pan. Carefully and slowly release the springs on the pan to unmold. If the springs are stubborn, coax them with a thin-bladed knife around edges.

Place the reserved ground dried pistachios on a baking sheet. Hold the dessert in one hand directly over the nuts. Tilt the cake slightly. With the other hand, pick up the ground nuts, and gently press them onto the sides and top of the Bavarian cream. Rotate the cake as you work until all the cream is covered. Press lightly with the side of a clean flexible metal icing spatula to ensure that the nuts adhere neatly.

Optional decoration: If using the P template, center it on top of the cake. Pour the cocoa into a sieve. Using the palm of your hand for better control of the powder's flow, gently tap the sieve to sprinkle it evenly over the P. Carefully lift the template.

Then slip under the paper a large wide spatula and transfer the dessert onto a serving plate.

Refrigerate until 15 to 30 minutes before serving.

La Fleur

A SOPHISTICATED milk-and-honey dessert, refined in its combination of flavors. The delicate honey cake contains a poached pear filling. After the cake has been frosted with a silky buttercream flavored with a pear liqueur, you can decorate the top with bees made of buttercream, if desired.

MAKES 6 TO 8 SERVINGS

Baker's Notes

☞ Prepare Pistachio Bavarian Cream and assemble the dessert at least 6 hours before serving. Once the cake is unmolded and decorated, you can store it in the refrigerator up to an additional 6 hours.

☞ This dessert may be prepared over a 2-day period.
First day: Bake Chocolate Génoise, prepare pistachios and infuse the milk for Bavarian cream.
Second day: Prepare Pistachio Bavarian Cream; assemble and decorate dessert.

☞ Blanching pistachios is a must for the filling's luscious pastel green color and unique flavor. Drying the nuts used to decorate the cake brings out their flavor and removes moisture.

☞ Almond extract intensifies the pistachio flavor.

Decorating Equipment: 8-inch stiff cardboard round, 14-inch pastry bag, 12-inch pastry bag, ⅜-inch (#4) round decorating tip, ¼-inch (#2) round decorating tip, small paper cone

	One 8-inch layer Honey Génoise (page 107)
½	cup Soaking Syrup (page 302)
2	medium pears, poached (page 272)
2 ½	cups Milk Buttercream (page 262), room temperature

Buttercream Bees, optional

1	ounce semisweet chocolate
1	ounce (¼ cup) sliced almonds
¼	cup Poire William liqueur (pear liqueur)
1	tablespoon lemon zest
2	tablespoons Poire William liqueur

Advance preparations: Prepare a layer of Honey Génoise as directed on page 107.

Prepare Soaking Syrup as directed on page 302.

Poach the pears following directions on page 272.

Prepare Milk Buttercream as directed on page 262.

Prepare the Buttercream Bees, if desired: Chop the chocolate into small pieces and melt in a 1-quart bowl that fits snugly over a bowl with hot tap water (120 degrees); set aside. Fit a 12-inch pastry bag with a ¼-inch open decorating tip and fill with ½ cup of the Milk Buttercream; pipe at least 12 small ovals about ¾ inch by ⅜ inch on a sheet of foil.

Fill the small handmade paper cone with the cooled but still liquid chocolate. Cut a tiny tip and then pipe three lines across each oval. After piping over at least 5 to 6 bees, place a small perfectly sliced almond on each side before the chocolate lines set too firmly. When all the bees are finished, slip a baking sheet that fits into your freezer under the foil. Freeze the sheet until you are ready to decorate.

☞ This dessert may be prepared over a 2-day period.
First day: Bake Honey Génoise; prepare Soaking Syrup; poach pears; prepare Milk Buttercream and the optional Buttercream Bees.
Second day: Assemble the dessert.

☞ Milk Buttercream's satiny, smooth consistency returns easily even after refrigeration.

☞ The purpose of the buttercream border is threefold: It provides a fence to hold in a lot of fruit, it supplies support for the next cake layer without squeezing the fruit out the sides, and it facilitates finishing the cake exterior neatly.

Understanding Cakemaking

Finishing the syrup and buttercream: Combine the Soaking Syrup, the ¼ cup liqueur and the lemon zest in a liquid measuring cup.

Place the remaining buttercream in a 3-quart mixing bowl. Slowly add the 2 tablespoons of liqueur, one teaspoon at a time, being certain it is absorbed before adding the next.

Drain the poached pears and cut them into small pieces, about ¼- to ½-inch cubes. Drain the diced fruit on paper towels to remove excess syrup.

Assembling the cake: Split the cake into two layers, each about ⅞ inch thick. Place the bottom cake layer, cut side up, on the cardboard round for easier handling. Moisten with about ½ of the dessert syrup, using a pastry brush. Spread a thin layer (about ¼ cup) of the buttercream over the moist layer, using a flexible metal icing spatula.

Spoon 1 cup of the buttercream into a 14-inch pastry bag fitted with a ⅜-inch round tip. (Reserve the remaining buttercream for frosting and decorating.) Pipe a ½-inch-thick coil of buttercream around the edge of the layer to form a border. Spoon the pear pieces into the center, and distribute them evenly to the border. Center the second cake layer on top, brush with the remaining syrup and spread a thin coating of buttercream on the sides and top of cake following the directions for frosting with buttercream on page 238. Refrigerate for 35 to 40 minutes, or until the buttercream is firm, then proceed with the second finishing coat of frosting.

Decorating the cake: Lightly outline 5 petals free-form with a toothpick in the buttercream. Slip a ¼-inch round decorating tip over the ⅜-inch tip *already attached* to the pastry bag. Refill pastry bag with the reserved buttercream if necessary. Holding the tip in place with one hand as you squeeze with the other, pipe the buttercream to trace the markings. Pipe a dot in the center where the petal meet. Remove five Buttercream Bees from the freezer and position them on top between the petals.

Storing the cake: Refrigerate until 1 hour before serving.

Lucerne Cheese Torte

A lemon-flavored génoise with a light unbaked cheesecake filling is frosted with whipped cream. The apricot-and-gelée glaze over the whipped cream creates a mirrorlike effect. This recipe is adapted from one created by the late Eduard Agopian.

MAKES 8 TO 10 SERVINGS

Decorating Equipment: 8-inch stiff cardboard round, cake decorating turntable, 14-inch pastry bag, ¼-inch (#2) round decorating tip

	One 8-inch layer Classic Génoise (page 104)
½	**cup Soaking Syrup (page 302)**
1	**recipe Cream Cheese Filling (page 254)**
¼	**cup fresh lemon juice, strained**

Apricot Gelée

½	cup apricot nectar
½	teaspoon gelatin
1	tablespoon sugar
¾	cup (6 ounces) heavy cream

Advance preparations: Prepare Classic Génoise as directed on page 104.
Prepare Soaking Syrup as directed on page 302.

Cutting the cake: The cake is cut in such a fashion that its exterior is left intact, but a core is removed. (See illustration on following page.)

Imagine a ½-inch-thick border around the outside edge of the cake. Now, using the tip of a short-bladed paring knife, cut along the imaginary line with a sawing motion around the entire cake, stopping short of the cake's bottom by ½ inch. Loosen the 6½-inch circle or inner core of the cake without disturbing the outer shell. Using a small serrated knife, such as a tomato knife, insert the blade into the side of the cake ½ inch from the bottom, creating a small slit. Keeping the knife horizontal and level, pivot the serrated edge in one direction, trying not to cut through the outer shell of the cake. (This will eventually loosen the entire bottom of the inner core.)

Remove the knife, insert it back into the slit with the serrated edge facing the opposite direction and pivot the other way. Repeat 3 more times, rotating the cake a quarter turn each time.

After completing 4 cuts, you should have loosened the core sufficiently to lift it out. Test it gently with a fork around the edge of the core; if you meet resistance anywhere, insert the serrated knife back into the nearest slit and pivot the blade again. Be patient and keep pivoting as well as tracing the top circle, and soon you'll be able to lift the core with the aid of the fork.

Remove the center core of the cake; it should measure about 6½ to 7 inches in diameter and be about 1 inch thick. Place the core on a flat work surface. Mentally divide it in

Baker's Notes

☞ This dessert may be prepared over a 2-day period.
First day: Bake Classic Génoise and prepare Soaking Syrup.
Second day: Prepare Cream Cheese Filling not more than ½ hour before assembling the dessert. Assemble the dessert at least 5 hours before serving.

☞ A day-old cake works best when you cut the cake as directed in this recipe. If the cake is fresh, freeze the layer for 30 to 45 minutes.

*Understanding
Cakemaking*

Top left: *Cutting an inner core to the cake.* Top right: *Separating the bottom cake core from the cake's outer shell.* Right: *Slicing the cake core in half.*

half horizontally. Now, using the paring knife, cut all the way around the side of the cake about ½ inch deep on that imaginary line. Slide a 12-inch knife into the cut. Holding the knife steady in that path, rotate the cake in a circle into the knife blade, cutting in a slow sawing motion all around, until the cake is evenly split into two ½-inch-thick layers.

Remove the top ½-inch layer, wrap it in plastic and save for future use. Split the remaining ½-inch layer into two ¼-inch-thick layers, using the same cutting procedure as above. (See page 235 for cutting thin layers.)

Remove the top ¼-inch layer and set aside. (Use a removable quiche bottom to aid in lifting, if necessary.)

Making the filling and syrup: No more than ½ hour before assembling the cake, prepare Cream Cheese Filling as directed on page 254, but wait until you assemble the dessert before adding the whipped cream. Set aside.

Combine Soaking Syrup and the lemon juice in a liquid cup measure.

Whip the ¼ cup cream from the recipe for Cream Cheese Filling until soft peaks form, and fold it into the cream cheese mixture just to incorporate it.

Assembling the cake: At least 4 hours before serving, place the shell of the cake on a cardboard round for easier handling. Using a pastry brush, coat evenly with a third of the dessert syrup inside the entire shell. Spoon about ¾ cup of the filling into the shell and smooth it to level. Place one of the thin cake layers on the filling and gently press so it adheres. Brush this layer with dessert syrup. Spoon more filling (about ¾ cup) over this. Then place the top layer of cake over the filling, and brush with the remaining third of the syrup.

Gently press the top layer down with your fingers until level with the edge. It now looks the way it did before the core was cut: a layer cake with no filling.

Making the gelée: Pour the apricot nectar into a small saucepan; sprinkle gelatin over its surface and set aside to soften (about 10 minutes). Add the sugar and place over low heat; stir just until dissolved. Set aside at room temperature to cool.

Whip the ¾ cup heavy cream until soft peaks form and the beaters make slowly closing tracks. Using a flexible metal icing spatula, frost the chilled cake as directed in the techniques of frosting cakes with whipped cream (page 239). When the sides and top are completely covered, spoon the remaining whipped cream into the pastry bag fitted with the decorating tip, and pipe a design around the edge of cake to form a border (it should look like successive S designs). Refrigerate the cake until the gelée is cool enough to pour onto the center of the cake's surface.

When the gelée is syrupy but still smooth and liquid (about 30 minutes), remove the frosted cake from the refrigerator and pour in the gelée slowly just to fill center portion of the cake. (Pour syrupy gelée onto a rubber spatula held ½ inch over the center of cake; this breaks the thrust of its flow so it pours gently.) The whipped cream border will keep the gelée from going down the sides. Refrigerate for 3 hours to set the filling and glaze.

Serving the cake: Remove from the refrigerator 30 minutes before serving.

Mocha Imperiale

NOTHING complements fondant like chocolate and coffee. Their richness masks the fondant's sweetness.

MAKES 8 TO 10 SERVINGS

Decorating Equipment: 8-inch stiff cardboard round, cake decorating turntable, small paper cone

	Nut Génoise (page 109)
½	recipe Classic Buttercream (page 260), room temperature
½	recipe Classic Fondant (page 302)
½	cup Soaking Syrup (page 302)
1	tablespoon *plus* 2 tablespoons Coffee Essence (page 269)
2	teaspoons dark rum
1	ounce semisweet chocolate
2	ounces walnuts, finely chopped

Advance preparations: Bake Nut Génoise as directed on page 109.

Prepare Classic Buttercream as directed on page 260; store in a covered container in the refrigerator.

Baker's Notes

☞ This dessert may be prepared over a 2-day period.
First day: Bake Nut Génoise; prepare Soaking Syrup, Classic Buttercream and Classic Fondant.
Second day: Assemble and decorate.

☞ You may want to review how to frost with buttercream (page 238) and how to glaze with fondant (page 242) before you assemble this dessert.

Understanding Cakemaking

Prepare Classic Fondant as directed on page 302; store in a covered container in the refrigerator.

Prepare Soaking Syrup as directed on page 302.

Prepare Coffee Essence as directed on page 269.

Combine Soaking Syrup and the 1 tablespoon Coffee Essence in a liquid measuring cup.

Place the buttercream in a 3-quart mixing bowl. Slowly add the 2 tablespoons Coffee Essence, mixing with a rubber spatula until it is creamy and smooth, resembling the consistency of mayonnaise.

Assembling the cake: Split the cake into two layers, each about ¾ inch thick.

Place the bottom layer, cut side up, on the cardboard round. Moisten with half the syrup, using a pastry brush. Spread a thin layer of buttercream, about ¼ cup, over the moist layer, using a flexible metal icing spatula.

Center the other layer on top, brush it with the remaining syrup and spread a thin coating of buttercream on the sides and top of the cake. Refrigerate for 35 to 40 minutes, or until the buttercream is firm; then proceed with the second, finishing coat. Refrigerate again for at least 1 hour. (This gives the buttercream time to chill and firm, so the warm fondant glaze doesn't melt the buttercream.)

Decorating the cake: Melt the chocolate in a small bowl over another small bowl half filled with 120-degree water. Stir occasionally until the chocolate is melted and smooth. Set it nearby still in the warm water, while you work with the fondant.

Prepare the fondant for glazing the cake's surface as directed on page 302. Add the rum. When it is the proper consistency, but before you remove the bowl of fondant from the water bath, fill the paper cone with melted chocolate. (Be certain to wipe the bowl dry before pouring the melted chocolate.) Set the filled paper cone nearby.

Now pour the fondant into the center of the cake and spread it right away with a flexible metal icing spatula to coat the surface.

Before the fondant sets, cut a small tip from the paper cone, and pipe lines over the glazed surface. Now draw the tip of a small paring knife back and forth over the lines, pulling the chocolate slightly to create a marbling effect. Wipe the knife tip clean between each stroke.

Pour the chopped walnuts onto a baking sheet. Hold the cake on its cardboard base in one hand directly over the nuts. Tilt the cake slightly, and with the other hand, gently press the nuts into the buttercream along the side of the cake until they are covered. Press lightly with the clean blade of a flexible metal icing spatula to ensure that the nuts adhere neatly.

Storing and serving the cake: Store at room temperature and serve the day assembled for best flavor and appearance.

Gâteau Rouge

THIS DESSERT is subtly flavored with cherries and red currants. A soft shade of red with lattice marks, it benefits from a simple decorating technique that looks professional. MAKES 8 TO 10 SERVINGS

Decorating Equipment: 8-inch stiff cardboard round, cake decorating turntable, 8-inch chef's knife

	One 8-inch layer Classic Génoise (page 104)
¼	cup Soaking Syrup (page 302)
1 ⅓	cups Classic Buttercream (page 260)
4	ounces (1 cup) walnuts
¼	cup *plus* 2 tablespoons maraschino liqueur
⅓	cup (4 ounces) currant jelly
2	teaspoons Cassis liqueur

Advance preparations: Prepare an 8-inch layer of Classic Génoise as directed on page 104.

Prepare Soaking Syrup as directed on page 302.

Prepare Classic Buttercream as directed on page 260.

With a chef's knife, chop the nuts on a cutting board into medium dice. Pour into a small bowl; set aside.

Making the syrup and buttercream: Combine Soaking Syrup and the ¼ cup maraschino liqueur in a liquid measuring cup.

Place Classic Buttercream in a 3-quart stainless steel mixing bowl. If it is cold and firm, it must be manipulated to a workable, spreading consistency (see page 238). When the buttercream is smooth, add the 2 tablespoons maraschino liqueur, one teaspoon at a time, being certain it is absorbed before adding the next. (Adding this liquid too quickly can cause curdling.)

Assembling the cake: Split the génoise into three equal layers, each about ¾ inch thick. (For specific details on techniques for splitting cake, see page 234.)

The layers are assembled so that the bottom becomes the top. This provides the precise, flat surface required for this dessert's finish. To aid in lifting the layers, use a wide metal spatula or the removable bottom from a quiche pan.

Turn the top layer upside down on the cardboard round, cut side up, and moisten with

Baker's Notes

☞ In order to glaze and decorate the cake properly, refrigerate the cake for at least 2 hours. Decorate and chill it again in the refrigerator at least 4 hours before serving.

☞ This dessert may be prepared over a 2-day period.
First day: Bake Classic Génoise; prepare Soaking Syrup and Classic Buttercream.
Second day: Assemble and decorate the dessert.

☞ Making buttercream ahead results in a smoother, more beautiful finish. If you do so, refer to page 238 for directions on how to transform cold, firm buttercream into a smooth spreadable consistency.

☞ The maraschino liqueur used in this dessert is not to be confused with thick red maraschino syrup. Maraschino liqueur has a light, clear, gentle taste of cherries.

Understanding Cakemaking

about one-third of the dessert syrup, using a pastry brush. With a flexible metal icing spatula, spread a thin layer of buttercream over the layer (be sure the buttercream reaches the edges). Center the middle layer on top, gently pressing this layer to level the cake. Brush with another third of dessert syrup; then spread a thin layer of buttercream. Now turn the last layer upside down and center it over the buttercream; brush it with the remaining one-third syrup.

Frost the sides and top with the buttercream. (To finish the sides and top of the cake with buttercream smoothly and neatly, two applications are best. You may want to review how to frost with buttercream on page 236.)

Place the cake in the refrigerator for at least 2 hours. The buttercream must be cold and firm before the cake is decorated.

Decorating the cake: Form a lattice pattern on the surface of the buttercream. Using the back, not the blade edge, of the 8-inch chef's knife, make parallel diagonal marks at equal intervals across the cake. Do not sink the knife into the buttercream more than 1/16 inch. Each time you pick up the knife, wipe it clean with a paper towel so that the next cut will be precise.

Now rotate the cake 90 degrees, and make parallel marks in the opposite direction, crossing the original lines to create a diamond pattern. Refrigerate the cake for at least 4 hours (or overnight) to harden the surface so that it is as firm as cold butter.

Pour the chopped nuts onto a baking sheet; set aside. Set a sieve over a 1-quart bowl. Place the cake on the turntable.

Heat the currant jelly in a small saucepan over low heat just to melt the jelly (not too hot, or it will melt the buttercream and remove the pattern). Once the jelly is melted, remove it from the heat and stir in the Cassis. Pour the jelly through the sieve into the bowl to make certain it is smooth and liquid.

Now pour all the melted jelly into the center of the cake. Using a light touch so as not to erase the marks in the buttercream, quickly spread it with a flexible metal icing spatula. Use short, quick strokes to distribute the glaze evenly to the edges, so a thin film covers the entire top. Notice how the surface is lightly tinted a soft red and that the scored

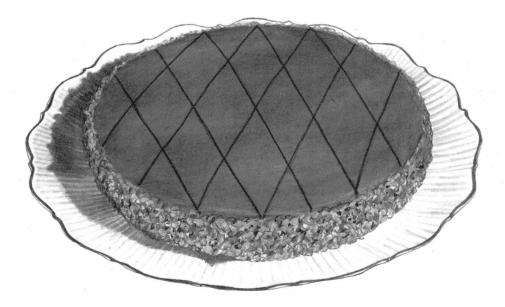

cuts are more pronounced because the jelly fills in the lines.

Hold the cake in one hand directly over the baking sheet of walnuts. Tilt the cake slightly, and with the other hand, gently press the nuts into the sides to coat. For a more finished look, ease some of the chopped nuts about ¹⁄₁₆ inch over the top edge or the seam of the cake where the glaze ends and the sides begin. Using a clean metal spatula, press the nuts into the buttercream with enough pressure so they adhere.

Storing the cake: Refrigerate until 1 hour before serving.

Jubilee Petal Cake

WHITE ON WHITE: an elegant wedding cake or a stunning conclusion to a formal dinner or celebration. Lemon zest spikes the flavor of white chocolate, and fresh coconut gives lightness and life to this simply assembled dessert.

(See photograph, page 155.)

MAKES 6 TO 8 SERVINGS

Decorating Equipment: 8-inch stiff cardboard round, cake decorating turntable

	One 8-inch layer Classic Génoise (page 104)
½	cup Soaking Syrup (page 302)
1	cup (4 ounces) freshly grated coconut (page 271)
	Seventy-five 1-inch-long, ¾-inch-wide White Chocolate Petals (page 292)
1	ounce semisweet chocolate
¼	cup dark rum
1 ¼	cups (5 ounces) heavy cream
2	tablespoons (25 grams) granulated sugar
1	teaspoon vanilla

Advance preparations: Prepare Classic Génoise as directed on page 104.

Prepare Soaking Syrup as directed on page 302.

Prepare freshly grated coconut as directed on page 271.

Prepare White Chocolate Petals as directed on page 292.

Grate the semisweet chocolate, using the smallest holes on a box grater over a sheet of waxed paper; or use a nut grinder or food processor. Store in a covered container until you assemble the dessert.

Combine Soaking Syrup and rum in a liquid measuring cup.

Whip the cream with the sugar and vanilla until soft peaks form; refrigerate until ready to use.

Assembling the cake: Split the génoise into three equal layers, each close to ⅝ inch thick. Lift the top two layers, one at a time, and set aside.

Place the bottom layer of cake, cut side up, first on a cardboard round to fit the cake, then on the turntable.

Moisten with about ¼ cup of the syrup, using a pastry brush. Remove the whipped cream

Baker's Notes

☞ This dessert may be prepared over a 2-day period.
First day: Bake Classic Génoise; prepare coconut, Soaking Syrup, White Chocolate Petals and grate semisweet chocolate.
Second day: Assemble the dessert.

from the refrigerator, and whisk briefly to combine the mixture again. Then spread ¾ cup of the whipped cream over the moist layer, using a flexible metal icing spatula, about 8 inches long, making sure the cream extends to the edges. Sprinkle the grated chocolate over the cream.

Center the middle layer of génoise over this and brush it with about ¼ cup syrup. Spread about ¾ of a cup whipped cream over the moist layer and sprinkle with about 3 tablespoons of the grated coconut. Center the last layer on the dessert.

Using the icing spatula, spread a thin layer of cream first on the sides and then on top of the cake. Now cover the sides and top again, rotating the cake on the turntable as you work as an aid to a smooth finish. Remember that the cream has already been whipped to its desired consistency, so any additional manipulation thickens the cream and can change its texture.

Decorating the cake: Place the remaining grated coconut on a baking sheet. Hold the cake in one hand directly over the coconut. Tilt the cake slightly, and with the other, gently press the coconut into the cream around the sides. Rotate the cake as you work until the sides are covered. Press lightly with the clean blade of a metal icing spatula to ensure that the coconut adheres neatly.

Starting along the edge of the cake, arrange White Chocolate Petals in 4 overlapping concentric circles.

Storing the cake: Refrigerate until 1 hour before serving.

Lemon Mist Torte

Tʜɪs sophisticated blend of whipped cream, airy lemon mousse and crisp, amber caramel was inspired by the lemon filling recipe a friend from Oregon, Dorothy Wiener, shared with me.

Mᴀᴋᴇs 12 sᴇʀᴠɪɴɢs

Decorating Equipment: 9-inch springform pan, round cutter, about 1 inch in diameter, 12-inch pastry bag, ⅜-inch (#4) round decorating tip

One 9-inch layer Classic Génoise (page 104)

Lemon Mousse Filling

⅓	cup water
3 ½	teaspoons gelatin
6	eggs, room temperature
¾	cup (150 grams) granulated sugar
¾	cup (4 to 5 lemons) lemon juice, strained
2	teaspoons lemon zest
½	cup (100 grams) granulated sugar
1	recipe All-Purpose Caramelized Sugar (page 305)
½	cup (4 ounces) heavy cream
½	cup (50 grams) unsifted powdered sugar

Baker's Notes

☞ This dessert may be prepared over a 2-day period.
First day: Bake Classic Génoise.
Second day: Prepare Lemon Mousse and assemble dessert at least 6 hours before serving the cake. Prepare caramel for glaze and whip cream to decorate.

☞ Fresh lemon juice is a must for flavor.

☞ For a note on uncooked egg whites, see page 31.

Advance preparations: Prepare a 9-inch layer of Classic Génoise as directed on page 104, except bake the batter in a 9-inch springform pan for 20 to 22 minutes.

Place the cake on a flat surface and divide it in half, each half ¾ inch thick. Lift the top layer onto a baking sheet and set it aside.

Using a small paring knife, trim a ½-inch border around the outer edge of the bottom layer. Place it inside the parchment-lined pan. (When the cake is trimmed, the filling flows around the layer and conceals it beautifully.)

Cut the top layer of the génoise with a serrated knife into 12 equal wedges like a pie. Using a round cutter, 1 inch in diameter (or the bottom of a ½-inch [#6] decorative tip), cut a circle of cake from each wedge close to the outside edge, coming to within ½ inch. Push the cake circle free from cutter with the tip of a chopstick or a wooden spoon. Reserve the 1-inch cake circles on a plate for later caramel glazing. Reform the wedges into a 9-inch circle on a large plate, and set aside. (If the wedges tear where the circle was stamped out, just patch them together when you replace them on the dessert. No one will know.)

Baking preparations: Lightly grease the sides of the clean 9-inch springform pan with almond oil (or an unflavored vegetable oil) to facilitate the later removal of the dessert. Insert a parchment paper or waxed paper round in the bottom to aid in removing this dessert before serving.

Making the Lemon Mousse: At least 6 hours before serving the dessert, pour the water into a liquid cup measure. Sprinkle with the gelatin to soften as it absorbs the liquid.

Separate the eggs, placing the whites in the bowl of a heavy-duty mixer, the yolks in the top of a 1½-quart double boiler. Whisk the yolks to combine. Pour the ¾ cup sugar into the yolks and whisk to combine. Add the lemon juice and whisk to blend.

Place the top of the double boiler over moderately bubbling boiling water and whisk continuously, back and forth, until a very foamy mixture thickens, triples in volume and reg-

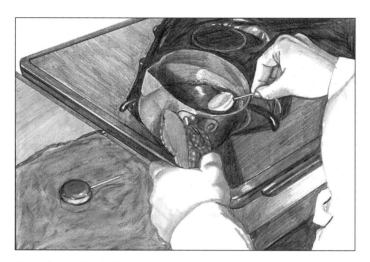

Dipping cake circles into caramelized sugar.

isters 170 degrees on a mercury candy thermometer (about 6 to 8 minutes).

Pour the lemon mixture into a 3-quart stainless steel mixing bowl, add the gelatin and stir until dissolved; then add the lemon zest. Place over a bowl of icy water (3 cups each ice and water) until the mixture is cooler and syrupy but still liquid. Stir occasionally to chill evenly and to prevent lumps.

When the lemon mixture is cooler and just beginning to thicken, though still syrupy (about 6 minutes), remove it from ice water bath. Then whip the egg whites on low speed until small bubbles appear (about 45 seconds). Then increase the speed to medium (#5), and gradually add the ½ cup sugar until shiny and glossy (not dry) peaks appear (about 3 minutes).

Whisk the cooler lemon cream smooth, breaking up any lumps. Then stir 1 cup of the meringue into the lemon mixture to lighten it; fold in the remaining meringue until it is incorporated.

Assembling the cake: Pour the lemon mousse into the cake-lined pan. Gently tap the pan on a counter to settle the filling around the cake. Smooth and level the top surface, using a rubber spatula. Place the 12 wedges on top, re-creating the original cake circle. Cover with plastic wrap and refrigerate to firm the mousse.

To prepare the cake circles to be coated with caramel so you don't burn your fingers, spear the side of each circle with a wooden toothpick. To prevent the cake circle from slipping off the toothpick, it must go in at least halfway. Repeat with remaining circles until you have a dozen cake "lollipops."

Prepare Caramelized Sugar in a 3-cup copper sugar pot or similar-size heavy-bottomed saucepan as directed on page 305. When the glaze is honey-colored, remove the pot from the heat.

Holding a cake circle by its toothpick and tilting the pot slightly, lower the circle into the glaze just enough to coat its top with a thin layer. Lift the cake and tilt it to allow the excess glaze to drip back into the pan. (See illustration.) Place the circle, glazed side up, on a sheet of foil. Repeat with the remaining circles and allow the caramel to cool and harden. If any caramel gets on the foil, it will release when cool. Any caramel strings can be cut away with scissors after the caramel has hardened.

Finishing the cake: Whip the cream until soft peaks form and refrigerate until ready to use. Fit the pastry bag with the decorating tip; set aside.

Remove the plastic wrap from the cake and run a thin table knife around the outer top edge, taking care not to disturb the shape of the mousse. Tilt the pan slightly to allow enough air to get to the bottom and to free the sides.

Pour the powdered sugar into a sieve. Using the palm of your hand, gently tap the sieve to sprinkle a thin, even layer over cake. Unmold the dessert by removing the springform rim carefully to avoid pulling or tearing the mousse. Using two metal spatulas crisscrossed, lift under the paper liner and transfer the cake to a serving plate.

Spoon the whipped cream into the pastry bag. Pipe a small amount of whipped cream into each empty circle. Pipe enough to make a rosette ¾ inch high in each hole.

Place a cake circle, caramel-glazed side up, directly on top of each whipped cream rosette. Repeat with remaining circles, remembering to remove the toothpicks.

Storing the cake: Refrigerate until serving time.

Recipes for Spongecakes

FOUNDATION CAKES

MORE CAKES

INDICATES ❁ EASY RECIPE

Spongecakes

Lᴵᴋᴇ ᴛʜᴇ génoise, the spongecake is made from many eggs and little or no fat. The major difference between the two is that for a spongecake, the eggs are always separated to develop two foams, one from the yolks; the other from the whites, whereas for a génoise, the foam is made by whippping whole eggs. The spongecake's final grain and texture are influenced by how much air is whipped into both the yolks and the whites.

These cakes are called cold-method sponges because you don't warm the eggs in a warm-water bath before you whip them, as you do to make a génoise. Spongecakes are leavened exclusively by the two natural leavenings. One form of leavening comes from whipping air into the yolks and whites to form millions of air bubbles; the other leavening agent is the steam, which evaporates from the liquid of the eggs and passes through air bubbles, expanding them and developing volume in the cake.

There are two types of spongecake. One is high in eggs and sugar and low in flour—a moist, rich, tender, spongy, open-grained cake. I classify this kind of cake as American. Like a butter cake, it is delicious on its own, eaten without any embellishment. You wouldn't think of soaking it with a dessert syrup, and if you didn't want to frost it with whipped cream or whatever is suggested, it would still make luscious eating.

The other type of sponge is high in eggs and flour, but lower in sugar—a lighter, springier, drier, finer-pored, denser texture. This group I classify as European. They are really at their best when enriched with a dessert syrup or other fillings creating a complexity of textures and flavors. The American and European spongecakes require different methods. Modifications of these two methods are used for my other sponge recipes.

Eᴳᴳꜱ ᴀɴᴅ Tʜᴇɪʀ Rᴏʟᴇ

The only set rule for making these cakes is that the eggs must be separated. After that, the ratio of yolks to whites, the proper stage for whipping each and the amount of sugar vary from recipe to recipe.

Eɢɢ-ʏᴏʟᴋ ꜰᴏᴀᴍꜱ

Tʜᴏᴜɢʜ almost half water, the yolk contains more protein than the white does, as well as all the egg's fat. It is therefore apparent that a yolk has less ability to foam to any great volume than the white since it contains so much fat. As you whip egg yolks, it is easy to guess the amount of air you incorporate because the color lightens. The addition of sugar, depending on the amount, can affect the whipped yolks' color and thickness, but you still cannot overwhip egg yolks as easily as you can egg whites. Though the fat decreases the chances for an enormous increase in volume, it stabilizes the foam so that when you make a cake, you can whip the yolks before the whites and let them stand without fear of losing too many air bubbles.

EGG-WHITE FOAMS

THE PROPER consistency to which you must whip the whites depends upon the texture and volume you need for a specific filling or cake. Whipping egg-white foams to their proper consistency as each recipe instructs will be neither guesswork nor a puzzle when you understand what happens as you whip.

An egg white is composed of protein (albumen) and water. The protein coagulates (goes from a liquid to a solid state) under two conditions: heat and whipping.

When you fry an egg, you see the heat transform the liquid of the white to solid. Heat's effect on an egg-white foam in the oven is similar, though it is not visible to you.

When you whip air into egg whites, the protein forms a film around the air bubbles, encapsulating them and expanding with them. As the bubbles increase in number, they become smaller, and the mass becomes thicker. These air bubbles along with the egg whites' liquid are suspended in this protein web. The key to whipping an egg-white foam successfully is to keep it elastic enough to be easily folded and incorporated into a batter or filling. Soft, shiny, smooth peaks with rounded tops form when you lift the whisk. These peaks can range from very soft to soft depending on their purpose in your recipe. Another way I judge the degree of softness is whether the egg-white foam sticks or slides in the mixing bowl. The thicker, soft foam sticks to the mixing bowl.

If the foam is whipped too long, the egg whites' liquid can no longer be held. It leaks out, so the elastic quality is gone, leaving the egg-white foam granular, dry and dull. What happens is that the whipping breaks up the liquid white, but as it incorporates air and thickens, the protein structure becomes firmer. The granular, inelastic characteristics are evidence that the egg-white foam is coagulating from being overwhipped.

Have you ever whipped an egg-white foam just until soft peaks form and then let it sit a few seconds before using it? Its surface becomes dry and dull. In this situation, surface coagulation occurs without your overwhipping the foam.

Both these egg-white foams are unstable mixtures; therefore, lightening a filling or batter with them is difficult because they will not blend smoothly and evenly. As a result, a filling's texture will be poor and the cake's volume will decrease in the oven because the overextended air bubbles break and the egg-white foam collapses.

If the egg-white foam is stable (soft, shiny, smooth peaks) when folded into a batter, the foam will retain its liquid, convert to steam, swell to leaven the mixture and coagulate (turn solid) after reaching a certain temperature.

Tips for Whipping Egg-White Foams Successfully

EQUIPMENT

SUCCESSFULLY whipping egg whites by hand or machine is possible, especially now that you know what is happening as you whip and what to look for. Throughout the book, I give directions for using either a heavy-duty mixer with the whisk attachment or an electric hand mixer with beaters. But egg whites can be whipped quite well by hand with a balloon whisk. Even large amounts can be whipped more quickly and with greater overall consistency by hand because the whisk reaches all parts of the mixing bowl. In addition, whipping by hand gives you more control over the final state of your egg-white foam because you develop a "feel" for when it is finished. If you are using a machine, I recommend you leave the finishing touches for hand whisking. I use the machine's whisk attachment to combine the entire mass. In this way, I can also judge if I have whipped the foam to the proper consistency.

For best results, when you whip egg-white foams for Classic Meringue (page 214), Classic Italian Meringue (page 265), Classic Royal Icing (page 269) and Classic Dacquoise (page 225), I recommend using an electric mixer. When you whip egg-white foams to be used for lightening fillings and batters, it is fine to do it by either machine or hand.

UTENSILS

THE BEST bowl for whipping egg whites is one that is made of stainless steel or copper. Its shape should be deep, and it should have sloping sides and a round bottom. The whisk you use should be in proportion to your bowl.

Plastic bowls are difficult to keep grease-free, glass bowls are slippery, and aluminum bowls may release small particles of metal when you whisk, graying the foam.

The only difference I can see between stainless steel and copper bowls is that the egg whites cling to the copper more. Some pastry chefs feel the copper reacts with the whites, lowering their pH (increasing their acidity), thereby strengthening their air-trapping ability and making it easier for the whites to stretch and expand. After lots of experimenting with both, my results were the same: I got close to 1 cup of foam per egg white. It was slightly faster and easier to whip in the copper bowl, but both foams looked the same after they had been whipped.

FRESHNESS OF EGGS

FRESH egg whites provide optimum flavor, aeration and structure for fillings and cakes. (A fresh egg white has body and is not runny when poured.) Some pastry chefs believe older egg whites foam better, but I am more concerned with the protein in the white, which is what traps the air. If the protein has deteriorated, the foam will not function as needed.

FAT

ANY TRACE of oil or yolk retards egg whites from reaching their optimum volume because the fat emulsifies into the whites' water, weighing them down and inhibiting volume. It is best to crack an egg when it is cold because the yolk is firmer and less likely to break. To make sure that your utensils are grease-free, moisten a paper towel with vinegar and wipe them before whipping.

CREAM OF TARTAR

MANY BAKERS believe that adding cream of tartar to egg whites lowers their pH and increases their acidity. The result is a physical reaction that makes it easier for the protein to stretch and extend yet maintain its stability. When I add cream of tartar to egg whites, it takes longer to whip the whites to the consistency I want, but the consistency of the foam is softer, making folding easier and smoother. The same is true when I add a small amount of sugar.

Cream of tartar's real value, though, is evidenced in the oven, where the whipped egg-white foam is a main contributor to a batter's volume and structure. The cream of tartar stabilizes the air bubbles in the heat, preventing them from collapsing before they set. When I tested these types of cake with and without cream of tartar, the results were dramatic. Using cream of tartar ensured greater volume.

SUGAR

WHEN YOU whip sugar into the foam, the whipping time increases before you attain the proper stiffness. This foam is smoother as well as more stable than a foam without sugar and doesn't break down and become liquid if you delay a bit before using it.

The sugar unites with the egg whites, giving it binding power so the foam will not separate quickly. At the same time it slows coagulation so you whip longer to get to the same consistency. Adding some sugar when whipping an egg-white foam reduces the risk of over-whipping.

TEMPERATURE

THE EGG WHITES' temperature affects the foam's stability. The best temperature is between 60 and 70 degrees. A cooler white is thicker and more viscous, trapping air more effectively; it may take longer to attain optimum volume but is less likely to be overwhipped.

The temperature at which the egg-white foam coagulates varies. It depends on how quickly it is heated, at what temperature and how much sugar is in the mixture. Yolks set at higher temperatures than whole eggs, and whites set at lower temperatures than yolks.

Classic American Spongecake

This moist, tender spongecake combines perfectly with an assortment of creams, such as the rich custard filling in **Boston Trifle** (page 171) and the strawberry mousse in **Strawberry Window Cake** (page 175).

For a simple dessert, split the cake into two or three equal layers; fill with fresh sliced strawberries, raspberries and/or blueberries and frost the top and sides with sweetened whipped cream.

MAKES ONE 9-x-2 ½-INCH ROUND CAKE

Baking Equipment: 9-inch springform pan

1	cup (100 grams) sifted cake flour
7	tablespoons (85 grams) *plus* 7 tablespoons (85 grams) *plus* 1 tablespoon granulated sugar
7	large eggs, room temperature
1	teaspoon vanilla
1	teaspoon cream of tartar

Baking preparations: Position rack in lower third of oven; preheat oven to 300 degrees.

This sponge bakes in an ungreased pan, enabling the batter to stick to the metal as it rises, allowing it to climb and expand.

Like most other foamy cakes and most chiffon cakes, this cake must cool upside down, elevated above the counter to preserve its structure. Since you're baking in a springform pan, which has no tube to fit into the neck of a bottle, you must make your own cooling area before the cake emerges from the oven.

The simplest way is to balance the pan on top of four sturdy glasses turned upside down on the counter. The pan's edges rest on the edges of the glasses' bases.

Ingredient preparations: Pour the flour and 7 tablespoons sugar in that order into a triple sifter. Sift onto a sheet of waxed paper and set aside.

Measure out the 7 more tablespoons of granulated sugar and place it in a small bowl; put the 1 tablespoon of granulated sugar in another small bowl; set aside.

Separate the eggs, placing the whites in the bowl of a heavy-duty mixer and the yolks in a 1½-quart bowl. (A deep bowl makes it more efficient for whipping the yolks thoroughly since it minimizes the surface area.)

Making the cake: With an electric hand mixer, whip the yolks on high speed (#10) for 3 to 5 minutes. Add the vanilla and continue whipping for 15 seconds to incorporate; the mixture should appear thicker, pale yellow and increased in volume. Test the consistency by lifting some of the mixture with the beaters. If it flows back into the bowl in ribbons that slowly dissolve on the surface, proceed to whipping the whites. But if the ribbons sink into the surface immediately, continue whipping until the yolks have the desired consistency.

(recipe continued on page 161)

Strawberry Window Cake
SEE PAGE 175 FOR RECIPE

Boston Trifle
SEE PAGE 171 FOR RECIPE

Jubilee Petal Cake
SEE PAGE 141 FOR RECIPE

Raspberry Cream Torte
SEE PAGE 190 FOR RECIPE

Chocolate Éclairs
SEE PAGE 382 FOR RECIPE

157

Chocolate Gemini
SEE PAGE 94 FOR RECIPE

Free-Form Puff Pastry Strip With Fruit
SEE PAGE 368 FOR RECIPE

159

Country Pear Galette
SEE PAGE 334 FOR RECIPE

Attach the bowl of whites to the mixer, and with the whisk attachment, whip on medium-low speed (#3) for 30 to 45 seconds to break them up. When small bubbles appear and the surface is frothy, stop the machine, and sprinkle the cream of tartar and the 1 tablespoon granulated sugar in the center. Resume whipping, increasing speed to medium (#5), for 4 to 5 minutes, or until the whites appear glossy and stiff but not dry or granular.

Detach the whisk and bowl, tapping the whisk against the side of the bowl with enough force to free the excess. Pour the yolks onto the whites (notice they float on the surface). Using just a few strokes, fold the two together with a rubber spatula. Don't be concerned if some of the yolks remain visible.

Sprinkle half of the 7 tablespoons sugar over the surface and fold it in to incorporate. Sprinkle with the remaining sugar, folding again to incorporate.

With the aid of a metal spatula, scoop a third of the flour and sprinkle it over the egg mixture; with a rubber spatula, fold to incorporate. Repeat two more times, folding just until incorporated after each addition.

Baking the cake: Gently pour the batter with the aid of a rubber spatula into the ungreased pan and smooth the surface level.

Bake for 55 to 60 minutes, or until the top is golden. (The batter hardly rises during the first 20 to 30 minutes of baking. The low oven temperature allows the batter to absorb heat slowly, so the rising is gradual. Toward the end of baking, the cake may mound high above the pan's rim. That's fine. As it cools, this dome will contract a bit.)

When done, the cake should feel spongy, springing back slightly upon being lightly touched. A toothpick inserted in the center comes out free of cake. If in doubt, baking 5 to 7 more minutes will not harm the cake.

Cooling the cake: Remove the spongecake from the oven, and immediately turn it upside down, positioning the edges of the pan on the inverted glasses.

Cool the cake for 2 hours; then turn the pan right side up, and place it on the counter. Though the cake is cool to the touch, let it sit for at least 1 more hour to cool the inside completely. (The cake's structure is less fragile when cool, making removal easier.)

To release the spongecake and maintain its shape perfectly, remove it from the pan as follows: Carefully loosen the cake crust that is stuck to the top rim of the pan; insert a thin metal spatula down 1/8 inch and free the crust all around the cake. Then tilt and rotate the pan, tapping it gently on the counter to free the sponge from the metal sides. Tap more if it is not completely released. Finally, release the spring mechanism and slowly remove the rim. (A thin, crusty layer of cake remains on the rim; it's delicious, too.)

Now tilt the cake on its side and gently tap the metal bottom on the counter. Rotate the cake as you tap until the removable bottom appears free. Additional tapping may be necessary before it comes off completely. Patience will ensure a perfectly shaped cake.

Storing the cake: If you plan to use the cake within a day, wrap it in plastic and store at room temperature.

To freeze, cover the plastic-wrapped package with foil and label it, indicating the contents and date. To protect the cake's delicate structure, place the foil-wrapped package in a sturdy container, such as a metal tin, before freezing it. Freeze for no longer than 10 days.

Baker's Notes

☞ Be organized. This batter goes together quickly.

☞ This cake can also be baked in a tube pan, but for decorating, it is more practical if there is no hole in the center.

☞ Large eggs, each weighing 2 ounces in the shell, are important for the cake's volume.

☞ The amount of sugar and a low oven temperature slow the baking process, but they contribute to a wonderful, moist cake. Do not remove the cake from the oven until a toothpick comes out clean.

☞ An experience years ago proved that this batter is nearly indestructible. After pouring it into its baking pan, I realized I had forgotten to fold in the sugar. Rather than begin again, I removed the batter to its original bowl, folded in the sugar, returned it to its baking pan and baked it. The cake baked perfectly!

Classic European Spongecake

THIS SPONGECAKE is less sweet and drier than the more delicate Classic American type. It has a smaller grain, with a stronger structure. These characteristics make it perfect for soaking with a dessert syrup. You may use this cake in place of Classic Génoise.

It is the foundation for Orange Mimosa (page 178).

MAKES ONE 8-X-2 ¼-INCH ROUND CAKE

Baking Equipment: 8-inch springform pan

1	cup (120 grams) unsifted cake flour
½	cup (100 grams) *plus* 2 tablespoons (25 grams) granulated sugar
6	egg whites, room temperature
5	egg yolks, room temperature
1	teaspoon vanilla

Baking preparations: Position rack in lower third of oven; preheat oven to 375 degrees.

This spongecake bakes in an ungreased pan, enabling the batter to stick to it as it rises so that it climbs and expands.

Ingredient preparations: Pour the flour into a triple sifter; sift onto a sheet of waxed paper to eliminate any lumps.

Measure the ½ cup sugar for the yolks and the 2 tablespoons sugar for the whites; set aside.

Place the whites in the bowl of a heavy-duty mixer and the yolks in a 2½- to 3-quart deep bowl.

Making the cake: With an electric hand mixer, whip the yolks on high speed (#10) for 30 seconds to combine. Add the ½ cup sugar in a steady stream and continue whipping until the mixture appears very thick, increased in volume and pale yellow (about 2 to 3 minutes). Add the vanilla toward the end of whipping. Test the consistency by lifting some of the whipped mixture with the beaters. If it falls back into the bowl in ribbons that slowly dissolve on the surface, proceed to whipping the whites. But if the ribbons sink into the surface immediately, continue whipping until the mixture has the desired consistency.

Attach the bowl of whites to the heavy-duty mixer with the whisk attachment, and whip on low speed (#2) until small bubbles appear and the surface is frothy, for 30 to 45 seconds. Increasing the speed to medium (#5), add 1 teaspoon of the 2 tablespoons sugar and whip until soft white peaks form (about 1 minute). Then, maintaining the same speed, add the remainder of the 2 tablespoons in a steady stream until the whites appear glossy and stiff but not dry or granular (about 2 minutes).

Fold a third of the meringue into the yolks to lighten them. Then add another third of the whites on top of the yolk mixture, sprinkle half the flour over this and fold to combine, scraping the sides of the bowl when necessary.

Baker's Notes

☞ This is a drier spongecake than Classic American Spongecake, with a more stable structure, so there is no need to turn it upside down to prevent its collapse while cooling.

☞ This batter may also be piped to form ladyfingers or other shapes.

☞ The additional egg white makes the cake springier.

Add the final third of whites on top of the yolk mixture, sprinkle with the remaining flour and fold, scraping the sides of the bowl when necessary. (Yolks are very thick, and folding seems tricky, but do not stop.) Fold just until smooth and incorporated.

Baking the cake: With the rubber spatula, gently scrape the batter into the prepared pan and spread it evenly. Bake for 40 to 45 minutes, or until the top is golden brown, springs back slightly when lightly touched and a toothpick inserted in the center comes out free of cake.

Cooling the cake: Remove the cake from the oven and place it on a rack to cool completely (about 1 to 2 hours). Then tilt and rotate the pan, tapping it gently on the counter to free the cake from the sides. Gently release the spring mechanism and carefully remove the rim. Now tilt the cake on its side and gently tap the metal bottom on the counter. Rotate the cake as you tap until the removable bottom appears free to be removed.

Storing the cake: If you plan to use the cake within a day, wrap it in plastic and store at room temperature.

To freeze, cover the plastic-wrapped package with foil and label it, indicating the contents and date. Freeze for no longer than 10 days.

Classic Spongecake Sheet

THE SIZE of this cake as well as its thickness and texture make it a baker's delight. You can cut it into a variety of shapes, and since it is thin, spongy and pliable, you can line a pan with it to form elegant desserts, such as **Pecan Chantilly** (page 192) and **Raspberry Cream Torte** (page 190).

MAKES ONE 12-X-15-INCH SPONGE SHEET

Baking Equipment: One 12-x-15½-x-½-inch baking sheet

½	cup (50 grams) sifted cake flour
4	large eggs, room temperature
2	tablespoons (25 grams) *plus* ½ cup (100 grams) granulated sugar
1	teaspoon vanilla

Baking preparations: Position rack in lower third of oven; preheat oven to 425 degrees.

Using a paper towel, lightly grease a small area in the center of the baking sheet with solid shortening. Then line the sheet with foil, leaving a 2-inch overhang at each short end. (The shortening holds the sheet of foil in place while it is being greased.) Sprinkle with all-purpose flour, shake to distribute and tap out the excess.

Ingredient preparations: Pour the flour into a triple sifter and sift onto a sheet of waxed paper to eliminate any lumps; set aside.

Baker's Notes

☞ The oven temperature is high so the cake bakes quickly without being overdried and inflexible.

☞ In order not to overbake, check it after baking 5 minutes.

Crack 2 of the eggs into the bowl of a heavy-duty mixer. Separate the remaining 2 eggs, placing the whites in a deep 1½-quart stainless steel bowl and adding the yolks to the 2 whole eggs. Set aside the 2 tablespoons sugar to use with the egg whites.

Making the cake: Attach the bowl to the heavy-duty mixer, and with the whisk attachment, mix the eggs for a few seconds on medium-low speed (#3), just to combine them. Increase the speed to medium (#5), and pour in the ½ cup sugar in a steady stream, whipping the ingredients for 3 to 3½ minutes. The mixture will appear lighter in color and thicker but still liquid enough to flow easily from the whisk when you raise it. Add the vanilla near the end of the whipping time. Detach the whisk and bowl and tap the whisk against the side of bowl to free any excess.

With an electric hand mixer, whip the whites on medium-low speed (#5) until small bubbles appear and the surface is frothy. Increase the speed to high (#10), pour in 1 teaspoon of the 2 tablespoons sugar, and whip until soft, white peaks form (about 1 minute). Maintaining same speed, add the remainder of the 2 tablespoons sugar in a steady stream, and continue whipping until thicker, glossy white (not dry or granular) peaks form (about 30 to 45 seconds).

With a rubber spatula, fold half the whites into the yolks until incorporated. (This lightens the mixture, making it easier to fold in the flour.) Scoop half the flour onto a metal spatula, and sprinkle it over the egg mixture, folding to incorporate with a rubber spatula. Repeat the procedure. (This entire sequence takes 1 to 1½ minutes.) Proceed from one addition to the next without stopping.

Baking the cake: With a rubber spatula, pour the batter from the bowl down the center of the baking sheet in a strip 5 to 6 inches wide. Spread the batter as evenly as possible with an 8-inch flexible metal icing spatula. Spread from the center to the sides and corners (the batter moves easily; don't rush). Use the sides of the pan as a guide; the batter should be level with them.

A spongecake sheet is thin and bakes quickly. To prevent the edges from burning or drying from uneven spreading of the batter, use this simple but effective test. Check the batter's uniformity by inserting a toothpick at various points. Begin at the corners and work toward the center (it's natural for the center to have more batter). The depth indicated on the toothpick should be the same at each point; adjust the batter if necessary.

Bake for 5 minutes; then check to see if baking is finished. The surface should be light golden. Press down lightly near the center with your fingertips; if it springs back, it's done. The short sides of the cake will begin to pull away from the foil, too. If the cake is not finished, return it to the oven for 1 to 3 more minutes, monitoring it carefully.

Cooling the cake: Remove the baking sheet from the oven and place it on a large rack. Using a thin-bladed knife, gently release any portion of the cake sticking to the long sides of the pan. Pull up on the foil overhangs, one at a time, to release the foil from the pan's edges. Finally, loosen the foil from the bottom of the pan by gently lifting the foil flaps.

Cover the baked spongecake sheet with another 12-x-15½-inch pan and invert. Remove original baking pan and peel off the foil carefully to avoid tearing the cake. Turn the foil over so that the sticky side faces up and reposition it on the cake. Cover it with the large cooling rack and invert right side up. Allow the sponge sheet to cool on the rack for at least 30 minutes to 1 hour.

Storing the cake: If you plan to use the cake later in the day, leave it, uncovered, on the rack.

To use within 2 days, slip a baking sheet under the foil and cake. Cover with foil and freeze.

Chocolate Spongecake Sheet

THIS THIN, pliable, bittersweet-chocolate-flavored sponge is a variation of Classic Spongecake Sheet. You'll thoroughly enjoy it in **Sacher Roulade** (page 187).

MAKES ONE 12-X-15-INCH SPONGECAKE SHEET

Baking Equipment: One 12-x-15½-x-½-inch baking sheet

½   cup (50 grams) unsifted cocoa powder
2   tablespoons (25 grams) unsifted cake flour
4   large eggs, room temperature
2   tablespoons (25 grams) *plus* ½ cup (100 grams) granulated sugar
1   teaspoon vanilla

Prepare Classic Spongecake Sheet as directed on page 163 with the following differences:

Ingredient preparations: Pour the cocoa and cake flour in that order into a triple sifter. Sift onto a sheet of waxed paper; set aside.

Making the cake: Combining the egg mixture and the cocoa-flour mixture takes about 1 to 1½ minutes. It's important to proceed from one addition to another so that the fat in the cocoa powder doesn't deflate the foamy structure.

Baking the cake: Bake for 7 to 8 minutes. It is better to underbake slightly (still 7 to 8 minutes) rather than to overbake if you are using it to roll. Then rolling will be easier.

Storing the cake: If you are rolling the sheet, do so right after cooling. (Don't wait more than 1 hour or too much moisture evaporates and the cake cracks during the rolling process.)

If you plan to cut circles or strips for other desserts, the cake may cool longer with no problem.

Nut Spongecake Sheet

Tᴴɪꜱ ᴛʜɪɴ, tender spongecake layer perfumed with fine-ground nuts is so delicious you'll be tempted to eat it before using it to make a dessert. If you make **Caramel Carousel** (page 180) with it, there will be some cake left over after you have assembled the dessert.

Mᴀᴋᴇꜱ ᴏɴᴇ 12-x-15-ɪɴᴄʜ ꜱᴘᴏɴɢᴇ ꜱʜᴇᴇᴛ

Baking Equipment: Two 12-x-15½-x-½-inch baking sheets

¼	cup (25 grams) sifted cake flour
3	ounces (½ cup plus) hazelnuts
½	cup (100 grams) *plus* ¼ cup (50 grams) granulated sugar
¼	cup (2 ounces) unsalted butter
4	large eggs, room temperature

Baking preparations: Position rack in lower third of oven; preheat oven to 400 degrees.

Using a paper towel, lightly grease a small area in the center of one of the baking sheets with solid shortening. Line the sheet with foil, leaving a 2-inch overhang at each short end. Grease the foil with shortening, using the paper towel. Then sprinkle with all-purpose flour, shake to distribute the flour and tap out the excess.

Ingredient preparations: Pour the flour into a triple sifter; sift onto waxed paper to remove any lumps and set aside. Grind the hazelnuts until they have the consistency of cornmeal. You need 1 cup minus 2 tablespoons ground (⅞ cup). Set aside.

Measure ½ cup sugar for the egg yolks and ¼ cup sugar for the egg whites; set aside.

Melt the butter in a small saucepan; pour into a 1-quart bowl; set aside.

Separate 3 of the eggs, placing the whites in a deep 1½-quart mixing bowl and the yolks in the bowl of a heavy-duty mixer. Add the remaining whole egg to the yolks.

Making the cake: Attach the bowl of yolks to the heavy-duty mixer. Add the ½ cup sugar and the ground hazelnuts. With the whisk attachment, whip on medium speed (#5) or until lighter in color, thicker and mousselike in texture (1 to 1½ minutes).

Using an electric hand mixer, whip the egg whites on medium speed (#5) for 30 seconds, or until small bubbles appear and the surface is frothy. Increase to high speed (#10), and add 1 teaspoon of the ¼ cup sugar, whipping until soft, white peaks form (about 1 minute). Then, maintaining the same speed, add the remaining sugar in a steady stream. Whip until thicker, stiffer but glossy, shiny peaks form (about 1 to 1½ minutes).

Scoop half the flour on a metal spatula and sprinkle it over the whipped yolk mixture. Using a rubber spatula, fold just to incorporate. Now fold in the last portion of flour.

Fold a third of the meringue at a time into the yolk mixture until incorporated.

Gently pour about 1 cup of the batter into the melted butter, and with the rubber spatula, fold until combined. Return butter mixture to reserved batter and again fold to combine.

Baking the cake: With a rubber spatula, scoop the batter onto the baking sheet. Pour

☞ I like to use a combination of nuts, such as 1 ounce Brazil nuts, 1 ounce hazelnuts and 1 ounce almonds.

☞ It's important to grind the nuts finely.

☞ This thin, moist spongecake sheet blends perfectly with other cakes, meringue or dacquoise disks and fillings.

☞ You can whip yolks and sugar with the ground nuts until they are thick and fluffy. That way you don't need to fold in the nuts later and you avoid reducing the cake's volume.

it down the center, forming a 4- to 5-inch-long strip. Using a flexible metal icing spatula, carefully spread the batter evenly over the pan, taking care not to deflate too much of the foamy structure.

Check to see if the batter is evenly distributed by inserting a toothpick at various points. Begin at the corners and work toward the center. It may look level but actually have more batter in the center. The depth on the toothpick should be the same at each point. Adjust the batter if necessary.

Bake for 5 to 6 minutes; then check to see if the baking is finished. The sponge should be golden. With your fingertips, test the center by pressing lightly. If the cake springs back without leaving an impression, it's done. The sides will also begin to contract from the foil portion of the pan.

Cooling the cake: Place the baking sheet on a large rack. Immediately pull up on the foil overhang to release it from the edges. Using a thin table knife, gently score all around the edges of the cake to loosen it from the pan.

Cover the cake with the other baking sheet and invert. Remove the top sheet and carefully peel off the foil. Turn the foil over so that the sticky side faces up and reposition it on the cake. Cover with the original baking sheet and invert right side up. Allow the cake to cool on the rack for at least 1 hour.

Storing the cake: If you plan to use the cake later in the day, leave it uncovered on the rack.

To use within 1 week, cover with foil, label with contents and date, then freeze.

Picq Sponge

THIS REMINDS me of a sponge ladyfinger recipe with ground nuts. Its light nutty texture combines marvelously with other ingredients and flavors for memorable desserts. It is adapted from a recipe I learned from a pastry chef, Philippe Picq.

This is the foundation for Dutch Soufflé Torte (page 184).

MAKES TWO 9-INCH OVAL SPONGE DISKS (9 x 6 ½ INCHES)

Baking Equipment: 17-x-14-x-½-inch baking sheet, 16-inch pastry bag, ½-inch (#6) round decorating tip

2	ounces (⅓ cup) hazelnuts
2	ounces (⅓ cup) blanched almonds
½	cup (50 grams) unsifted powdered sugar
¾	cup (75 grams) sifted cake flour
¼	cup (50 grams) granulated sugar
3	large eggs, room temperature

Baking preparations: Position rack in lower third of oven; preheat oven to 350 degrees.

Fit the pastry bag with the decorating tip.

Piping batter into ovals.

☞ The batter is versatile; you can pipe smaller shapes to make individual desserts.

☞ You can pipe two 9-inch circles instead of ovals.

☞ The yolks make the sponge moist; the whites make it light.

☞ If you pipe the batter through too small a decorating tip, it deflates because of the pressure you must use to press it through the tip.

☞ Scoop the batter into the pastry bag carefully; rough handling can deflate it, too. Using a bowl scraper is very efficient (see the equipment section, page 20).

Line the baking sheet with parchment paper to fit. Make a pattern by drawing and cutting a 9-x-6½-inch oval from stiff cardboard. Then trace two ovals on the parchment. These ovals are your guide for piping the batter on the parchment paper.

Ingredient preparations: Grind the nuts separately until they have the consistency of cornmeal, producing ½ cup ground hazelnuts (packed) and ½ cup ground almonds (packed). Combine the nuts. Sift the powdered sugar into a small mixing bowl to remove lumps and combine it with the ground nuts. Stir to blend and remove 3 tablespoons of this mixture to another small bowl. Then add the flour to the larger amount of ground nuts and stir to blend.

Measure the ¼ cup granulated sugar and set aside for the egg whites.

Crack and separate the eggs, placing the whites in the bowl of a heavy-duty mixer and the yolks in a 1½-quart mixing bowl.

Making the sponge disks: Add the reserved 3 tablespoons of the sugar-nut mixture to the yolks, and with an electric hand mixer, whip on high speed (#10), until pale yellow and thick in texture (2 to 3 minutes).

Attach the bowl of whites to the mixer, and with the whisk attachment, whip them on medium-low speed (#2) for 30 seconds, or until small bubbles appear and the surface becomes frothy. Increase to medium speed (#5), add 1 teaspoon of the ¼ cup granulated sugar and whip until soft, white peaks form (about 1 minute). Maintaining the same speed, add the remainder of the sugar in a steady stream, and continue whipping until glossy white, thicker peaks form (about 1½ to 2 minutes).

Pour the yolk mixture over the whites; fold the two together with a rubber spatula. Sprinkle with half of the flour-nut mixture and fold. Repeat the procedure; fold just until combined.

Forming the sponge disks: Scoop the batter into the pastry bag fitted with the ½-inch round decorating tip. Pipe a 4-inch line lengthwise, beginning in the center of the oval. Use this line as a guide, spiraling the batter around it. Continue until you reach the pencil mark. Apply just enough pressure to the pastry bag so the amount forced from it is no larger than the ½-inch diameter of the pastry tip.

Baking the sponge disks: Bake for 15 to 18 minutes, or until light brown and springy but firm to the touch. (You do not want them crisp inside and out like a meringue.)

Cooling the sponge disks: Remove the pan from the oven; lift the parchment onto a large cooling rack. When it is cool, peel the paper from each oval.

Storing the sponge disks: If you plan to use the sponge disks within 24 hours, wrap in foil and store at room temperature.

To freeze, cover the foil-wrapped package with another sheet of foil; label the package, indicating the contents and date. Freeze for no longer than 1 week.

Sponge Ladyfingers

THESE sponge ladyfingers are ideal for lining a container decoratively before filling it, as in the classic dessert **Charlotte Malakoff** (page 182).

MAKES TWENTY-EIGHT 5 ½-INCH-LONG LADYFINGERS

Baking Equipment: Two 12-x-15½-x-½-inch baking sheets, 16-inch pastry bag, ½-inch (#6) round decorating tip

1 ¼	cups (125 grams) sifted cake flour
¼	cup (50 grams) *plus* ¼ cup (50 grams) granulated sugar
4	large egg whites, room temperature
6	large egg yolks, room temperature
1	teaspoon vanilla
1	cup (100 grams) unsifted powdered sugar

Baking preparations: Position rack in lower third of oven; preheat to 350 degrees.

Line each baking sheet with baking parchment to fit. Using a pencil and ruler, draw parallel lines on the paper 5½ inches apart across the 12-inch (short) side of each pan in rows ½ to 1 inch apart. These lines are guides for piping the desired length of the ladyfingers.

Fit the pastry bag with the ½-inch round decorating tip; set it near the prepared baking sheets.

Ingredient preparations: Pour the flour and ¼ cup granulated sugar in that order into a triple sifter. Sift onto a sheet of waxed paper; set aside.

Measure the additional ¼ cup sugar; set aside until whipping egg whites.

Place the whites in the bowl of a heavy-duty mixer and the yolks in a deep 1½-quart mixing bowl.

Making the ladyfingers: With an electric hand mixer, whip the yolks on high speed (#10) for 3 to 5 minutes, or until the mixture thickens, increases in volume and appears pale yellow. Add the vanilla near the end of the whipping time. Test the yolks' thickness by lifting the beaters. If the mixture falls back into the bowl in ribbons, remaining

Baker's Notes

☛ This sponge recipe has more yolks than whites and more flour than other sponge recipes, so the ladyfingers bake more perfectly with less cracking on the surface.

☛ These ladyfingers are spongier and drier than Génoise Ladyfingers (page 118) because this recipe combines two foamy mixtures and contains no butter. However, these ladyfingers are tender because of the fat from the additional yolks.

Piping ladyfinger batter between the marked lines.

awhile on the surface, proceed to whipping the whites. But if the ribbon dissolves into the surface immediately, continue whipping until the yolks have the desired consistency. Detach the whisk and bowl, and tap the whisk against the side of the bowl with enough force to free the excess.

Attach the bowl of whites to the heavy-duty mixer, and with the whisk attachment, whip them on medium-low speed (#3) for 30 seconds, or until small bubbles appear and the surface is frothy. Increase the speed to medium (#5), adding 1 teaspoon from the other ¼ cup granulated sugar, and continue whipping until soft, white peaks form (about 1 minute). Then, maintaining the same speed, add the remaining granulated sugar in a steady stream. Continue whipping until thicker, stiffer, glossy peaks form (about 2 minutes).

Immediately pour the yolks over the meringue. Using just a few strokes, fold the two mixtures together with a rubber spatula. Don't be too concerned if some of the yolks are still visible.

With the aid of a metal spatula, scoop a third of the flour mixture and sprinkle it over the surface, folding with the rubber spatula. Repeat two more times, just until the ingredients are incorporated.

Forming the ladyfingers: Immediately scoop all the batter into the pastry bag. (The foam structure is fragile and unstable, so if part of the batter remains in the bowl and is scooped into the bag later, it will decrease the batter's volume too much.)

Holding the bag at a 45-degree angle to the baking sheet and about ½ inch above it, pipe the batter into 5½-inch-long ladyfingers, using the lines drawn on the parchment paper as guides (see illustration). Pipe the batter leaving ½- to ¾-inch space between. Remember, pressure is applied on the batter-filled bag with one hand while the other hand guides the direction of the flow. Each time a ladyfinger is completed, stop applying pressure on the bag and lift up the tip, moving it away from you and over the piped ladyfinger to cut off the flow of batter.

Pipe rows of ladyfingers until both baking sheets are full. You will have 14 to 15 ladyfingers on each sheet.

Baking the ladyfingers: Pour the powdered sugar into a sieve. Using the palm of your hand, gently tap the sieve to sprinkle the sugar over the ladyfingers. Bake for about

10 to 11 minutes, or until the ladyfingers are barely colored and firm but still spongy when pressed with a finger.

Cooling the ladyfingers: Remove the sheets from the oven and transfer the parchment paper with the ladyfingers on it to a cooling rack. Release the ladyfingers while they are warm. (Because of their length, it is easier at this time; when they are cool, they are less flexible and could crack and break.) Slide a pancake-type spatula carefully under the ladyfingers, approaching them from their sides rather than their tips (lifting from either end might break or crack them, too). Cool on racks.

Storing the ladyfingers: If using the ladyfingers the next day, freeze them when they are cool. (Ladyfingers stale quickly unless soaked with dessert syrup.) Place them in a plastic container with waxed paper between the layers. Freeze for no longer than 10 days.

Boston Trifle

ONE EXTRAORDINARILY hot Fourth of July, after we juggled a Boston Cream Pie with a rapidly melting chocolate glaze while traveling by car to a friend's party, this dessert was born. In order to save it, I had to put the dessert into a bowl.

Later this fluffy, rum-laced custard layered between a moist, light spongecake and topped with a thin chocolate coating became a best-seller in my baking business.

(See photograph, page 154.)

MAKES 8 SERVINGS

Special Equipment: 2½- to 3-quart glass bowl

One 9-inch Classic American Spongecake (page 152)
1   cup (4 ounces) Chocolate-Butter Glaze (page 289)
¼   cup Chocolate Flakes (page 282)

Custard Filling
1 ⅓   cups half-and-half
½   cup (100 grams) granulated sugar
4   egg yolks
½   cup (100 grams) granulated sugar
¼   cup (35 grams) unsifted all-purpose flour
1   teaspoon vanilla
1   teaspoon dark rum
1   cup (8 ounces) heavy cream

Advance preparations: Prepare Classic American Spongecake as directed on page 152.

Prepare Chocolate-Butter Glaze as directed on page 289, and store in a covered container in the refrigerator if not using right away.

Prepare Chocolate Flakes as directed on page 282. Store in a covered container in the freezer until ready to use.

Baker's Note

☞ This dessert may be prepared over a 2-day period.
First day: Bake Classic American Spongecake and Custard Filling.
Second day: Assemble dessert and make glaze.

Making the filling: Pour the half-and-half into a 1½-quart heavy-bottomed saucepan, add the ½ cup sugar and stir to combine. In a 1-quart bowl, whisk the egg yolks and the remaining ½ cup sugar to combine. Add the flour and whisk to combine. Bring the half-and-half mixture just to a boil over medium heat. Remove and pour half of the hot liquid over the yolk mixture, whisking to combine. Pour the yolk mixture into saucepan and over medium heat, bring it to a boil again, stirring constantly. When it is thick and smooth, remove it from the heat, pour it into a 3-quart mixing bowl to cool, and cover the surface with plastic wrap to prevent a crust from forming on the cream. (This bowl allows room for folding in the whipped cream later.) Pierce the plastic with the tip of a knife to let steam escape so the custard cools faster. Refrigerate.

Assembling the trifle: Split the cake evenly into three layers, each about ⅞ inch thick, using a 12-inch serrated knife in a sawing motion. (You may want to review the techniques for splitting a cake into layers on page 234.)

Lift the top two layers, one at a time, and set aside (this is easy because each layer is spongy and thick).

Stir the vanilla and rum into the cold custard. Whip the heavy cream in a 1½-quart mixing bowl to the Chantilly stage, or until it clings softly to the beaters. It should be thick enough to create swirls in the bowl but liquid enough to move if the bowl is tilted. Fold the cream into the custard mixture.

Place the bottom cake layer in the bowl and cover it with half the filling. Spread evenly with a rubber spatula. Center the middle layer on top, and cover it with the remaining filling. Center the last layer on top. Cover the dessert with plastic wrap and refrigerate.

Finishing the trifle: Spoon 1 cup of Chocolate-Butter Glaze into a 1-quart bowl over a bowl of hot tap water (120 to 130 degrees). Stir until liquid and smooth.

Spread the glaze over the top of the dessert evenly with a metal or rubber spatula. Sprinkle Chocolate Flakes around the rim of the dessert.

Storing the trifle: Refrigerate for up to 1 to 2 hours before serving.

Hazelnut Sponge With Raspberry Whipped Cream

FINE-GROUND hazelnuts and egg bread used in place of flour produce this fragrant torte. Its stunning decoration couldn't be simpler—a pale pink cream, tinted from raspberry jelly and topped with one of nature's most beautiful fruits, the raspberry.
MAKES ONE 10-X-2 ¾-INCH TUBE CAKE, 10 TO 12 SERVINGS

Baking and Decorating Equipment: 10-inch tube pan with removable bottom, long-necked bottle, 9-inch stiff cardboard round, cake decorating turntable

6	ounces (1 ⅓ cups) hazelnuts
2	ounces (about 1 slice) egg bread
½	cup (100 grams) *plus* ¼ cup (50 grams) granulated sugar
8	large eggs, room temperature
1	teaspoon cream of tartar

Raspberry Whipped Cream

1 ½	cups (12 ounces) heavy cream
½	cup raspberry jelly
1	cup fresh raspberries

Baking preparations: Position rack in lower third of oven; preheat oven to 350 degrees.

This batter is baked in an ungreased pan, enabling it to stick to the sides as it rises, setting the foamy structure.

Have a long-necked bottle nearby to rest the baked cake on after baking.

Ingredient preparations: Lightly toast the hazelnuts on a baking sheet in a preheated 350-degree oven for 10 to 12 minutes. Remove from oven and cover with a kitchen towel until cool. This will make removing the skins easier. Rub a handful at a time to remove the skins. Do not try to remove the stubborn ones. Then grind until the mixture has the consistency of cornmeal. You need 2 cups ground.

Place the bread in a food processor fitted with a metal blade and process until it is fine crumbs. You need 1 cup of crumbs.

Now combine the ground nuts, bread crumbs and ½ cup sugar in a 1½-quart bowl; set aside.

Measure the ¼ cup sugar for later; set aside.

Crack and separate the eggs, placing the whites in the bowl of a heavy-duty mixer and the yolks in a deep 1½-quart bowl.

Baker's Notes

☞ Another name for the hazelnut is filbert. Toasting brings out its flavor. Removing as much of the dark skin as possible is best; some pastry chefs feel the skins add bitterness.

☞ It's important to grind the nuts properly since they take the place of flour as well as provide flavor (see the section on nuts in the equipment section, page 23).

☞ The egg bread (also called challah) takes the place of flour, lending structure and flavor to the cake. It is available in supermarkets and bakeries.

☞ The 8 eggs in their shells should weigh a total of 1 pound.

☞ The oil in the nuts gives tenderness to the cake's texture.

Understanding Cakemaking

☞ This moist cake may remain in the tube pan a day before removal.

☞ For the jelly in Raspberry Whipped Cream, choose a brand that is soft and smooth, not one that is lumpy and filled with pectin.

Making the cake: Reduce oven temperature to 325 degrees. With an electric hand mixer, whip the yolks on high speed (#10) until the mixture thickens, increases in volume and appears pale yellow (3 to 5 minutes). Test the consistency by lifting some of the yolks with the beaters. If the mixture falls back into the bowl in ribbons, slowly dissolving on the surface, proceed to whipping the whites. If the yolks fall from the beaters in drops rather than in ribbons or sink into the surface, continue whipping until they have the desired consistency and color.

Attach the bowl to the heavy-duty mixer, and with the whisk attachment, whip the whites on medium-low speed (#3) for about 30 to 45 seconds, or until small bubbles appear and the surface becomes frothy. Stop the mixer and sprinkle the cream of tartar into the center. Resume whipping, increase the speed to medium (#5) and continue to whip until glossy white, stiff (not dry or granular) peaks form (4 to 5 minutes).

Detach the whisk and bowl and tap the whisk against the side of the bowl to free the excess. Pour the yolks over the whites. Fold the two mixtures together with a rubber spatula. Don't be concerned if some of the yolks are still visible.

With the aid of a metal icing spatula, scoop the ¼ cup of sugar and sprinkle it over the mixture, folding with the rubber spatula with a few strokes.

With the metal spatula, scoop up one-third of the ground nut mixture and sprinkle it over the surface, folding with the rubber spatula. Repeat two more times.

Baking the cake: With a rubber spatula, gently scrape the batter into the pan and smooth it until level.

Bake for 45 to 50 minutes, or until the cake feels spongy, springs back slightly when lightly touched in the middle and a toothpick inserted in the center comes out free of cake.

Cooling the cake: Remove from the oven; immediately invert the pan onto the neck of the bottle. Allow it to cool for at least 2 hours. To remove the cake, slip a flexible metal spatula carefully down its side, slowly tracing around the perimeter to release the cake sticking to the pan. Try to keep the spatula in contact with the pan to guarantee as smooth-sided a cake as possible.

When the sides are free, push under the removable bottom to release the cake from the outer portion. Tilt the cake with the removable bottom still attached on its side, tapping it on counter surface to loosen. Rotate and tap until the cake appears free. Then place a rack on top of the cake's top, invert onto rack and remove the metal bottom of the tube.

Storing the cake: If using the cake the following day, wrap it in plastic wrap and store at room temperature.

To freeze, wrap the plastic-covered cake in foil. To protect its delicate shape in the freezer, place it in a sturdy plastic container or a tight-fitting metal container. Label the container, indicating the contents and date. Freeze for no longer than 1 week.

Prepare Raspberry Whipped Cream: Pour the heavy cream into the bowl of a heavy-duty mixer. Add the jelly. Whisk by hand briefly to blend the ingredients. Then attach the mixer and whip until soft peaks form and the beaters make tracks in the cream that slowly close.

Decorating the cake: Place the sponge on the cardboard round, then on the turntable.

Apply a thin coating of the cream around the sides and on the top of the cake with a flexible metal icing spatula. You'll notice that manipulating the cream continues to thicken it. This is fine because it will patch the cake, filling in its imperfections. (The nuts make the surface rather coarse.) Now apply another coating of the cream over this thin layer. Fill the hole left from the tube pan with the whipped cream, then smooth its surface using the metal spatula and rotating the turntable to produce a neat finish to the dessert. (See frosting techniques on page 239.)

Place the fresh raspberries on top.

Serving the cake: Remove from refrigerator 1 hour before serving.

Strawberry Window Cake

Aᴍᴀᴊᴇꜱᴛɪᴄ dessert for a large group. Not only is the basket-weave finish on the outside picturesque, but every slice reveals a window of fresh strawberry mousse in the middle.

(See photograph, page 153.)
Mᴀᴋᴇꜱ 18 ᴛᴏ 20 ꜱᴇʀᴠɪɴɢꜱ

Baking and Decorating Equipment: 4-x-15-x-4-inch-high angel loaf pan, stiff cardboard rectangle (about 3 x 14 inches), 16-inch pastry bag, ¼-inch (#2) round pastry tip

Cake
1 ½	cups (150 grams) sifted cake flour
¾	cup (150 grams) *plus* ⅔ cup (130 grams) *plus* 2 tablespoons (25 grams) granulated sugar
10	eggs, room temperature
1 ½	teaspoons vanilla
1 ½	teaspoons cream of tartar
1	recipe Strawberry Mousse (page 255)

Frosting
2	cups (1 pint) heavy cream
¼	cup (50 grams) granulated sugar
2	teaspoons vanilla

Decoration
1	pint fresh strawberries
2	cups (1 pint) heavy cream, optional
¼	cup (50 grams) granulated sugar, optional
2	teaspoons vanilla, optional

Baker's Notes

☞ The basket-weave design is an optional finishing touch. If you prefer a smooth finish, just use the amount of cream, sugar and vanilla called for in the frosting and omit these ingredients in the decoration.

☞ Cool the cake for at least 12 hours. Make the filling at least 4 to 6 hours ahead.

☞ This dessert may be prepared over a 2-day period.
First day: Bake sponge-cake.
Second day: Prepare filling; assemble and decorate.

Understanding Cakemaking

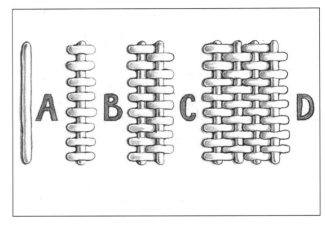

Clockwise from top left:
Removing the interior of the cake to form a tunnel. Filling the tunnel. Making the basket-weave pattern.

☞ Sometimes I split this spongecake in half vertically, providing two cakes for two different desserts. You can freeze the other for another time.

☞ A large spongecake needs to be inverted after baking to set its structure while it cools. If it is not, the cake's texture will compact as the steam escapes.

Baking preparations: This batter must bake in an ungreased pan to encourage it to stick to the pan as it rises. Prepare a place for the cake to cool when it emerges from the oven. Inverting a tube pan is easily accomplished over a long-necked bottle. If you are baking in a springform pan, balance the empty pan on top of four sturdy glasses turned upside down, in such a way that the pan's rim rests on the edges of the glasses' bases.

Ingredient preparations: Pour the flour and the ¾ cup of sugar in that order into a triple sifter. Sift onto a sheet of waxed paper; set aside.

Measure the ⅔ cup of sugar and the 2 tablespoons sugar; set aside.

Separate the eggs, placing the whites in the bowl of a heavy-duty mixer and the yolks in a 1½-quart bowl. (A deep bowl this size makes it more efficient for whipping the yolks thoroughly since it minimizes the surface area.)

Making the cake: With an electric hand mixer, whip the yolks on high speed (#10) for 3 to 5 minutes. Add the vanilla, and continue whipping for 15 seconds to incorporate; the mixture should appear thicker, pale yellow and increased in volume. Test the consistency by lifting some of the mixture with the beaters. If it flows back into the bowl in ribbons that slowly dissolve on the surface, proceed to whipping the whites. But if the ribbons sink into the surface immediately, continue whipping until the yolks have the desired consistency.

Attach the bowl of whites to the heavy-duty mixer, and with the whisk attachment, whip on medium-low speed (#3) for 30 to 45 seconds to break them up. When small bubbles appear and the surface is frothy, stop the machine, and sprinkle the cream of tartar and the 2 tablespoons granulated sugar in the center. Resume whipping, increasing speed to medium (#5), for 4 to 5 minutes, or until the whites appear glossy and stiff but not dry or granular.

Detach the whisk and bowl, tapping the whisk against the side of the bowl with enough force to free the excess. Pour the yolks onto the whites (notice they float on the surface). Using just a few strokes, fold the two together with a rubber spatula. Don't be concerned if some of the yolks remain visible.

Sprinkle half of the ⅔ cup sugar over the surface, and fold to incorporate. Sprinkle with the remaining sugar, folding again to incorporate.

With the aid of a metal spatula, scoop a third of the flour and sprinkle it over the egg mixture; with a rubber spatula, fold to incorporate. Repeat two more times, folding just until incorporated after each addition.

Baking the cake: With a rubber spatula, gently scrape the batter into the pan and smooth the surface level.

Bake for 60 to 70 minutes, or until the top crust is golden, the cake feels spongy, springs back slightly when touched and a toothpick inserted in the center comes out clean.

(Don't worry if the batter hardly rises during the first 30 minutes of baking. The low oven temperature allows the batter to absorb the heat slowly; therefore, rising is gradual.)

Cooling the cake: Remove the spongecake from the oven; immediately turn it upside down on top of the four glasses or invert it over the neck of a bottle. Cool it inverted for 12 hours. This length of time allows the spongecake to cool completely, making perfect removal possible.

To release the spongecake and maintain its shape perfectly, carefully loosen the cake's crust stuck to the top rim of the pan by inserting a thin metal spatula down ⅛ inch and loosening the crust all around the cake. Next slip a flexible metal icing spatula carefully down the sides of the pan, and slowly trace around the perimeter to release the cake clinging to the pan. Try to keep the spatula against the pan to ensure as smooth-sided a cake as possible. Then tilt and rotate the pan, and tap it on the counter to free the sponge from the metal sides. Continue to tap until the cake appears completely released.

When the sides appear free, place the cardboard on top of the cake and invert the pan, firmly rapping it on the counter as you invert it. This process may have to be repeated. Remove the baking container when cake is free. (Do not rush; be certain the sides are free before rapping it on the counter, or the spongecake will tear.) Cool for at least 12 hours.

Assembling the cake: You are going to remove a tunnel of cake from the center of the loaf without disturbing the outside walls. With the cake upside down on the cardboard, make an incision all around it, 1 inch from the top with a 2-inch paring knife. Then slip a 12-inch serrated knife through the marked portion, slicing the inch-thick lid from the top in a sawing motion. Remove the cake lid; set it nearby. (See illustration.)

Beginning ¾ inch in from the edges of the cake, make a 2-inch-deep incision down into the cake, moving the knife up and down in a sawing motion as you cut around the cake. An inch should remain uncut at the bottom; this forms the shell for the mousse.

To remove the center section efficiently, creating a tunnel, cut it into 2-inch-wide rectangles. Using the tines of a fork, lift out each piece. (You may freeze them in a plastic bag to make cake crumbs to decorate another dessert.)

Preparing the filling: Prepare Strawberry Mousse as directed on page 255. When it is ready, pour it into the tunnel, reposition the sponge lid on top, and gently press in place. Wrap it in plastic wrap and refrigerate for at least 4 hours for the mousse to set.

Frosting the Dessert: Whip the heavy cream with the sugar and vanilla until it stands in soft peaks and the beaters form light tracks. Frost the sides and top of the cake with a thin layer of the cream. (You may want to review techniques for frosting with whipped cream on page 239.)

Optional decoration: If you are not making the basket-weave design, cut the strawberries in half and place them on top of the cake. If you are making the basket-weave, whip the cream with the sugar and vanilla as directed for the frosting. Fill the pastry bag fitted with the decorating tip with the whipped cream. Pipe a basket-weave pattern around the sides of the dessert (see illustration on page 176). Cut the strawberries in half and place them on top of the cake to resemble a basket filled with fruit.

Storing the cake: Refrigerate for up to 1 hour before serving.

Orange Mimosa

Slicing into this unusually shaped dessert reveals layers of Grand Marnier-soaked spongecake, orange-flavored buttercream and small pieces of candied orange slices, which taste like the finest orange marmalade.

Makes 10 to 12 servings

Baking and Decorating Equipment: Stainless steel mixing bowl, at least 6-cup capacity, or a Zuccoto mold, stiff cardboard round, cake decorating turntable

Candied Orange Slices
    1   recipe Soaking Syrup (page 302)
    24   orange slices, each ⅛ inch thick (3 thin-skinned naval oranges)

    One Classic European Spongecake (page 162)
    2   tablespoons Grand Marnier liqueur

Filling and Frosting
    ½   recipe Classic Buttercream (page 260)
    1   tablespoon Grand Marnier
    1   teaspoon orange zest

    5   candied orange slices
    Candied mimosa, optional

Advance preparations: Prepare Candied Orange Slices as follows: Bring Soaking Syrup to a boil in a 2½-quart heavy-bottomed saucepan. Add the orange slices, reduce heat to medium-low and simmer gently for 1 hour. Remove from heat and set aside at room temperature until cool. Remove the orange slices from the syrup, using a slotted spoon. Transfer to a rack over a baking sheet and let drain and dry for about 3 to 4 hours or overnight. Reserve the leftover syrup for the dessert. After drying the candied orange slices, if you are not using them right away, store them in a covered plastic container at room temperature.

Prepare Classic European Spongecake as directed on page 162, with the following differences:

Baking preparations: Using a paper towel, grease the inside of the bowl with solid shortening. Dust generously with all-purpose flour; tilt to distribute and tap out the excess.

Baking the cake: The batter comes close to the top of the bowl, and during baking it rises above it; this is fine; it settles a bit after baking.

Bake for 35 to 40 minutes, or until the top is golden brown, the cake springs back slightly when lightly touched and a toothpick inserted in the center comes out free of cake.

Making the syrup: Pour ¾ cup of the reserved Soaking Syrup in a liquid measuring cup, add the 2 tablespoons Grand Marnier and stir to blend.

Making the buttercream: Prepare Classic Buttercream as directed on page 260. Slowly add first the 1 tablespoon Grand Marnier, then the orange zest.

Assembling the cake: Up to 1 day before serving, trim the bottom of the cooled cake so it is level. With a 12-inch serrated knife, split the cooled spongecake into four equal layers, using a sawing motion. Each layer will be about 1 inch thick, but different sizes in diameter.

Place 14 of the candied orange slices on a cutting board and chop them into coarse pieces

Baker's Notes

☞ This dessert may be prepared over a 2-day period.
First day: Bake Classic European Spongecake; prepare Soaking Syrup and Candied Orange Slices.
Second day: Prepare Classic Buttercream and assemble dessert. The dessert may be assembled up to 1 day before serving.

☞ Candied Orange Slices should be prepared at least 1 day before assembling the cake. They are so delicious that you may want to double the recipe. After drying the slices overnight, toss them in granulated sugar and give to friends as gifts. These slices keep well, so you can make them 1 week to 10 days in advance.

☞ Candied mimosa are tiny balls of sugar-coated blossoms, usually colored yellow. They are sold in specialty sections in food stores.

☞ After baking, the cake will settle ½ inch lower than it originally rose. This occurs because the baking container was greased and floured. The end product is still fine in texture, taste and form.

Understanding Cakemaking

with an oiled knife; the oil keeps the orange from sticking to the knife. (Or place the orange slices in the bowl of a food processor fitted with the steel blade, and use short on/off spurts until the oranges are chopped finely; do not purée them.)

Arrange the widest layer, cut side up, on a stiff cardboard round. Moisten with ¼ cup of soaking syrup, using a pastry brush. Then spread 3 tablespoons buttercream evenly and thinly, using a flexible metal icing spatula. Sprinkle with one-third of the chopped candied orange pieces. Moisten the next layer with 3 tablespoons syrup, 2 tablespoons buttercream, then some of the orange pieces. Center the third layer on top, and moisten with 2 tablespoons syrup, 1 ½ tablespoons buttercream and the orange pieces. Moisten the fourth layer's cut surface with 2 tablespoons syrup. Then center this last layer, and gently press to form an even dome shape.

Using the same metal spatula, frost the cake on the turntable with a thin film of the buttercream. Refrigerate for 30 minutes to 1 hour. Remove from the refrigerator and mask the cake with the remaining buttercream. (This will at first seem to be too much buttercream, but it is the most efficient way to cover the dome shape smoothly.) As you finish smoothing the buttercream over the cake's surface, remove any extra buttercream. Work with the aid of the turntable and the spatula to accomplish a neat finish (see techniques for frosting with buttercream, page 238).

Serving the cake: Remove from the refrigerator at least 1 hour before serving. Garnish with 5 reserved orange slices and the candied mimosa, if using. Slice with a serrated knife, using a sawing motion.

Caramel Carousel

Tʜɪɴ ᴄɪʀᴄʟᴇs of nougatine decorate a sumptuous dessert of two thin layers of Nut Spongecake filled with a fragrant Caramel Bavarian Cream Filling.
Mᴀᴋᴇs **8 ᴛᴏ 10 sᴇʀᴠɪɴɢs**

Decorating Equipment: 8-inch springform pan

> **One Nut Spongecake Sheet (page 166)**
> 8 **nougatine circles (page 309)**
> 1 recipe Caramel Bavarian Cream (page 250)
> ¼ cup (25 grams) unsifted powdered sugar

Advance preparations: Prepare Nut Spongecake Sheet as directed on page 166. When baking is completed, invert as directed onto a rack, remove the foil liner, then turn over the foil so that the sticky side faces up and reposition it back on the cake. Cover with a large cooling rack and invert right side up.

Prepare the nougatine as directed on page 309. After rolling the hot nougatine ¼ inch thick (or less) with the oiled rolling pin, hammer an inverted ½-inch (#6) decorating tip into the nougatine to cut out a circle. To form perfect circles, the nougatine must not be too hot or too cold. If it is too hot, the circle either will not form or will stick to the tip after you hammer. If it is too cold, it will crack after being hammered. (You can put the

thin nougatine on a baking sheet and into a preheated 325-degree oven for a short time to soften it a bit so you can work with it again.)

Store the circles in an airtight container at room temperature for up to 1 week. Nougatine crumbs for decorating or adding to fillings may be made by processing the remaining nougatine in a food processor, fitted with the steel blade.

Using the removable bottom of the springform pan as your guide, trace around it with the tip of a sharp paring knife on top of Nut Spongecake Sheet to form the bottom layer of cake for the dessert. Repeat this process to form the top layer of cake for the dessert.

Prepare Caramel Bavarian Cream as directed on page 250 and chill for 4 to 6 hours.

Assembling the cake: Lightly grease the sides of the springform pan with almond oil (or an unflavored vegetable oil) to facilitate the removal of the Bavarian cream from the pan later without disturbing its smooth surface. Insert a parchment paper round in the bottom to aid in removing the dessert before serving.

Next, place a nut spongecake circle inside the parchment-lined pan. Pour Caramel Bavarian Cream into the cake-lined pan. Top with the other nut spongecake circle and press lightly on the cake so it is level. Cover the pan with foil and refrigerate to firm the Bavarian cream (about 4 hours).

Finishing the cake: On the day of serving, remove the foil and run a thin-bladed table knife around the outer top edge of the cake, taking care not to disturb the shape of the Bavarian cream. Tilt the pan slightly to allow enough air to get to the bottom and to free the sides.

Pour the powdered sugar into a sieve. Using the palm of your hand, gently tap it to sprinkle a thin layer evenly over the cake. Unmold the dessert by removing the sides carefully to avoid pulling the Bavarian cream. Using two metal spatulas crisscrossed or a large, wide metal spatula, lift under the parchment liner and transfer the cake to a serving plate.

Serving the cake: Refrigerate until serving time. Place the nougatine circles on top just before serving.

Baker's Notes

☞ This dessert may be prepared over a 2-day period.
First day: Bake Nut Spongecake Sheet; prepare Caramel Bavarian Cream and nougatine circles.
Second day: Decorate.

☞ Make Caramel Bavarian Cream and assemble the dessert at least 4 to 6 hours before serving.

☞ Any leftover nougatine is delicious eaten as candy.

Understanding Cakemaking

Charlotte Malakoff

A CLASSIC dessert with a unique twist to guarantee a dramatic and delicious ending to any dinner. I saw this presentation in a magazine; I would love to meet the creative person who thought of lining a child's pail with ladyfingers.

(See photograph on the cover.)

MAKES 6 TO 8 SERVINGS

Baking and Decorating Equipment: 6-inch-high child's metal sand bucket, stiff cardboard round, 14-inch pastry bag, ½-inch (#6) round decorating tip, #5A decorating tip

Eighteen 5 ½-inch-long Sponge Ladyfingers (page 169)
1 ounce (¼ cup) sliced almonds

Filling
4 ounces (¾ cup) blanched almonds
4 ounces (1 stick) unsalted butter, room temperature
¾ cup (150 grams) granulated sugar
3 tablespoons kirsch or maraschino liqueur
½ teaspoon vanilla
½ teaspoon almond extract
1 cup (½ pint) heavy cream

Decoration
½ cup (4 ounces) heavy cream
1 tablespoon granulated sugar
1 teaspoon vanilla

Advance preparations: Prepare Sponge Ladyfingers as directed on page 169, but pipe through a ½-inch (#6) open decorating tip that has been flattened from its round shape to almost an oval by being pinched between the thumb and forefinger. (Altering the tip is permanent but worth it for this dessert. The ladyfingers will bake wider but thinner than usual so they will fit next to each other more neatly in the container.) If you freeze the ladyfingers, you can line your container with them as they are. They will defrost quickly.

Toast the 1 ounce of sliced almonds on a baking sheet in a preheated 350-degree oven for 5 to 10 minutes.

Preparing the mold: Tear off a piece of foil 16 inches long. Fold it in half and then in half again. Fit this strip down inside the contour of the sand bucket, leaving a few inches of overhang on both sides of the container.

Trace the container's bottom, and cut circles of waxed paper and stiff cardboard to fit the bottom. Place the cardboard in the bottom on top of the foil; then put the waxed paper circle on top of the cardboard. (The bottom need not be covered—it will become the decorated top later.)

Arrange the ladyfingers slightly overlapping each other around the inside of the bucket. When fitting the last ladyfinger into the bucket, tuck it behind the one next to it. In this way all the ladyfingers are overlapping, with no evidence of which is the first and which is the last in the mold. Now gently push the ladyfingers from their upright position so they fit diagonally into the bucket. This is easy; one ladyfinger will follow the other.

Making the filling: Grind the almonds in a nut grinder or other rotary-type mill until they have the consistency of cornmeal. You need 1½ cups ground.

Place the butter in the bowl of a heavy-duty mixer. With the flat beater (paddle) attachment, cream the butter on medium speed (#5) until it is lighter in color, clings to the sides of the bowl and has a satiny appearance (as though it were a cake batter), about 30 to 45 seconds.

Maintaining the same speed, add all the sugar in a steady stream. Then stop the mixer, and scrape the mixture clinging to the sides into the center of the bowl. Continue creaming until the mixture is almost white in color and fluffy in texture, with almost no feeling of grittiness when rubbed between the thumb and forefinger (about 4 to 5 minutes). Maintaining the same speed, gradually (teaspoon by teaspoon) pour in the kirsch, vanilla and almond extract, whipping for an additional 1 to 2 minutes. Then stir in the ground almonds with a rubber spatula until they are incorporated.

Using an electric hand mixer, whip the 1 cup cream to the Chantilly stage, or until it clings softly to the beaters. It should be thick enough to create swirls in the bowl but liquid enough to move if the bowl is tilted. Fold it into the butter-almond mixture with the rubber spatula.

Assembling the dessert: Spoon the filling into the ladyfinger-lined mold. Tap it lightly on the counter to settle the filling into the container. Cover with foil and refrigerate until firm.

Remove the foil cover and pull the foil strips up, lifting them to loosen the dessert. When you are assured the mold is free from the container, place a serving plate on top. Invert the dessert onto it, and remove the container, foil strips, cardboard and waxed paper circle. If any loose powdered sugar falls from the ladyfingers onto the serving plate, remove it with a clean pastry brush.

Finishing the dessert: Whip the ½ cup cream with the sugar and vanilla until soft peaks form and the beaters make softly closing tracks. Place in the pastry bag, fitted with the #5A decorating tip. Pipe one layer of star-shaped rosettes to cover the surface, then pipe another row over the first and then another row on top of the second. Decorate by sticking the toasted sliced almonds in the cream.

Serving the dessert: Remove from the refrigerator 1 hour before serving. To serve, slice in half horizontally with a serrated knife, using a sawing motion. Place this top half on another plate and cut wedges for your servings. Spoon a small dollop of whipped cream next to each serving.

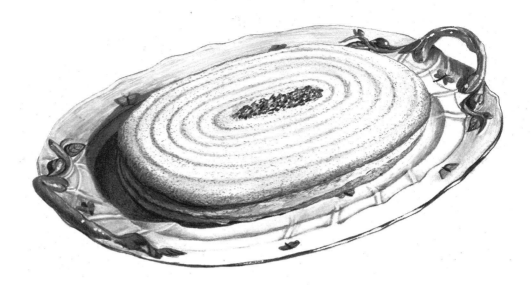

Dutch Soufflé Torte

THIS EASILY assembled dessert, with its creamy hazelnut-flavored filling sandwiched between two nutty sponge cake ovals, proves that simplicity can be stunning. MAKES 10 TO 12 SERVINGS

☞ This dessert should be prepared over a 2-day period.
First day: Bake Picq Sponge and prepare Hazelnut Bavarian Cream Soufflé; you want the filling to chill and set.
Second day: Assemble and decorate. The dessert may be assembled up to 6 hours before serving.

Decorating Equipment: ½-inch (#6) round decorating tip, 16-inch pastry bag

	Two 9-x-6 ½-inch Picq Sponge oval disks (page 167)
1	recipe Hazelnut Bavarian Cream Soufflé (page 253)
½	cup (50 grams) unsifted powdered sugar
2	teaspoons chopped hazelnuts

Advance preparations: Prepare two 9-x-6½-inch Picq Sponge oval disks as directed on page 167.

Prepare Hazelnut Bavarian Cream Soufflé the day before assembling.

Assembling the dessert: When the sponge disks are completely cool, you may begin.

If the disks are not level, shave off any uneven areas with a knife. Set one disk on top of the other to compare shapes and trim where necessary so that both disks match in shape.

Place one of the disks, flat side up, on a clean cutting board. Fill the pastry bag, fitted with the decorating tip, with the cold soufflé and pipe it onto the disk in the same manner you piped the sponge batter to form the oval shape. (Pipe any excess filling over the first layer.) Top with the other disk, the flat side touching the filling. Press to level the dessert. (Piping is the most efficient way to spread the filling easily and evenly. Also, the manipulation of the filling through the pastry tip softens its consistency, deflating it slightly and leaving just the right amount of body. This body facilitates cutting and serving and keeps the filling from penetrating the spongy disks too soon and making them soggy.)

Decorating the cake: Pour the powdered sugar into a small sieve and tap the sieve to coat the top of the dessert lightly. Place a few chopped nuts in the center of the oval.

Slip two flexible metal icing spatulas under the dessert, crisscross them, and transfer it to a serving plate.

Refrigerate until 30 minutes before serving.

Serving the dessert: Slice with a serrated knife, using a sawing motion.

Indianerkrapfen
(SPONGY CREAM PUFFS)

R OUND, HOLLOW, spongy pastries called othellos, glazed with apricot and chocolate and filled with whipped cream, form this classic Austrian specialty.
MAKES 15 SERVINGS; 2 ½ TO 3 DOZEN OTHELLOS

Baking and Decorating Equipment: Two 12-x-15½-x-½-inch baking sheets, 16-inch pastry bag, ½-inch (#6) round decorating tip, #9 open star decorating tip

Othello Batter
- ½ cup (70 grams) all-purpose flour
- ¼ cup cornstarch
- 3 tablespoons (35 grams) *plus* ¼ cup (50 grams) granulated sugar
- 5 large eggs, room temperature
- 1 teaspoon vanilla

Glazes
- 1 cup strained apricot jam
  Double recipe Viennese Chocolate Glaze (page 291)

Filling
- 2 cups (1 pint) heavy cream
- ¼ cup (50 grams) granulated sugar
- 1 teaspoon vanilla

Baker's Notes

☞ This dessert may be prepared over a 2-day period.
First day: Bake othellos and glaze them.
Second day: Assemble the dessert.

☞ Othello batter is similar to a sponge ladyfinger batter, though spongier, lighter and less sweet. Combining all-purpose flour and corn-starch makes a flour similar to cake flour. This combination makes a more tender othello.

Understanding Cakemaking

Piping batter into half globes.

Hollowing the baked othellos.

Baking preparations: Position rack in lower third of oven; preheat oven to 350 degrees.

Fit the pastry bag with the ½-inch round decorating tip.

Line the baking sheets with baking parchment paper to fit.

Making the othellos: Pour the flour, cornstarch and 3 tablespoons sugar in that order into a triple sifter. Sift on waxed paper to distribute the ingredients evenly; set aside.

Measure ¼ cup sugar for the egg whites; set aside.

Crack and separate the eggs, placing the whites in the bowl of a heavy-duty mixer and the yolks in a 1-quart mixing bowl.

With an electric hand mixer, whip the egg yolks on high speed (#10) until the mixture appears pale yellow, increases in volume and thickens slightly (about 3 to 5 minutes). Add the vanilla and continue whipping for 30 seconds more. To test the consistency, lift the beaters. If the mixture falls back into the bowl in ribbons and remains on the surface, proceed with whipping the whites. If the ribbon sinks into the surface immediately, continue whipping until it has the desired consistency.

Attach the bowl to the heavy-duty mixer, and with the whisk attachment, whip the whites on medium-low (#3) for 30 seconds, breaking them up. When small bubbles appear and the surface is frothy, increase the speed to medium (#5) and add 1 teaspoon of the ¼ cup of sugar until soft peaks appear (about 1 minute). Continue whipping while adding the remaining sugar in a steady stream until thick, white, shiny peaks form (about 1½ to 2 minutes more).

Detach the whisk and bowl; tap the whisk against the side of the bowl to free the excess. Pour the yolks over the whites. Fold the two mixtures together with a rubber spatula. Don't be too concerned if some of the yolk is still visible.

With the aid of a flexible metal icing spatula, scoop half the flour mixture and sprinkle it over the egg mixture. Fold in with a rubber spatula, repeating until the ingredients are combined.

Baking the othellos: Spoon all the batter into the pastry bag, and pipe the batter on the parchment-lined baking sheet, forming small domes or half globes, 2¼ inches in diameter, spacing them 1 inch apart. (See illustration.)

☞ You can also glaze each othello shell with coffee or chocolate-flavored fondant to vary Indianerkrapfen's flavor. Use the glazing technique in this recipe.

☞ To test if Viennese Chocolate Glaze is the correct consistency to coat the cakes, I pour a small amount over a slice of bread.

Bake for 8 to 11 minutes, or until they are light golden and, when touched in the centers with fingertips, feel firm and spongy, not leaving an impression but springing back.

Remove the baking sheet to a cooling rack, and while each othello is warm, slide a metal spatula under it to release it from the parchment paper. Each spongy ball must be hollowed, and it is easier to hollow each while it is warm. Working on the flat side, trace ¼ inch from the edge all around with the tip and blade of a small paring knife, using an up-and-down sawing motion. With the tip of the knife, lift out the cut portion. You can also use your fingertips to pull out half of the sponge inside to create a shell. (The leftover sponge pieces may be used to make crumbs for coating a cake.) Repeat with the other baked forms.

Allow the shells to cool completely, drying them in the air for a couple of hours on racks. You may proceed to glaze them, or freeze them in a sturdy plastic container for up to 1 week.

Glazing the othellos: The day before or early in the day before serving, shave off from each shell's surface the tiny tip that formed from piping, using a small paring knife. Then place the dried shells on racks. Heat the apricot jam and coat each shell's surface with a pastry brush. Allow the glaze to air-dry until not too sticky, at least 1 hour. (To hasten this process, see the fan method, page 127.) The apricot glaze creates a smooth finish; drying it enables the next glaze to flow over the surface rather than stick to it.

Place a rack of apricot-glazed shells over a jelly roll pan. Prepare Viennese Chocolate Glaze as directed on page 291. Spoon the warm, liquid glaze over each shell to cover its surface. The glaze that accumulates in the pan under the rack may be reused. Pour it into a bowl and set the bowl into another container of hot water (120 degrees), adding Stock Syrup (page 302), if necessary. Stir until the glaze has a smooth consistency, then coat the remaining shells. Allow the glaze to set completely on the shells before handling.

Assembling the dessert: No more than 2 hours before serving, whip the cream with the sugar and vanilla. Spoon it into the pastry bag, fitted with the #9 open star decorating tip. Pipe an exaggerated amount of cream (about 3 tablespoons each) into 12 of the hollow glazed shells. Place the 12 remaining glazed shells on top of each dollop of whipped cream.

Sacher Roulade

THE SACHER torte is Vienna's most famous dessert. The classic version is a chocolate spongecake covered with a layer of apricot preserves and a rich, candylike chocolate glaze. I tasted 17 different Sachers in a two-week period in Austria, which included a visit to the Austrian National Library in search of the book with "the" original recipe. I missed the copy machine's office hours, and since I was leaving the city the next morning, I had no choice but to copy the recipe by hand. Have you ever copied a language you don't speak?

This dessert is based on my favorite recipe, with the added touch of turning it into a roulade.

MAKES 8 TO 10 SERVINGS

Decorating Equipment: 12-x-15½-x-½-inch baking pan, 10-x-15-x-1-inch jelly-roll pan, baking parchment, two small paper cones

One Chocolate Spongecake Sheet (page 165)

Filling
½   cup seedless raspberry jam
2   tablespoons framboise liqueur

Glaze
⅓   cup seedless raspberry jam
1   recipe Viennese Chocolate Glaze (page 291)

Baker's Notes

☞ This dessert may be prepared over a 2-day period.
First day: Bake Chocolate Spongecake Sheet; fill and roll.
Second day: Glaze and decorate.

☞ Scoring every inch of the cake with a paring knife makes it flexible and easier to roll.

☞ I choose a raspberry jam that tastes like fresh fruit, not overly sweet, thickened juice. Using apricot jam is also a traditional choice.

☞ As you roll up the cake, if splits or cracks occur, do not stop, just roll on! The technique used here for reducing the circumference and condensing the filled cake roll will disguise any splits or imperfections.

Advance preparations: No more than 1 hour before rolling the dessert, bake Chocolate Spongecake Sheet as directed on page 165.

After removing it from the oven, place the baking pan on a large rack, and with a thin-bladed knife, gently release any portion of the cake sticking to the long sides of the pan. Pull up on the foil overhangs, one at a time, to release foil from the pan's edges. Finally, loosen the foil from the bottom of the pan by carefully lifting the foil flaps.

Cover the baked spongecake sheet with another 12-x-15½-x-½-inch baking sheet and invert. Remove the original baking sheet, peel off the foil carefully to avoid tearing the cake, and turn the foil over so that the sticky side faces up; reposition it back on the cake. Cover with the large cooling rack and invert right side up.

To facilitate rolling up the spongecake sheet, trim ⅛ inch from the two long sides to remove any crisp edges that might inhibit its flexibility. (The cake should still be on top of the foil used during baking.)

To ensure that the end flap of the sponge fits snugly once it is rolled, cut the edge of the short end farthest from you differently. Using a small paring knife, make a slanting cut, from top to bottom, along its length; you'll notice that the bottom edge extends out farther than the top edge. When the cake is rolled, this beveled edge will lie flat against the surface of the cake roll.

Now score every inch of the cake's surface with the paring knife, never cutting completely through. (See illustration on the following page.)

Making the filling: Combine the ½ cup raspberry jam and the framboise in a small bowl. Using a flexible metal icing spatula, spread a thin film of the mixture evenly over the spongecake sheet. (This adds sweetness and moisture to the bittersweet chocolate cake.)

Rolling the cake: At least 2 hours before glazing, place the trimmed sponge still on its foil on your counter with the beveled edge away from you and the length of the cake perpendicular to you. Using your fingertips, roll the sponge jelly-roll fashion, using the foil to assist you in lifting and rolling. At the end of the rolling, secure the end by pressing it slightly to adhere. Discard the baking foil.

The circumference of the cake roll is about 8 inches. This next technique condenses its circumference to about 7 inches, giving the roll a rounder, more uniform shape.

Place the roulade across the bottom third of an 18-inch sheet of baking parchment. Bring the top edge of the paper toward you, and drape it over the roulade, allowing a 2-inch overhang. Place the edge of a rimless baking sheet at a 45-degree angle to the roulade and your

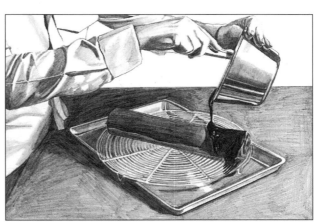

Top left: *Scoring the cake's surface.* Top right: *Rolling the cake.* Bottom left: *Compressing the cake roll.* Bottom right: *Applying chocolate glaze.*

work surface. Press against the roulade, trapping the 2-inch overhang, and push, simultaneously pulling the bottom portion of paper toward you. This push-pull motion creates a resistance that results in compressing the roulade.

You can proceed to glaze the roulade right away if you wish. Or you can wrap the compressed roulade still in its parchment paper to reinforce the cinching and leave it at room temperature for 3 to 4 hours before glazing. You can also leave it at room temperature overnight or freeze it for up to 1 week.

Glazing the cake: Up to 6 hours before serving, unwrap the roulade and place it on a rack over a 10-x-15-x-1-inch jelly roll pan. Melt the ⅓ cup raspberry jam in a 3-cup saucepan over low heat, making the jam smoother and easier to apply. Glaze the roulade, using a pastry brush. Allow it to air-dry for about 1 hour, or until it is not so sticky to the touch (to speed the process, see the fan method on page 127). This thin film of jam fills imperfections on the roulade, providing a smooth surface for the chocolate glaze to flow over.

Assemble the ingredients for the chocolate glaze while the jam glaze is drying. When ready, prepare Viennese Chocolate Glaze as directed on page 291, and pour it from the container immediately while it is warm and liquid. Pour from one end of the roulade to the other, down the cake's center. Leave about ¼ cup of the glaze in the mixing bowl for decoration later.

Understanding Cakemaking

Tap the rack against the pan to assist the glaze to roll down the sides of the roulade. Use a small flexible metal icing spatula, if necessary, to cover any areas that the glaze missed.

Optional decoration: When the chocolate glaze is cooler and has a piping consistency (about 5 minutes later), spoon it into a paper cone and cut an opening in the tip (less than ¼ inch). Pipe a continuous S pattern on top. If the glaze becomes too firm, place the bowl over warm water, and add Stock Syrup (page 302) until it is the correct consistency for piping.

Apply dots of jam from another paper cone in between the chocolate lines. With the aid of a long, wide metal spatula, place the cake on a serving platter.

Serving the cake: Store at room temperature, and serve 2 to 3 thin slices per serving. Use a serrated or sharp knife with a sawing motion as you slice. Traditionally, the slices are served with whipped cream, so pipe a large swirl on each plate if you wish.

Raspberry Cream Torte

THIS FRESH, colorful, fruity dessert is fun to make and has a mesmerizing geometrical design. (**See photograph, page 156.**)
MAKES 8 TO 12 SERVINGS

Decorating Equipment: 12-x-15½-x-½-inch baking sheet, 8-inch square cake pan with straight sides

One Classic Spongecake Sheet (page 163)

Filling
½　cup seedless raspberry jam
1　recipe Raspberry Mousse (page 256)

½　cup strained apricot jam

Advance preparations: Prepare Classic Spongecake Sheet as directed on page 163. When the baking is completed, invert as directed onto a rack and remove the foil liner. Turn foil over so that the sticky side faces up and reposition it back on the cake. Cover with large cooling rack and invert right side up. Allow to cool.

For easy removal when you unmold the dessert, line the pan with a strip of parchment paper about 14 inches long (allowing a few inches' overhang on two ends). Fold the overhangs down, outside the pan, taping them in place if desired.

Cutting the cake: Trim the short edges of the cake. Cut about 1/16 inch from each side, using kitchen scissors or a small serrated knife. Several strips will be measured, then stacked together to form the pattern.

Spread the raspberry jam in a very thin, even film over the surface of the sponge sheet, extending to the edges.

☞ I use a straight-sided square pan since the dessert's two layers (cake and mousse) look best when unmolded. But most 8-inch square pans are 8 inches across the top and less than that on the bottom. If you can't find anything but a pan with sloping sides, by all means use it. You'll use less cake when assembling the dessert, but the finished dessert will still be beautiful and delicious.

☞ Prepare Raspberry Mousse and assemble the dessert 4 to 6 hours before serving.

☞ Though the batter is spread evenly, the baked spongecake sheet may develop crisp edges during baking since the heat is conducted to these sections first. Trimming these edges before assembling desserts is wise.

Place a ruler next to one of the longest (15-inch) edges. With a paring knife, mark ½-inch-long notches every 1½ inches along the entire length. Repeat on the opposite side, so that the notches line up directly across from each other. With a small paring knife, score lightly in a straight line (not cutting through the cake) from one notch to the other, using a ruler as a guide. Now cut through the scored lines, using scissors or a small serrated knife, forming 10 strips of spongecake, each 1½ inches wide.

Stack three jam-covered strips on top of each other, lining up the edges exactly. Repeat this procedure two more times. You now have 3 stacks with 3 layers in each. (There will be 1 leftover strip.)

Transfer the 3 stacks to the baking sheet, and freeze them for 30 to 45 minutes, or until firmer. Freezing reduces the sponginess and stickiness, making the next step of slicing the stacks easier and more efficient.

Assembling the torte: Remove one 3-layer stack at a time from the freezer, and place it on a clean cutting board. With a small serrated knife, cut each with the jam-coated side up into slices ¼ inch wide. (From now on, you'll pair 2 slices together at a time, making bundles.) Each stack will yield about 20 slices.

Press 2 slices together just enough to make them adhere to each other. Because the 2 slices are compressed gently, each bundle appears to have 6 uniform layers. Tuck the bundle into the upper left-hand corner of the parchment-lined pan, sticky side up. With fingertips, gently compress the bundle, making 6 uniform layers but reducing its length from 2 inches to 1½ inches. Make another bundle by pressing 2 slices together and place it next

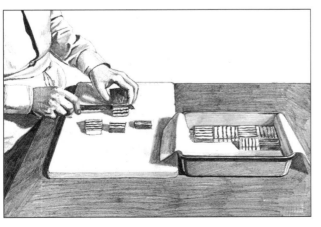

Clockwise from top left:
Scoring jam-covered cake to form 1½-inch strips. Stacking the strips. Slicing stacked strips into pieces and arranging them into a geometrical pattern inside the pan.

Understanding Cakemaking

to the first. This time turn the bundle 90 degrees so that it is perpendicular to the first one. Notice a basket-weave pattern beginning to form.

Continue adding bundles in rows across the pan, alternating their direction each time to maintain the basket-weave pattern. As each bundle is placed in the pan, compress it together slightly like an accordion, reducing its length from 2 inches to 1½ inches. You should have five rows of bundles across with 5 bundles in each row for a total of 25 (2-ply) bundles. Set aside while you prepare the filling.

Making the mousse: Prepare Raspberry Mousse as directed on page 256. Pour it into the cake-lined pan. Cover with foil and refrigerate for 4 to 6 hours to set.

Glazing the torte: Slide a thin-bladed table knife between the mousse and the two sides, not touching the parchment paper. Then tilt the dessert to loosen each side. Gently lift the top two parchment overhangs, pulling just to free the dessert without removing it.

Place the serving plate on top of the dessert in the pan and invert it onto the plate. Lift the pan gently to remove it and then the parchment paper.

Heat the apricot jam in a small saucepan just to melt it. Brush over the cake portion.

(If a thicker coating of glaze is desired, pour the melted jam into the center of the cake, and spread it over the surface with a metal spatula.)

Serving the torte: Refrigerate until serving time.

Pecan Chantilly

A THIN, moist cake wrapped around velvety Pecan Bavarian Cream with chocolate glaze and caramelized pecans on top.
MAKES **8** TO **10** SERVINGS

Decorating Equipment: 9-x-5-inch Pyrex (1½-quart) loaf pan, 8-x-4-inch stiff cardboard rectangle

One Classic Spongecake Sheet (page 163)
1 recipe Glossy Cocoa Glaze (page 289)
14 caramelized pecan halves (page 306)
1 recipe Pecan Bavarian Cream (page 251)

Advance preparations: Prepare Classic Spongecake Sheet as directed on page 163. When baking is completed, invert as directed onto a rack, remove the foil liner and turn it over so that the sticky side faces up and reposition it back on the cake. Cover with a large cooling rack and invert right side up.

Prepare Glossy Cocoa Glaze as directed on page 289.

Prepare the caramelized pecan halves as directed on page 306.

Baking preparation: Cut a rectangle from cardboard to fit base of dessert (approximately 8 x 4 inches).

Cutting the cake: Before cutting the spongecake sheet to its specific length and width, trim ⅛ inch from each of the shorter edges. These two cake edges must be pliable before the dessert is assembled. Use kitchen scissors for cutting the cake; it is easier than a knife. (The cake can still be on its baking foil on its baking sheet.)

Place a ruler next to one of the short sides, and make a notch 8 inches from one end. Repeat this procedure on the opposite short side to line up the notches directly across from each other. With a small paring knife, score lightly in a straight line (not cutting through the cake) from one notch to the other, using a ruler as a guide. Cut along the scored line with kitchen scissors, making two pieces of sponge: one about 8 x 14 inches and the other about 4 x 14 inches. (See illustration on the following page.)

The large piece lines the pan as well as forms a lid that folds over the filling. The small strip forms the ends. Each end piece should measure approximately 4 x 2¼ inches. To be exact and guarantee a snug fit, wait until you insert the large strip into the Pyrex pan; then measure the ends again before you finally cut the end pieces.

Do not line the pan with parchment paper before you insert the spongecake strip; the moisture from the dessert would cause the cake to stick to the lining, and the finish on the cake would not be smooth. In this instance, the completed dessert unmolds easily without a liner.

Insert the large piece of spongecake into the pan by positioning one end of the cake strip flush with a rim. Carefully tuck the cake into the pan so that it fits the contour. The portion of the cake extending beyond the other rim will eventually form the lid. Careful! This flap could break or tear if it is allowed to hang unsupported from the pan. Rest it on a stack of books so it will not tear while you prepare the filling. Insert the two end pieces, trimming if necessary to make them fit snugly.

Filling the cake: Prepare Pecan Bavarian Cream as directed on page 251. Using a rubber spatula, guide the filling into the cake-lined pan and smooth the top until level. Drape the cake flap over the filling as if you were closing the lid of a treasure chest.

Baker's Notes

↪ A Pyrex container is useful for viewing the dessert's assembly.

↪ For this dessert, the 9-x-5-inch (1½-quart) loaf pan requires an 8-x-14-inch sheet cake.

↪ Prepare Pecan Bavarian Cream and assemble the dessert at least 6 hours before serving.

↪ If you don't have a loaf pan of the size called for here, you can use another pan, provided you calculate the size of the inside so you can cut the cake to the proper dimensions. Measure the depth of the pan down its longest side and the width across its top. The sum of twice the width plus twice the depth is how long the cake should be. The length of the long side of the pan is the cake's width.

Understanding Cakemaking

Clockwise from top left:
Trimming the spongecake sheet to fit the pan's shape. Lining the loaf pan with the cake. Trimming excess cake after filling and covering the dessert.

Where the two pieces of cake meet at the rim's edge, trim the excess with the scissors. Cover the top with plastic wrap and refrigerate for at least 4 to 6 hours or overnight. For a neat, trim package, make sure that the flaps rest right up against the rim of the pan.

Glazing the cake: Remove the chilled dessert from the refrigerator. Tilt the pan with the dessert gently back and forth until you can see that the cake lining the pan is being released. (Tilting allows air to get under it, too.) Place the strip of cardboard on top; invert the dessert onto it; then carefully lift off the pan. Place the dessert on a rack over a jelly roll pan and allow it to sit at room temperature for about 30 minutes to remove some of its chill.

Meanwhile, reheat Glossy Cocoa Glaze. Before you use the glaze, pat any moisture from the dessert with a paper towel.

Pour the glaze in a slow, steady stream from the bowl down the length of the dessert, beginning at one end and moving to the opposite. Coat the entire cake, including the ends. Then place caramelized pecan halves on top decoratively. Allow the dessert to set for about 30 minutes before transferring it to a serving plate. Scrape the leftover glaze from the jelly roll pan into a container. (Store in refrigerator and reheat over low heat to use again.)

Serving the cake: Remove from refrigerator 30 to 60 minutes before serving.

Recipes for Angel Food Cakes

Recipe for a Chiffon Cake

Angel Food Cakes

How DOES the angel food cake achieve its airy volume and its fine, even, tender texture without any baking powder or fat? This one-bowl cake, which is simple to assemble, owes its success to the proper whipping of egg whites. When the cake is in the oven, some volume builds from the air cells you have whipped into the whites. But most of the volume is produced by the steam which evaporates from the liquid in the egg whites and passes through the air cells of the egg whites, expanding them.

THE INGREDIENTS AND THEIR ROLE

EGG WHITES

For BEST results, I prefer that the temperature of the egg whites be cooler than room temperature, around 60 degrees. Cooler whites are more viscous and do not incorporate air as quickly as whites at room temperature, but the air bubbles that form hold better. The result is egg whites whipped to their optimum, not their maximum, capacity, leaving room for them to expand in the oven. You need wet and shiny whites with soft peaks that end when they are lifted from the whisk. If you whip the whites too stiff, incorporating other ingredients will require extra folding, and in the process you're bound to lose volume. At the same time these overextended air cells can collapse and deflate during the baking process. (See the tips for whipping egg-white foams successfully on page 150.)

SUGAR

Sugar is the ingredient that helps give the angel food its tenderness. But the point at which you add it is crucial. I have experimented with whipping different amounts of sugar into the egg-white foam at different stages. Whipping a small amount of sugar into the whites at the beginning produces a smoother, softer and more stable foam for folding in the remaining sugar, flour and salt. Too much sugar prevents optimum aeration, creating a heavy syrup formation, which burdens the whites.

In the oven, the sugar interacts with the coagulation (setting) of the egg and flour proteins. If the oven is too low, this amount of sugar will absorb liquid from the egg whites, turn syrupy and weep out of the batter, pulling down the air cells and decreasing the cake's volume. On the other hand, you don't want the oven to be too hot, or the cake's outer structure will set before it can fully expand and bake through.

FLOUR AND FLAVORINGS

I USE CAKE flour in my angel food cakes because its low protein content and fine particles help produce a delicate, tender cake.

Salt enhances the flavor of angel food cakes, regardless of what other ingredients you choose to add.

CREAM OF TARTAR

CREAM of tartar produces a whiter Classic Angel Food Cake (page 198). Its stabilizing action on the egg-white foam is most apparent in the oven, where air cells hold up longer without collapsing before they coagulate. As in some spongecakes, this is important because the high percentage of sugar can slow coagulation in the oven.

BAKING PANS

THE TRADITIONAL tube pan is not necessary for all angel food batters. It is advantageous in the case of a heavy batter with a high fat content, such as Chocolate Angel Food Cake (page 199) made with cocoa powder, or with recipes requiring large amounts of batter. The tube pan's even heat distribution, coming from both the center and the outside edges, allows these batters to bake more quickly, avoiding the risk of weeping and loss of volume.

☞ I bake the cake in the 9-inch springform since 9-inch tube pans are difficult to find. A hole in the center is not necessary for successfully baking this size angel food cake. This shape cake is nice for variety and is easy to decorate. A 9-inch angel food tube pan (with or without removable bottom) may be used, too.

☞ You can make a Walnut Angel Food Cake with this batter by reducing the flour to ⅔ cup (75 grams) unsifted cake flour. After sifting it with the ½ cup of granulated sugar, add ⅔ cup (2 ounces) finely ground walnuts. Assemble, bake and cool following the directions below.

☞ A dry (ungreased) tube pan allows the batter to cling to the sides and rise to its full height.

☞ This cake goes together quickly, so have all your ingredients and utensils at hand.

☞ Whipping the whites with a little sugar, then folding in some sugar produces a more tender cake than one with all the sugar whipped into the whites at one time.

☞ If the vanilla is added too soon, it will interfere with the volume of the egg whites. Add it in the last moments of whipping the whites.

Classic Angel Food Cake

THIS fine-textured vanilla-flavored cake is a sentimental favorite among our American-style cakes. It's excellent with fresh fruit or ice cream.

This is the foundation for Duchess Cake (page 203).

MAKES ONE 9-x-1 ¾-INCH ROUND CAKE

Baking Equipment: 9-inch springform pan

1	cup (7 or 8 large) egg whites
1 ¼	cups (125 grams) sifted cake flour
½	cup (100 grams) granulated sugar
¼	teaspoon salt
2	tablespoons (25 grams) *plus* ⅓ cup (65 grams) granulated sugar
1	teaspoon cream of tartar
1	teaspoon vanilla

Ingredient preparations: Place fresh, cold egg whites in the bowl of a heavy-duty mixer. Set aside until 60 degrees, slightly below room temperature.

Pour flour, ½ cup sugar and salt in that order into a triple sifter. Sift onto a sheet of waxed paper; set aside.

Measure the 2 tablespoons of sugar and the ⅓ cup sugar and have at hand.

Baking preparations: Position rack in lower third of oven; preheat oven to 350 degrees.

Since you're baking in a springform pan with no tube to fit into the neck of a bottle, you must make your own cooling area. The simplest way is to balance the empty pan on top of four sturdy glasses turned upside down on the counter. The pan's edges rest on the glasses' bases.

Making the cake: Attach the bowl with the egg whites to the mixer, and with the whisk attachment, beat them on low speed (#2) for 1 to 1½ minutes. When small bubbles appear and the surface is frothy, stop the machine and sprinkle the cream of tartar over the top. Resume whipping, increase the speed to medium (#5) and pour in the 2 tablespoons sugar in a steady stream. Whip until the whites have increased to several times their original volume, have thickened and form soft, droopy white peaks rather than stiff, straight, inelastic ones (about 2 minutes). Add the vanilla in the final moments of whipping.

Detach the whisk and bowl and use the whisk attachment to whip entire mass for 5 to 10 seconds to bring the entire egg-white foam uniformly together.

Sprinkle half of the ⅓ cup sugar over the whipped whites and fold with a rubber spatula, using as few strokes as possible. Sprinkle with the remaining sugar and fold again, using a minimum number of strokes to preserve the foam structure.

Scoop a third of the flour mixture onto a metal spatula and sprinkle it over the egg whites; fold in with a rubber spatula. Repeat two more times, folding just until incorporated.

Baking the cake: Holding the bowl close to the ungreased pan, guide the batter into the pan, using a rubber spatula. Spread its surface smooth. (This batter almost pours into the pan, unlike most conventional angel food batters. There's no need to run a spatula through the batter because few, if any, air pockets exist.)

Bake for 25 to 30 minutes, or until the top is light golden, the cake feels spongy and springs back when touched, and a toothpick inserted in the middle comes out free of cake.

Cooling the cake: Remove the cake from the oven, and immediately turn it upside down, positioning the edges of the pan on the inverted glasses. Cool it for 1 hour; then turn the pan right side up and place it on the counter.

To remove from the springform, slip a flexible metal spatula carefully down the side of the pan and slowly trace around the perimeter to release any cake sticking to the pan. Unlock the springform rim and remove it.

Cover the cake with a rack, invert, and carefully remove the bottom of pan. Turn right side up.

Storing the cake: If you plan to use the cake within a day, wrap it in plastic wrap and store it at room temperature.

To freeze, cover the plastic-wrapped package with foil and label it, indicating the contents and date. (Or place it in a sturdy container before freezing to protect it.) Freeze for no longer than 1 week.

☞ Angel food cakes must cool upside down to preserve their structure.

☞ You may freeze the angel food, but its spongy structure will not survive a long period. Its texture also can pick up odors in the freezer.

Chocolate Angel Food Cake

THIS IS an exceptional angel food cake, not only because of its undeniably chocolate flavor but because of its surprising moistness. It's delicious served on its own.

This is the foundation for Cinderella Cake (page 204).

MAKES ONE 10-X-2-INCH CAKE

Baking Equipment: 10-inch angel food tube pan with removable bottom

1	cup (7 or 8 large) egg whites
½	cup (50 grams) unsifted cocoa powder
¼	cup (25 grams) sifted cake flour
½	cup (100 grams) granulated sugar
¼	teaspoon salt
1	teaspoon cream of tartar
1	teaspoon vanilla
2	tablespoons (25 grams) *plus* ½ cup (100 grams) granulated sugar

Make the cake by following each step for Classic Angel Food Cake (page 198), with the following differences:

Ingredient preparations: Pour the cocoa, flour, ½ cup sugar and salt in that order into a triple sifter. Sift onto a sheet of waxed paper; set aside. (It's easier to fold these

☞ Bake in a tube pan since as the cake bakes, the fat from the cocoa weighs on its structure. The tube aids in baking more evenly, distributing the heat and quickly setting the structure.

☞ At first you will think the amount of batter is not enough. But it rises quite a bit, surprising you.

☞ Don't be concerned if your batter deflates somewhat while you fold in the cocoa mixture. That is to be expected because cocoa powder, though dry like flour, is heavy with cocoa butter. And as it incorporates into the batter, it becomes moist, making it heavier.

☞ To prevent the batter from deflating too much during folding, try not to lift the rubber spatula above the batter's surface. Rather, keep it in the batter under the surface. Also, do not twist the spatula in your hand. Allow your wrist to move the utensil.

ingredients into the whites if they're together.)

Have the cream of tartar, vanilla, the 2 tablespoons sugar and the ½ cup sugar at hand.

Baking preparations: Position rack in lower third of oven; preheat oven to 325 degrees.

Making the cake: The egg whites should be whipped a little stiffer than for Classic Angel Food Cake. But they should still look soft and be elastic (not dry or granular) for optimum folding in of the dry ingredients. (If the whites are too stiff, they lose their potential to rise while in the oven. Also, the batter can be deflated while folding in the other ingredients because you overfold in attempting to incorporate them.) When you have finished whipping the whites, take the whisk in hand and whip the mixture for 4 to 5 seconds to bring the foamy structure together.

Baking the cake: Bake for 30 to 35 minutes, or until the top is not shiny but dull brown, the cake springs back when touched and contracts from the sides slightly. Do not overbake or the cake will be dry.

Cooling the cake: Remove from the oven and invert over a long-necked bottle for 1 to 2 hours, or until cool.

To remove, slip a flexible metal spatula carefully down the side of the pan and slowly trace around the perimeter to release any cake sticking to the pan. Try to keep the spatula against the pan to ensure as smooth-sided a cake as possible.

When the sides are free, push on the removable bottom to release it from the pan completely. Tilt the cake on its side with the removable bottom still attached and tap the bottom against the counter gently to loosen cake. Rotate the cake, tapping the bottom a few more times, until it appears free. Cover the cake with a rack, invert and remove the bottom of the pan.

Chocolate Angel Food Sheet

Tᴏ THIS THIN, pliable layer of cake uses a mixture of chocolate and water instead of cocoa powder to flavor the batter to create a moist flavorful cake.

This is the foundation for Chocolate Angel Food Roll (page 202).

Mᴀᴋᴇꜱ ᴏɴᴇ 12-x-15-x-½-ɪɴᴄʜ ᴄʜᴏᴄᴏʟᴀᴛᴇ ᴀɴɢᴇʟ ꜰᴏᴏᴅ ꜱʜᴇᴇᴛ

Baking Equipment: 12-x-15½-x-½-inch baking sheet

⅔	cup (5 large) egg whites
2	tablespoons unsifted cake flour
⅓	cup (65 grams) granulated sugar
4	ounces semisweet chocolate
2	tablespoons hot tap water

Ingredient preparations: Place the fresh, cold egg whites in the bowl of a heavy-duty mixer. Set aside until 60 degrees, slightly below room temperature.

Pour the flour into a triple sifter and sift it onto a sheet of waxed paper to remove any lumps.

Measure the granulated sugar; set aside.

Cut the chocolate into matchstick-size pieces and place them in a 3-quart stainless steel bowl that fits snugly over another large mixing bowl. (This saves transferring the melted chocolate to another bowl later when you combine it with the meringue and flour.) Fill the lower bowl halfway with hot tap water (120 degrees), place the bowl with the chocolate on top and add the 2 tablespoons hot water to the chocolate.

Wait 1 minute before stirring to allow the chocolate to absorb the heat from the water underneath as well as from the water poured over it. Then stir the mixture to distribute the heat. When some of the chocolate has liquefied, wait another minute and then stir again. Continue this procedure until the mixture is smooth and liquid.

Baking preparations: Position rack in lower third of oven; preheat oven to 375 degrees.

Using a paper towel, lightly grease a small area in the center of the baking sheet with solid shortening and line the pan with foil, leaving a 2-inch overhang at each short end of the pan. (The dab of shortening holds the foil in place.) Lightly grease the foil with shortening and sprinkle with all-purpose flour. Shake pan to distribute flour and tap out the excess.

Making the cake: Attach the bowl of whites to the heavy duty mixer, and with the whisk attachment, whip the whites on medium-low speed (#3) until small bubbles appear and the surface is frothy (about 30 seconds). Increasing the speed to medium (#5), pour in 1 tablespoon of the ⅓ cup sugar in a steady stream, and whip until soft white peaks form (about 1 minute). Maintaining the same speed, add the remaining sugar in a steady stream, and continue whipping until thicker, glossy white peaks form (about 1½ minutes).

Detach the whisk and bowl. Using the whisk attachment, whip the mass by hand for 5 to 10 seconds to bring the entire egg-white foam uniformly together. Tap the whisk against side of bowl to free excess. Pour the flour onto the meringue and fold just to combine with a rubber spatula.

Scoop the meringue into the mixing bowl containing the melted chocolate and fold to combine with a rubber spatula. (Folding the meringue into the chocolate instead of the reverse keeps the deflating of the meringue's foamy structure to a minimum.)

Baking the cake: Using a rubber spatula, scrape the batter down the center of the prepared baking sheet in a strip 4 to 5 inches long. Spread the batter as evenly as possible with an 8-inch metal spatula. Do not be afraid of moving the batter. Direct it with the spatula as though the spatula were your hand. Use the sides of the pan as a guide. The batter should be level with them.

The angel food sheet is thin and bakes quickly. To produce an even layer, check the uniformity of the batter's depth by inserting a toothpick at various points. Begin at the corners and work toward the center. The depth on the toothpick should be the same at each point; adjust the batter if necessary.

☞ This cake is similar to a chocolate meringue but it's not as dry or crisp.

☞ Adding water to chocolate provides more moisture to the batter and thins the melted chocolate enough so folding it into the other ingredients is easy, preventing it from solidifying and forming tiny chips. (Do not let the chocolate mixture cool for too long before you incorporate it, or tiny chips will form.)

☞ You can cut this cake into strips and layer it with a filling rather than roll it.

Understanding Cakemaking

Bake for 7 to 8 minutes; then check to see if the baking is finished. The angel food sheet should feel spongy when pressed near the center; the top should appear set, not shiny, and the sides of the cake may contract slightly from the pan. Don't overbake or the chocolate may scorch.

Cooling the cake: Remove the baking sheet from the oven and place it on a large rack. Using a thin-bladed knife, gently release any portion of the cake sticking to the long sides of the pan. Pull up on the foil overhangs, one at a time, to release foil from pan's edges. Finally, loosen foil from the bottom by gently lifting up on foil flaps.

Cover the cake with another 12-x-15½-inch pan and invert. Remove the original baking sheet and peel off foil carefully to avoid tearing the angel food. (It is especially delicate while warm.) Turn the foil over so that the sticky side faces up and reposition it back on the cake. Cover with a large rack and invert right side up. Allow the angel food to cool on the rack for 45 minutes. After this time it is cool yet still flexible enough to be manipulated. Lift it by the foil ends off the rack to the countertop if you plan to roll it. (Leave the cake on its loosened baking foil.)

Storing the cake: If you plan to roll the cake, it is best to do so 45 to 60 minutes after baking. If you plan to cut it into strips to use later in the day, leave it, uncovered, on the cooling rack.

To use within 2 days, slip a baking sheet under the foil and cake, cover with foil and freeze.

Chocolate Angel Food Roll

WRAPPED like a present in a pliable compound called Plastic Chocolate, this dessert delights everyone. It consists of an airy, thin angel food cake rolled around whipped cream and enrobed in chocolate.

MAKES 8 TO 10 SERVINGS

One Chocolate Angel Food Sheet (page 200)

Filling
¾	cup (6 ounces) heavy cream
1	tablespoon granulated sugar
1	teaspoon vanilla
1	recipe Plastic Chocolate (page 293)

Advance preparation: Prepare Chocolate Angel Food Sheet up to 1 hour before filling.

Making the filling: On the day of serving, whip the heavy cream with the 1 tablespoon sugar and vanilla on high speed (#10) if you are using an electric hand mixer. Whip until peaks stand up on the surface when the beater or whisk is lifted. Tracks made from pulling the beaters or a rubber spatula through the center of the cream remain (see piping stage, page 240). Such stiffness is useful because it gives body and support to the thin cake as it rolls. You want the cream barely to move while you roll the cake.

Filling and rolling the cake: Scoop the whipped cream onto the angel food sheet, and spread it evenly in a thin layer with an 8-inch flexible metal icing spatula. Spread the filling to every edge but one short end; on this end, leave a 2-inch border free of filling. (The filling should be spread approximately ¼ inch thick.)

Now turn the cake, with the foil still underneath, so that the short end with the filling is directly in front of you (parallel with the edge of the counter) and the short end without filling faces away from you. Grasp the foil nearest you, and begin rolling up the cake by flipping over the edge of the cake onto itself. Continue to roll the cake up, using the foil as an aid, until it forms the shape of a log. As you roll, some of the cream filling moves to the end of the cake that was not covered originally.

Transfer the roll onto a baking sheet (you can pick up the roll with your hands easily, but if in doubt, use a metal spatula), cover the roll with foil and refrigerate while making Plastic Chocolate for decoration. Don't worry if there are some cracks on the roll; the decoration covers the entire roll.

Making Plastic Chocolate: Up to 30 minutes before decorating the roll, prepare Plastic Chocolate as directed on page 293. When its consistency is like soft clay, roll it to form a paper-thin sheet as the recipe directs, until it is about 18 inches by 6 inches. Don't rush when rolling it out.

Decorating the cake: Remove Chocolate Angel Food Roll from the refrigerator, place it lengthwise over the lower third of the chocolate sheet, and lift the lower portion of the Plastic Chocolate sheet over the roll. Lift the other portion over, then rotate the roll so the seam is not visible. Each end of the Plastic Chocolate sheet will overlap the angel food roll; pinch the chocolate sheet lightly, gathering it decoratively. Brush off some of the powdered sugar from rolling the Plastic Chocolate from the dessert's surface. Lift onto a serving platter.

Serving the cake: Remove from refrigerator at least 1 hour before serving since its texture and flavor are never at their best cold.

Duchess Cake

A vanilla angel food covered with a creamy orange-flavored frosting. Crisp cookies in the shape of butterflies give a whimsical finishing touch. **(See photograph, page 66.)**

Makes 8 to 10 servings

Decorating Equipment: Stiff cardboard round, cake decorating turntable

    One Classic Angel Food Cake (page 198)
6   **Miniature Butterflies, optional (page 273)**
1   **recipe Orange Sabayon Frosting (page 268)**

Baker's Notes

☞ Prepare Chocolate Angel Food Sheet up to 1 hour before filling and rolling. Make Plastic Chocolate up to 30 minutes before decorating the roll.

☞ Don't be concerned with the cake's appearance on the ends when you have finished rolling; the entire roll will be concealed in Plastic Chocolate, page 293.

☞ Flavor the filling with 1 tablespoon of your favorite liqueur instead of the vanilla if you wish.

☞ This dessert may be prepared over a 2-day period.
First day: Bake Classic Angel Food Cake; prepare Miniature Butterflies.
Second Day: Prepare Orange Sabayon Frosting and assemble the dessert.

☞ The Miniature Butterflies are optional.

Advance preparations: Prepare Classic Angel Food Cake as directed on page 198. When it is cool, invert it onto a stiff cardboard to fit the cake.

Prepare Miniature Butterflies, if desired, as directed on page 273, and store them in an airtight metal container at room temperature until ready to decorate the cake.

Frosting the cake: On the day of serving, prepare Orange Sabayon Frosting as directed on page 268. Place the cake on the turntable and frost the top and sides of the cake (you may want to review frosting techniques for different consistencies, page 238). Finish the sides, top and base of the cake smoothly with the aid of a flexible metal icing spatula and turntable.

Storing and serving the cake: Refrigerate the dessert if it is not to be served within the next 2 hours. Remove it from the refrigerator 1 hour before serving for the dessert's best flavor.

If using Miniature Butterflies, decorate just before serving to keep their crispness.

Cinderella Cake

LIKE ITS namesake in the fairy tale, this simple cake gets dressed up enough to go to anybody's party.

MAKES 8 TO 10 SERVINGS

Decorating Equipment: 9-inch stiff cardboard round, cake decorating turntable, 12-inch pastry bag, #3 open star decorating tip

	One 9-inch Chocolate Angel Food Cake (page 199)
30 to 40	**Chocolate Rings, optional (page 283)**
1	**recipe Cocoa Whipped Cream (page 288)**
½	**cup (4 ounces) heavy cream**
2	**teaspoons granulated sugar**

Baker's Note

☞ This dessert may be prepared over a 2-day period.
First day: Bake Chocolate Angel Food Cake and prepare Chocolate Rings.
Second day: Frost and decorate.

Advance preparations: Prepare Chocolate Angel Food Cake as directed on page 199. Prepare Chocolate Rings, if using, as directed on page 283. After the piped circles have set, place the foil-lined baking sheet in a cool room. To store Chocolate Rings for more than 1 day, carefully slip a small spatula under each ring, transfer it to an airtight metal container and store the container in a cool room. (You may even freeze these shapes in their sturdy container to ensure they remain dry if you live in a very humid climate.)

Making and applying the frosting: On the day of serving, mix the ingredients together for Cocoa Whipped Cream as directed on page 288. Refrigerate for at least 30 minutes before whipping.

Place the cake first on the cardboard round, then on the turntable. Fit the pastry bag with the tip.

Whip Cocoa Whipping Cream until soft peaks form. Frost the sides and top of the cake with a thin film of the cream; then fill in the hole in the cake from the tube pan. Next finish the sides and top of the cake. (You may want to review frosting techniques on page 239.)

Decorating the cake: Whip the ½ cup of heavy cream with the sugar until soft peaks form and a track in the bowl closes slowly but not completely (decorating stage). Spoon the mixture into the pastry bag and pipe six spirals on top of the cake. Then stick five or six chocolate rings into each whipped cream spiral to resemble a crown or tiara.

Storing and serving the cake: Remove from refrigerator up to 2 hours before serving.

Chiffon Cake

~

THIS TENDER, light and fluffy cake resembles a butter cake in formula and preparation. But because its shape and texture are close to that of a spongecake and because its leavening relies mainly on an egg-white meringue, it belongs in the sponge (or foam) category.

Traditional recipes for chiffon cake call for unflavored oil, which gives moistness and a tender crumb but imparts no flavor, rather than for melted butter. To offset blandness, I add salt, spices and sometimes fruit puree, or even cocoa powder or chocolate.

Making chiffon cakes is not difficult. The yolks are mixed briefly with the other ingredients. Then a light meringue is whipped and folded into the yolk mixture. The egg-white foam is important, but chiffon cakes always contain baking powder as an extra assurance of volume.

Classic Banana Chiffon Cake

A RUM CREAM covers this moist, tender, banana-flavored cake, which is permeated with spices.

MAKES ONE 10-X-3 ¼-INCH TUBE CAKE, 12 TO 14 SERVINGS

Baking and Decorating Equipment: 10-inch angel food tube pan with removable bottom, 10-inch stiff cardboard round, cake decorating turntable, 12-inch pastry bag, ¼-inch (#2) round decorating tip

2	cups (240 grams) unsifted cake flour
1 ⅓	cups (265 grams) granulated sugar
1	tablespoon baking powder
1	teaspoon salt
¼	teaspoon nutmeg
½	teaspoon cinnamon
2	tablespoons (25 grams) granulated sugar
1	cup (7 or 8 large) egg whites, room temperature
5	egg yolks, room temperature
2	large ripe bananas
½	cup unflavored vegetable oil
1	teaspoon vanilla
1	recipe Rum Cream (page 263)
1	banana

Baking preparations: Position rack in lower third of oven; preheat oven to 325 degrees.

A dry (ungreased) tube pan allows the batter to cling to the sides and rise to its full height. Place a long-necked bottle or large metal funnel nearby for inverting the baked cake.

Baker's Notes

☞ This dessert may be prepared over a 2-day period.
First day: Bake Classic Banana Chiffon Cake. Second day: Prepare Rum Cream and decorate.

☞ This recipe may seem to contain a lot of salt, but it is important for flavor.

☞ A tube pan with a removable bottom facilitates the cake's removal from the pan, resulting in the best shape. If you use a standard tube pan with no removable bottom, be certain to cool the cake for several hours before removing it.

☞ I mash ripe bananas with a pastry blender.

☞ A round, not flat, wooden toothpick is important for testing doneness. A thin toothpick might slip through the chiffon's spongy texture, appearing clean and not providing an accurate test.

☞ The filling and frosting use the 3 leftover yolks from the cake.

Ingredient preparations: Place a triple sifter over a large 3-quart mixing bowl. Pour in the flour, 1⅓ cups sugar, baking powder, salt and spices in that order, and sift into the bowl; set aside.

Measure the 2 tablespoons of sugar for the egg whites; set aside.

Place the egg whites in the bowl of a heavy-duty mixer and the yolks in a small bowl.

Mash the 2 bananas in a 1½-quart mixing bowl (you need 1 cup), add the oil, egg yolks and vanilla and stir to combine.

Making the cake: Pour the banana mixture into the center of the dry ingredients. Stir to combine with a rubber spatula until the batter is smooth and homogeneous (except for the banana pieces).

Attach the bowl with the whites to the mixer, and with the whisk attachment, whip them on low speed (#3) until small bubbles appear and the surface is frothy (about 45 seconds). Increase the speed to medium (#5), add 1 teaspoon of the 2 tablespoons sugar, and whip until soft white peaks form (about 1 minute).

Maintaining the same speed, add the remaining sugar in a steady stream, and continue to whip until thicker, glossy white (but not dry) peaks form (about 1½ to 2 minutes). Detach the whisk and bowl. Using the whisk attachment, whip the mass by hand for 5 to 10 seconds to bring the egg-white foam uniformly together.

Scoop a third of the meringue onto the banana mixture, and fold to lighten with a rubber spatula. Then fold in the remaining meringue until combined.

Baking the cake: Pour the batter into the pan, and spread it evenly with a rubber spatula.

Bake for 50 to 55 minutes, or until the top springs back slightly when touched and a toothpick inserted in the center of the cake comes out free of cake.

Cooling the cake: Remove pan from oven, and immediately invert it over the long-necked bottle to cool for 2 to 3 hours.

When it is cool, slip a flexible metal spatula carefully down one side of the pan and slowly trace around the perimeter to release the cake sticking to the pan. Try to keep the spatula against the pan to ensure as smooth-sided a cake as possible.

When the sides are free, push up on the removable bottom to release the cake completely. Tilt the cake with the bottom still attached on its side, and tap it gently against the counter to loosen it. Rotate the cake, tapping it a few more times, until it appears free. Cover the cake with a rack and invert; remove the bottom of pan.

Storing the cake: If you plan to use the cake within a day, wrap it in plastic and store at room temperature.

To freeze, cover the plastic-wrapped package with foil and label it, indicating its contents and the date. Freeze for no longer than 1 week.

Making the Rum Cream: On serving day, prepare Rum Cream as directed on page 263.

Assembling the cake: Place the cake first on the cardboard round, then on the turntable. Fit the pastry tip into the pastry bag. Frost the top and sides of the cake as soon as you have folded the whipped cream into the Rum Cream, filling the hole left from the tube pan. Finish frosting the dessert with the aid of the turntable and the flexible metal icing spatula.

Decorating the cake: With the clean edge of the metal icing spatula, mark the cake's surface very lightly in the frosting with four, two-sided open triangles, each line connecting to the other (resembling a four-pointed star). Spoon the remaining frosting into the pastry bag and pipe onto the marked lines. In between each design, pipe small dots the size of a dime. Just before serving, place a banana slice on top of each of the piped dots.

Serving the cake: Remove from the refrigerator up to 2 hours before serving for best flavor and texture.

Recipes for Meringues

Recipes for Dacquoise

Meringues

~

A MERINGUE is composed of egg whites that have been whipped with the addition of sugar. The texture of a meringue—it can be soft or hard—depends on the ratio of sugar to each white. This ratio influences the method you use to create all varieties of meringue. For example, it is not difficult to whip 6 tablespoons of sugar into 3 egg whites to obtain a shiny, smooth mixture with good volume to fold into a cake batter. But incorporating three times as much sugar into the same number of egg whites requires another method to accomplish the same goal. (See Classic Italian Meringue, page 265.)

A meringue that is low in sugar will always remain in a soft form whether you fold it into a mousse or a Bavarian cream, or use it as part of a filling for a soufflé or spread it on a pie, or even smooth it on a cake and then broil it, as in baked Alaska. Soft meringues can also be poached and served as desserts in their own right: Île flottante (floating island) and oeufs à la neige (eggs in snow) are two famous examples. A meringue with little sugar will never become crisp no matter how you choose to use it.

A meringue with a high proportion of sugar to egg whites, on the other hand, may be soft or hard; its texture depends on whether you choose to fold it into another mixture, bake or boil it as a topping, or dry it in the oven. Piped shapes of meringue with a high proportion of sugar are generally dried in a low oven so as to evaporate the meringue's moisture. The high percentage of sugar forms a more concentrated, sugary network, so drying the meringue sets a crisp, firm, honeycomblike structure. But I know some pastry chefs who prefer a warmer oven so that the sugar will caramelize, adding color and flavor to the meringue. Sometimes, I pipe small shapes of meringue and place them in a moderately hot oven so that the outside sets and the inside remains soft.

MAKING MERINGUES

THERE ARE three methods for making meringues, either soft or hard. The most common is the **Cold Method** where sugar is added (sometimes in stages) to cool or room-temperature egg whites (see Classic Meringue, page 214). Another method warms the egg whites with granulated sugar before whipping; hence the name **Warm-Method Meringue** (see Swiss Meringue, page 264). The other method involves adding a cooked sugar syrup to whipped whites (see Classic Italian Meringue, page 265).

Whether a meringue is called a Swiss meringue or a French meringue should not confuse you. The great pastry chefs themselves differ on nomenclature. The important thing is that the recipe and its technique bring you success. Since all meringues begin with an egg-white foam, you may want to review my tips for whipping egg-white foams (page 149).

When I need a soft meringue for topping pies, cakes, tarts or baked Alaska or for folding into fillings such as chocolate mousse, the warm method is my favorite because it is easy and it does not break down as quickly as the cold-method meringue. As with the cold method, either a soft or firm meringue can be made, depending on the proportion of sugar to the whites. Though the recipe can vary from equal amounts of sugar and egg whites to twice the amount of sugar to egg whites, the method remains the same.

It involves whisking the egg whites and sugar in a bowl to combine, then warming the mixture to 100 degrees over a water bath (hence the name "warm method"). This method dissolves the sugar into the whites to form a syrupy solution so that the egg whites reach the desired stiffness after being whipped until completely cool.

This method eliminates any doubt you might have about when to add the sugar. Although beading—tiny syrupy drops on top of a baked meringue topping—can appear as a result of overcooking the meringue, the warm method reduces the risk of beading because the sugar is completely dissolved, producing a more stable meringue.

Whether to bake or dry the meringue depends on what you need: For the meringue topping on a pie, you would bake it quickly at a higher temperature; for meringue mushrooms or disks, dry them in a low oven until crisp and chalky in appearance.

Like the cold- and warm-method meringues, an Italian meringue can remain soft or be dried until it is crisp. But Italian meringues have a higher percentage of sugar than all other meringues, so another method is required to incorporate the amount of sugar in order to make them. It involves first boiling a sugar syrup, then pouring it onto whipped egg whites. The heat of the sugar syrup immediately expands the protein-coated air cells, partially cooks them and sets the structure, thereby producing the most stable soft meringue.

An Italian meringue is perfect for adding to mousses, ice creams, sorbets, fillings, ganaches—anything that requires lasting lightness. Since it maintains its light structure and gives body to the mixture, it can substitute for gelatin or whipped cream. Italian meringue's versatility extends to the dessert's exterior too. Use it to top pies, cakes or baked Alaska.

You can pipe Classic Italian Meringue to form disks, mushrooms, swans, igloos or Beehive Vacherin (page 221). An Italian meringue's formula can be as high as 6 tablespoons sugar (75 grams) to 1 egg white (25 grams), making a crisper meringue after it has dried in the oven than the cold- or warm-method meringues. Since I usually make Italian meringue to incorporate into Bavarian cream, lemon curd or mousse or to top a dessert, I prefer a recipe with less sugar because the dessert has its own sweetness.

FLAVORING MERINGUES

SUGAR need not be the only flavoring in your meringue. Add 2 teaspoons Coffee Essence (page 269) or lemon, orange or tangerine zest before drying or baking it.

Because the primary rule in making egg-white foams is a meticulous avoidance of fat, you should add ground or melted chocolate, cocoa powder, melted butter or a nut oil only after you have formed the whipped mixture.

The addition of an ingredient changes not only the meringue's texture and flavor but also its name. Folding finely ground nuts into meringue makes it a dacquoise.

Classic Meringue

This meringue is not overly sweet so it adapts irresistibly to a variety of fillings. Folding a part of the sugar in at the end contributes to its delicate texture.

You can also pipe shells and serve them with ice cream or alone.

This is the foundation for Beehive Vacherin (page 221).

MAKES THREE OR FOUR 8-INCH DISKS

Baking Equipment: 16-inch pastry bag, ½-inch (#6) plain decorating tip, two 14-x-17-inch baking sheets

2	tablespoons (25 grams) *plus* ½ cup (100 grams) granulated sugar
¾	cup (75 grams) unsifted powdered sugar
¼	cup (50 grams) granulated sugar
⅔	cup (about 5 large) egg whites, room temperature

Baking preparations: Position one rack in lower third of oven and the second rack in upper third; preheat oven to 225 degrees.

Fit the pastry bag with the decorating tip.

Line each baking sheet with parchment paper to fit. For making disks, trace two 8-inch circles on each paper with a pencil. (For other shapes, draw the designs or pipe them directly on the paper.)

Ingredient preparations: The sugar will be added in three stages to produce maximum volume and optimum texture. Pour each quantity of sugar into three small mixing bowls so it is ready when you whip the whites.

Pour the 2 tablespoons granulated sugar into one bowl.

Pour the ½ cup granulated sugar into another bowl.

Pour the powdered sugar and the remaining ¼ cup granulated sugar in that order into a triple sifter over a third bowl and sift. Sifting the two together separates the powdered sugar particles.

Set each bowl aside. The powdered sugar gives the meringue more body for piping and requires less moisture to dissolve (granulated sugar needs more moisture).

Making the meringue: Pour the egg whites into the bowl of a heavy-duty mixer. Attach the bowl to the mixer, and with the whisk attachment, beat the whites on medium-low speed (#3) until small bubbles appear and the surface is frothy (about 30 to 45 seconds). Increase the speed to medium (#5); then pour in the 2 tablespoons granulated sugar in a steady stream. Continue whipping, until soft white peaks form, about 45 seconds. (Sugar added at this stage unites the mixture and keeps it from separating.)

Maintaining medium speed (#5), gradually add ½ cup granulated sugar in a steady stream. (The whites may appear to deflate slightly at this point, but it's only temporary. Just continue whipping, and the volume will be restored.)

Continue whipping until thick, stiff, glossy white peaks form, about 2 minutes. When a small amount rubbed between your thumb and forefinger feels smooth, not granular, indicating the sugar has dissolved and has been incorporated into the egg whites, proceed to the next step.

Detach the whisk and bowl and tap the whisk against the side of the bowl with enough force to free the excess. Sprinkle all the powdered sugar mixture over the meringue and fold the two together with a rubber spatula just until incorporated. (Overmixing causes the grains of undissolved sugar to rupture the air bubbles and decreases volume.)

Filling and piping the meringues: Without delay, scoop all the meringue into the pastry bag fitted with the decorating tip.

Before piping meringue disks, squeeze the equivalent of a half teaspoon in a corner of each baking sheet under the parchment paper to hold it in place during the piping.

Now pipe the disks as follows: Beginning in the center of the circle, pipe meringue in a continuous, widening spiral until it reaches the traced mark. Hold the pastry bag perpendicular to the baking sheet, 1½ to 2 inches above the area you are piping. Always apply enough pressure to create a string of meringue (no larger than the pastry opening) which will be directed into its place as you pipe. As you pipe, allow your body, not your arms, to move. The hands hold and apply pressure on the pastry bag while the arms stay in place next to your body. Your hand movements will be quite steady, forming the spirals inside the marked circles more easily. Lift the tip slightly to cut off the flow of meringue when you have completed a disk. Repeat the procedure until all the disks have been formed.

If the spirals do not fall neatly next to one another or if the string of meringue should abruptly break during piping, no problem. Just continue to pipe as best you can. After the meringues have dried in the oven and before you assemble the dessert, any flaws may be modified easily.

Pipe a couple of small disks 1½ inches in diameter with any extra meringue in the pastry bag on each baking sheet as samples to test if larger disks are finished drying and ready to remove from the oven.

Drying the meringues: Place baking sheets in the oven on the racks. Dry the disks in the 225-degree oven for 60 to 75 minutes, rotating pans halfway during that time to ensure even drying.

After 60 minutes, test to see if meringues are completely dried and ready to come out of the oven by removing one sample from the baking sheet. If it releases easily and, after cooling for 5 to 10 minutes, snaps in half and is uniformly crisp, the other meringues are done. Don't worry if the meringue disks are still in the oven; an additional few minutes will not harm them. (The drying time and testing are relevant for other shapes, too.)

Storing the meringues: If the sample indicates the meringue is sufficiently dry, remove the baking sheets from the oven and place on racks for about 30 minutes, or until cool. Then slide an 8-inch metal icing spatula under the shapes, releasing them from the paper.

To keep the meringues crisp, store them at room temperature in airtight metal containers for up to 1 week.

Baker's Notes

☞ Fresh egg whites are very important in meringues. Their fresh protein whips up better and gives strength to the air bubbles' framework.

☞ Don't hesitate to use this recipe to pipe individual shapes, such as ovals, small balls, letters of the alphabet, swans—anything your imagination dictates. Whatever you pipe will not change shape in the oven. Piping is easy with this recipe because of its high proportion of sugar. It's the sugar in the meringue that stabilizes the air bubbles.

☞ This meringue must be dried in the oven to evaporate its moisture slowly. Should the oven temperature be too high, the outside of the meringue will expand rapidly, drying and setting its shape quickly. The inside, on the other hand, will not dry, will be underdone, chewy and sticky and the outside will separate from the inside.

☞ If it is rainy or humid, you may have to dry the meringue in the oven 15 to 30 minutes longer than on a dry day.

☞ If the meringue begins to color, your oven temperature is too high and the sugar is caramelizing.

Chocolate Meringue

COCOA POWDER not only changes Classic Meringue's flavor but makes it less sweet. Chocolate Meringue Mushrooms make wonderful gifts at Christmas. They are used to decorate Cranberry-Chocolate Eistorte. You can also pipe shells to serve with vanilla ice cream or frozen yogurt.

This is the foundation for Chambéry Lemon Torte (page 217).

MAKES FOUR 8-INCH DISKS OR 5 DOZEN CHOCOLATE MERINGUE MUSHROOMS

Baking Equipment: Two 12-x-15½-x-½-inch baking sheets, 16-inch pastry bag, ½-inch (#6) round decorating tip

2	tablespoons (25 grams) *plus* ½ cup (100 grams) granulated sugar
¾	cup (75 grams) unsifted powdered sugar
¼	cup (50 grams) granulated sugar
⅓	cup (40 grams) unsifted cocoa powder
⅔	cup (about 5 large) egg whites, room temperature

Make the meringue as for Classic Meringue on page 214, with the following differences:

Preparations: Preheat oven to 225 degrees. After placing the granulated sugar in separate bowls, pour the powdered sugar, remaining ¼ cup granulated sugar and cocoa powder in that order into a triple sifter over a third bowl, and sift; set aside until whipping the whites.

Making meringue disks: Pipe as directed on page 215.

Making meringue mushrooms: Fill the pastry bag, fitted with the decorating tip, with the meringue mixture and pipe a small dot under a corner of the parchment paper to anchor it to each baking sheet. Pipe out cap shapes, holding the bag at a 30-degree angle to the baking sheet and slightly above it.

Pipe an assortment of cap sizes, ½ inch to 1½ inches in diameter for variety, spacing them about ½ inch apart. Squeeze on the pastry bag, allowing the meringue to flow into a round shape, without moving the tip's position, then stopping pressure when the desired width is reached. To release the meringue and avoid a point, rotate the tip in a clockwise motion and lift the bag away.

To pipe out the stems, hold the pastry bag perpendicular to the parchment-lined baking sheet with the tip about ¼ inch above. Squeeze and hold this position to build a small base of meringue; then lift the pastry tip up about 1 inch, still applying pressure on the bag. Stop when you achieve the desired height. The stem sizes depend upon the amount of pressure you exert on the bag. Do not worry if caps and stems are not perfectly shaped.

Bake in the preheated 225-degree oven for 50 to 65 minutes, or until the caps and stems can be removed without sticking to the parchment. Remove the baking sheets to cooling racks. If you are not using the mushrooms the day they are baked, store the pieces in an airtight metal container for up to 1 week.

Baker's Notes

↪ When forming disks with the pastry bag, I find it is easier if I move my body while holding my arms against my sides. This provides a steady foundation and more control for forming spirals for the disks. This technique also applies to piping designs or writing on the tops of cakes.

↪ I pipe 7½-inch disks because they expand and dry to 8-inch circles in the oven.

↪ If you are making Chocolate Meringue Mushrooms, you'll need 1 recipe Classic Royal Icing for assembling and decorating them.

Decorating and storing the mushrooms: With the tip of a small paring knife, gently bore a small hole in the underside of each cap. Set upright on a baking sheet.

Make a small paper cone as directed on page 244. Then prepare Classic Royal Icing as directed on page 269. Fill the paper cone with 2 to 3 tablespoons of the icing and decorate many of the mushroom caps with dots, giving a whimsical polka-dot effect. Dry the icing for about 30 to 60 minutes. (To speed the drying, place the baking sheet of decorated caps in a preheated 200-degree oven for 10 to 15 minutes.) Cover the remaining icing with plastic wrap to prevent its drying.

To attach the stems to the caps, pipe a dot of icing into the hole; then press the stem tip to fit. Place the assembled mushrooms on a baking sheet until the icing has dried.

If you are not serving the mushrooms right away, store them in airtight metal containers at room temperature.

Chambéry Lemon Torte

MERINGUE takes two forms in this dessert: a crunchy cake layer and a fluffy frosting. The combination of chocolate meringue layers and lemon filling is subtle and refreshing.

MAKES 10 TO 12 SERVINGS

Decorating Equipment: 8-inch stiff cardboard round, 14-inch pastry bag, ³⁄₁₆-inch (#1) round decorating tip, cake decorating turntable, sugar shaker, template of a lemon, optional (page 131)

	Three 8-inch disks Chocolate Meringue (page 216)
1	**recipe Classic Lemon Curd (page 258)**
½	**recipe Classic Italian Meringue (page 265)**
4	**ounces (1 stick) unsalted butter, room temperature**
1	**cup (100 grams) unsifted cocoa powder**
¼	**cup (25 grams) unsifted powdered sugar**

Advance preparations: If using, prepare a template from acetate as directed on page 131. Trace a picture of a lemon with leaves from an art book.

Prepare Chocolate Meringue disks as directed on page 215. (Pipe three 7½-inch circles on the baking parchment. As the meringues dry in the oven, they will expand to 8 inches.) Dry them in a preheated 225-degree oven for 60 to 75 minutes, rotating the pan halfway through to ensure even drying. Store in an airtight container at room temperature until ready to use.

Prepare Classic Lemon Curd as directed on page 258. Cover the surface with plastic wrap, pierce the wrap to allow steam to escape and refrigerate. Remove from the refrigerator 1 hour before making the buttercream and frosting to remove its chill.

Using the 8-inch cardboard round as a guide, trim any uneven edges from the meringue disks with a small paring knife. Rest the knife against the cardboard as you cut. Also, if a disk is not level, trim any unevenness from its surface. Then place one disk on the card-

Baker's Notes

☞ This dessert may be prepared over a 3-day period.
First day: Prepare Chocolate Meringue disks and Classic Lemon Curd.
Second day: Finish lemon buttercream, prepare Italian Meringue and assemble dessert.
Third day: Serve the dessert.

☞ This dessert should be made the day before serving. The flavors mellow, and the meringue softens perfectly.

☞ Italian Meringue is used to lighten the frosting since it will hold up longer than others.

☞ If a meringue disk should break, don't worry. No one will know. Merely patch it together like a puzzle piece when you assemble the dessert.

board for easier handling of the dessert.

Prepare recipe for Classic Italian Meringue as directed on page 265. (You will only need ½ recipe for this torte.)

Making and piping the buttercream: Divide the lemon curd in half; reserve one-half (¾ cup) in a 3-quart mixing bowl for the frosting.

Place the butter in a 1½-quart mixing bowl. With an electric hand mixer, whip on medium speed (#5) for 40 to 45 seconds, or until light and fluffy. With the mixer running, add the lemon curd, a tablespoon at a time, and continue whipping until smooth. If necessary to achieve a smooth consistency, increase the speed and whip until the mixture is homogeneous.

Fit the 14-inch pastry bag with a ³⁄₁₆-inch (#1) round decorating tip and fill it with the lemon buttercream.

Lift the meringue disk, pipe a dot of buttercream on the cardboard ½ inch from one of its edges, and reposition the meringue disk back on it. (This dot of buttercream holds the dessert on the cardboard once it firms in the refrigerator. It is not centered on the cardboard so the majority of the slices release easily when cut without sticking in the center.)

Pipe thin strings of buttercream, as in forming a meringue disk, in a continuous spiral over the meringue; top with a second disk. (Piping distributes a very thin layer of buttercream more evenly and more efficiently in this case than if the buttercream were spread with a metal spatula.) Press down lightly with fingertips so the two layers are level and adhere. Repeat the piping procedure, and place the last chocolate disk on top, upside down. (The flat side is now face up and will provide the most level finish for this dessert.) Press the top meringue disk down gently to adhere.

Making the frosting: When the Italian Meringue is cool, remove ½ cup from the bowl containing the ½ recipe and discard. (Unless it is removed, it will make the lemon frosting too light and sweet.)

Spoon the remaining meringue into the bowl with the reserved lemon curd and fold together with a rubber spatula. The consistency resembles that of a stiff meringue or whipped cream. Place the dessert on the turntable.

Scoop all the frosting on top of the dessert. Using an 8-inch flexible metal icing spatula, maneuver the frosting, smoothing from the top and down the sides. Rotate the turntable as you work to finish the cake neatly and smoothly.

Refrigerate the dessert for at least 12 hours so that the flavors blend and the meringue softens slightly from the moisture in the filling and frosting.

Serving the torte: Pour the cocoa into the sugar shaker. Hold the dessert over the sink, and dust its sides and top with the cocoa. Pour the powdered sugar into a small sieve. Lay the template of the lemon on top of the dessert, if using, and lightly dust it with the powdered sugar. Remove the template. Return the dessert to the refrigerator for up to 2 hours before serving.

Cranberry-Chocolate Eistorte

THIS DESSERT is both delicious and unusual. The mushrooms are optional, but give it personality. Cranberry is too special a taste to reserve for the holidays. Freeze the berries, and enjoy the pairing of chocolate and cranberry out of season. The coolness and supersmoothness of this dessert make it a welcome finale to a summer meal.

MAKES 6 TO 8 SERVINGS

Decorating Equipment: 8-inch round straight-sided cake pan, 8-inch stiff cardboard round, cake decorating turntable

Chocolate Meringue Mushrooms, optional (page 216)

Cranberry Sorbet
1 ¾	cups water
2	cups (400 grams) granulated sugar
12	ounces (3 cups) cranberries, washed and picked over
3	tablespoons lemon juice
½	cup orange juice

1	recipe Chocolate Whipped Cream (page 288)

Advance preparations: Prepare Chocolate Meringue Mushrooms, if using, as directed on page 216. Store in an airtight metal container at room temperature until ready to use.

Making the sorbet: Place the water and sugar in a heavy 2½-quart saucepan over medium-low heat. Stir occasionally until the sugar dissolves. Pour in the cranberries, increase heat to medium and bring to a boil. Continue to boil, stirring occasionally and reducing the heat if necessary to prevent an overflow, until all the cranberries have popped and a pink foam covers the surface (about 4½ minutes). Remove from heat and let cool for 10 to 15 minutes.

☞ This dessert may be prepared over a 2-day period.
First day: Prepare Chocolate Meringue Mushrooms and cranberry sorbet.
Second day: Prepare Chocolate Whipped Cream, assemble and refreeze.

☞ You need an ice cream maker for the Cranberry Sorbet, but you can buy 1 quart of any sorbet or ice cream and substitute it if you wish.

☞ Fresh or frozen cranberries may be used.

Pour the cranberry mixture into the bowl of a food processor fitted with the steel blade (it will fit in the standard-size processor bowl), and process with on and off spurts just until the cranberries are chopped finely but not pureed (about 30 seconds). Pour into a large, shallow stainless steel bowl and refrigerate for at least 2 hours.

Place the 8-inch cake pan in the freezer, so that it will be very cold for molding the sorbet later.

When the cranberry mixture is chilled, stir in the lemon and orange juices. Then prepare the sorbet in an ice cream maker according to the manufacturer's instructions.

Scoop the sorbet into the cold pan. Smooth and level it with a rubber spatula, cover with foil and freeze it for at least 12 hours, or until firm.

Unmolding the sorbet: Choose a baking sheet that fits in the freezer and place it in the refrigerator to chill before unmolding the sorbet.

Fill a large, shallow bowl with cool water. Remove the sorbet mold from the freezer, and run a thin-bladed knife down the side of the pan and around the perimeter of the sorbet to loosen it. Hold the pan in water just to its rim for 30 to 45 seconds. Remove, tilt and rotate the pan to see if sorbet is being loosened from sides. Return the pan to the water if necessary. Remove the baking sheet from the refrigerator.

Wipe excess water from the pan and cover the sorbet with the cardboard round, then the chilled baking sheet. Invert the pan, shaking and tapping it gently until the sorbet slips out. If the surface area is slightly melted, smooth the top and sides with an 8-inch metal icing spatula. Return the sorbet to the freezer.

Making the whipped cream: Prepare Chocolate Whipped Cream as directed on page 288.

Assembling the dessert: When the Chocolate Whipped Cream is finished, remove the molded sorbet from freezer. Lift under its cardboard with the aid of a metal spatula; hold the sorbet in one hand, and with the other, coat the sides with the cream with a flexible metal icing spatula. Rotate the dessert on its cardboard and smooth the sides until they are completely frosted. Now place the dessert on the turntable, and mask the top and sides with the cream as directed on page 238.

Return the dessert to the freezer until serving time.

Serving the dessert: Garnish with Chocolate Meringue Mushrooms, if using, before serving. Serve each portion on chilled plates.

Beehive Vacherin

THIS BEAUTIFUL, whimsical meringue is functional; it insulates the ice cream inside, preventing it from melting rapidly.

MAKES 8 TO 10 SERVINGS

Baking Equipment: Two ovens, four 12-x-15½-x-½-inch baking sheets, 16-inch pastry bag, ½-inch (#6) round decorating tip, ¼-inch (#2) round decorating tip, math compass

1	recipe Classic Meringue (page 214)
1	quart ice cream, any flavor

Optional Decoration

6 to 8	meringue bees (instructions, page 222)
12 to 20	sliced almonds

Baking preparations: Fit the pastry bag with the ½-inch (#6) pastry tip.

Line the four baking sheets with parchment paper to fit. Using a compass, make circles on each baking sheet as follows:

First pan: ½-inch, 5¼-inch and 1¾-inch circles, side by side.

Second pan: two 7½-inch circles, side by side. Inside one circle, trace a 6¼-inch circle, and inside the other, draw a 5¾-inch one.

Third pan: two 7½-inch circles side by side. In one circle, draw a 4¾-inch circle, and inside the other, draw a 4½-inch one.

Fourth pan: one circle, 6¾-inches and one circle, 6¼ inches, side by side. Inside one circle, draw a 3½-inch circle, and inside the other, draw a 2½-inch one.

Position one rack in lower third of oven and second rack in upper third; preheat oven to 225 degrees. Repeat with other oven.

Advance preparations: Prepare Classic Meringue as directed on page 214. Reserve about 1 cup in a small bowl, cover with plastic wrap, and refrigerate for final assembling of beehive. (This is the adhesive for "gluing" the beehive together; refrigerating it will slow down its natural inclination to break down.)

Without delay, scoop the remaining meringue into the pastry bag. Squeeze the equivalent of a half teaspoon in a corner of each baking sheet under the parchment paper to hold it in place.

Piping the meringue: Place the first baking sheet on the work surface. Beginning in the center of one of the 7½-inch circles, pipe a string of meringue in a continuous, widening spiral until the outer edge reaches the traced pencil line. Lift the tip slightly to cut off the flow of meringue when completed. (This disk forms the base of the beehive.) Repeat this procedure of spiraling in the 1¾-inch circle, but overlap the strings on top of each other slightly to form a tip; this will be the top of the beehive.

The remaining circles are rings of meringue rather than solid disks. Using the circle as a guide, pipe a continuous string of meringue around another circle. Stop applying pressure on the meringue-filled pastry bag and at the same time, lift the tip slightly when you return to the starting point, to cut the flow of meringue. Repeat until all other circles have been traced with the meringue. You should have one 7½-inch disk and 13 other rings of varying diameters, plus the top.

Making the optional decoration: To form the decorative bees, if using, slip the ¼-inch (#2) tip directly over the outside of the other tip, and holding it in place with the hand that guides the pastry bag, pipe six ½-inch-long ovals of meringue on one of the baking sheets. Tuck a slice of almond on each side of an oval to resemble the bee's wings. Repeat for remaining bees.

Finally, pipe a few very small disks or ovals on a baking sheet as samples to test if beehive disk and rings are finished drying.

Baker's Notes

☞ This dessert may be prepared over a 2-day period.
First day: Prepare meringue rings.
Second day: Assemble the dessert.

☞ You may want to refer to my suggestions for piping with a pastry bag on page 243.

☞ To draw circles of varying diameters on parchment paper, use a simple compass, available at stationery or department stores.

☞ Different-size rings of meringue will be piped, some inside the others to save baking sheet space. (This will require 2 ovens and 4 baking sheets.) After the rings are dried and cooled, they will be put together in a graduated stack to resemble a beehive.

☞ Should a meringue ring break while you are assembling the dessert, don't worry; just fit it in place as though it were a jigsaw puzzle.

Baking the meringue: Bake for 1 hour, rotating the baking sheets after 30 minutes to ensure even drying. Check one of the samples of meringue. If it releases easily from the baking sheet and after cooling for 5 minutes, appears uniformly crisp inside and out when snapped in half, the other meringues are done.

Cooling the meringues: Remove the baking sheets from the ovens and place on racks to cool completely. (If you are making the meringues in advance, store them in airtight containers at room temperature until assembly.)

Assembling the dessert: Preheat oven to 225 degrees; place a rack in the lowest position possible.

Two parts will be assembled to make the beehive: the base or the bowl, which will hold the scoops of ice cream, and the lid, which will form the top of the beehive.

Gently scrape any uneven areas on the rings with a small knife so the fit will be as smooth and neat as possible.

Scoop the reserved 1 cup meringue into a pastry bag fitted with the ¼-inch (#2) tip. Place the 7½-inch meringue disk on one half of a baking sheet. (The lid portion of the beehive will be formed next to it later.) Pipe a row of small meringue dots around the edge of the disk. Place one of the 7½-inch meringue rings upside down on top of the disk in such a way that the dots of meringue "glue" the two together. Repeat the procedure, gluing the remaining 7½-inch rings together with dots of meringue. Make sure that each ring is layered upside down and centered as it is stacked; this will make a smoother fit of all rings together. To ensure a neat finish, press each ring down gently with your fingertips so it will adhere to the raw meringue.

Once the four 7½-inch rings have been glued to form the base, glue the remaining rings together to form the top of the beehive. Place the 6¾-inch ring on the other half of the baking sheet. Beginning with the next smallest size and decreasing in size thereafter, glue the remaining 9 rings together with dots of meringue. Remember to press down slightly on each ring to ensure that each sticks to the other. Check your work so the beehive is aligned correctly and appears straight.

Place 3 to 5 bees at various spots on the beehive with dots of raw meringue.

Drying the dessert: Place the two parts of the beehive (the base and its lid) in the oven and dry them for 1 hour. Remove from the oven and cool.

Serving the dessert: A few hours before serving, place scoops of ice cream on a foil-lined baking sheet and keep on a freezer shelf until serving time.

Before serving, place the base of the beehive on a serving plate. Mound the ice cream scoops inside and top with the lid.

Dacquoise

ADACQUOISE is meringue paste with the addition of fine-ground nuts. Other names for this mixture are japonais or broyage. This nutty meringue paste is usually formed into thin shapes by piping, stenciling or drawing free-form, and then is dried in the oven until crisp. The dacquoise is always used in combination with cakes and creams to create a dessert that melts smoothly in your mouth. I make my dacquoise using the Cold Method, but the Warm Method (see page 212) works well too.

The proportion of nuts and sugar to egg whites can vary to produce different textures. Classic Dacquoise (page 225) is similar to Classic Meringue (page 214) with the addition of some ground nuts. As with meringues, the more sugar incorporated, the less quickly the egg-white foam will break down and become runny. Folding ground nuts into Classic Dacquoise without affecting the volume of the egg-white foam is easy. Because the proportion of nuts is low in relation to the ratio of sugar to egg whites, you can dry the mixture as though it were a meringue.

In Basler Dacquoise Sheet, on the other hand, more ground nuts and less sugar are used to create a nuttier taste. You can bake this mixture to set its structure quickly since it is low in sugar. Traditionally, meringues are baked in a low oven, but in this instance, a slow drying process would dissolve all the foaminess before its structure set. The faster baking results in a stronger dacquoise with a glorious toasted-nut flavor. I like my dacquoise crisp and thin, but if you pipe the mixture thicker before baking, you will get a chewier result, similar to a macaroon.

A small amount of melted butter may be folded into a dacquoise that has a large amount of ground nuts in relation to the sugar and egg whites to make it less brittle and more tender. Though cornstarch and flour in a dacquoise recipe can stabilize the egg-white foam and contribute texture, you'll find these two ingredients unnecessary if you whip the egg whites correctly. (You may want to review my tips for whipping egg-white foams successfully on page 149.)

Classic Dacquoise

Tᴏ HIS IS a variation of a classic meringue, with the addition of nuts. The nuts add flavor and texture and disguise some of the sweetness.

This is the foundation for Chocolate Délice (page 227).

Mᴀᴋᴇꜱ ᴛʜʀᴇᴇ 8-ɪɴᴄʜ ᴅɪꜱᴋꜱ

Baking Equipment: One 14-x-17-x-½-inch baking sheet, one 12-x-15½-x-½-inch baking sheet, 16-inch pastry bag, ½-inch (#6) round decorating tip

- ⅓   cup (2 ounces) unblanched almonds
- ¼   cup (50 grams) *plus* 2 tablespoons *plus* ⅔ cup (130 grams) granulated sugar
- ⅔   cup (5 large) egg whites, room temperature

Baking preparations: Position one rack in lower third of oven and second rack in upper third; preheat oven to 225 degrees.

After fitting the pastry bag with the tip and lining the two baking sheets with parchment paper to fit, draw three 8-inch circles, using a saucepan lid or cake pan as a guide.

Ingredient preparations: Using a nut grinder or rotary-type grater, grind the nuts until they have the consistency of cornmeal; you need ⅔ cup ground. Combine with the ¼ cup sugar in a small bowl and set aside.

Pour the 2 tablespoons sugar into another small bowl.

Pour the ⅔ cup sugar into a third bowl.

Making the dacquoise: Pour the egg whites into the bowl of a heavy-duty mixer. Attach the bowl to the mixer and with the whisk attachment, whip the whites on low speed (#2) for 30 to 45 seconds, or until small bubbles appear and the surface is frothy. Increase the speed to medium (#5); then pour in the 2 tablespoons sugar in a steady stream. Continue whipping until soft, white peaks form, about 45 seconds.

Maintaining medium speed, gradually add the ⅔ cup sugar in a steady stream. Continue whipping until a small amount rubbed between your thumb and forefinger feels smooth, not granular, about 2 minutes.

Detach the whisk and bowl and tap the whisk against the side of the bowl with enough force to free excess. Sprinkle the almond-sugar mixture over the meringue and fold the two together with a rubber spatula.

Piping the dacquoise: Without delay, scoop all the mixture into the pastry bag fitted with the decorating tip.

Beginning in the center of a marked circle, pipe meringue in a continuous, widening spiral until the outer edge reaches the pencil line. Lift the tip slightly to cut off the flow of meringue when you have completed piping. Repeat on the other circles.

Pipe a couple of disks about 1½ inches in diameter with any extra dacquoise mixture in the pastry bag on each baking sheet. These are samples to test if larger disks are dried and ready to be removed from the oven.

Baker's Notes

☞ It is especially important that the nuts be ground properly so they will be as fine as cornmeal and dry, not oily.

☞ You may substitute another nut for the almond. The important thing is that you use the same amount that the recipe specifies once the nuts are ground (⅔ cup ground) and that you use firm nuts that grind well. In substituting, keep in mind that the nuts should be as close to cornmeal consistency and as dry as possible after they are ground. First measure them out using the weight given in the recipe, then grind as I recommend.

☞ You can pipe large or small disks with this mixture.

Drying the dacquoise: Place in the preheated oven and bake for 65 to 75 minutes, or until dry but not colored. Test for doneness by examining the sample. If it releases easily and, after cooling for 5 to 10 minutes, snaps in half and is uniformly crisp, the other disks are done. This additional time in the oven will not harm the dacquoise. Please note that while the disks are warm, they will not always be crisp when removed from the oven. If they have baked the proper time, they will become crisp after cooling.

Cooling and storing the dacquoise: If the sample indicates the meringue is sufficiently dried, remove it from the oven. Lift the disks with the parchment paper and transfer to a large rack to cool completely. When they are cool, slip a spatula under each disk to release it. If you want to store the disks for some time before using, merely cut around the parchment paper with kitchen scissors and place them in airtight metal containers. This gives more support to the disks and keeps them from breaking. Store at room temperature for no more than 1 week.

Basler Dacquoise Sheet

A THIN, crisp, not too sweet dacquoise, full of flavorful ground nuts—an asset to a grand multilayered dessert.

This is the foundation for Gift Box Gâteau (page 229).

MAKES ONE 12-x-15 ½-x-½-INCH SHEET

Baking Equipment: 12-x-15½-x-½-inch baking sheet

5	ounces (1 scant cup) unblanched almonds
½	cup (100 grams) *plus* 3 tablespoons (35 grams)granulated sugar
½	cup (4 large) egg whites, room temperature

Baking preparations: Position rack in lower third of oven; preheat oven to 350 degrees.

Line the baking sheet with aluminum foil, leaving a 2-inch overhang at each short end of the pan.

Ingredient preparations: Using a nut grinder or a rotary-type grater, grind the nuts until they are the consistency of cornmeal; you need 1½ cups ground.

Combine the ground almonds and ½ cup sugar in a small bowl; set aside.

Pour the 3 tablespoons sugar into another small bowl.

Making the dacquoise: Pour the egg whites into the bowl of a heavy-duty mixer. Attach the bowl to the mixer and with the whisk attachment, whip the whites on low speed (#2) until small bubbles appear and the surface is frothy (about 30 to 45 seconds). Increase the speed to medium (#5); then pour in 1 teaspoon of the 3 tablespoons sugar. Continue whipping until soft white peaks form (about 45 to 60 seconds). Then add in a steady stream the remaining tablespoons sugar and whip until thicker, smooth white (not dry or granular) peaks form (about 1½ minutes).

Detach the whisk and bowl, and with the whisk attachment, whip the mass by hand for 5 to 10 seconds until the egg whites foam. Sprinkle the almond-sugar mixture over the meringue, and fold the two together with a rubber spatula, just until combined.

Baking the dacquoise: Using a rubber spatula, scrape the mixture down the center of the baking sheet in a strip 4 to 5 inches long. Spread as evenly as possible with an 8-inch flexible metal icing spatula. Direct the batter with the spatula as though the spatula were your hand. Use the sides of the pan as a guide. The mixture should be level with them.

Check the uniformity by inserting a toothpick at various points. Begin at the corners and work toward the center. The depth indicated on the toothpick should be the same at each point; adjust if necessary.

Bake for 25 to 30 minutes, or until light brown and crisp. Remove from the oven, and with a thin-bladed knife, gently release the dacquoise that might be sticking to the sheet. Pull up on the foil overhangs, one at a time, to release the foil from the edges. Finally, loosen the foil from the bottom by carefully lifting up on the flaps. Transfer the dacquoise sheet to a large cooling rack.

(The dacquoise has to be removed at this time because as it cools, it becomes crisper, making cracking and breaking quite possible.) Cool for about 30 minutes.

Storing the dacquoise: Leave the dacquoise on its baking sheet and cover it with foil for up to 1 day. (This is not recommended if you live in a very humid climate.)

Chocolate Délice

Nutty dacquoise layers are interspersed with dark chocolate and whipped cream and covered with sweetened toasted almonds. This attractive dome-shaped dessert must be made ahead and frozen before serving.

Makes 6 to 8 servings

Decorating Equipment: 8-inch stiff cardboard round, cake decorating turntable

1   recipe Classic Dacquoise (page 225)
1   recipe Decorator's Sliced Almonds (page 270)

Ganache Cream
    4   ounces semisweet chocolate
    ⅓   cup (3 ounces) cup heavy cream

Filling and Frosting
    1 ½   cups (12 ounces) heavy cream
    ⅓   cup (65 grams) granulated sugar
    1   teaspoon vanilla

Advance preparations: Prepare Classic Dacquoise as directed on page 225. Prepare

☞ This dacquoise is full of ground nuts, producing a denser mixture than Classic Dacquoise (page 225).

☞ It bakes at a higher temperature than Classic Meringue or Classic Dacquoise because there is less sugar, and it sets more quickly than other mixtures with more sugar, which slows setting. This higher temperature also toasts the nuts and produces a wonderful flavor.

☞ Foil rather than baking parchment is used on the baking sheet since the dacquoise bakes quite crisp and foil makes its removal easier.

☞ Don't be afraid of manipulating this mixture while spreading it as evenly as possible on the baking sheet before baking. You don't have to rush.

☞ The cooling time is short so a dessert can be assembled soon after baking it.

Understanding Cakemaking

Decorator's Sliced Almonds as directed on page 270. Store in an airtight metal container until ready to use.

Making Ganache Cream and frosting: When ready to assemble the dessert, prepare Ganache Cream by chopping the chocolate into matchstick-size pieces, then placing them in a 1-quart mixing bowl. Pour the ⅓ cup heavy cream into a 1-quart saucepan and heat just to boiling. Pour the cream over the chocolate and stir with a whisk until the mixture is glossy and smooth. Set aside to cool.

Whip the 1½ cups heavy cream with the sugar and vanilla in a 3-quart bowl or the bowl of a heavy-duty mixer until soft peaks form and the beaters make tracks in the bowl that stay in place but do not move to close (piping stage, page 240). Store the whipped cream in the refrigerator until the ganache is cooler and has a spreading consistency.

Assembling the dessert: Using the 8-inch cardboard round as a guide, trim any uneven edges from one of the dacquoise disks with a small paring knife. Rest the knife against the cardboard as you cut.

For the second disk, use a 7-inch saucepan lid as a guide to reduce its 8-inch diameter. (This reduction is merely for the sake of drama; it creates a natural curve which, when frosted with whipped cream, will form a dome shape.)

Now check if each disk is level; trim with the knife if necessary. Place the 8-inch dacquoise disk on the cardboard round.

Decorating the cake: Spread the surface of both dacquoise disks with ganache, using a rubber spatula. Remove the whipped cream from the refrigerator; since it has been in the refrigerator for a while, whisk it briefly to unify the whipped mass again. Spread the larger disk with some of the cream, about ¾ cup. Place the 7-inch dacquoise layer on top, pressing gently to level it.

Place the dessert on the turntable. Spread the remaining cream over the top and sides with a flexible metal icing spatula. To finish the dome shape, rotate the turntable with one hand, while moving the spatula from the bottom of the dessert upward along its contour to the center top. Continue this procedure, forming the dome.

Place Decorator's Sliced Almonds on a baking sheet. Hold the cake in one hand directly over the pan filled with almonds. Tilt the cake slightly, and with the other hand, gently press the nuts into the cream. Rotate the dessert until it is almost covered. Sprinkle the top to cover it completely. Press lightly with the clean blade of a metal icing spatula to ensure that the nuts adhere neatly.

Place on a baking sheet in the freezer for an hour to firm the cream. Then, to ensure the dessert is protected in the freezer, place it with its cardboard round in the top of a metal container. Now invert the bottom of the metal container and place it over the dessert. (To avoid disaster and to remind yourself of this different type of storage, mark "Top" on the inverted tin's bottom.)

Serving the dessert: Remove from the freezer to the refrigerator up to 2 hours before serving.

Gift Box Gâteau

Tᴴɪꜱ ᴜɴɪQᴜᴇ cake for a wedding, anniversary or any other celebration features thin layers of dacquoise, kirsch-soaked génoise and a combination buttercream-pastry cream. The cake is then coated with dacquoise crumbs and finished with a ribbon.
Mᴀᴋᴇꜱ 12 ᴛᴏ 14 ꜱᴇʀᴠɪɴɢꜱ

Decorating Equipment: Stiff cardboard, cake decorating turntable, 30-inch-long ½-inch-wide gold polyester ribbon, optional

	One Basler Dacquoise Sheet (page 226)
½	**recipe Classic Buttercream (page 260)**
1	**recipe Classic Pastry Cream (page 248)**
6	**tablespoons Soaking Syrup (page 302)**
	One Génoise Sheet (page 117)
3	**tablespoons kirsch**
⅔	**cup Basler Dacquoise Sheet crumbs (page 226)**

Advance preparations: Prepare Basler Dacquoise Sheet as directed on page 226; use a large metal spatula to free it from the baking sheet, to lift under it and to remove it to a large rack to cool. If you are assembling dessert the next day, lift it back onto baking sheet after it is completely cool and cover it with aluminum foil.

Prepare Classic Buttercream as directed on page 260; refrigerate it if you are using it the next day.

Prepare Classic Pastry Cream as directed on page 248; cover its surface with plastic wrap and refrigerate until ready to use.

Prepare Soaking Syrup as directed on page 302.

At least 1 hour before assembling the dessert, prepare Génoise Sheet as directed on page 117 If you are assembling the dessert the next day, cover the génoise with aluminum foil after it has cooled completely. Before assembling, invert it onto another baking sheet, care-

Baker's Notes

☞ This dessert may be prepared over a 2-day period.
First day: Bake Dacquoise Sheet; prepare Classic Buttercream, Classic Pastry Cream and Soaking Syrup.
Second day: Bake Génoise Sheet and assemble.

☞ This dessert is best if served the day after assembling.

☞ The combination of buttercream and pastry cream is irresistibly delicious.

Understanding Cakemaking

229

fully remove the foil and turn it over so that the sticky side faces up. Then invert the génoise right side up.

Trimming the cakes: Mark the cake with the help of a ruler into three 4-x-12-inch strips.

Mark the dacquoise as for the génoise to make three 4-x-12-inch strips. Another strip will be left over; save it for decorating the dessert. Cut the strips with a small paring knife, using short up-and-down movements, rather than pulling the blade straight through the pastry.

Making the filling and frosting: About 1 hour before using, remove the buttercream from the refrigerator to a 3-quart mixing bowl. Remove the pastry cream from the refrigerator, and stir it with a rubber spatula until it is creamier. Now stir the buttercream until it is creamy and soft, close to the pastry cream's consistency. (If you forgot to remove the buttercream in time, see page 238 for a softening technique.)

Add ¼ cup of the pastry cream to the buttercream, stirring with the rubber spatula until it has been incorporated. Continue until all the pastry cream has been added to produce a smooth mixture. Do not add the pastry cream too quickly. If the creams do not combine well, merely stir them vigorously until smooth.

Assembling the dessert: Cut a strip of stiff cardboard to fit the rectangular shape of a dacquoise strip. Have the filling and frosting at hand and pour the kirsch into the Soaking Syrup.

Place one of the dacquoise strips on the cardboard. Spread a thin layer (about ¼ cup) of the buttercream with a flexible metal icing spatula. (Should a dacquoise strip break, merely patch it together as though it were a puzzle. No one will know.) Top with a strip of génoise, and brush with 2 to 3 tablespoons of the dessert syrup.

Continue layering, ending with a strip of génoise. After assembling all the layers with the buttercream, cut any uneven edges from the dessert's short ends with kitchen scissors. (The dacquoise does not shrink in the oven as does the génoise.) Then spread a thin coating over the sides and top with the remaining buttercream.

Making the dacquoise crumbs: Place the leftover dacquoise strip on waxed paper, and roll the rolling pin over it back and forth until the crumbs resemble dry breadcrumbs or cornmeal (this will yield about ⅔ cup). Pour the crumbs onto a baking sheet, and holding the cake in one hand, pat the crumbs over the sides and top of the dessert.

Storing, decorating and serving the dessert: Refrigerate on a baking sheet for at least 2 hours, but overnight is best. After 2 hours, cover the dessert with plastic wrap to prevent any odors from penetrating it.

When the buttercream is firmer, remove the plastic wrap and, if you like, tie the ribbon around the dessert as though it were a gift. Place on a serving plate and serve.

Fillings, Frostings, Glazes, Toppings and Finishing Touches

~

Splitting and Frosting Cakes Perfectly

SPLITTING A CAKE HORIZONTALLY
INTO THICK LAYERS

THIS IS A two-step process, requiring a 2-inch paring knife and a 12-inch serrated knife. This method produces level layers, the thickness of which will always be precisely what you want them to be.

Set the cake, right side up, on your cutting surface; this gives you the most level base to work from. Place your hand on top of the cake. Then bend over the side of the cake slightly until your eyes are just above the level of the cake; this gives you the best perspective for a straight, even cut. With the 2-inch paring knife, make an incision all around the cake about 1 inch deep where you wish to split it. Move the paring knife in and out in a sawing motion, simultaneously rotating the cake with your other hand until you have circumnavigated the entire cake. Be careful to maintain the incision at the same level all around the layer.

Now place your 12-inch serrated knife, blade side in, straight into the precut path at one edge of the cake. Rotate the cake as you cut through the entire layer, pushing it into the knife while simultaneously sawing back and forth.

Left: *Marking the cake layer before splitting it.* Right: *Slicing the cake layer.*

Left: *Slicing the first thin cake layer, using yardsticks as a guide for your knife.* **Right:** *Slicing another thin layer.*

SPLITTING A CAKE HORIZONTALLY INTO THIN LAYERS

S PLITTING a cake into thin layers can make any baker nervous. When I began teaching, I looked for some sort of guide. It had to be something everyone has around the house. The answer turned out to be yardsticks. For best results, I recommend buying three yardsticks and splitting them in half to yield six 18-inch sticks, each less than ¼ inch thick. By stacking them one on top of another, you can vary the thickness of the layers you wish to cut.

To proceed, place your yardsticks equally on each side of the cake, back and front. You can place one yardstick on each side or stack two or three on each side, depending on the thickness you desire. Using the top stick as your level, rest a 12-inch serrated knife on the stick or sticks with your hand centered on the cake to steady it. (You will cut the layer bottom side first.) Saw slowly through the cake. The handle of the knife should be off the cutting surface to allow greater freedom of movement. After you have cut each layer, remove the top portion; if fragile, slide a removable quiche bottom under the just-cut thin layer and set it aside. Replace the uncut portion between the yardsticks. Be sure your knife rests on top of the yardsticks at all times to cut a level layer. Refrigerating or partially freezing the cake before you split it can facilitate your cutting the thin layers in this technique.

PREPARING THE CAKE FOR FROSTING

F ROSTING a cake to seal in freshness and to impart contrast in flavors and textures is simple. But frosting a cake for the purpose of decorating requires a smooth finish, which is somewhat more difficult to achieve.

I T IS important to begin with a level cake (see previous page for directions on how to split a cake into even layers). Besides looking more appetizing, it is easier to frost. You won't have to adjust any unevenness, and therefore, you'll need less frosting. When a level surface is especially important for your decorative finish, turn the cake right side up before you split and frost it. Remember that chilling or partially freezing some fragile cakes makes the trimming process easier and produces fewer crumbs.

Place your cake bottom on a stiff piece of cardboard (be sure the bottom is trimmed level so that it will balance on the cardboard properly). Place a dot of frosting on the cardboard; this secures the cake to the cardboard, especially if you need to refrigerate the cake after it has been frosted. I usually prefer to have the piece of cardboard equal the exact size of the cake, providing maximum access and flexibility when I frost the sides; if necessary, place the cake on top of the cardboard and trim the cardboard to the proper size with kitchen scissors. If you want a thicker coat of frosting, allow some overhang of the cardboard instead of trimming it flush; this will serve as a guide for your spatula.

If a cake is to be soaked with a dessert syrup, some pastry chefs brush the bottom of the cake with a thin coating of melted chocolate and chill it until firm before they place it on the cardboard. Even if you're not using chocolate in the dessert, the technique keeps the syrup in the cake layers instead of letting it leak through the bottom.

A sturdy decorating turntable is invaluable for frosting and decorating; it allows you to rotate the cake as you work, to reach all surfaces and to produce a smooth, beautifully finished product.

A flexible metal icing spatula, measuring about 1 inch in width, is the best utensil for spreading and manipulating frosting.

The frosting's consistency and the size and shape of the cake will dictate the method you use to frost it.

I like to frost my cakes in two stages, using two separate coats of frosting. The first coat sets a foundation for applying a smooth finish by sealing the crumbs and filling in imperfections, or it conceals a cake that is darker than its frosting. Generally, the first and second coats are the same frosting, but you may use a different type for each, such as a jam glaze beneath fondant.

When frosting a cake, you're working with two dimensions: its sides and top. When I begin, if the cake is manageable and permits it (usually 10 inches or less), I simply hold it in one hand and frost the sides first. It is best to balance the cake on your outstretched fingertips rather than on your palm; this makes it easier to rotate. This method gives excellent control and an eye-level perspective.

Applying the First Coat

This technique is used for frostings (such as buttercreams, meringues or whipped creams) that have enough body to cling to the spatula.

Apply a dab of frosting to the side of the cake. Without lifting the spatula, spread the frosting away from you in a smooth, even stroke, moving forward, around and down. The spatula should avoid touching the cake, or it will pick up and spread crumbs on the frosting. Scrape the spatula on the edge of the bowl between strokes to get rid of excess frosting and crumbs, which could make tracks and mar the finish of your final coat.

After the sides have been completely sealed with a thin coat, place the cake on your turntable. Next apply a thin coat to the top. (You never frost the top in your hand because it requires different leverage and perspective.)

If you are using a butter-based frosting, such as a buttercream, refrigerate the cake for about 30 to 60 minutes until the first coat is firm. This ensures that the second coat will spread smoothly over the first without integrating with it or smearing it.

Refrigeration is not necessary for frostings, such as Italian meringue, that must be applied right after they have been made. With these, proceed to apply the second coat immedi-

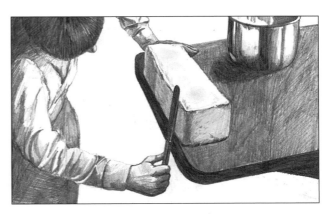

Top left: *Applying the frosting to a round cake layer.* Top right: *Smoothing the sides.*
Bottom left: *Smoothing the top.* Bottom right: *Using the edge of the counter as a guide for smoothing the frosted sides of a square or rectangular cake.*

ately since any lapse of time will change the frosting's texture and affect its spreadability.

When frosting with whipped cream, you will notice that the amount of manipulation used to apply the first coat stiffens the cream. The second coat, though applied immediately after the first, will appear to be softer and less whipped since you do not need to work it as much to achieve a silky, smooth finish.

APPLYING THE SECOND COAT

Unlike the first coat, which forms the foundation and seals your cake, the second coat is decorative. Nonetheless, the procedure for applying the frosting to the sides and top is the same. Simply repeat the steps given for applying the first coat. When you have finished putting a thin second coat on the sides, place the cake on the turntable. When you apply the second coat to the top, it should be thicker than any of the others. This thicker application allows you to make a smooth, level finish to the cake as you remove the excess frosting.

SMOOTHING THE SIDES AND TOP

To smooth the sides, rotate the turntable while you rest the spatula lightly against the cake, perpendicular to the turntable.

Fillings and Frostings

You will notice a ridge or seam where the sides of the frosting meet the top of the cake. If you were to frost first the top and then the sides, this seam would remain, but frosting the top last makes it possible to eliminate it.

Beginning at the seam, hold the spatula flat, and draw it from this outer edge of the cake to the center, using a light stroke. Now rotate the cake on its turntable an eighth of a turn, and repeat this technique with the spatula. Continue until the seam has disappeared and the top is smooth.

To tidy up the bottom edges after the cake has been completely frosted, run the flat side of the spatula underneath the cardboard and rotate the turntable.

When using a butter-based frosting, you may dip your spatula in hot water occasionally and spread it over the sides and top of the cake. The liquid evaporates, leaving a sleek, glossy finish.

FINISHING A SQUARE OR RECTANGULAR CAKE

ANY CAKE too large to hold in your hand must be frosted on either a counter or a turntable. You proceed as for smaller cakes, frosting first each side separately and then the top. Finish the sides by placing the edge of the cake parallel to the counter edge. Rest your spatula perpendicular to the edge and draw it against the cake's side with a steady stroke. The counter edge serves as your guide. Slip the spatula under the cardboard, lift, and turn the cake to finish its other sides in the same way. Then smooth the top as previously directed.

FINISHING WITH SOFT FROSTINGS

SOME FROSTINGS, such as those that have had whipped cream folded into them, are so soft that you cannot pick them up on a spatula to apply first and second coats. With these, one layer of frosting is thick enough to hide any flaws and give a soft, smooth finish. Because of their texture, it is easier and less messy to apply these frostings on a turntable. Pour most of the frosting on top of a cake in its center. Then work from the top, and draw the excess down over the sides until the cake is covered. Smooth the sides and top with the aid of the flexible metal icing spatula and turntable as previously directed.

SPREADING THE DIFFERENT FROSTINGS

BUTTERCREAM

FRESHLY MADE buttercream is very light and fluffy since you have just incorporated a lot of air into it. This consistency makes it easy to spread in a thin layer, giving you the advantage of needing less frosting to work with, making your dessert less rich.

However, there are times when it is more convenient to prepare the buttercream in advance and refrigerate it until you are ready to use it. If this is the case, allow the buttercream to stand at room temperature for about 1 hour; then mix it together with a rubber spatula until smooth. Or use the following method to bring it to a smooth and very spreadable consistency.

Place chunks of the amount of buttercream you need in the bowl of a heavy-duty mixer. Place this bowl over a shallow pan, such as a 10-inch skillet, filled with 1 inch of hot tap water (120 degrees). When the buttercream begins to melt around the edges of the bowl, remove it from the water, wipe the bowl dry and then attach it to the mixer. (Your goal is to bring the buttercream to a thin, spreading consistency resembling mayonnaise rather than the airy, whipped consistency of freshly made buttercream.) Using the paddle attachment, mix the pieces of buttercream on low speed (#2) until the mixture is homogeneous and smooth (about 1 to 2 minutes). If it is still too firm, repeat the hot-water process. Don't be alarmed if the buttercream looks curdled while you work it; increase your mixing speed (#3 or #4) just until it is smooth.

When the buttercream reaches a soft, satiny, smooth consistency resembling mayonnaise, it is ready to apply to the cake.

WHIPPED CREAM

HEAVY CREAM must have at least 30 percent butterfat content, but 36 to 40 percent butterfat whips lighter. Heavy cream whips best when the bowl and beaters (or whisk) are chilled; the friction of whipping may warm the cream and begin turning it into butter. This is especially true for large amounts because the longer you must whip cream to reach the proper consistency, the easier it is for it to loose its chill. You may avoid this either by whipping large quantities of heavy cream over a bowl of ice water to keep it cold all during the whipping process or by whipping it in two stages: first, whipping it until the cream begins to thicken but forms no peaks and refrigerating it for up to 3 hours, and second, just prior to using it, whipping it to the desired stage of thickness. I prefer whipping any amount exceeding 2 cups in a heavy-duty mixer with the whisk attachment. For small amounts (up to 2 cups), I prefer whipping it by hand or an electric hand mixer in a chilled, deep 1½-quart bowl. A small amount of heavy cream doesn't take long to thicken (about 2 to 3 minutes), so whipping just before using it poses no problems.

But no matter which method I choose to whip the cream, I always finish the process by hand with a whisk. This gives me control over the cream's finish, allowing me to stop and test for the desired degree of thickness. I can also scrape the sides of the bowl more efficiently than with an electric mixer, thus uniting the entire mixture.

I add granulated sugar and vanilla *before* whipping; I've never experienced a problem with the sugar's dissolving or hindering the cream's development because generally I use no more than 2 tablespoons of sugar per cup of cream. (I do not recommend using powdered sugar because the cornstarch in it affects taste and texture.)

Even after the cream has been whipped to the desired consistency, any kind of manipulation—whether folding, filling a pastry bag, piping or spreading—will continue to thicken it.

A heavy cream with 30 percent butterfat content does not keep its body after being whipped. Generally, it's difficult to determine the butterfat content of heavy cream without consulting directly with the specific dairy. If the whipped cream you put on your cake loses its shape and begins to appear runny after being refrigerated for a couple of hours, you can add a small amount of gelatin to the whipped cream the next time to stabilize the emulsion. For 1 cup heavy cream, sprinkle ½ teaspoon powdered gelatin over 1 tablespoon cold water. When the gelatin has softened, place it over very low heat just to dissolve it. Whip the cream to the desired consistency; then fold about ¼ cup of the cream into the gelatin mixture. Pour this into the whipped cream, and fold to combine. Frost the cake immediately.

How thick you whip your cream depends on what it is being used for. Will it serve as a frosting or filling? Will it be blended with the other ingredients? If you are folding it into a mixture, what stage will give the smoothest result? I find that most people think that heavy cream should always be whipped the same, no matter what its purpose: very, very thick.

The key to success in whipping cream is to bring it to just the right stage and to be able to recognize when it has reached that stage. To judge its thickness, draw a beater or whisk through the middle; this will leave a track or furrow. The stability of the track will tell you how thick the cream is.

Bavarian Stage: This stage requires the least amount of whipping. You manipulate the cream until it just begins to thicken; it will not stick to the beater, but rather drips back into the bowl and quickly mixes into the rest of the cream. Any track made in the Bavarian stage will melt quickly. Cream at this stage is used for folding into other ingredients, such as mousses, to impart lightness to texture.

Chantilly Stage: This cream is whipped a little longer than for the Bavarian; it will cling softly to the beater. It should be thick enough to create swirls in the bowl but liquid enough to move if the bowl is tilted. It has more body than the Bavarian stage, though any track you make in it will soften almost immediately. This cream might accompany a slice of cake or be folded into Orange Sabayon Frosting (page 268) to frost Duchess Cake (page 203).

Decorating Stage: This cream is whipped beyond the Chantilly stage, and as its name implies, it is usually (but not always) used for decorating or frosting. When whipped, it should form soft peaks and have enough body to be lifted onto a spatula without falling off. The track made in it will close very slowly but not completely.

Piping Stage: This cream is a little stiffer, with the track staying in place awhile, then moving only slightly. The peaks should still be soft but more defined. This cream is primarily used for piping, but this amount of body is necessary in assembling some desserts. When you pipe with whipped cream, the smaller the tip you use, the less you should whip it, since squeezing it through a small opening continues to manipulate the cream. You need body for piping, but not as much as you may think to create the desired amount of detail.

GLAZES

GLAZES may be used alone or as base coats for other frostings. A glaze can give a cake a smooth finish and high sheen, seal in its moisture, fill in imperfections and add to the complexity of flavors. Because they are thin, glazes are applied differently from all other frostings.

APRICOT GLAZE

AN APRICOT glaze usually serves as the foundation for another frosting, such as fondant, a chocolate glaze or a transparent glaze. It imparts an elegant tang and a lush color, but other fruit glazes may be substituted.

My apricot glaze is made from jam or preserves that have been warmed and strained to remove any pieces of fruit. When you heat it a little, you can remove the fruit more easily before straining it through a sieve.

Place the cake (on its cardboard base) on a cooling rack over a jelly roll pan. This setup will catch any excess glaze, which is reusable. Warm the strained apricot jam until it becomes thin and liquid; then pour it in the center of the cake. Using a flexible metal icing spatula, spread the glaze to the outside edges, leaving a thin, even layer on top; then push the excess down the sides. Touch them up with the spatula to cover completely.

If your glaze is being used as a base coat, allow it to dry awhile—just until its surface is not too sticky to the touch—before you apply another glaze, such as Classic Fondant (page 302) or Chocolate-Butter Glaze (page 289). This will allow the second coat to slip over freely, retaining its own identity and not mixing with the apricot glaze.

CHOCOLATE GLAZES

A CHOCOLATE glaze may be the only glaze, applied in two coats as both sealer and finishing glaze, or a second flavor over a jam glaze or buttercream base. The function and application will depend on the type.

Sugar-Syrup-Based Chocolate Glazes: Similar to fondant, these are applied only as finishing glazes and must be used immediately after they have been made because their consistency changes as they cool. Therefore, to apply, you must pour them while they are still warm and thin.

Place the cake (on its cardboard base) on a cooling rack over a jelly roll pan. Pour the glaze onto the center of the cake, and spread it across the top with a flexible metal icing spatula, encouraging the glaze to drip down the sides. Smooth the sides quickly to cover. This provides a thin, shiny coating to the cake.

Butter-Based Chocolate Glazes: These can be used as both sealer and finishing coat on a cake. The glaze may be allowed to cool and thicken after being made; then it is applied in a thin layer with a metal spatula for a first coat. Because it is butter-based, this glaze may then be placed over a water bath until it reaches body temperature to liquefy it without harming its texture.

To glaze the cake, place it (on its cardboard base) on a cooling rack over a jelly roll pan to catch any excess, which is reusable. Pour the glaze onto the center of the cake, manipulating the metal spatula to spread it across the top in an even and thin layer, pushing the excess over the sides. Use the spatula to help cover the sides completely (see illustration page 91).

An alternate method is to pour the glaze on the center of the cake, then to lift the cake with its cardboard base about 1 inch above the cooling rack and tilt it gently back and forth until the glaze covers the top and flows over the sides. Replace the cake on the rack, and touch up the sides with a flexible metal icing spatula. This guarantees a flawless finish on top, though a bit thicker coating than the method previously described.

FONDANT

Fondant is very sweet, so only a thin coat should be applied. Since a thin coat would emphasize any imperfections in a cake, it is necessary for an apricot glaze or buttercream to be used as a foundation to ensure a smooth finish.

In order to work with fondant successfully in glazing cakes or petits fours, it must be melted and thinned to make it fluid enough to handle. You must thin it with a solution most like itself—i.e., Soaking Syrup (page 302)—to maintain its crystalline structure. (Water is too thin and would disrupt its structure.)

For best results, heat only the amount of fondant you need. Pour some Soaking Syrup into a small saucepan and heat just to warm it. Put the fondant in a small bowl or saucepan in a water bath filled with about 110-degree water. It is best to use a saucepan that will not color the fondant as you stir it. To maintain the water's temperature, place it on very low heat.

Stir the fondant with a rubber spatula until it is melted. Then add the coloring and/or flavoring. Add the syrup as needed to make the glaze thin enough for your specific purpose. If you're spreading it on top of a cake, it need not be as liquid as if you were pouring it to glaze petits fours. For best results in maintaining the fondant's crystalline structure, heat it to at least body temperature but no higher than 105 degrees. Stir slowly, keeping the fondant moving to heat it evenly, but do not whip air into it. These considerations will provide a satiny, smooth, sparkling finish.

If you are working with a buttercream foundation on a cake, chill the cake before you cover it with fondant so the warmth of the fondant won't melt the buttercream. Pour the fondant into the center of the cake; then spread it with a flexible metal icing spatula. As the fondant cools, it becomes less fluid, so work without delay.

When you glaze petits fours, these forms should be neat since any discrepancies will show through the glazed surface. You may either pour fondant over them (on a rack over a jelly roll pan) or spear them in the bottom with a fork, then dip them into the fondant.

Pastry Bag Techniques

FILLING A PASTRY BAG

When selecting a pastry bag, first choose one not too small, or you may find it difficult to keep the filling from creeping out the end as you pipe. Next, slide the decorating tip you wish to use inside it to the end. (You may need to snip the bag's opening a little to accommodate the size of your tip.) Twist the bag a few times just behind the tip, and push this twisted section into the tip itself. This seals the end of the bag so that it can be filled.

Fold the bag about halfway down to form a cuff that covers your hand. This makes filling easier and keeps your hand clean at the same time.

As a rule, you should fill a bag no more than half to two-thirds full, in order to exercise firm control over the pressure when you pipe.

There are some mixtures which benefit from having the entire recipe put into the bag at once. Cream puff pastry, for example, dries and forms a crust on its surface if left in the bowl uncovered. Putting all this mixture into the pastry bag at once protects it against the air and prevents this problem. A light, airy ladyfinger batter with its delicate structure is also best scooped all at once. If left in a bowl, it naturally begins to deflate. Then the extra manipulation used in lifting this semideflated mixture to the bag compounds the problem, and the result will be a loss in the volume and quality of your ladyfingers.

If you need assistance when filling a pastry bag with a mixture, you can brace the pastry bag inside a large glass or bowl.

USING A PASTRY BAG

ONCE THE bag is filled, twist it down to the mixture to push it into the tip; as you decorate, hold the twisted section between your thumb and forefinger. Continue to twist as the mixture lessens, always forcing it into the tip. Control of the piping process is achieved through a combination of different elements: the size of your pastry tip, the amount of pressure you apply, the speed with which you move the bag and the height at which you hold the tip. The bag is held at different angles (usually 45 degrees and 90 degrees), depending on the shape you're piping. Coordinating the amount of pressure with a steady movement of the pastry bag will ensure smooth results. The amount of pressure required will depend on the consistency of your mixture and the shape you are piping. Practice makes perfect.

Rest the tip of the bag firmly between your index and middle fingers. When changing to another tip, I frequently place this other tip over the one already inserted and hold it in position with my fingers as I pipe.

PIPING

TO MAINTAIN a steady movement needed for smooth piping, brace your arms against your body, and move slowly in the direction you are piping. A gentle pressure will create a flow of mixture the same size as your tip; heavier pressure will increase the size of the flow, making it larger than the tip. Raising the tip slightly, along with increased pressure, will make the shape not only wider but thicker. You can actually double the diameter of the mixture emerging by increasing the pressure and moving the bag slower.

PIPING LINES

HOLD THE pastry bag at a 90-degree angle as you pipe, until you have the desired length. To stop piping, release pressure on the bag; then rotate the tip in a clockwise motion and lift the bag away. Remember, the amount of pressure and the height of your tip above the surface dictate the width and thickness of the line. This technique is especially useful when piping éclairs and ladyfingers.

PIPING SPIRALS

DRAW A circle as a guide; then begin piping in its center, about 1 inch above the surface. The string of mixture emerging from the bag should be the size of the tip. Work from the center outward, surrounding the initial curl of mixture and enlarging the spiral shape by using each preceding section as your guide. To stop piping, rotate the tip and pull away gently. This technique is especially useful for meringue or sponge disks.

PIPING CIRCLES OR OVALS

Draw the size of the circle or oval as a guide. Position your tip 1½ inches above the work surface, and pipe about a 2-inch-long string of the mixture to direct it into the shape you're piping. This technique is useful when you are outlining shapes with meringue, whipped cream, etc.

PIPING SOLID SHAPES

To pipe oval forms, rest the tip of the bag at a 45-degree angle to the surface; apply enough pressure for the mixture to flow slightly larger than the tip, moving slowly so that the diameter will increase to the desired width.

To pipe circular forms, hold the pastry bag at a 90-degree angle to the surface, about ½ inch above the surface; pipe out the mixture, raising the tip as necessary, to create the height and width of your circle.

USING HANDMADE PAPER CONES

I like to use handmade paper cones if I need only a small amount of a mixture such as chocolate, royal icing or buttercream for decorating. They are quick to make and have the added advantage of being disposable. You may snip the tip of the cone off with scissors, but I find I have better results if I try to roll the tip to the size opening I need. Sometimes the cut surfaces of the opening will make squiggly rather than straight, even lines when you pipe. To make a paper cone (see illustration):

From waxed or parchment paper, cut an 11-x-8-x-8-inch triangle (or fold a square of paper into a triangle). Hold the triangle in one hand with the longest side at the bottom and the thumb of your other hand in the center.

Bring the lower left-hand corner B up to corner A and hold together to begin to form a cone.

Wrap corner C around the front of the cone until it meets point AB.

Fold ABC into the cone until the fold is level with the front to hold the paper cone together. To reinforce the corners and seam, you can tear a small tab on either side of the back middle seam. Fold this tab into the cone.

Fill the paper cone half full; fold the two sides toward the middle; fold the top down to enclose the mixture. Cut the tip if necessary before piping.

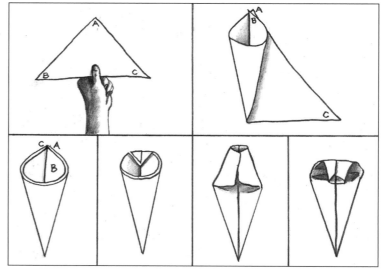

Recipes for Fillings, Frostings, Glazes, Toppings and Finishing Touches

FILLINGS

FROSTINGS, GLAZES AND TOPPINGS

*can also be used as a frosting

Classic Crème Anglaise

CRÈME ANGLAISE, also called custard sauce, is the foundation for a variety of magnificent creams: ice cream, pastry cream, soufflé and Bavarian cream. It is easy to make but requires attention.

MAKES 1 ¾ CUPS

Cooking Equipment: Mercury candy thermometer, 1½ quart mixing bowl, 1½-quart heavy-bottomed saucepan

1	cup (8 ounces) milk
¼	cup (50 grams) granulated sugar
1	vanilla bean
3	large egg yolks

Ingredient preparations: Rest a sieve on top of a 1-quart mixing bowl to strain the crème anglaise after cooking.

Pour the milk and half the sugar into a 1½-quart heavy-bottomed saucepan (the addition of some sugar raises the temperature of the milk faster and prevents the milk from scorching the pan). Split the vanilla bean in half with a small paring knife, scrape the seeds out and place them in the milk.

Making and storing the crème anglaise: Place the egg yolks in a 1-quart mixing bowl and whisk just to combine; whisk in remaining sugar.

Place the saucepan over medium heat, and bring the milk just to a boil. Turn off heat; then pour about half the milk into the egg-sugar mixture, whisking continuously until they are combined. Pour the mixture back into the saucepan; whisk to combine; then return to medium-low heat.

Stir constantly with a wooden spoon, remembering to reach the entire bottom surface of the pan. (This is a delicate moment, so do not rush the heating or the yolks may curdle.)

Cook until the candy thermometer registers 165 to 170 degrees (about 45 seconds). If you are not using a thermometer, look for steam, meaning the mixture is approaching the correct temperature. Do not allow the mixture to boil, or it will curdle. The custard should be thick enough to nap the spoon and leave a clear path when your finger is drawn down its center. Remove it from the heat, and quickly pour it through the sieve.

Set it aside for 5 to 10 minutes, stirring occasionally. Then cover and refrigerate it. It will thicken slightly as it cools.

Serve within 2 to 3 days.

Baker's Notes

☞ When you add sugar to yolks, combine immediately; otherwise, the sugar will set the yolk and some of its ability to thicken will be reduced.

☞ The track the sauce leaves on a wooden spoon is a helpful indication that it is ready. If you cook it until it is visibly thicker, you will curdle it.

☞ If your vanilla bean is brittle, preventing easy removal of seeds, allow it to steep in the hot milk for 2 to 3 minutes, or until it is soft. Then slit it in half vertically, scrape out the seeds and proceed as directed.

☞ In place of the vanilla bean, you can flavor with vanilla extract after the crème anglaise has cooled.

☞ You may also perfume it after making it with coffee, liqueur, liquor or melted chocolate. Before making the crème anglaise, you can infuse the milk with fresh mint, ground nuts or tea leaves as though you were making tea to flavor it.

Classic Pastry Cream

Pastry cream is crème anglaise with the addition of cornstarch or flour and sometimes butter for flavor. With whipped cream folded in, it becomes the base for Diplomat Cream (below); with whipped egg white, it becomes Vanilla Soufflé (page 249).

Makes 1 ½ cups

1   cup (8 ounces) milk
¼   cup (50 grams) granulated sugar
1   vanilla bean
3   large egg yolks
2   tablespoons all-purpose flour
1   ounce (2 tablespoons) unsalted butter

Ingredient preparations: Rest a sieve on top of a 1-quart mixing bowl to strain the pastry cream after it has been cooked.

Pour the milk and half the sugar into a 1½-quart saucepan. Split the vanilla bean with a small knife, scrape out the seeds and place them in the milk.

Place the egg yolks in a small bowl and whisk to combine. Add the remaining sugar and whisk to combine. Then stir in the flour and set aside.

Making the pastry cream: Bring the milk mixture just to a boil over medium heat. Turn off heat and pour about half the milk mixture into the yolk mixture, whisking until combined. Pour the mixture back into saucepan; whisk to combine; then return to medium-low heat.

Cook, stirring constantly, until the mixture comes to a boil (about 1 to 2 minutes). At this time it will thicken. Continue to stir and simmer until it is smooth and thick (for about 1 minute). Remove from heat and add the butter, stirring until melted and incorporated; then pour the cream through the sieve into the mixing bowl.

Cover the surface of the pastry cream with plastic wrap, and poke 6 to 8 slits in it with the tip of a knife to allow steam to escape.

Storing the pastry cream: Refrigerate for up to 3 days.

Diplomat Cream

This pastry cream, its texture lightened by a small amount of whipped cream, has a rich flavor without an overly sweet taste.

Makes 2 cups

1   recipe Classic Pastry Cream (page 248)
¼   cup (2 ounces) heavy cream
1   teaspoon vanilla

Baker's Notes

☞ In terms of thickening power, 1 tablespoon cornstarch is the equivalent of 2 tablespoons flour. Both have their usefulness, depending upon the dessert and the texture the cream needs.

☞ I use flour in this classic version. Since it is thicker, it prevents sogginess better. When you thicken the cream with cornstarch, the consistency may be described as light and short, not as thick as the flour version. In some recipes I advise using cornstarch.

☞ You may omit the vanilla bean; then add 1 teaspoon vanilla extract when the cream is cool.

☞ For a delicious filling, combine equal amounts of pastry cream and Classic Buttercream (page 260) as in Gift Box Gâteau (page 229).

☞ Add melted chocolate, liqueur, ground nuts or freshly grated coconut for other flavor variations.

Baker's Note

☞ You can also lighten this cream by folding half a cup of meringue into the recipe.

Stir the cold pastry cream until smooth. Pour the heavy cream and vanilla into a deep 1-quart mixing bowl and whip until soft peaks form. Fold into the pastry cream.

Use without delay as a filling or frosting.

Vanilla Soufflé

FOLD IN raspberries or other fresh fruits and serve this in small bowls if you wish.

This soufflé is used in Soufflé Feuilleté (page 372).

MAKES 2 CUPS

3	eggs
1	cup (8 ounces) milk
¼	cup (50 grams) granulated sugar
1	vanilla bean
2	tablespoons all-purpose flour
1	teaspoon granulated sugar

Baker's Note

☞ For a note on uncooked egg whites, see page 31.

Ingredient preparations: Rest a sieve on top of a 1-quart mixing bowl to strain the pastry cream after it has been cooked. Place the egg whites in a 1½-quart mixing bowl. Place the yolks in a small bowl and whisk to combine.

Pour the milk and 2 tablespoons of the ¼ cup sugar into a 1½-quart saucepan. Split the vanilla bean with a small knife, scrape out the seeds and place them in the milk.

Add the remaining 2 tablespoons sugar to the egg yolks and whisk to combine. Then stir in the flour and set aside.

Making the pastry cream base: Bring the milk mixture just to a boil over medium heat. Turn off heat and pour about half the milk mixture into the egg mixture, whisking until combined. Pour mixture back into saucepan; whisk to combine; then return to medium-low heat.

Cook, stirring constantly, until the mixture comes to a boil (about 1 to 2 minutes). At this time it will thicken. Continue to stir and simmer until it is smooth and thick (for about 1 minute). Remove from heat, then pour the cream through the sieve into the mixing bowl.

Set aside in a 1½-quart mixing bowl to cool slightly for at least 30 minutes.

Finishing the soufflé: Whip the egg whites until soft peaks form. Then add the 1 teaspoon sugar and continue to whip until thicker, elastic (but not dry or granular) peaks form. Fold a third of the whites into the cooled pastry cream base to lighten; then fold in the remaining just until combined.

Use without delay as a filling or simply a soufflé.

Caramel Bavarian Cream

This is caramel-flavored crème anglaise bound by gelatin and lightened with very softly whipped cream.

It is used in Caramel Carousel (page 180).

Makes 3 cups

It is used in Caramel Carousel (page 180).

Baker's Notes

☞ For the sake of the caramel flavor, don't be afraid to let the sugar turn a very dark amber.

☞ Using sugar cubes for caramelizing sugar is more efficient than using granulated sugar. They gradually melt and color more evenly.

☞ You can use ¼ cup granulated sugar if you don't have cubes on hand.

Cooking Equipment: 3-cup copper sugar pot or comparable-size heavy-bottomed saucepan, mercury candy thermometer

25	(50 grams) small sugar cubes
½	cup (4 ounces) heavy cream
1	cup (8 ounces) milk
3	tablespoons water
2	teaspoons gelatin
1	cup (8 ounces) heavy cream
3	egg yolks

Ingredient preparations: Place the sugar cubes into a 3-cup copper sugar pot or comparable-size heavy-bottomed saucepan and melt them over medium-low heat. At the same time, pour the ½ cup heavy cream into a small saucepan and warm it over low heat.

When the sugar is melted, raise the heat to caramelize it. Swirl the pan from time to time to distribute the heat evenly. (You want the sugar to color darker than usual so that its flavor will carry through the other ingredients.) When the sugar is a dark amber color, remove it from the heat. Pour the warm heavy cream, all at once, into the pan. (Careful, it will bubble up.) Begin stirring the mixture right away with a wooden spoon. If some of the sugar hardens, put the mixture over very low heat, and stir it occasionally until it melts into the cream. Then pour this into a liquid cup measure and add enough milk to make 1½ cups.

Pour the water in a small bowl, sprinkle the gelatin over it and set aside until softened.

Pour the 1 cup heavy cream into a deep 1½-quart mixing bowl, and whip it until it clings softly to the beaters and is thick enough to create swirls in the bowl but liquid enough to move if the bowl is tilted (Chantilly Stage, page 240). Refrigerate until ready to use.

Making the crème anglaise: Rest a sieve on top of a 1½-quart mixing bowl to strain the filling after it has been cooked.

Place the egg yolks in a 1½-quart heavy-bottomed saucepan and whisk to combine. Add the 1½ cups caramel-flavored milk and whisk to blend. Place over medium heat and stir constantly over the entire bottom with a wooden spoon until the mixture registers 165 to 170 degrees on the candy thermometer and is thick enough to coat the back of the spoon.

Finishing the Bavarian cream: Immediately remove from the heat and pour the cream through the sieve into the mixing bowl. Stir in the softened gelatin until dissolved and set over a large bowl filled with ice water. Stir the mixture occasionally to prevent it from sticking to the cold sides of the bowl and to redistribute the temperature. When it is syrupy and cooler than room temperature (about 9 minutes), fold in the chilled, lightly whipped cream with a rubber spatula.

Pour into a container or cake-lined pan and refrigerate at least 4 hours or until cold and set.

Pecan Bavarian Cream

USE AS pie filling in a baked crust, or serve on its own in a bowl.

This is the filling for Pecan Chantilly (page 192).
MAKES 3 ½ CUPS

This is the filling for Pecan Chantilly (page 192).

Cooking Equipment: Mercury candy thermometer

2	ounces (½ cup) pecans
2	tablespoons dark rum
2	teaspoons gelatin
1	cup (8 ounces) heavy cream
3	large egg yolks
¼	cup (50 grams) granulated sugar
1	cup (8 ounces) milk

Preparations: Grind the pecans with a nut grinder to the consistency of cornmeal to yield about ⅔ cup ground.

Pour the rum into a small bowl, sprinkle the gelatin over it and set aside until softened.

Pour the cream into a 1½-quart deep mixing bowl, and using an electric hand mixer, whip on medium-high (#8 to #10) until very soft peaks form and it is thick enough to create swirls in the bowl but liquid enough to move if the bowl is tilted (Chantilly Stage, page 240). Refrigerate until ready to use.

Making the crème anglaise: Rest a sieve on top of a 3-quart mixing bowl to strain the filling after it has been cooked.

Place the egg yolks in a 1-quart mixing bowl and whisk to combine. Add 2 tablespoons of the ¼ cup sugar and whisk until completely incorporated.

Pour the milk and remaining sugar into a 1½-quart saucepan and place over medium heat to bring just to a boil.

Remove from the heat; then pour about half of it into the egg mixture, whisking until blended. Pour the mixture back into saucepan and whisk. Return to medium-low heat and cook the mixture, stirring constantly, until it registers 170 degrees on a mercury candy thermometer and is thick enough to coat the back of a spoon (about 2½ minutes).

Finishing the Bavarian cream: Remove from the heat and pour through the sieve on top of the 3-quart mixing bowl. Stir in the softened gelatin to dissolve; then add the ground nuts and set over a larger bowl of ice water.

Baker's Note

☞ Make this creamy filling at least 4 to 6 hours in advance so it has time to chill and set.

Stir the mixture occasionally to distribute the cold and prevent lumpiness. When the mixture is syrupy and cooler than room temperature (about 20 to 25 minutes), fold in the chilled, lightly whipped cream with a rubber spatula until combined.

Pour into a container or cake-lined pan and refrigerate for at least 4 hours or until cold and set.

Pistachio Bavarian Cream

Y OU CAN serve this prettily colored cream in parfait or champagne glasses with a cookie or ladyfingers or simply alone.

This is the filling for Pistachio Cake (page 131).
MAKES 3 ½ CUPS

This is the filling for Pistachio Cake (page 131).

Baker's Notes

☞ The pistachio flavor and the texture of the cream are so pure and delicate that your freezer will never be without pistachios once you have tried this dessert.

☞ Make the Pistachio Bavarian Cream at least 4 to 6 hours in advance so it has time to chill and set.

Cooking Equipment: Mercury candy thermometer

4	ounces (¾ cup) pistachio nuts
2	cups (1 pint) milk
3	tablespoons water
2	teaspoons gelatin
1	cup (8 ounces) heavy cream
¼	teaspoon almond extract
4	large egg yolks
½	cup (100 grams) granulated sugar

Ingredient preparations: Blanch the pistachios as described on page 132. Grind them to make 1 cup (small nut pieces flavor the milk faster).

Rest a sieve on top of a 3-quart mixing bowl to strain the filling after it has been cooked.

Combine the milk and ground pistachios in a 1½-quart saucepan and bring just to a boil over medium heat. Remove from the heat and let steep for 10 to 15 minutes. Pour through a second sieve to strain; extract milk from the nuts by pressing them against the sides of the sieve with a rubber spatula. Discard the nuts (their flavor is now in the milk) and measure the flavored milk, adding more milk if needed to make 1½ cups.

Pour the water into a small bowl, sprinkle the gelatin over it and set aside until softened.

Pour the cream and almond extract into a 1 ½-quart deep mixing bowl, and with an electric hand mixer, whip the cream on medium to high speed (#8 to #10) until peaks barely form. Refrigerate until ready to use.

Making the crème anglaise: Whisk the egg yolks in a 1-quart mixing bowl to combine, add half the sugar and whisk until completely incorporated.

Return the pistachio-flavored milk with the other half of sugar to medium heat and bring just to a boil. Remove from heat and pour about half into the egg mixture, whisking until blended. Pour mixture back into saucepan, whisk and return to medium-low heat.

Cook the mixture, stirring constantly with a wooden spoon, until it registers 165 to 170 degrees on the candy thermometer and is thick enough to coat the back of the spoon (about 45 to 60 seconds).

Finishing the Bavarian cream: Immediately remove from the heat and pour the mixture through the sieve into the mixing bowl. Add the gelatin; stir to dissolve; then set over a larger bowl of ice water. Stir the mixture occasionally to distribute the cold and prevent any lumpiness. When the mixture is syrupy and cooler than room temperature (about 8 to 10 minutes), fold in the chilled, lightly whipped cream with a rubber spatula until combined. If it goes beyond the syrupy stage and develops more body than desired, remove from the cold-water bath and whisk the partially setting mixture until smooth. Then fold in the cream.

Pour into a container or cake-lined pan and refrigerate for at least 4 hours or until cold and set.

Hazelnut Bavarian Cream Soufflé

A HAZELNUT-FLAVORED pastry cream that is bound with gelatin and lightened with a soft meringue. It may be served on its own in small bowls lightly sprinkled with toasted hazelnuts.

This is the filling for Dutch Soufflé Torte (page 184).

MAKES 3 ½ CUPS

1	ounce (2 tablespoons) hazelnuts
1	cup (8 ounces) milk
2	tablespoons water
1	teaspoon gelatin
3	eggs
2	tablespoons (25 grams) granulated sugar
2	tablespoons all-purpose flour
2	tablespoons (25 grams) granulated sugar
2	ounce (2 tablespoons) unsalted butter
1	tablespoon granulated sugar

Ingredient preparations: Grind the hazelnuts in a nut grinder to the consistency of cornmeal.

Combine the ground nuts and milk in a 1½-quart saucepan. Bring just to a boil over medium heat. Remove from heat, stir and allow to steep, uncovered, for 10 to 15 minutes.

Pour the milk through a sieve into a 1-quart mixing bowl. Using a rubber spatula, remove excess milk by pressing nuts against the sieve's screen. Discard the nuts (their flavor is now in the milk). You now have ¾ cup hazelnut-flavored milk.

Rest a sieve on top of a 3-quart mixing bowl to strain the filling after it has been cooked.

Pour the 2 tablespoons water into a liquid measuring cup. Sprinkle the gelatin over the water; set aside to soften.

Separate the eggs, placing the whites in a deep 1½-quart stainless steel mixing bowl and the yolks in a shallow 1½-quart bowl.

Whisk the egg yolks to combine, add the 2 tablespoons sugar and whisk until the mixture is pale yellow. Then add the flour and incorporate.

Baker's Notes

☞ Make the hazelnut pastry cream 4 to 6 hours before serving so it can chill and set.

☞ The hazelnuts are ground to increase their surface area; this allows their flavor to be infused more quickly.

☞ In this instance, the measurement of ground nuts need not be precise, as, for example, in a cake batter.

☞ For a note on uncooked egg whites, see page 31.

Fillings and Frostings

Making the hazelnut pastry cream: In a 1½-quart saucepan, bring the hazelnut-flavored milk and 2 tablespoons sugar to a boil over medium heat. Remove from the heat and pour about half the milk mixture into the egg yolk mixture, whisking until combined. Pour back into the saucepan, stirring again to blend. Then cook over moderate heat, stirring constantly over the entire bottom of the pan, until the mixture comes to a boil. Reduce heat to low and continue to cook, stirring constantly until thick and smooth (about 1 minute).

Finishing the Bavarian cream soufflé: Remove from the heat and pour through the sieve into the mixing bowl.

Stir in the softened gelatin and butter until dissolved.

Whip the egg whites on low speed with an electric hand mixer until foamy and frothy. Then increase speed, add the 1 tablespoon sugar in a steady stream and whip until soft white peaks form. Fold into the warm cream. Cover its surface with plastic wrap, poking holes with the tip of a small knife blade to allow steam to escape.

Refrigerate until set, about 4 hours; or store up to 2 days in the refrigerator.

Cream Cheese Filling

Tʜɪs ɪs really cream-cheese buttercream with whipped cream added to make it a delectable filling.

It is for the filling of Lucerne Cheese Torte (page 134).

Mᴀᴋᴇꜱ 1 ½ ᴄᴜᴘꜱ

Cooking Equipment: 3-cup copper sugar pot or comparable-size heavy-bottomed saucepan, mercury candy thermometer

4	ounces cream cheese, room temperature
1 ½	ounces (3 tablespoons) unsalted butter, room temperature
1	tablespoon sour cream
1	teaspoon lemon zest
2	large egg yolks
2	tablespoons water
¼	cup (50 grams) granulated sugar
¼	cup (2 ounces) heavy cream

Ingredient preparations: In a 2- to 3-quart mixing bowl manipulate the cream cheese with a rubber spatula until smooth. Gradually add the butter, stirring until smooth and homogeneous. Lastly, stir in the sour cream and lemon zest; set aside.

Making the filling: Place the egg yolks in the bowl of a heavy-duty mixer and with the whisk attachment, whip them on medium speed (#5) until light in color and fluffy in texture (about 2 minutes). Detach whisk and remove bowl; set whisk close by to use later.

Combine the water and sugar in the sugar pot or saucepan. Place over low heat, swirling the pot occasionally to distribute heat until the sugar completely dissolves (about 2 minutes). Keep a pastry brush in a small glass of water to wash down any sugar crystals that

Baker's Note

☞ You may use an electric hand mixer instead of a heavy-duty mixer since you are making a small amount.

form along the sides of the pot.

As soon as the sugar has dissolved, increase heat to high and boil until it registers 238 degrees (soft ball stage) on the mercury candy thermometer (about 5 minutes).

Quickly pour the syrup into the center of the whipped yolks and whisk vigorously by hand to combine, using the mixer's whisk attachment.

Reattach the bowl and its whisk to the mixer and whip on medium speed (#5) until the egg yolk mixture thickens, increases in volume, lightens in color and texture and cools to room temperature (about 4 minutes).

Whisk into the cream cheese mixture until blended smoothly.

Finishing the filling: Whip the heavy cream in a deep 1½-quart mixing bowl until soft peaks form. Then fold into cream cheese buttercream. The consistency is soft and thin, but after refrigeration, the cream cheese and fat become firm to give the filling body and texture.

Strawberry Mousse

THIS FRUIT mousse uses sweetened fresh fruit puree as a base before gelatin is added to bind it and whipped cream to lighten it. It is adapted from Craig Claiborne's Strawberry Mousse. It may be served alone in champagne glasses with a strawberry on top.

This is the filling for Strawberry Window Cake (page 175).

MAKES 3 ½ CUPS

¼	cup (2 ounces) Grand Marnier
2 ½	teaspoons (1 package) gelatin
1	pint fresh ripe strawberries
1	cup (8 ounces) heavy cream
½	cup (100 grams) granulated sugar

Ingredient preparations: Pour the liqueur into a small bowl, sprinkle the gelatin over it and set aside until softened.

Remove and discard stems from the strawberries; rinse under cold water; then cut each strawberry into 6 to 8 small pieces to yield a total of 2 to 2¼ cups.

Making the mousse: Pour the cream into a deep 1½-quart mixing bowl and whip it with an electric hand mixer on high speed (#10) just until it appears to thicken and develop some body. (The cream, though very softly whipped, is still liquid enough to flow from the beaters when lifted.) Refrigerate until ready to use.

Put the strawberry pieces in a 10-inch skillet. Sprinkle the sugar over them and stir to combine. (Do not let them sit after the sugar has been added.) Place over low heat, stirring until the sugar is completely dissolved. Remove from heat and stir in the softened gelatin until dissolved.

Finishing the mousse: Pour the mixture into a 3-quart mixing bowl; set aside to cool to room temperature, stirring occasionally. (It may take 1 hour to cool. If you are in

Baker's Notes

☞ Make this mousse at least 4 to 6 hours in advance so it has time to chill and set.

☞ Strawberries absorb water rapidly, so usually they are not submerged in water unless they are filthy. In this recipe, however, it is important to wash them in water to impart extra moisture, so that the added sugar will dissolve quickly when it is heated. Then the strawberries need not be overheated, reducing their flavor.

a hurry, place the bowl over a larger bowl of ice water, and stir until proper temperature is reached.) Then fold in the chilled, lightly whipped cream with a rubber spatula until combined. Spread or pour in the cake immediately. Refrigerate until set, about 4 hours.

Raspberry Mousse

YOU CAN serve this mousse alone topped with a single perfect fresh raspberry.

This is the mousse for Raspberry Cream Torte (page 190).

MAKES 3 CUPS

1	package (12 ounces) frozen red raspberries
2	tablespoons (25 grams) granulated sugar
1	cup (8 ounces) heavy cream
2	tablespoons water
2	tablespoons framboise liqueur
2	teaspoons gelatin
¼	cup (50 grams) granulated sugar

Baker's Notes

☞ Make this mousse at least 4 to 6 hours in advance so it has time to chill and set.

☞ Packages of frozen raspberries are slightly sweetened.

☞ Thaw the raspberries before pureeing them.

Ingredient preparations: Place the frozen raspberries in the bowl of a food processor fitted with steel blade. Sprinkle with the 2 tablespoons sugar and set aside (about 1 to 1 ½ hours) until defrosted.

Pour the cream into a deep 1½-quart mixing bowl, and with an electric hand mixer, whip it on medium-high speed (#8 to #10) until soft peaks form. Refrigerate until ready to use.

Making the mousse: Combine the water and liqueur in a small dish. Sprinkle surface with the gelatin and set aside to soften.

When the berries are completely defrosted, process with on/off bursts until pureed. Pour puree into a sieve, and push it through with the aid of a rubber spatula, straining seeds from puree; if necessary, add water to make 1 cup.

Pour ¼ cup of the raspberry puree into a 1-quart heavy-bottomed saucepan. Stir in the ¼ cup sugar, and place over low heat, swirling pan occasionally, until sugar is dissolved. Then increase the heat, and bring syrup just to a boil so that it is hot enough to dissolve the gelatin.

Remove from heat and stir in softened gelatin until it is dissolved.

Finishing the mousse: Pour the mixture and the reserved puree into a 2- to 3-quart mixing bowl, and set over a larger bowl filled with ice water. Whisk occasionally until the mixture becomes syrupy and cooler than room temperature (about 5 minutes).

Then fold in the chilled, lightly whipped cream with a rubber spatula until the mixtures are combined. Pour into a container or cake-lined pan and refrigerate at least 4 hours or until cold and set.

Lemon Mousse

Y OU MAY serve this mousse in a soufflé dish on its own.

This is the mousse for Lemon Mist Torte (page 142).

MAKES 8 CUPS

Cooking Equipment: Mercury candy thermometer, 1½-quart double boiler

⅓	cup (3 ounces) water
3 ½	teaspoons gelatin
6	large eggs
¾	cup (150 grams) granulated sugar
¾	cup strained fresh lemon juice (4 to 5 lemons)
2	teaspoons lemon zest (1 to 2 lemons)
½	cup (100 grams) granulated sugar

Ingredient preparations: Pour the water into a small bowl, sprinkle the gelatin over it and set aside until softened.

Separate the eggs, placing the whites in the bowl of a heavy-duty mixer and the yolks in the top of the double boiler. Stir the yolks with a whisk to combine; then add the ¾ cup sugar slowly, whisking until blended. Pour in the lemon juice and zest; whisk to combine.

Making the mousse: Place the yolk mixture over boiling water (moderately bubbling) so that the bottom of the pot just touches the water, and cook over medium heat, whisking back and forth continuously for 6 to 8 minutes to create a very foamy mixture. As it foams and thickens, tripling in volume, continue to cook it until the candy thermometer registers 170 degrees.

Then remove the container from the water, add the softened gelatin and stir until dissolved. Pour into a 2- to 3-quart mixing bowl and set over a larger bowl of ice water, whisking occasionally until the mixture becomes syrupy and cooler than room temperature (about 6 minutes).

Making the meringue: Attach the bowl of egg whites to the mixer, and with whisk attachment, whip on low speed (#3) until small bubbles appear and the surface is frothy (about 30 to 45 seconds). Increase speed to medium (#5), and add 1 teaspoon of the ½ cup sugar. Continue whipping for 30 to 45 seconds, or until soft white peaks form. Then add the remainder of the sugar in a slow, steady stream, whipping until stiff, glossy peaks form.

Finishing the mousse: Whisk the cooled lemon mixture once or twice until smooth. Then fold in about 1 cup of the meringue with a rubber spatula to lighten. Now fold in the remaining meringue until incorporated. Pour into a container or cake-lined pan and refrigerate until cold and set, about 4 hours or overnight.

Baker's Notes

☞ Make this mousse at least 4 to 6 hours in advance so it has time to chill and set.

☞ Lemons can vary in tartness. I find them sweeter in the spring and summer than in the fall and winter so a slight sugar adjustment may be necessary. (I'd suggest adding an additional tablespoon to the ½ cup in the recipe.)

☞ The most intense lemon flavor comes from the zest—not from its juice.

☞ If you wish a softer filling, reduce the gelatin to 2 ½ to 3 teaspoons.

☞ For a note on uncooked egg whites, see page 31.

Classic Lemon Curd

THIS lemon curd has a nicely balanced taste, neither too eggy nor too tart. It may be used as a frosting, and it is the foundation for a variety of fillings. You can add butter, fold in whipped cream or meringue, or top it with meringue. Lemon curd spread over caramel cream (page 307) in a baked tart is a fabulous blend. Combined with fresh fruits, such as peaches, strawberries, papayas, mangoes, bananas or blueberries, it is glorious.

This is used in Chambéry Lemon Tart (page 217).

MAKES 1 ½ CUPS

Cooking Equipment: Mercury candy thermometer

2	large eggs
2	egg yolks
½	cup (100 grams) granulated sugar
6	tablespoons strained fresh lemon juice (2 lemons)
2	teaspoons lemon zest (1 lemon)
4	ounces (1 stick) unsalted butter, chilled and cut into 8 pieces

Making the lemon curd: Place the eggs and egg yolks in a 1½-quart heavy-bottomed saucepan and whisk to combine. Add the sugar, lemon juice and lemon zest, whisking to combine after each addition.

Add the pieces of chilled butter and place the saucepan over medium heat, stirring constantly over the entire bottom with a rubber spatula. Cook for 2 to 3 minutes, or until the mixture begins to develop body and thicken. As the butter melts, it is incorporated into the mixture. It is important to regulate the heat so the mixture never boils. Boiling could cause curdling and the butter to separate from the curd.

The curd is finished and thick enough when the candy thermometer registers 160 degrees. Immediately remove it from heat.

Cooling the lemon curd: With the rubber spatula, scrape the curd into a shallow 1½-quart mixing bowl to cool. Cover it with plastic wrap, pressing the wrap onto the surface to keep the top from drying and forming a crust. This provides a completely smooth, thick lemon curd when cold. If the surface is not covered, it dries, forming lumps. Poke 5 to 7 small slits in the plastic with the tip of a knife blade to allow steam to escape; then refrigerate up to 10 days.

Lime Curd

USE as you would lemon curd; it's particularly delicious with mangoes and papayas.

This is the filling for Melon and Lime Curd Tart (page 348).

MAKES 1 ½ CUPS

Baker's Note

☞ Zest of lemon is grated from the yellow part of the lemon, not the pith, which is bitter. The natural pectin in the skin helps thicken the curd. If you want more lemon flavor, add zest, not juice.

☞ Lemon curd keeps fresh for 10 days in the refrigerator.

Cooking Equipment: Mercury candy thermometer

2   large eggs
2   egg yolks
½   cup (100 grams) granulated sugar
6   tablespoons strained fresh lime juice (3 limes)
2   teaspoons lime zest (2 limes)
4   ounces (1 stick) unsalted butter, chilled and cut into 8 pieces

Preparation: Prepare as for Classic Lemon Curd (page 258) but substitute lime juice and zest for the lemon.

Baker's Note

☞ Limes are less acidic and sweeter than lemons.

Lemon Almond Cream

Tʜɪs ɪs lemon curd with a subtle almond flavor.

It is the filling for Lemon Parfait Cake (page 83).
Mᴀᴋᴇs ¾ ᴄᴜᴘ

Cooking Equipment: Mercury candy thermometer

3   egg yolks
1   tablespoon unsalted butter, room temperature
2   tablespoons almond paste, room temperature
½   cup (100 grams) granulated sugar
¼   cup fresh lemon juice, strained (1 to 2 lemons)
4   teaspoons lemon zest (2 lemons)
¼   cup (2 ounces) water

Baker's Notes

☞ If lemons are not too tart, cut the sugar to ⅓ cup.

☞ Store this filling for no longer than 1 day after it is made because the lemon's acid breaks down the consistency over time.

Making the filling: Place the egg yolks in a 1½-quart heavy-bottomed saucepan and stir them only to combine. Add the butter, almond paste, sugar, lemon juice and lemon zest. Mix until blended; then stir in the water. (If the almond paste is not completely smooth now, it will dissolve while the filling is cooked.)

Place the pan over medium-low heat and cook, stirring constantly; smash the almond paste against the sides if it is not already dissolved. When mixture is thick enough to coat the back of a spoon (about 4 to 5 minutes and registering 165 degrees on a mercury candy thermometer), pour it into a 1-quart mixing bowl. Cover with plastic wrap and refrigerate until cold. As it chills, it will thicken.

Classic Buttercream

Baker's Notes

☞ About 2 cups butter-cream will frost an 8- or 9-inch cake.

☞ Small amounts of honey, ground nuts, citrus zest, diced dried fruits, Praline Powder (page 309), cake crumbs, liqueur, jam, diced marrons, molasses, fresh mint, maple syrup, pastry cream or meringue may be added to Classic Buttercream for variety.

☞ For Chocolate Buttercream, see page 286.

☞ High-quality butter (i.e., low water content) improves your butter-cream's quality.

☞ Some pastry chefs say the amount of butter should be double the sugar's weight. I add enough to give it the flavor and the necessary smoothness.

☞ The buttercream's texture is lighter (more airy) when it is freshly made.

☞ Since it keeps well in the freezer, I like to make more than one batch at a time. I find it easier to scoop it out by the portion when it's cold or frozen and put it right on my scale.

☞ For a note on eggs, see page 31.

THIS RECIPE begins by adding a hot sugar syrup to whipped egg yolks. That is also the first step for many other creams, fillings and parfaits, including **Rum Cream** (page 263). MAKES 4 CUPS (ABOUT 1 ½ POUNDS)

Cooking Equipment: Mercury candy thermometer, 5-cup copper sugar pot or comparable-size heavy-bottomed saucepan

1	pound (4 sticks) unsalted butter
8	egg yolks
⅓	cup water
1	cup (200 grams) granulated sugar

Ingredient preparation: Remove the butter from the refrigerator allowing enough time for it to reach room temperature. It should be pliable but not melting soft. (If butter is too firm, it's difficult to create an emulsion.) If the butter weeps with droplets of water on its surface, wrap or pat it with a towel to remove or blot excess moisture.

Making the buttercream: Place the egg yolks in the bowl of a heavy-duty mixer, and with the whisk attachment, whip them on medium speed (#4) until light in color and fluffy in texture (about 4 to 7 minutes). Whipping the yolks reduces chance of their curdling when hot syrup is added. Detach the whisk and remove the bowl, setting both near the sugar syrup.

While whipping the yolks, pour first the water, then the sugar into the sugar pot (or comparable-size thick-bottomed saucepan); stir or swirl to combine. Place over low heat, swirling the pot occasionally to distribute heat, until the sugar completely dissolves (about 3 minutes).

As soon as the sugar has dissolved, increase to high heat, and boil until it registers 238 degrees (soft ball stage) on the candy thermometer (this takes 2 to 3 minutes). Dip a pastry brush in water and wash down any sugar crystals that appear around the sides of the pot during the boiling.

Quickly pour the syrup into center of the whipped yolks. (If you pour the sugar syrup down the side of the mixer while the whisk is moving, it splatters around the bowl.) Then, holding the mixer's whisk in your hand, whisk vigorously to combine. (The hot syrup cooks the yolks, and the vigorous whisking action distributes the heat and prevents curdling.)

Finishing the buttercream: Without delay, reattach the bowl with its whisk to the mixer and whip on medium speed (#5) until the egg yolk mixture thickens, increases in volume, lightens in color and texture and cools to body temperature (about 5 minutes). Then reduce the speed to low (#2), and whip it until very light and fluffy and cools to room temperature (about 5 to 6 minutes); you can hold some ice cubes against the bowl to hasten the cooling of the mixture.

Add the butter slowly, as if you were adding oil when making mayonnaise, to create a smooth, homogeneous mixture. On medium speed (#5), add a chunk (about 1 tablespoon)

of softened butter, and toss it into the mixture. Whip to incorporate; then repeat the procedure with a similar amount of butter. The first pieces of butter will appear to melt into the mixture. Continue adding butter, a tablespoon or two at a time, until the entire amount has been incorporated. (When half or more of the butter has been added, the mixture will appear lumpy; that is fine. Continue adding the butter, and toward the last addition the mixture will magically become smooth.)

If, while you add the butter, the buttercream appears to be curdling, increase the speed to medium-high (#6 to #7). When the butter is completely incorporated (emulsified), go back to the medium speed and again add the butter. If, when all the butter has been added, the mixture is not smooth, add 1 tablespoon of cold butter at a time until it is homogeneous.

Storing the buttercream: If you are not using the buttercream soon, transfer it to a sturdy container, and refrigerate it for up to 1 week, or freeze it for up to 1 month. Flavor it as you desire or according to recipe's instructions.

To restore buttercream to a smooth, spreadable, consistency: If time permits, leave the necessary amount of buttercream out of the refrigerator until the proper consistency (perhaps 1 hour). To hasten this process, place the buttercream, in pieces, in the bowl of a heavy-duty mixer. Rest it briefly in a shallow pan, such as a 10-inch skillet, filled with 1 inch of hot tap water (about 120 degrees). When some of the buttercream just begins to melt around the sides, remove it from the water bath. Wipe the bowl, and place it on the mixer with the flat beater (paddle) attachment. (The flat beater is used since our goal is a spreading, not an airy, whipped consistency.) Mix the pieces of buttercream on medium-low speed (#2 or #3) until homogeneous and smooth. If the buttercream is still too firm, repeat the hot-water procedure. Do not give up; the buttercream may look slightly curdled before it is smooth; increase the mixer's speed if necessary. Should the buttercream get too thin, return it to the refrigerator awhile; then mix it. (This is the same procedure as the hot-water treatment, but in reverse.)

Orange Buttercream

THIS MAKES an excellent filling and frosting for **Almond Paste Génoise** (page 110).

MAKES 4 CUPS (ABOUT 1 ½ POUNDS)

Cooking Equipment: Mercury candy thermometer, 5-cup copper sugar pot or comparable-size heavy-bottomed saucepan

1	pound (4 sticks) unsalted butter
8	egg yolks
⅓	cup water
1	cup (200 grams) granulated sugar
2	teaspoons orange zest (1 orange)
2	to 4 tablespoons orange liqueur

Fillings and Frostings

Prepare as for Classic Buttercream, following each step on page 260 with the following difference:

After adding the butter, add the 2 teaspoons orange zest, then the 2 to 4 tablespoons orange liqueur, 1 teaspoon at a time.

Coffee Buttercream

THIS IS delicious with any chocolate cake. Coffee Essence is a good keeper and will last for weeks stored at room temperature.

MAKES 4 CUPS (ABOUT 1 ½ POUNDS)

Baker's Note

☞ For a note on eggs, see page 31.

Cooking Equipment: Mercury candy thermometer, 5-cup copper sugar pot or comparable-size heavy-bottomed saucepan

    1   pound (4 sticks) unsalted butter
    8   egg yolks
    ⅓   cup water
    1   cup (200 grams) granulated sugar
    2   to 4 tablespoons Coffee Essence (page 269)

Prepare as for Classic Buttercream, following each step on page 260 with the following difference:

After adding the butter, add the 2 to 4 tablespoons Coffee Essence (page 269).

Milk Buttercream

MILK gives this frosting a richer, more satiny texture than classic buttercream. It is easy to work with and easy to use after refrigeration.

MAKES 2 ½ CUPS (ABOUT 1 ½ POUNDS)

Cooking Equipment: Mercury candy thermometer

Baker's Notes

☞ About 2 cups buttercream will frost an 8- or 9-inch cake, excluding decoration.

☞ Any leftover buttercream retains its exceptionally smooth, velvety texture.

☞ For a note on eggs, see page 31.

    12   ounces (3 sticks) unsalted butter
    1   large egg
    1   egg yolk
    ½   cup (4 ounces) milk
    1   cup (200 grams) granulated sugar

Ingredient preparation: Remove the butter from the refrigerator in enough time for it to reach room temperature. It should be pliable but not melting soft. (If the butter is too firm, it's difficult to create an emulsion.) If the butter weeps with droplets of water on its surface, wrap or pat it with a towel to remove or blot excess moisture.

Making the buttercream: Place the egg and the egg yolk into the bowl of a heavy-duty mixer, and with the whisk attachment, whip on medium speed (#5). Continue whipping until the egg foams slightly and increases in volume (about 1 minute).

Pour the milk and then the sugar into a 2½-quart heavy-bottomed saucepan and stir or swirl to combine. Place over low heat, swirling pan occasionally until the sugar completely dissolves (about 1 minute).

Increase heat to medium-high and boil syrup until it registers 220 degrees on the candy thermometer (about 10 minutes).

With the mixer on medium speed (#5), pour the syrup in a steady stream down the side of the bowl onto the eggs. Whip until it cools to body temperature (about 98 to 99 degrees), about 10 minutes.

Maintaining medium speed, break off about 1 tablespoon of the softened butter (70 degrees) and toss it into the mixture. Whip until it is completely incorporated before repeating the procedure. The first pieces of butter will appear to melt into the mixture. Keep adding the butter, a tablespoon or two at a time, until the entire amount has been incorporated. (When half or more of the butter has been added, the mixture will appear lumpy. That is fine. Continue adding the butter, and toward the last addition, the mixture will magically become smooth.)

If, while you are adding butter, the buttercream appears to be curdling, increase the speed to medium-high (#6 to #8). When the butter has been completely incorporated, reduce to medium speed again, and resume adding the butter.

Storing the buttercream: Transfer to an airtight storage container and refrigerate it for up to 1 week, or freeze for up to 1 month. Flavor it according to recipe's instructions.

Rum Cream

THE FOUNDATION of this frosting is a sugar syrup combined with egg yolks and flavored with vanilla and rum; then whipped cream is folded into it.

Rum Cream is used to frost Classic Banana Chiffon Cake (page 207).
MAKES 2 CUPS

Baker's Note

☞ For a note on eggs, see page 31.

Cooking Equipment: Mercury candy thermometer, 3-cup copper sugar pot or comparable-size heavy-bottomed saucepan

3	large egg yolks
2	tablespoons water
½	cup (100 grams) granulated sugar
1	teaspoon vanilla
2	tablespoons dark rum
1	cup (8 ounces) heavy cream

Ingredient preparations: Place the egg yolks in the bowl of a heavy-duty mixer, and with the whisk attachment, whip on medium speed (#5) until light in color and fluffy in texture. Detach the whisk and remove the bowl, setting whisk close by to use later.

Pour the water, then the sugar into the sugar pot; stir or swirl to combine. Place over low heat, swirling the pot occasionally to distribute heat until sugar completely dissolves (about 3 minutes).

Making the rum cream: As soon as the sugar has dissolved, increase heat to high, and boil until it registers 238 degrees (soft ball stage) on the candy thermometer. Have a pastry brush in a small glass of water at hand to wash down any sugar crystals that form along the sides of the pot.

Quickly pour the syrup into the center of the whipped yolks and whisk vigorously by hand to combine, using the mixer's whisk attachment.

Reattach bowl and its whisk to the mixer, and whip on medium speed (#5) until the egg yolk mixture thickens, increases in volume, lightens in color and texture and cools to room temperature (about 4 minutes).

Finishing the rum cream: When the yolk mixture has cooled to room temperature, remove the bowl from the mixer and stir in the vanilla and rum.

Whip the heavy cream in a deep 1½-quart mixing bowl until soft peaks form and tracks made in the cream close slowly but not completely. Then fold it into the egg-yolk mixture with a rubber spatula until combined. (The consistency is soft.) Frost any cake without delay.

Swiss Meringue

Nᴏᴛ ᴀs sweet as Italian Meringue, this is a particularly easy one to make.

It is used to decorate the top of Milano Rice Tart (page 353).
Mᴀᴋᴇs 2 ½ ᴄᴜᴘs

| ½ | cup (about 4 large) egg whites |
| 10 | tablespoons (125 grams) granulated sugar |

Ingredient preparations: Pour the egg whites into the bowl of a heavy-duty mixer, and using the whisk attachment, break them up by hand. Add the sugar and whisk briefly to combine. Rest the bowl in a shallow pan, such as a 10-inch skillet, filled with 1 inch of water that feels hot to the touch (120 degrees). To prevent the whites from setting, whisk continuously until the mixture reaches body temperature (about 30 to 45 seconds).

Making the meringue: Attach the bowl to the mixer, and with the whisk attachment, whip on medium speed (#5) until the mixture has cooled to room temperature and increased in volume, forming thick, shiny, stiff peaks that are still elastic but are not dry or granular. Test the consistency by lifting the whisk from the mixture. This process will take about 4 to 5 minutes. Remove the bowl and its attachment from the mixer and use the meringue without delay.

Baker's Notes

☞ Use this meringue immediately after it has been made.

☞ You may want to refer to the Warm-Method Meringue on page 212 before proceeding.

☞ For a note on uncooked egg whites, see page 31.

Classic Italian Meringue

This meringue may be used alone to top cake, or it can be folded into another mixture, such as a mousse, Bavarian cream, pastry cream or lemon curd. You can bake or broil it. You can even count on it to insulate ice cream from melting too quickly, as in a baked Alaska. Add butter to it, and you have **Italian Meringue Buttercream** (page 267). Makes 3 ½ cups

Cooking Equipment: 3-cup copper sugar pot or similar 3-cup heavy-bottomed saucepan, mercury candy thermometer

- ⅓   cup (about 3) egg whites, room temperature
- 2   tablespoons (25 grams) granulated sugar
- 3   tablespoons water
- ½   cup (100 grams) granulated sugar

Ingredient preparations: Place the egg whites in the bowl of a heavy-duty mixer. Set the 2 tablespoons sugar nearby.

Cooking the sugar syrup: Pour the water, then the ½ cup sugar into the copper sugar pot or saucepan (add the water first so the sugar will dissolve rather than stick to the bottom). Stir or swirl the pot to combine the ingredients and moisten the sugar. Place over low heat to dissolve the sugar. When it has completely dissolved, raise the heat to medium-high. Wash down any sugar crystals clinging to the side of the pan by dipping a pastry brush into water in a glass and then brushing the crystals away from the sides into the sugar syrup. Continue to dip into water and wash the sides as needed. (Or place a lid on top for 1 minute as the mixture begins to boil; it catches the steam and drops moisture back into the pot, washing down the sides.) Continue to boil, uncovered, until the syrup registers 210 degrees on the mercury thermometer (this temperature is merely a guideline, suggesting when to begin whipping the egg whites).

Whipping the egg whites: As the syrup continues to boil, attach the bowl to the heavy-duty mixer, and using the whisk attachment, whip the whites on medium-low speed (#4) for 30 seconds. When small bubbles appear, producing a frothy surface, increase the speed to medium (#5), and add 1 teaspoon of the 2 tablespoons sugar. Maintaining same speed, continue whipping until soft white peaks form. Add the remainder of the sugar in a steady stream.

Finishing the meringue: Simultaneously continue boiling the syrup and checking the thermometer as the whites whip until the syrup registers close to 245 degrees. Remove it from the heat. Its temperature will continue to rise as it waits for the whites. When the syrup registers 248 to 249 degrees and the whites are thick, stiff and glossy but not dry or granular, pour the hot syrup in a slow, steady stream near the side of the bowl onto the whipped whites. Do not pour the liquid directly onto the wire whisk attachment. As the hot syrup is poured onto the whipped whites, the mixture immedi-

↦ The water merely moistens the sugar. If you accidently add too much, that's no problem; just cook the mixture longer until it reaches the proper temperature.

↦ The sugar syrup can be held until the egg whites are whipped, but whipped egg whites cannot wait for the sugar syrup to reach its proper temperature. If the sugar syrup cooks too quickly, add water to it and continue to cook it to stall for time.

↦ The freshness of the whites is more important for flavor than any other factor.

↦ Some Italian meringue recipes instruct you to cook the sugar syrup to between 235 and 248 degrees. The higher the temperature, the more evaporation in the syrup and the drier, firmer and stiffer the meringue will be. (In areas of high humidity, cook the syrup to 248 degrees.) In any case, remove the mixture from the heat just under the desired temperature so the heat of the pan finishes the cooking.

ately expands, almost tripling its volume. After all the syrup has been incorporated, continue to whip it for 2 to 3 more minutes. The mixture will thicken and form glossy, stiff peaks and will have a marshmallowlike appearance.

Cooling the meringue: Reduce speed to low (#2 to #3), and continue whipping to set the meringue's structure (about 8 to 10 minutes), until the meringue is at room temperature and very thick.

If the Italian meringue is incorporated into another mixture before it is thoroughly cooled, its heat could dissolve the other mixture, including its sugar particles. If necessary, transfer the meringue to a large plate, spreading it with a rubber spatula over the surface to cool completely (about 15 to 30 minutes) before it is combined with another mixture.

Maple Italian Meringue

Fluffy and delicately flavored with maple, this frosting is easy to spread between layers and over cake.

This is used to frost Victorian Maple Cake (page 82).

MAKES 5 ½ CUPS

Cooking Equipment: Mercury candy thermometer

½ cup (about 4 large) egg whites, room temperature
2 tablespoons (25 grams) granulated sugar
1 cup pure maple syrup

Ingredient preparations: Place the egg whites in the bowl of a heavy-duty mixer. Set the 2 tablespoons sugar nearby.

Boiling the syrup: Pour the maple syrup into a 1½-quart heavy-bottomed saucepan. Bring to a boil over medium heat, and continue boiling until the syrup reaches a temperature of about 230 degrees. (This temperature is merely a guideline for when to begin whipping the egg whites.)

Whipping the egg whites: As the syrup continues to boil, attach the bowl to the mixer, and with the whisk attachment, whip on low speed (#3) until small bubbles appear (about 30 seconds). Increase speed to medium (#5), and pour in the sugar in a steady stream. Continue whipping until stiff but not dry peaks form (about 2 minutes).

Meanwhile, continue boiling the maple syrup until the temperature registers 238 degrees on the mercury candy thermometer (about 2 minutes).

Finishing the meringue: With the mixer still on medium speed (#5), slowly pour the hot syrup in a steady stream directly down the side of the bowl. (If the hot liquid lands on the beater, it will splatter.) The meringue expands as the syrup is incorporated.

Whip for about 2 minutes, or until fully expanded. Then decrease the speed to low (#2),

☞ If you overwhip the egg whites, your finished mixture will look curdled. Therefore, add some sugar to the whites while they are being whipped to reduce the chance of your overwhipping them. The sugar keeps the whites smoother and softer.

Baker's Note

☞ This recipe is not difficult, but it requires organization and close attention. Remember that you can heat the syrup and hold it for a few moments, but once you've whipped the whites to the proper stage, you must proceed. (See Classic Italian Meringue recipe on page 265.)

and continue whipping for about 5 to 7 minutes to stabilize the meringue's texture as it cools to room temperature and thickens.

Italian Meringue Buttercream

THE LIGHT, not-too-sweet consistency of this meringue buttercream is perfect for summertime use. Its pristine white color makes it ideal for frosting a wedding cake. MAKES 3 CUPS (ABOUT 1 POUND 2 OUNCES)

12	ounces (3 sticks) unsalted butter, room temperature
⅓	cup (about 3 large) egg whites, room temperature
2	tablespoons (25 grams) granulated sugar
3	tablespoons water
½	cup (100 grams) granulated sugar

Ingredient preparation: The butter must be prepared so it will blend smoothly into the Italian meringue. Place the butter in a 1½-quart mixing bowl and whip it with an electric hand mixer on medium speed until creamy and light (about 1 to 2 minutes). Set aside until time to add to the Italian meringue.

Making the Italian meringue buttercream: Prepare as for Classic Italian Meringue following each step as directed on page 265. Whip the egg whites on low speed until cool, setting the fully expanded, fluffy texture.

Then, with the mixer on medium speed (#5), add the butter to Italian Meringue mixture, 1 tablespoon at a time. Continue whipping until a smooth, mayonnaiselike consistency is achieved (about 3 to 4 minutes). Should the mixture appear curdled at any time while the butter is being added, increase the mixer's speed until the butter is smooth. Then reduce to medium speed and continue adding the butter.

Flavoring the buttercream: After adding the butter, pour in liquid flavoring (orange juice, vanilla, Coffee Essence, etc.) teaspoon by teaspoon, with the mixer still on medium speed.

To flavor with zests, remove bowl from the mixer and stir in the zest with a rubber spatula.

Storing the buttercream: If you are not using the buttercream right away, store in a sturdy container for up to 1 week in the refrigerator, or for up to 1 month in the freezer.

To use the buttercream after storage, allow it to reach room temperature; then mix it together until smooth.

Baker's Notes

☞ For an orange or lemon flavor, add 1 tablespoon of fine-grated zest from oranges or lemons and 3 tablespoons juice. Or you can add Coffee Essence (page 269) to taste.

☞ For a more intense orange or lemon flavor, substitute citrus juice for the water and add the zest and juice at the end.

☞ For chocolate Italian meringue buttercream, melt 4 ounces semisweet chocolate until smooth. When the chocolate is cooler but still liquid, stir in about 1 cup of the buttercream. Then incorporate it into the larger bowl of buttercream.

☞ The structure of this frosting is lighter (more airy) when it's freshly made.

Orange Sabayon Frosting

S IMILAR to an orange or lemon curd but without any butter, this frosting is excellent on angel food, chiffon or an orange génoise.

It is used in Duchess Cake (page 203).

MAKES 2 ⅔ CUPS

Baker's Notes

☞ This will frost a 10-inch angel food, chiffon or orange génoise.

☞ You may substitute another fruit juice for the orange juice.

☞ Reducing the orange juice intensifies its flavor.

Cooking Equipment: 1½-quart double boiler, mercury candy thermometer

2	small sugar cubes
1	orange
1	cup (8 ounces) fresh orange juice
5	egg yolks
½	cup (100 grams) granulated sugar
1	cup (8 ounces) heavy cream
1	tablespoon Grand Marnier

Ingredient preparations: Rub each side of the sugar cube against the orange skin to capture its flavor (the cubes will turn orange).

Pour the juice into a 1-quart heavy-bottomed saucepan. Bring to a boil over medium heat, reduce heat and simmer until reduced to ½ cup (about 13 minutes). Add the orange-flavored sugar cubes, stir until dissolved and set aside to cool slightly.

Making the frosting: Place the egg yolks in the top of the double boiler; whisk just to combine; then pour in the sugar and whisk until blended. Stir in the juice.

Place the pan over lightly boiling water. Cook, stirring constantly with a rubber spatula, until the mixture begins to thicken (about 3 to 4 minutes) and registers 175 degrees on the mercury candy thermometer. Stir to keep eggs from curdling, but not to foam the mixture. Remove the top portion of the double boiler from the heat, and pour the orange cream into a 1-quart mixing bowl. Cover the surface with plastic wrap to prevent a film from forming while cooling. Refrigerate until cold, 3 hours or overnight.

Finishing the frosting: When the orange mixture is cold, whip the heavy cream with the Grand Marnier until thicker than Chantilly Stage (page 240). Stir a couple of tablespoons of the whipped cream into the cold orange mixture until smooth. Then fold in the remaining cream until blended. Frost the cake without delay.

Translucent Sugar Glaze

O NCE DRY, this simple, no-cook glaze forms a thin film over a cake or cookie crust. It may also be used as a decoration.

MAKES ¾ CUP

Baker's Note

☞ You can vary the flavor and instead of water, add lemon, lime, tangerine or orange juice or even rum or coffee to the powdered sugar.

½   cup (50 grams) unsifted powdered sugar
4   teaspoons water

Pour the sugar into a triple sifter and sift into a 1-quart mixing bowl. Add the water and stir with a rubber spatula until blended and smooth. The consistency should be thin enough so that a transparent film will cover the baked good. Adjust the consistency by adding water if it is too thick or sugar if it is too thin. Use immediately.

Classic Royal Icing

THIS IS one of the most useful recipes in the pastry repertoire. It may be applied directly to the dessert as a decorative touch, or designs may be piped ahead on aluminum foil, then allowed to dry, stored in an airtight container and placed on the dessert when it is time to decorate it.

MAKES ½ CUP

1   cup (100 grams) unsifted powdered sugar
2   tablespoons (1 large) egg white
⅛   teaspoon cream of tartar

Mix all the ingredients in a deep 1½-quart mixing bowl with an electric hand mixer until blended. Then, on medium-high speed, whip the ingredients until the mixture is thick and white and has a creamy, marshmallowlike consistency (about 5 minutes). This is important since it makes the icing elastic and easy to spread. If you are not using the icing right away, cover the surface with plastic wrap to prevent it from drying.

When you are ready and if you are piping it, fill a small handmade paper cone half full with the royal icing, and adjust the tip according to your purpose. (See page 244 for directions on how to pipe with a handmade paper cone.)

Coffee Essence

HAVE THIS intense coffee syrup on hand to flavor buttercreams, dessert syrup, pastry cream or crème anglaise.

MAKES 7 TABLESPOONS

Cooking Equipment: 3-cup copper sugar pot or comparable-size saucepan

1   tablespoon instant coffee
¼   cup hot tap water
50   small (100 grams) sugar cubes

Place the instant coffee in a small bowl, add the water and stir to combine; set aside.

Pour about half the sugar cubes into the sugar pot or saucepan. Dissolve the sugar over very low heat, swirling to distribute the heat evenly. As the sugar dissolves and liquefies,

Baker's Notes

☞ Classic Royal Icing is a delicious addition when spread in a thin layer on puff pastry before baking.

☞ It may be colored or flavored with chocolate (see page 291).

☞ Whipped, it's elastic enough to pipe script and figures as well as to pipe strings of the icing from one object to another.

☞ If you want to dip cookies (such as Pfefferneuse) into this icing, don't whip the ingredients. Sift the powdered sugar and add 1 teaspoon lemon juice and enough egg whites until it has a thin consistency for dipping.

☞ For a note on uncooked egg whites, see page 31.

Baker's Notes

☞ If you don't have sugar cubes, you may substitute ½ cup granulated sugar. I prefer sugar cubes because their shape regulates how the sugar melts—gradually and evenly, from the bottom up. As the bottom layer melts, it forms a very hot sugar syrup that hastens the melting of the rest of the cube.

☞ You may store this in a small jar on a cool shelf for several weeks.

add the remaining sugar. When the sugar has completely dissolved, raise the heat to medium-high, and cook until it is a deep amber color (darker than honey). Remove from heat; pour in the coffee (careful, it will bubble madly at first); then stir with a small wooden spoon to combine. If some of the caramelized sugar solidifies, place it over very low heat and stir it occasionally until it is melted. Set aside to cool; then pour into small jar to store.

Ground Almond Frangipane

Sometimes named Almond Cream, this almond filling is baked in tarts, tartlets or puff pastry dough. You can vary the flavor by adding, for example, small amounts of currants, grated chocolate or fine-chopped candied citron. You can substitute another nut for the traditional almond or even fold in a soft meringue before baking for a change in texture.

It is the filling for Papillon (page 376).
MAKES 1 ½ CUPS

(page 376)

4	ounces (¾ cup) blanched almonds
4	ounces (1 stick) unsalted butter, room temperature
½	cup (100 grams) granulated sugar
2	large eggs
2	teaspoons dark rum
¼	teaspoon almond extract

Process the almonds in a nut grinder (or other rotary-type grater) until they have the consistency of cornmeal and yield 1 cup ground.

Place the butter in a 1½-quart mixing bowl, and beat it with an electric hand mixer until smooth and soft, as though you were making a butter cake. Add the sugar and continue to beat until combined. Add the eggs, one at a time, and then the rum and almond extract. Stir in the nuts until combined. (Whipping air into the mixture isn't important; just blend the ingredients together smoothly.)

Pour into a container, cover and refrigerate if not using right away. Use within 3 days or freeze up to 1 month.

Baker's Notes

☞ You may also make this in your food processor, using the steel blade for a creamier mixture. Process the ground nuts, sugar and butter (cut into 8 pieces) for about 15 to 25 seconds, until chunky. Add the eggs and flavorings and process until creamy.

☞ As a filling, put ½ recipe of the frangipane in a partially baked tart shell and bake in a preheated 350-degree oven until the tart shell is golden brown. Remove, cool and pipe lemon curd on top or arrange fresh fruit over it.

☞ For a note on uncooked eggs, see page 31.

Decorator's Sliced Almonds

These nuts are perfect for coating or decorating desserts. Their flavor is delicious, and since they are coated and toasted, they do not absorb moisture as quickly as plain sliced nuts. You'll enjoy their crunchy texture and their not-too-sweet flavor.

These are a finishing touch for Chocolate Délice (page 227).
MAKES 1 ½ CUPS

(page 227)

2	tablespoons (1 large) egg white
4	ounces (1 ½ cups) sliced almonds
2	tablespoons (25 grams) granulated sugar

At least 15 minutes before baking, position rack in lower third of oven; preheat oven to 325 degrees.

Place the egg white in a 3-quart mixing bowl; pour in the almonds; then sprinkle the sugar over the almonds. Toss with a rubber spatula to coat the nuts.

Spread the coated nuts in a thin layer on a baking sheet and bake for 20 to 30 minutes, or until lightly toasted and dry. Toss the nuts every 5 to 7 minutes during the baking to redistribute them so that they dry and toast evenly. Remove from oven to a rack to cool. Store them in an airtight tin at room temperature for up to 10 days.

Freshly Grated Coconut

THE FLAVOR of fresh coconut cannot be matched by canned or packaged coconut.

MAKES 2 ½ CUPS

Special Equipment: Hammer and nail

One 2-pound coconut

Draining the liquid: With a nail or screwdriver, carefully puncture two of the holes, or eyes, found at one end of the coconut. Drain the liquid by shaking over a bowl or sink.

Cracking the shell: Place the coconut, eyes down, in the palm of one hand. Tap around the top with the hammer. Soon the coconut's shell will crack all the way around so that you can lift off its top. Continue tapping the remaining shell to break off additional pieces. The coconut meat will naturally break into pieces. Using a vegetable peeler, remove the thin brown skin from the meat.

Grating and drying: You can use a food processor fitted with a shredding disk, a Mouli grater or an electric grater (with a coarse- or fine-shredding disk) for grating coconut for fillings and decorations. After you have grated the coconut meat, spread it on a baking sheet in a thin layer.

Preheat oven to 300 degrees. Place the baking sheet in the oven and dry the shredded or grated coconut for about 25 minutes. Toss the coconut every 5 minutes to ensure its drying evenly. Continue to dry the coconut for 10 to 12 more minutes if you want it lightly toasted.

Storing the grated coconut: Allow the coconut to cool. Then store it in a covered container and refrigerate it for up to 2 days, or freeze for up to 1 month.

Baker's Notes

☞ This method for opening coconut is the best. Freezing or heating it may help you open it, but the flavor will not be at its freshest.

☞ Don't buy a coconut with any sign of mold around its three eyes; it's a sign that the meat is rancid.

☞ Drying and toasting the grated coconut intensifies its flavor. I like to dry the grated coconut without changing its color by baking it in the oven for a short time for most of my decorating. However, toasting it longer until it turns a light brown makes it flavorful and pretty too.

☞ Like all nuts, the coconut should be dried or roasted at a low temperature. If the temperature is too high, it can suddenly burn.

Poached Pears

Baker's Note

☞ It's best to use *slightly* underripe pears for poaching.

POACHED Pears are delicious served plain or with Classic Caramel Cream (page 307).

These are used in La Fleur (page 132).

MAKES 4 PEAR HALVES

    2   medium-size (8 ounces each) underripe pears
    1   recipe Poaching Syrup (page 302)

Peel the firm pears with a vegetable peeler, following the contour of the fruit as closely as possible. (This is particularly important when you prepare fruit that will be visible, such as in a tart.) Cut each pear in half and with a paring knife or melon baller, clean out the seed area.

Pour Poaching Syrup into a 1½-quart saucepan and bring it to a boil over medium heat. Add the fruit and return the syrup to a simmer. To prevent the pears from turning brown, cover them with a paper towel to keep their surfaces moist. Simmer very lightly over low heat, for about 15 minutes, or until a tip of a knife blade inserted into a pear half meets no resistance. Let the fruit cool in the poaching syrup.

Refrigerate in the syrup for up to 3 days.

Streusel

Baker's Notes

☞ Working the streusel with your fingertips gives the best consistency.

☞ Streusel keeps and freezes beautifully. Use the amount needed and keep the remaining portion in a container in the refrigerator or freezer.

THIS STREUSEL is good for baking on top of pies or coffee cakes, providing sweetness and crunch.

It is the topping for Flag-Raising Apple Pie (page 329).

MAKES 2 ½ TO 3 CUPS

    ½   cup (100 grams) light brown sugar, packed
    ½   cup (100 grams) granulated sugar
    1   cup (140 grams) unsifted all-purpose flour
    4   ounces (1 stick) unsalted butter, room temperature

Combine the sugars in a small bowl with your fingertips, breaking up any lumps. Add the flour and mix to combine.

Cut the butter into 8 pieces and scatter them over surface. Work the butter in with your fingertips until the mixture resembles coarse crumbs.

Storing the streusel: Refrigerate it in an airtight container for up to 1 week or freeze for up to 1 month.

Miniature Butterflies

This batter is usually used to make delicate, crisp cookies known as cigarettes.

The butterflies are a finishing touch for Duchess Cake (page 203 and see photograph, page 66).
Makes 6 dozen

Decorating Equipment: 12-x-15½-x-½-inch nonstick baking sheet, small paper cone

7	tablespoons (100 grams) unsalted butter, room temperature
1 ¼	cups (125 grams) unsifted powdered sugar
½	cup (about 4 large) egg whites, room temperature
1	teaspoon vanilla
12	tablespoons (100 grams) unsifted all-purpose flour
1	recipe Classic Royal Icing, optional (page 269)

Advance preparations: Trace a butterfly pattern using the one on the following page as a guide onto a piece of thin cardboard. (The cardboard from a shoe box is the perfect thickness.) Carefully cut out the butterfly shape to give you a pattern for forming the cookies.

Baking preparations: At least 15 minutes before baking, position the rack in the lower third of the oven; preheat oven to 350 degrees.

A nonstick baking sheet is useful for these cookies since they must be removed while warm to bend their shape. If the nonstick coating is old, grease it very lightly with unsalted butter. (Don't use too much butter; the batter will spread too thin during baking, making the cookie too fragile.)

Making the batter: Rinse out a 1½-quart mixing bowl with hot tap water and wipe dry. Place the butter in the bowl and cream it with an electric hand mixer on medium speed until it is creamy and has the consistency of mayonnaise. (The heat in the bowl aids in reaching this consistency.) Add the powdered sugar, about 2 tablespoons at a time, and beat until each addition of sugar is absorbed by the butter before you add more. Beat until light and fluffy.

Whisk the whites briefly to break them up and make them thinner. With a heavy-duty mixer on medium speed, gradually add the whites. Wait for each portion to be incorporated before adding the next. Add the vanilla. (If the mixture looks curdled, beat it on high speed for about 1 minute; then add 1 to 2 tablespoons of the flour toward the end of this time.) Tap the beaters against the edge of the bowl to remove any excess.

Stir in the flour with a rubber spatula in two or three additions until the batter is smooth.

Shaping and baking the butterflies: Position the cardboard stencil on the baking sheet and drop a small amount (about 1 teaspoon) inside it. Spread it thinly inside the stencil with a small offset metal spatula. Carefully lift the stencil. Repeat this procedure

Below: *Butterfly pattern for making a stencil.* Top right: *Spreading batter over the stencil while baked cookies cool on a cake pan rim.* Bottom right: *Piping Classic Royal Icing to decorate the butterflies.*

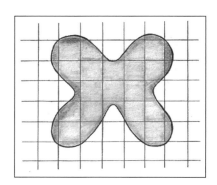

until 6 to 8 butterflies have been formed on the baking sheet. Bake in the preheated 350-degree oven for 5 to 7 minutes; then remove from baking sheet with a metal spatula, and drape each one over the edge of a cake pan to bend slightly. (If the cookies harden before they are removed from the pan, return them to the oven just until they soften.) Repeat with the remaining batter.

Decorating and storing the butterflies: To decorate the butterflies, if desired, place them on plastic wrap when they are crisp and cool. Then prepare Classic Royal Icing (page 269) and pipe antennas through a small paper cone. When the icing is hard and dry (about 1 hour), it releases easily from the plastic wrap. (The antennas break more easily if they are released from aluminum foil or waxed paper.)

Store butterflies in an airtight metal container at room temperature for 2 to 3 days.

Working With Chocolate

Recipes for Chocolate Frostings, Fillings, Glazes and Finishing Touches

Introduction

W HEN YOU work with chocolate, you need to have two things: patience and the right temperature. If you have these, the techniques that follow should guarantee success and save you from the problems all of us have confronted when working with chocolate: tightening, seizing in a fudgelike mass or lumping.

MELTING CHOCOLATE

L EARNING to melt chocolate properly is one of the most important techniques because the chocolate must be in liquid form when you add it to cake batters, glazes, ganache and buttercreams.

Since chocolate melts in your mouth quickly at 98.6 degrees, it's obvious that little heat is required to melt any brand of real chocolate—no matter what the amount. Excessive or direct heat will not only scorch the chocolate, sacrificing its flavor, but it may also separate the cocoa butter from the chocolate solids. Your goal in melting chocolate is to liquefy it, not to cook or heat it.

To accomplish this, I prefer the water-bath (bain-marie) method, in which the chocolate is melted in a bowl that fits snugly over a container half filled with water at 120 degrees (tap water: hot to the hand). Such a setup prevents steam from rising into the chocolate, which can cause it to "seize," that is, lump or tighten into a mass. (There is hardly any steam in 120-degree water.) When melting a large quantity of chocolate, the water will have to be replaced as it cools.

MELTING BITTER, SEMISWEET (ALSO CALLED BITTERSWEET) OR DARK CHOCOLATE

M ELTING chocolate to a creamy, smooth liquid slowly and gradually over the 120-degree water bath is the key to success. To make this process as quick as possible, chop the chocolate into matchstick-size pieces on a dry cutting board with a chef's knife. This allows a greater surface area to be reached at once and speeds the melting process. Then place the pieces into the bowl over the water and wait until about 10 percent of the chocolate has melted before stirring. If you stir too soon, not enough chocolate will have melted, hence the liquid chocolate will adhere to the unmelted pieces and merely resolidify. Replace the water with 120-degree water when it feels cooler. The melted chocolate should never exceed a temperature of 110 degrees. An instant bi-therm thermometer is a valuable aid when you melt chocolate. Just be certain to wipe it dry after testing the water before dipping it into the liquid chocolate. With this method, it usually takes me 5 to 7 minutes to liquefy 4 ounces of chocolate.

Two questions I am frequently asked are (1) may I cover the bowl of chocolate fragments while they are melting? and (2) can the water surround the bowl rather than just touching the bottom? The answer to both, from my experience, is yes. Covering the chocolate will help contain the temperature and hasten melting. If any condensation forms on the lid, the water in the bottom container is too hot. As for surrounding the bowl with water, the additional warmth hastens the melting too.

MELTING MILK OR WHITE CHOCOLATE

MELTING MILK or white chocolate requires more careful attention. If these chocolates have any contact with moisture or if they are melted over water that exceeds 95 to 110 degrees, they tend to tighten, seize or lump quickly. Too much heat affects the milk proteins in the chocolate (a process known as denaturing), causing it to become lumpy.

If any kind of chocolate tightens or seizes into a fudgelike mass during melting, before you add it to another mixture, add small amounts of clarified unsalted butter or vegetable shortening, about a teaspoon at a time. Most of the time it is moisture that creates this unworkable state. If the chocolate is overheated, however, nothing you do will restore its original flavor or gloss.

MELTING CHOCOLATE WITH OTHER INGREDIENTS

MELTING chocolate with other ingredients such as milk, heavy cream and butter is not tricky, provided the amount of these other ingredients isn't so small that the chocolate scorches. When you melt chocolate with other ingredients, you reduce its chances of burning.

There is no formula for how much liquid may be melted with a given amount of chocolate to guarantee that it will not tighten or seize because each brand of chocolate is a recipe itself (and its formula is unknown). From experience, I have discovered that the more fat in the chocolate, the more liquid you need to melt with it. But I've had no problem melting as much as 6 ounces of chocolate with 3 ounces of butter or as much as 4 ounces of chocolate with ¼ cup of heavy cream or milk. I prefer to place the ingredient(s) with the chocolate (chopped into small pieces) in a heavy-bottomed saucepan over low direct heat, and stir until three-quarters of the chocolate has melted. Then I remove it from the heat and allow the residual temperatures of the pan and the liquid to complete the melting. When adding water to unmelted chocolate, do not stir right away—allow most of the chocolate to melt first.

One procedure for melting chocolate that seems to contradict the water-bath method is to pour boiling water over chocolate pieces, drain the water from the bowl, then stir. Voilà, melted chocolate. How does this happen? The water is 212 degrees. Some of the water's heat quickly transfers to the chocolate, cooling the water. But since the water doesn't remain hot for any length of time, the chocolate doesn't scorch. The chocolate pieces do absorb some of the water before draining, but the amount is not enough to cause the chocolate to tighten or seize.

Another procedure for melting that might seem strange, too, is pouring heavy cream that has been brought just to a boil over pieces of chocolate. The two ingredients are stirred together until the chocolate is melted and the mixture smooth. Again, the heat of the heavy cream is immediately dissipated by the chocolate. The chocolate uses the heat of the cream and liquefies in it, and there is sufficient liquid so the chocolate doesn't tighten. Should you add the heavy cream very slowly, stirring in one teaspoon, then another, tightening would occur. The chocolate reacts immediately to the addition of a small amount of liquid, changing its consistency.

These two procedures are commonly used when melting chocolate for such recipes as chocolate mousse, ganache creams or truffles. The resulting mixtures are quite shiny because the cocoa butter in the chocolate has been completely melted; stirring the mixture distributes it and produces the sheen.

ADDING LIQUIDS TO MELTED CHOCOLATE

If you add liquids to already-melted chocolate in very small amounts, the liquid will probably cause the chocolate to tighten or seize. If, however, you add a reasonable amount all at once and the chocolate still isn't a smooth emulsion, then the problem is due to an imbalance in temperature. The cocoa butter in the chocolate just begins to soften but is not liquid at 75 degrees. So if you were to add cold milk from the refrigerator (42 degrees) to 110-degree melted chocolate, it's easy to understand why the chocolate would begin to resolidify and prevent the mixture from becoming smooth. If the liquid you add is even a few degrees above or below that of the chocolate, the cocoa butter may separate (too hot) or resolidify (too cool). The temperature of the liquid must be as close as possible to the temperature of the chocolate before you mix the two together.

I find that a whisk, rather than a rubber spatula, blends the liquid into the melted chocolate quicker and more efficiently. Don't use a metal utensil since its cooler temperature can lower the temperature of the chocolate. Also, if you use a wooden spoon, be certain to earmark it for chocolate use only, unless you like garlic-flavored chocolate.

ADDING MELTED CHOCOLATE
TO OTHER INGREDIENTS OR MIXTURES

To incorporate melted chocolate successfully into whipped cream without melting the cream or to whipped egg whites without deflating them, the chocolate should still be liquid, but neither too warm nor too cold. The same rule applies when you add melted chocolate to batters, buttercreams and the like. The best procedure is to stir a small portion of the mixture into the liquid chocolate, diluting and tempering the chocolate for even distribution into the larger portion.

TEMPERING CHOCOLATE

If you are using chocolate that is first melted and then resolidified, as for molding shapes, dipping candies or as a decoration, you must temper it so that it remains firm and shiny.

If you unwrap a bar of chocolate, you will notice its high gloss, clear design and "snapping" quality when you break it. That is tempered chocolate. Melt it, however, and allow it to resolidify, and it will be dull, perhaps grayish in appearance, without its clean "snap." Melting the chocolate caused it to lose its "temper."

Tempering, which directly affects the cocoa butter, refers to the successive heating, cooling and reheating of chocolate to stabilize the cocoa butter crystals. If the chocolate is heated and cooled improperly, then some of the unstable cocoa butter crystals surface, producing any of several problems: a dull finish, gray appearance or a refusal to set up firmly. Proper tempering makes it possible to mold the chocolate (it contracts from the sides as it cools), gives it a shiny surface and helps it to set up quickly.

There are several methods for tempering chocolate. The most reliable, time-consuming, and best known is the double-boiler method, a three-step process that requires three changes of water. I prefer another reliable method that involves less guesswork. I call this the Short Tempering Method (see below) because it involves only two steps.

Before you begin the Short Tempering Method, assemble the utensils and molds near your work area. Give yourself 30 to 60 minutes for the tempering process and the chocolate work to follow. Should your attempt not be successful, you may remelt the chocolate and try tempering again as long as no other ingredient has been added to it. The chocolate is fine for any other purpose even if it didn't temper properly—don't throw it away.

You may work with any amount of chocolate, but the larger the quantity, the easier it is to maintain its tempered state for some length of time. Three pounds of chocolate may seem like a large amount until you melt it.

Once you have tempered the chocolate, you will want to maintain its temper as long as possible. While working with a portion of the chocolate, keep the bowl of tempered chocolate in a 94-degree water bath. This will maintain the temper for some time (it's not possible to give a time because the amount of chocolate dictates that). Unfortunately, your chocolate will not maintain its temper indefinitely and you may have to retemper it for the same project.

Humidity, like moisture, is a great enemy to chocolate. If you are tempering under very humid conditions, I suggest working in as small an area as possible with one or two inexpensive dehumidifiers.

SHORT TEMPERING METHOD

CHOP 1 pound of chocolate into matchstick-size pieces on a dry cutting board with a chef's knife, reserving one piece of chocolate that weighs approximately 1 ounce. (If tempering 8 ounces of chocolate, reserve a ½-ounce piece of chocolate; if tempering 3 pounds of chocolate, reserve a 3-ounce chunk, etc.) Place the chocolate pieces in a bowl that fits snugly over another saucepan or bowl (a double boiler is fine too) half filled with water no hotter than 120 degrees. As the chocolate melts, the water will cool, so be prepared to replace the water occasionally. (After melting chocolate several times, you'll become accustomed to the feel of 120-degree water, thus eliminating the need to check it with a thermometer.)

When all the chocolate is creamy and liquid and registers 110 degrees on a mercury or bi-therm thermometer, remove the bowl from the container of water, wiping any moisture from the bottom. At this point, you have melted all the cocoa butter crystals, thereby untempering the chocolate. (I call this stage of melted chocolate virgin chocolate.)

Now drop in the reserved chunk of chocolate (tempered chocolate) and stir it around in the melted chocolate. (Do not stir too quickly or too slowly.) As you stir, the chocolate piece melts, inoculating the liquid chocolate with stable cocoa butter crystals (some chefs call this seeding) and at the same time you are lowering the temperature of the chocolate, cooling it. Stir until a thermometer registers 88 to 91 degrees (for dark chocolate) or 85 to 87 degrees (for milk chocolates), removing what remains of the chunk of chocolate. (A small amount applied with a wooden spoon or rubber spatula to your lower lip should feel cool when it is at the proper temperature.)

The process of stirring, the temperature of the room and the relative humidity all contribute to the tempering process. If the temperature of the chocolate falls below the recommended degrees, then the chocolate will either be too thick or set, making it impossible to work with. And any temperature above the recommended degrees will cause your chocolate to lose its temper.

CHOCOLATE FINISHING TOUCHES

YOU CAN produce a variety of shapes with chocolate to decorate your desserts with flair. It's not difficult; it merely requires practice, patience and an eye to the chocolate's temperature. Some of the shapes are made from the bar of chocolate itself; others are made from chocolate spread thinly on a baking sheet.

When I work from a bar of chocolate, I like to use a 13-ounce bar available in most specialty food stores and supermarkets. (Any larger portion of chocolate is fine also.) These sizes give me something to hold on to with a greater surface area for creating the shapes.

When I work with chocolate that I spread thinly on a baking sheet, I prefer to temper the chocolate first. This way, it releases from the baking sheet neatly and easily. You can spread melted chocolate on the baking sheets without tempering it, but forming the shapes from this chocolate can be frustrating.

The key to making a variety of shapes successfully—whether from the chocolate bar or the thin layer of chocolate—is the temperature of the chocolate. In this case, the temperature range is so narrow that only your senses can tell you if the chocolate is ready for a particular shape.

When working with a bar of chocolate for the finishing touches that follow, experimenting with its surface temperature alters its consistency and makes possible a variety of shapes. The same is true when working from the thin sheet of chocolate on the baking sheet. To adjust the surface temperature of a bar of chocolate or a thin sheet of chocolate, place it under a light source such as a gooseneck desk lamp, about 6 inches from the bulb. Obviously, you cannot leave the chocolate for a second because it is affected quickly. Its surface should not be warmed beyond room temperature; if it begins to shine, it is too warm and too soft to form any shape. The cooler the surface, the finer, more brittle the shapes; the warmer surface is more supple and will provide thicker, curlier shapes.

CHOCOLATE FLAKES

WITH A 2-inch paring knife, scrape the tip of the blade firmly but gently down the bar of chocolate. If the chocolate's surface area is cool, you will get fine flakes; if it's slightly warm, the shapes will be very small corkscrews.

SMALL CHOCOLATE PENCIL SHAVINGS

HOLD A shallow, miniature tartlet tin upside down in one hand and draw its edge down the bar's surface firmly. Besides being easy to hold, the tartlet tin has a good edge for this task, and it forms shavings that are broader than those made by a knife blade.

CHOCOLATE SHAVINGS OR CURLS

STAND the chocolate bar on its end, and scrape a vegetable peeler down the edge. If the chocolate's edge is cool, you will get shavings; if it's slightly warm, you will get curls.

LARGE CHOCOLATE SHAVINGS OR LONG CIGARETTES

PLACE the bar of chocolate in front of you and perpendicular to the edge of the counter; brace one end of the chocolate bar against your body. Grip a metal pastry scraper firmly in both hands and with the blade tilted toward you but almost parallel with the bar, scrape down the bar, pulling it forward toward yourself.

If the chocolate's surface area is cool, you will get large shavings; if it's slightly warm, the chocolate will curl into long, thin cigarettes. (See illustration, page 284.)

CHOCOLATE RINGS

MAKE a small paper cone (for instructions on how to do so, see page 244); set aside. Cover a cutting surface with aluminum foil. (Chocolate releases easily from foil, and the foil gives it a special sheen.) Press the wide end of a ½-inch round decorating tip into the foil to make circular impressions.

Temper 4 ounces of chocolate, using the Short Tempering Method on page 281. When the chocolate is the correct temperature, pipe in the circular impressions on the foil. Remove to a cooler room until set.

When ready to use as decoration, gently slip a small metal spatula under each ring to release the chocolate from the foil. (See illustration, page 284.)

CHOCOLATE CIGARETTES

TO MAKE cigarettes that are more perfectly shaped than the ones described above, temper the chocolate using the Short Tempering Method on page 281 so they will release neatly and easily from the baking sheet.. Spread about 7 ounces of the chocolate in a paper-thin layer on the back of a 14-x-17-x-½-inch baking sheet, preferably one that is rimless on three sides with a ½-inch lip at only one end. Hook this lip over the edge of a counter for steady support.

Mark the thin chocolate sheet with the aid of a ruler and the tip of a paring knife with lines to indicate how wide you want the cigarettes to be (I suggest anywhere from 1½ to 8 inches wide), then mark across each strip every 2 inches for each cigarette.

Tilt a pancake-type metal spatula upside down at a 45-degree angle to the baking sheet. Brace the baking sheet with one hand and push the spatula slowly forward, scraping and

Making fine chocolate flakes.

Forming chocolate curls after slightly softening chocolate from a lamp's heat.

Making indentations on foil with a pastry tip.

Piping chocolate rings in the indentations.

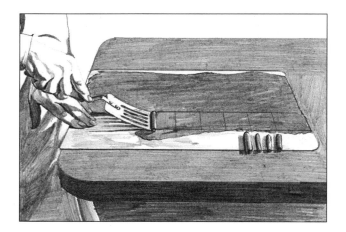

Forming chocolate cigarettes.

Forming a chocolate strip.

lifting the chocolate to the end of the 2-inch section. If the chocolate doesn't curl up in front of the spatula in a continuous piece, it is too cold. Either wave the chocolate-coated baking sheet several inches above a warm burner or position the gooseneck lamp several inches above the chocolate just until it appears to be less brittle and more supple. You can test the chocolate's consistency in one corner of the baking sheet with your finger or the metal spatula. (See illustration, page 284.)

CHOCOLATE STRIPS

You can wrap these supple strips around cakes and desserts that are lightly covered with whipped cream or buttercream.

Temper the chocolate and apply it to the baking sheet as directed above for Chocolate Cigarettes. Then, using a pancake-style metal spatula, push with one hand to lift a strip of chocolate; hold the top edge of the forming strip of chocolate with the fingertips of your other hand. Keep a light, steady tension on the top edge as the strip lengthens; this should be a smooth, synchronized movement between the right and left hand.

The chocolate's temperature is important; it must be supple enough to pull away in one piece (see Chocolate Cigarettes). If too cold, it will crumble; if too warm, it will be soft and form no shape.

The width of the metal spatula will determine the width of the chocolate strip unless you want to mark the thin chocolate strip the exact width of your cake before you begin to lift the strips from the baking sheet. Each time you lift a strip, apply it and fit it to the side of the cake while it is supple. (See illustration, page 284.)

STORING CHOCOLATE FINISHING TOUCHES

I prefer making different chocolate shapes ahead, storing each type in a covered plastic container and freezing them for later. Lift them into the containers with the aid of a pastry scraper. The chill keeps the chocolate dry, but it's especially important for the small fragments of chocolate as the heat of your fingers or hand can melt them when you apply them as decoration. Chilling prevents this from happening quickly.

Chocolate Buttercream

For a note on eggs, see page 31.

A VERY versatile frosting and filling, to which finely chopped nuts may be added.

MAKES 4 CUPS (1 ½ POUNDS)

1	pound (4 sticks) unsalted butter
8	egg yolks
⅓	cup water
1	cup (200 grams) granulated sugar
4	ounces unsweetened chocolate, melted

Prepare as for Classic Buttercream, following each step on page 260, with the following difference:

After adding the butter, stir in about 1 cup of buttercream into the cooler but still liquid chocolate. Then incorporate this mixture into the larger bowl of buttercream

Bittersweet Chocolate Frosting

This will frost two 8- or 9-inch cake layers.

Manipulating the butter until it's soft and smooth, similar to the consistency of mayonnaise, gives body to frosting without adding air bubbles. Combining it gradually with chocolate maintains its dark, rich brown color.

If the weather is cold, add 4 ounces instead of 3 ounces of butter. The chocolate tends to harden in cool weather and the additional butter keeps its softer and satiny.

For a note on uncooked eggs, see page 31.

THE CONSISTENCY of this frosting is neither too thick nor too thin; it is perfect for spreading. Though it is known as Hungarian Frosting, I call it Bittersweet because of its taste.

This is the frosting for Chocolate Gemini (page 94).

MAKES 1 ½ CUPS (14 OUNCES)

3	ounces (6 tablespoons) unsalted butter, room temperature
4	ounces unsweetened chocolate
1	cup (100 grams) powdered sugar
2	tablespoons hot tap water
2	large eggs, room temperature
1	teaspoon vanilla

Ingredient preparations: If you don't have time to let the butter soften, fill a 1½- to 2-quart stainless steel mixing bowl with hot tap water. Pour out the water, wipe the bowl dry and drop in the butter. Using a rubber spatula, mash the butter against the sides of the bowl until it is very soft, smooth and homogeneous (the consistency of mayonnaise). If the butter remains too cold or lumpy, suspend the bowl over a larger bowl filled with hot tap water for a few seconds. You don't want to melt the butter, though the butter touching the sides and bottom of the bowl may begin to. This is no problem; stir quickly to distribute the heat.

If the butter is firm and cold from the beginning of this process, continue to expose it to the hot water and stir as necessary. Be patient; it will soon be smooth. Then set it aside.

Making the frosting: Cut the chocolate into matchstick-size pieces and place them in a 2- or 3-quart stainless steel bowl that fits snugly over another mixing bowl half filled with hot tap water (120 degrees) to touch the bottom of the bowl of chocolate. Stir occasionally until the chocolate is smooth and liquid. (If necessary, replace hot water if it cools.) When the chocolate is melted, remove it from the water.

Pour the sugar into a triple sifter and sift it on top of the melted chocolate, without stirring. Add the hot water; then stir to combine with a rubber spatula. The mixture will thicken like chocolate paste. Add 1 egg and stir to combine before adding the other egg. (Stirring quickly to incorporate the egg is fine, but whisking is not recommended. It introduces too much air, thereby lightening the frosting's rich dark color.) Stir in the vanilla.

Finishing the frosting: Add about ½ cup of the chocolate mixture to the bowl of butter, stirring with a rubber spatula to combine until smooth. Add this mixture to the remaining chocolate, and stir until it is smooth and homogeneous. For best results, use as soon as you finish making it.

Chocolate Sabayon Buttercream

Excellent as a filling or frosting, this may also be piped.

Makes 1 ½ cups

Cooking Equipment: 1½-quart double boiler, mercury candy thermometer, 5-inch sieve

4	ounces (1 stick) unsalted butter, room temperature
2	ounces unsweetened chocolate
2	ounces semisweet chocolate
3	large eggs
⅔	cup (130 grams) granulated sugar

Ingredient preparations: Fill a 1- or 2-quart stainless steel mixing bowl with hot tap water. Pour out the water, wipe the bowl dry and drop in the butter. Using a rubber spatula, smash the butter against the sides of the bowl until it is very soft, smooth and homogeneous (the consistency of mayonnaise). If the butter remains too cold or lumpy, suspend the bowl over a larger bowl filled with hot tap water for just a few seconds. The butter touching the sides and bottom of the bowl may begin to melt; just stir quickly to distribute the heat. If the butter is firm and cold from the beginning of this process, continue to expose it to the hot water and stir as necessary. Be patient; it will soon be smooth. Then set it aside.

Cut the chocolates into matchstick-size pieces; place them in a 1½-quart mixing bowl; rest the sieve over the bowl and set aside.

Making the buttercream: Crack the eggs into the top section of the double boiler and whisk to combine the yolks and whites. Add the sugar, whisking to combine.

Set the top section over lightly boiling water so that bubbles break and just touch the

Baker's Notes

☞ For best spreading, prepare this recipe just before using.

☞ The method of whisking the eggs over bubbling water—not to foam them but to prevent their curdling while the mixture thickens and the eggs cook—gives a special gloss to the frosting.

☞ You can add chopped nuts to the finished frosting if you like.

bottom of the pan. Cook, whisking constantly in a circular, stirring motion to prevent the eggs from setting, until the temperature registers 165 degrees on a mercury candy thermometer and the mixture begins to thicken slightly (about 3 minutes). Some foam will form on the surface from stirring with the whisk; that is fine.

Wipe the bottom of the bowl and pour the hot mixture through the sieve, using a rubber spatula to hasten its flow (the sieve filters any particles of egg). Stir until the chocolate dissolves. Then set aside at room temperature to cool for 15 to 25 minutes, stirring occasionally.

Finishing the buttercream: Pour ½ cup cooled chocolate into the bowl of butter, stirring with a rubber spatula to combine smoothly. Return the mixture to the remaining chocolate, and stir, scraping the sides and bottom of bowl, until the buttercream is a homogeneous mixture. (This procedure retains the chocolate's rich dark brown color.)

For best results (shine and spreadability), use immediately after making to fill and frost a cake.

Cocoa Whipped Cream

An easy-to-prepare filling and frosting.

This is the frosting for Cinderella Cake (page 204).
MAKES 2 CUPS

>   ½   cup (100 grams) granulated sugar
>   ¼   cup (25 grams) unsifted cocoa powder
>   1   cup (8 ounces) heavy cream

Pour the sugar and cocoa powder into a deep 1½-quart mixing bowl; stir with a rubber spatula to blend. Add the cream and combine. Refrigerate for at least 30 minutes before whipping to give the sugar and cocoa time to dissolve. Then whip with an electric hand mixer until soft peaks form. Frost immediately.

Chocolate Whipped Cream

This has a rich chocolate flavor without being sweet.

This is the frosting for Cranberry-Chocolate Eistorte (page 219).
MAKES 2 ½ CUPS

>   4   ounces semisweet chocolate
>   2   tablespoons water
>   1   cup (8 ounces) heavy cream

Chop the chocolate into matchstick-size pieces and place them in a 1-quart mixing bowl that fits snugly over another bowl half filled with hot tap water (120 degrees). When the chocolate is smooth and melted, remove 2 tablespoons water from the bowl below and pour it over the melted chocolate. Whisk until smooth and glossy. Let the chocolate sit over the water and proceed to whip the heavy cream.

Pour the cream into a deep 1½-quart mixing bowl and whip until soft peaks form on the surface but the cream remains somewhat liquid underneath. (You can detect how liquid it is by wiggling the bowl.)

Remove the chocolate from its water bath. It should be at body temperature, no hotter or cooler. Pour in a third of the softly whipped cream and whisk immediately to combine the two. (Note that the cream slightly deflates from the warmth of the chocolate.) Now pour all the chocolate cream into the remaining cream and whisk together until it is incorporated. The cream should be smooth with soft peaks. Additional whisking after the two mixtures are blended will stiffen the cream's consistency; too much additional manipulation will change its smooth texture. Use immediately as a frosting or filling.

Chocolate-Butter Glaze

WHEN THIS glaze is liquid and at about body temperature, it can be poured or spread over a cake. When it cools close to room temperature, it has enough body to be piped in a design on the cake.

MAKES 1 SCANT CUP (9 OUNCES)

    4   ounces semisweet chocolate
    2   ounces unsweetened chocolate
    3   ounces (6 tablespoons) unsalted butter

Chop the chocolates into matchstick-size pieces with a chef's knife on a dry cutting board. Place first the butter, then the chocolate pieces in the top portion of a 1½-quart double boiler (or a 1-quart mixing bowl that fits snugly over a saucepan or another mixing bowl). Fill the bottom vessel half full with hot tap water (120 to 130 degrees) and place the chocolate/butter bowl on top to melt. You may put the double boiler on the stove over a very low flame just to maintain the water's temperature while melting the mixture if you wish.

Stir occasionally to blend until the mixture is smooth, shiny and liquid. Remove from the water, and use according to the instructions for glazing on page 240.

You may make this glaze ahead and store it in an airtight container in the refrigerator up to 2 weeks. To liquefy, heat over a water bath, being careful that the temperature of the water doesn't exceed 130 degrees.

Glossy Cocoa Glaze

THIS not-too-sweet glaze does not lose its gloss when refrigerated because it's made with cocoa powder instead of chocolate.

This is the glaze for Pecan Chantilly (page 192) and Chocolate Éclairs (page 382).

MAKES 2 CUPS

Baker's Note

☞ The preparation can be a bit tricky if the chocolate is not kept liquid while being incorporated with the whipped cream. The temperature of the chocolate and whipped cream is important to avoid small chips of chocolate from appearing.

Baker's Notes

☞ One recipe glazes an 8-inch cake layer.

☞ If in doubt, double the recipe. The decorative finish is more attractive if you don't have to skimp with the glaze. Any leftover glaze keeps in an airtight, covered container for up to 3 weeks in the refrigerator.

☞ Make the glaze at least 1 hour before you plan to apply it to the cake. It is perfect for coating any imperfections on the cake's surface. (See Glazes, page 240.)

☞ When made with a good-quality chocolate (one high in chocolate liquor and cocoa butter), the glaze's gloss and flavor will be superior to that produced by a brand of lesser quality.

☞ Semisweet chocolate is also known as bittersweet.

1 cup (8 ounces) heavy cream
1 tablespoon light corn syrup
1 cup (200 grams) granulated sugar
1 cup (100 grams) unsifted cocoa powder
1 ounce (2 tablespoons) unsalted butter
1 tablespoon vanilla

Baker's Notes

☞ Don't boil the glaze, or you'll scorch it and the fats will separate from the mixture.

☞ While the glaze mixture is cooking, the heat melts the cocoa butter in the cocoa powder and also dissolves the sugar, thus giving shine and luster to the glaze.

Combine the cream and corn syrup in a 1½-quart heavy-bottomed saucepan.

Pour the sugar and cocoa powder into a triple sifter and sift them onto waxed paper (sifting is imperative for a smooth glaze). Add the sugar-cocoa mixture to the saucepan and stir to combine. Add the butter and place over very low heat, stirring constantly, until the butter melts and the glaze is smooth (about 7 minutes).

When the glaze is smooth and warm (never hot; otherwise, separation may occur), remove it from heat and stir in the vanilla. Its consistency resembles a chocolate sauce and thickens upon cooling.

To apply the glaze, pour it over the cake. (See Chocolate Glazes, page 241.) You may apply a second coat to perfect the surface. After the first application, allow the glaze to set (about 30 minutes), then reheat the remaining glaze and pour it over the cake a second time.

You may make this glaze ahead and store in an airtight container in the refrigerator up to 2 weeks. To liquefy, place in a heavy-bottomed saucepan over very low heat, stirring to prevent scorching.

Regal Chocolate Glaze

A BITTERSWEET-flavored glaze, with the rich taste of chocolate.

It is the glaze for Chocolate Rhapsody (page 124).
MAKES ¼ CUP

2 ounces semisweet chocolate
1 ounce (2 tablespoons) unsalted butter
2 tablespoons water

Chop the chocolate into matchstick-size pieces. Place the butter in a 1-quart mixing bowl. Add the chocolate, fit the bowl snugly over another bowl half filled with hot tap water (120 to 140 degrees) and stir until melted and smooth. Remove from the bottom container, take 2 tablespoons water from it, add it to the chocolate-butter mixture and stir until smooth.

Pour or spread the mixture over the surface you wish to glaze while the glaze is warm and liquid. (For instructions on glazing a cake, see page 240.)

Viennese Chocolate Glaze

THIS RICH chocolate glaze is sweeter and more candylike than any other glaze in this book.

This is used to glaze Indianerkrapfen (page 185) and Sacher Roulade (page 187).

MAKES 1 CUP

6	ounces semisweet chocolate
7 to 12	tablespoons Stock Syrup, room temperature (page 302)
1	tablespoon unflavored vegetable oil

Chop the chocolate into matchstick-size pieces and place them in a 1-quart container that fits snugly over a container half filled with hot tap water (120 degrees).

When the chocolate is liquid and smooth, remove it from the bottom container and add 7 tablespoons warm syrup and the oil. Stir until smooth and slightly thinner than honey. If you want it thinner, add more Stock Syrup.

Then pour or spread without delay. (See page 240 for instructions on how to glaze a cake.)

Baker's Notes

☞ To test the glaze's consistency for coating, I pour a small amount over a slice of bread. If it's too thick, I add more Stock Syrup.

☞ If your Stock Syrup is in the refrigerator, heat it in a small saucepan to 70 degrees.

Cocoa Piping Syrup

WHATEVER design you pipe on the cake or petit fours, this mixture remains shiny even after refrigeration.

MAKES 3 TABLESPOONS

¼	cup (25 grams) unsifted cocoa powder
2	tablespoons Stock Syrup (page 302)

Mix the ingredients together in a small mixing bowl to make a thick, smooth paste. Then place over another bowl half filled with hot tap water (120 degrees). Stir until the mixture heats to body temperature, but no more than 100 degrees. The heat from the water bath melts the cocoa butter in the cocoa powder, thinning the mixture and making it glossy.

Fill a handmade paper cone half full, cut its tip and pipe out decorations (page 244).

Chocolate Royal Icing

THIS MAY be used like Classic Royal Icing (page 269). The addition of cocoa powder is a color and flavor variation.

MAKES ½ CUP

1	cup (100 grams) unsifted powdered sugar
¼	cup (25 grams) unsifted cocoa powder
2	tablespoons (1 large) egg white
⅛	teaspoon cream of tartar

Baker's Note

☞ For a note on uncooked egg whites, see page 31.

Fillings and Frostings

Prepare following each step as directed in the recipe for Classic Royal Icing on page 269, adding cocoa powder along with the other ingredients.

White Chocolate Petals

Tʜɪs ʀᴇᴄɪᴘᴇ is adapted from Gaston Lenôtre's Dark Chocolate decoration.

The petals are a finishing touch for Jubilee Petal Cake (page 141 and photograph, page 155).

Mᴀᴋᴇꜱ 75 ᴘᴇᴛᴀʟꜱ

3   ounces white chocolate
1   teaspoon lemon zest

Place the chocolate in a bowl that fits snugly over another bowl half filled with 110-degree water. When almost all the chocolate is melted, remove it from the water bath and add the lemon zest. Stir until the chocolate is smooth.

Place a long (18-inch) sheet of aluminum foil on a flat work surface. Dip the back side of a table teaspoon into the chocolate and smear it gently onto the foil, moving the spoon toward you. Repeat the procedure using about ¼ teaspoon chocolate for each petal.

Allow the petals to set until firm. (You can speed up the process by refrigerating them for about 5 minutes; then remove them and allow to stand until they are completely firm.) When the petals are completely firm, slip the blade of a small metal spatula under each one to release it from the foil. Remove and place in an airtight container up to 3 days.

Baker's Notes

☞ You have to be cautious when melting white chocolate because of its milk content. Excessive heat changes the protein in the milk, resulting in lumpy chocolate.

☞ Choose a white chocolate you enjoy eating for making this recipe.

☞ I add lemon zest to white chocolate to perk up the flavor and take the edge off its sweetness.

☞ When you shape the petals, it's best if your room is cool and dry.

Applying the melted chocolate to the foil with the back of a spoon.

Plastic Chocolate

ADDING corn syrup to melted chocolate produces a chocolate compound that has the consistency of soft clay after it has stood for a while at room temperature. It's an easy mixture to work with for a variety of decorations.

This is rolled around Chocolate Angel Food Roll (page 202).

MAKES ½ CUP

4	ounces semisweet chocolate
3	tablespoons light corn syrup

Chop the chocolate into matchstick-size pieces, and place them in a 1-quart mixing bowl that fits snugly over another bowl half filled with hot tap water (120 degrees). When the chocolate is smooth and liquid, remove the bowl from the container of water.

Add the corn syrup and stir with a rubber spatula until smooth and elastic but no longer creamy (about 30 seconds). At first the mixture is thin and shiny; as you continue to stir, it thickens and becomes dull. Wrap it in plastic and set aside until the mixture is firmer yet still pliable (like soft clay) but is not as hard as a Tootsie Roll (about 20 to 30 minutes). The length of time depends upon the temperature of your room. (If the mixture gets too firm, knead it in your hands since their heat while working the mixture softens it a bit.) Never refrigerate or it will be unworkable.

Forming a chocolate sheet: To form sheets or ribbons, work with the plastic chocolate after it has rested and developed some body, but not so long after that the chocolate hardens completely.

To form a single sheet from the plastic chocolate, lightly sprinkle your work surface with powdered sugar, and roll the plastic chocolate recipe into a thin layer with a rolling pin as though it were dough or marzipan. Continue to dust the work surface with powdered sugar as necessary. After applying the chocolate sheet as you wish to the dessert, brush the excess powdered sugar from its surface if you like.

Forming chocolate ribbons: To form ribbons, pinch off pieces that range in size from a walnut to a golf ball, depending on your preference. Dust them with powdered sugar and roll paper-thin in a long strip like a ribbon with a rolling pin. You can cut and trim the ribbons to fit the sides of your cake precisely if you wish, using a ruler and a pastry wheel.

To form ribbons if the plastic chocolate hardens, break off approximately 2 teaspoons of mixture, flatten it and dust lightly with powdered sugar. Then run it through the kneading rollers of a pasta machine, notching down gradually as you do for making pasta. Place these thin ribbons around and/or over your cake.

Baker's Notes

☞ You can cut different shapes from the chocolate sheets. For example, frost the cake with a thin coating of whipped cream. Then, with a ruler and pastry wheel, cut strips of Plastic Chocolate in widths that match the cake's height. Then fit as many strips as are necessary to go around the cake to cover the whipped cream.

☞ You can form small ribbons to twist and shape into roses.

☞ You can substitute white chocolate for the semisweet. Melt the white chocolate slowly over 110-degree water.

☞ Make sure that each tablespoon of corn syrup is a level measurement.

Working With Sugar

Sugar Syrup Recipes

Introduction

Stages of Sugar Syrups

Sugar Syrup Recipes

Introduction

Ⅰ N BAKING, sugar crystals not only add sweetness but also retain moisture, prolong freshness, assist in creaming and whipping processes, aid in yeast fermentation and contribute good crust color. When used as a major ingredient, such as for fondant, nougatine, caramel and hard candy, the sugar must be in a liquid form and plays an important part in determining texture.

The sugar we are concerned with is sucrose, which is the same as table sugar and originates from the sugarcane or sugar beet. Chemically it is known as a disaccharide, or complex sugar; it is composed of two monosaccharides, or simple, sugars: dextrose (glucose) and levulose (fructose).

A sugar solution is a mixture of sugar and water. This is the basis of a wide variety of products, from a simple poaching syrup to a brittle caramel. The amount of sugar in relation to the amount of water, whether or not it is cooked and for how long are the three determining factors for sugar solutions.

If you add some sugar to a pint of water, the sugar will dissolve and disappear. Only by tasting will you know whether it is there. If you continue to add sugar, it will dissolve and disappear until the water has reached the saturation point and will hold no more. Any sugar added after this will drop to the bottom and be visible.

If a cold saturated solution is heated, almost twice as much sugar can be dissolved into it. The hotter the water, the greater amount of sugar it will hold. At boiling point, hot solutions reach their maximum level of saturation.

If you allow a hot saturated solution to cool, it will precipitate some of the excess sugar in the form of sugar crystals. Because of the drop in temperature, the liquid cannot sustain the sugar in a dissolved state. Suppose, however, you continue to heat it, gradually evaporating away the water. In that case, the solution will become more and more dense as the proportion of sugar to water increases. The concentration of sugar in both hot and cold supersaturated solutions produces crystallization.

SUGAR BOILING

Ⅼ UGAR solutions are boiled to form a syrup that will vary in its concentration or density and thus can be used to make a variety of desserts. It may be added to other ingredients to form buttercreams, Italian meringue or marzipan. It may also be used by itself as a dessert syrup or a poaching syrup or even be caramelized to decorate a cake.

The longer a sugar syrup is boiled, the more concentrated it becomes and the harder it sets when it cools, so the stage to which you allow your syrup to cook will precisely determine the final texture of your product. Since evaporation of the water is what determines the final concentration, the initial proportion of water to sugar is not the most crucial element. If you begin with a large amount of water, you simply must cook the syrup longer before it reaches high-sugar density. There should always be enough water to dissolve the sugar, however, and best results are obtained if the syrup requires only brief boiling before it reaches the desired consistency. Since the majority of the syrups we use for our confections are supersaturated solutions, we must always be concerned with the degree of crystallization.

Crystallization is the inclination of the sugar in a cold or hot supersaturated solution to return to its natural crystalline structure. It occurs because there is insufficient moisture to maintain the sugar in solution.

Crystallization need not be undesirable. It lends texture to many confections. Fudge, for example, can vary in its consistency from grainy (where you feel the grit of sugar crystals when you eat it) to smooth and creamy. Other confections like fondant, marzipan or caramels, however, are not supposed to vary in texture. The final texture is always determined by controlling crystallization.

GUIDES FOR AVOIDING PREMATURE CRYSTALLIZATION

WHEN BOILING sugar syrups, I prefer using a copper sugar pot or a heavy-bottomed enamel-coated pan. These pans have smooth surfaces that are not likely to catch any undissolved granules of sugar that could recrystallize the entire solution later when recrystallization is undesirable.

There are other ways to avoid premature crystallization. One is to be certain that all the sugar is dissolved before the syrup boils. Another is to wash down the sides of the pan frequently once the syrup boils, either with a pastry brush dipped in water or by placing a lid on top and letting the condensed steam wash the sides. The boiling syrup should not be stirred since some of the syrup may be deposited on the sides of the pan and can crystallize too. Swirling the syrup to distribute the heat evenly is fine.

During the boiling of the syrup, the sucrose breaks down from a complex sugar into the two simple sugars dextrose and levulose; this process is called inversion. The more sucrose inverted into simple sugars, the less you have to worry about crystallization because the fewer crystals there are to control.

To reduce the possibility of crystallization in the syrup, it is also common practice to add other simple sugars, such as corn syrup or glucose, which cannot crystallize. Confectioners call this cutting the grain.

Adding an acid, such as cream of tartar or lemon juice, during the boiling process hastens the inversion of some of the sugar.

Adding butter to the syrup lubricates the mixture, preventing a crystal network from forming; confectioners call this greasing the sugar.

GUIDES FOR CONTROLLING CRYSTALLIZATION

Now that you have boiled your syrup to the proper stage, you want to control the formation of the crystals that will provide the characteristic texture.

Crystals form from the manipulation of the syrup; the temperature of the syrup when it is worked determines their size. If the syrup is very hot, the crystal formation is large; if it is cooler, it is smaller.

One way to control the size of the crystals is by seeding—adding a crystal of the desired size to a supersaturated solution. This begins a chain reaction, in which the syrup uses the seed as a pattern, or nucleus, to determine its crystalline structure. For example, when manipulating the syrup to make fondant, you can add a remnant from a previous batch to serve as a nucleus. Because you are placing it in a supersaturated solution, the fondant seeds will not dissolve or be absorbed but will merely act as a pattern.

TESTING THE STAGES OF SUGAR BOILING

Sugar syrups go through various stages. Temperature is one indication of the stage of the syrup, but testing its consistency is a more reliable measure.

Mercury candy thermometers measure the temperature in Fahrenheit degrees. You should first test to determine the accuracy of the thermometer because the syrup's stage must be precisely correct for some products. To test your thermometer, bring some water to a boil and plunge your thermometer into it; it should read 212 degrees. If it does not, adjust or compensate for it. Don't forget to read the temperature at eye level. Before using the candy thermometer, place it in a glass of warm water. This prevents the shock resulting from plunging a cold thermometer into hot liquid and reduces the risk of breakage. It also gives you a reading of your mixture's temperature more quickly.

Professionals working with sugar usually judge the stages by hand-testing the syrup. Considered the most accurate method, this is done by first plunging your fingers into ice water, then immediately dipping them onto the surface of the boiling sugar syrup and back into the ice water. Since I am a coward, I dip a spoon into the syrup and drop some of it into cold water. Then I feel the consistency of the cooled syrup.

Stages of Sugar Syrups

The table below summarizes the different stages to which sugar can be boiled .

Stage	Temperature Range	Characteristics
Thread	230-234	Touch the surface with your finger, join the forefinger with your thumb, and when you pull them apart, a thread forms.
Soft ball	234-240	The mixture will feel sticky and loses its shape when you press it.
Firm ball	244-248	A firm but pliable ball forms.
Hard ball	250-266	When manipulated with fingers, a much firmer ball is formed, but it is still sticky. Syrup is thicker than the firm ball stage, and the temperature rises more rapidly.
Soft crack	270-290	A thin skin is formed at this stage and will crack when touched. Sugar syrup at this stage sticks to your teeth.
Hard crack	300-310	A very thick skin is formed and snaps when it is broken.
Caramel	320-365	The color of the sugar syrup turns from a light to dark amber.

Poaching Syrup

Poaching fruits low in acid in a syrup prevents their turning brown once they are peeled and exposed to the air. Poaching any fruit in this sugar syrup rather than in water also preserves its flavor.

MAKES 6 CUPS

2	pounds (4 cups) water
1	pound (2 ¼ cups) granulated sugar
½	vanilla bean
1	strip lemon peel

Pour the water into a 2-quart saucepan. Add the sugar and stir to combine. Add the vanilla bean and the strip of lemon peel, removed from the lemon with a vegetable peeler. Bring just to a boil, stirring until the sugar is dissolved.

If you are not using the syrup immediately, cool, then pour it into a sturdy container and refrigerate it for 1 week or freeze for up to 3 months.

Baker's Notes

☞ This particular sugar syrup is easy to make. Don't worry about the sugar recrystallizing because the proportion of sugar to water is low.

☞ Each sugar syrup recipe in this chapter uses 1 pound of sugar with varying amounts of water, so that the water to sugar ratio is easily determined. The proportion for this syrup is two to one in weight ratio.

Soaking or Stock Syrup

Combining this soaking syrup with a flavoring, such as a liqueur, creates a syrup used in assembling some desserts.

MAKES 2 ½ CUPS

10	ounces (1 ¼ cups) water
1	pound (2 ¼ cups) granulated sugar

Pour the water into a 1½-quart saucepan. Add the sugar; stir to blend; then bring to a boil over medium heat.

Remove from heat and cool. Pour into a container with a lid and refrigerate up to 6 months.

Baker's Notes

☞ A dessert syrup should be evenly applied when it is brushed on a génoise layer. As a pastry chef advised me, "The last bite must be as good as the first."

☞ Another purpose for this syrup is for thinning fondant and chocolate glazes.

Classic Fondant

Fondant is an icing made by cooking a sugar syrup, then cooling it and manipulating it until it has an opaque white color and is creamy smooth. Ideally, fondant leaves a thin, hard, glossy finish after it has been dipped or spread on cakes.

This is used to glaze Mocha Imperiale (page 137).

MAKES 1 ¼ CUPS (1 POUND)

Cooking Equipment: Mercury candy thermometer, 10-x-15-x-1-inch jelly-roll pan, 5-cup copper sugar pot

½   **pound (1 cup) water**
2   **tablespoons light corn syrup**
1   **pound (2 ¼ cups) granulated sugar**

Pan preparation: Sprinkle the jelly roll pan with water. (It is best to use a brushed aluminum pan since working the syrup in a pan of another material could color the fondant gray.) Set the pan aside.

Cooking the sugar syrup: Pour the water, corn syrup and sugar in that order into a 5-cup copper sugar pot or a 1½-quart heavy-bottomed saucepan. Swirl the pot to combine the ingredients and moisten the sugar. Place over low heat and stir occasionally until the sugar is dissolved (about 5 to 7 minutes). When it has dissolved (the solution appears translucent), stop stirring, raise the heat to medium-high and boil the mixture until it registers 235 degrees (soft ball stage, page 301) on the mercury candy thermometer. Dip a pastry brush into a glass of water to wash down any crystals of sugar that form on the sides of the pot; during the boiling, continue to wash any crystals from the sides. (Or place a lid on top for a few seconds when the mixture begins to boil in order to catch the steam and drop moisture back into the pot, washing down the sides in the process.)

When you reach the soft ball stage (about 5 to 7 minutes), remove the pot from the heat and dip its bottom into cold water to stop the cooking process. Pour the syrup into the jelly roll pan to cool for about 5 to 7 minutes, or until 110 degrees (warm to the touch). For the best crystal formation, do not work the syrup if it is more than 110 degrees.

Working the syrup: Manipulate the outside portion of the syrup toward the center with a moistened pastry scraper or a pancake type of spatula to cool it evenly. As the syrup begins to lighten and thicken, massage it back and forth, kneading it with the scraper or spatula. (The texture changes because the syrup is cooler, and it becomes whiter since crystals are forming and air is being trapped as you work.)

Stop working the mixture when it is smooth, creamy and opaque. If you are not using the mixture right away, scrape it into a sturdy container, place a damp towel over the surface before putting on the lid, and allow the fondant to ripen for at least 12 hours (during this time the structure relaxes and becomes softer) or refrigerate for up to 1 year.

If the fondant becomes difficult for you to work and crumbly, place it in a heavy-duty mixer with the paddle attachment and, on low speed (#2), let the machine knead it until it is smooth and creamy (about 5 to 10 minutes). If, on the other hand, the syrup never changes from a syrupy stage, remaining thin, you probably didn't cook it to a high enough temperature. Add ½ cup water and recook it to the soft ball stage; then proceed again in working the syrup to make fondant.

Melting the fondant: In order to work with fondant successfully in glazing cakes or petits fours, it must be melted and thinned to make it fluid enough to handle. It must be thinned with a solution most like itself (Stock Syrup, page 302) to maintain its crystalline structure. (Water is too thin and would disrupt its structure.)

Pour some Stock Syrup in a small saucepan and heat just to warm it.

For best results, heat only the amount of fondant you need. Put it in a small saucepan over a larger pan filled with hot tap water. (Do not use a saucepan that will color the fondant as you stir it.) To maintain the water's temperature, place the pan on very low heat. Stir the fondant with a rubber spatula until it is melted. Then add the coloring and/or flavoring as the specific recipe indicates. Add stock syrup as needed to make the fondant thin enough for your purpose. If it is to be spread on top of a cake, it need not be as liquid as if it were being poured to glaze petits fours.

For best results in maintaining fondant's crystalline structure, heat the fondant to at least body temperature but no higher than 108 degrees. Stir it slowly, keeping it moving to heat it evenly, but do not whip air into it. Chill the object(s) to be glazed briefly in the freezer before the glazing, so the fondant will set up quickly. For the technique of applying the fondant, see page 138.

Classic Marzipan

A SMOOTH almond mixture, sweeter than almond paste, marzipan can be rolled into thin sheets or strips to decorate a cake or other dessert. It can also be colored and shaped into small flowers, fruits or vegetables as confections.

Though you can buy marzipan, I prefer making my own for several reasons. It is better-tasting, less sweet and easier to handle than the purchased variety. It isn't difficult to make, and it remains fresh for several weeks if it is carefully wrapped and refrigerated.

Thanks to Doug Basegio, owner of the Woodside Bakery in Woodside, California, for sharing this recipe.

MAKES 1 ¾ CUPS (1 ½ POUNDS)

Cooking Equipment: Mercury candy thermometer, 5-cup copper sugar pot or a 1½-quart heavy-bottomed saucepan

1	pound (scant 2 cups) almond paste, room temperature
⅓	cup (3 ounces) water
2	tablespoons light corn syrup
1	cup (200 grams) granulated sugar
	Powdered sugar
	Cornstarch

Ingredient preparation: Place the almond paste in the bowl of a heavy-duty mixer, and mix on low speed (#2 or #3) with the flat beater (paddle) attachment, just to break it up into several pieces.

Cooking the sugar syrup: Pour the water, corn syrup and granulated sugar into the 5-cup copper sugar pot or the 1½-quart heavy-bottomed saucepan. Swirl the pot to combine the ingredients. Place over low heat and stir occasionally until the sugar dissolves (about 5 to 6 minutes). Then stop stirring, raise the heat to medium-high and boil the mixture until it registers 250 degrees (firm ball stage, page 301) on the mercury candy thermometer. Dip a pastry brush into a glass of water to wash down any crystals of sugar that form on the sides of the pot. This cooking process takes about 3 minutes.

Baker's Note

☞ The sugar syrup will be cooked to the firm ball stage (page 301), 250 degrees, before being added to the almond paste. As it reaches this temperature, the bubble formation becomes thicker, smaller and slower to develop since liquid has evaporated.

Combining the paste and syrup: When the sugar syrup has reached the firm ball stage, begin mixing the almond paste on low speed (#2 to #3); as you mix, without delay, pour the sugar syrup onto the almond paste. (Avoid pouring syrup on the beater or down the sides of the bowl.) When all the syrup has been added, stop the mixer and scrape the sides of the bowl, pushing the mixture into the center. Increase the speed to medium (#5) and mix for about 3 minutes.

Reduce the speed (#2) and mix until the mixture lightens in color (ivory-white) and is cool to the touch (about 2 minutes).

Finishing the marzipan: Lightly dust your work surface with powdered sugar and knead the marzipan gently by hand until it is pliable and no longer sticky (about 2 minutes). Use the powdered sugar sparingly, about 3 tablespoons in all.

Storing the marzipan: If you are not using the marzipan right away, form it into a sausage shape, wrap it in plastic, then wrap it in foil and refrigerate for up to 2 months.

Tinting the marzipan: Set aside the amount needed, wrapped in plastic, until it reaches room temperature. Then unwrap and place it on a clean work surface. (A clean surface is essential; otherwise, the marzipan picks up stray bits and mars the dessert's appearance.) Flatten the marzipan with the palm of the hand to a small disk and add drop(s) of food coloring in the center. Knead to distribute the coloring evenly, sprinkling the work area lightly with cornstarch to reduce the marzipan's stickiness. (Cornstarch is used now, rather than powdered sugar, because the sugar attracts moisture, causing sweating on the marzipan's surface. Using cornstarch is especially important if you plan to roll the marzipan in a thin layer to cover a cake.)

All-Purpose Caramelized Sugar

I USE THIS all-purpose caramel for glazing cream puffs, thin cake layers and small cake circles, as in **Lemon Mist Torte** (page 142); for making spun sugar, for shaping cages or crowns and for pulling sugar to form ribbons.

MAKES 2 CUPS

Cooking Equipment: 5-cup copper sugar pot or a 1½-quart heavy saucepan stainless steel mixing bowl

¼	cup water
½	cup light corn syrup
1	cup (200 grams) granulated sugar

Cooking the sugar syrup: Pour the water, corn syrup and sugar into a 5-cup copper sugar pot or a 1½-quart heavy-bottomed saucepan. Swirl the pot to combine the ingredients and moisten the sugar. Place over low heat and stir occasionally until the sugar is dissolved (about 5 to 6 minutes). When the sugar has dissolved, stop stirring, raise the heat to medium-high and boil the mixture until it reaches the color the specific recipe

Baker's Notes

☞ You can use a copper sugar pot, a heavy-bottomed saucepan or a shallow frying pan to caramelize the sugar.

☞ The corn syrup keeps the caramelized sugar more pliable and less brittle while it is hot and makes it more resistant to humidity when it is firm.

Fillings and Frostings

directs (for example, a light amber color takes 7 to 9 minutes). Dip a pastry brush into a glass of water to wash down any crystals of sugar that form on the sides of the pot while the sugar solution cooks. The syrup may begin to color in one section of the pot first. Swirl the pot to distribute the heat evenly. When the sugar syrup begins to smoke, this is an indication that the temperature is high and color will deepen rapidly.

Test to see if the color is correct for your purpose. Then dip the bottom of the pot into cold water to stop the cooking process. (If you are using a copper pot, it may be wise to stop cooking the syrup before the desired caramel stage and allow the pot's heat to continue to raise the temperature.)

GLAZING SMALL PASTRIES

Follow each step in preparing All-Purpose Caramelized Sugar (page 305). When it is amber-colored, dip individual pieces into the caramel. The caramel is easier to reach if the pot is tilted. (If dipping many items, you may want to dip the pot in cold water to stop the cooking process, thus preventing further color change.)

GLAZING A CAKE LAYER

Warm the cake layer to be glazed in a preheated 200-degree oven for a few minutes. Remove the layer to a clean cutting board. Pour some of the caramel over the cake and spread it quickly in a thin layer with a flexible metal icing spatula. Cut individual cake portions with an oiled knife blade while the caramel is still warm and pliable.

GLAZING NUTS

Skewer the bottom of each nut with a toothpick. Place a strip of aluminum foil on a work surface and place an orange in the center. (The foil makes cleanup easy; the orange holds the speared nuts while the glaze sets.)

When the caramel is amber-colored, remove the pot from the heat and dip the bottom of the pot into cold water to stop the cooking process.

Dip one skewered nut at a time and stick it into the orange to set until it is cool and firm. If the caramel becomes too thick for a thin coating, return it to a very low heat to melt it again. Its color will not change because not enough heat accumulates to change it.

Continue to dip the nuts. When they are firm and cool to the touch, remove the toothpicks from the orange. Trim extra caramel and strings from each nut with scissors; then remove the toothpick. If you are not using the nuts that day, store them in an airtight container for up to 1 week.

MAKING SPUN SUGAR

Spun sugar is a dramatic finishing touch for many desserts. When the caramel is honey-to amber-colored, stop its cooking by dipping the bottom of the pot into cold water. Then allow the caramel to cool for about 3 minutes. (This cooling period is necessary to allow the caramel to form golden strings; if the caramel is too hot, small beads will drop when it is lifted on a fork.)

Dip the tines of a fork or a cutoff whisk into the syrup which has a color and consistency similar to that of honey. Pull up and lift the golden strings that form (they will not be too hot to touch). You may wrap them around your hand to form a nest or around the

☞ If you use a copper sugar pot, the heat remains longer than in other metals so that the caramelized sugar's temperature continues to rise after you remove it from your heat source. Either stop short of the desired temperature and color you wish and allow the residual heat in the pan to complete the cooking, or continue heating the mixture until it is close to the stage you want. Then plunge the pan into ice water to stop the cooking.

☞ When the sugar syrup cooks to the caramel stage, it may be difficult to get an accurate perspective on its color just by looking into the pot. Instead drop a dot of the sugar solution onto something white to give you the best frame of reference.

☞ Glaze for cakes or cream puffs should be lighter in color than that for spun sugar, caramel stages or crowns.

☞ You can reliquefy this caramel over very low heat if it gets too thick or solidifies.

outside of a cake. If you are not using the strands right away, place them in an airtight metal container for a couple of hours before using on a dessert.

MAKING CARAMEL CROWNS OR CAGES

Follow the directions for spun sugar above.

The only difference between a crown or a cage is the size. Lightly grease the outside of a stainless steel mixing bowl (for a cage) or the outside of a ladle (for a crown) with solid shortening. Dip a fork into the caramel sugar syrup, lift it and zigzag it back and forth over the lightly greased surface. (Put a mitt on the hand holding the ladle or container in case some of the sugar drops.) Continue until the bowl or ladle is covered with enough caramel strings to form a cage or crown.

Wait for a few seconds after applying the last few strings of caramel; then gently lift the form off. (If it is allowed to cool completely on the container or ladle, it will stick to it and perhaps crack when removed.)

Store in an airtight metal container at room temperature for a couple of hours before placing it on a dessert.

MAKING CARAMEL RIBBONS

When the caramel is amber-colored, stop its cooking by dipping the bottom of the pot in cold water. Then pour the caramel onto a marble slab or into a baking pan with sides. Manipulate the outer portion of the syrup toward the center with a moistened pastry scraper to cool it evenly. When it is thicker and cooler (careful, it is still very hot; some people use surgical or rubber gloves), pick up a section of the caramel, and pull it as though it were taffy. Shape it into ribbons or bows for decoration.

Store in an airtight metal container at room temperature for a couple of hours before using on a dessert.

Classic Caramel Cream

CARAMEL cream which is sugar melted and heated to the caramel stage with cream added after, is wonderful over ice cream or fruit.

This is used in Banana Caramel Tart (page 349).

MAKES ⅔ CUP

Cooking Equipment: 3-cup copper sugar pot or a 1-quart heavy-bottomed saucepan

¼	cup water
¾	cup (50 grams) granulated sugar
⅓	cup heavy cream

Cooking the sugar syrup: Pour the water and sugar into the 3-cup copper sugar pot or the 1-quart heavy-bottomed saucepan. Swirl the pot to combine the ingredients and moisten the sugar. Place over low heat and stir occasionally until the sugar is dissolved. When the sugar has dissolved, stop stirring, raise the heat to medium-high and

Baker's Notes

☞ To make a caramel syrup thin and clear, add ½ cup water instead of heavy cream after you have caramelized the sugar.

☞ To make a thinner caramel cream for serving over ice cream, poached pears and peaches, or as a base for flavoring buttercreams, use ½ to ⅔ cup of heavy cream instead of the ⅓ cup in this recipe.

☞ To make a divine chocolate-caramel cream, add this caramel cream to 4 ounces melted dark chocolate.

☞ Another flavor variation is to substitute ⅓ cup coffee or ⅓ cup orange juice for the heavy cream in the recipe.

boil the mixture. Dip a pastry brush into a glass of water to wash down any crystals of sugar that form on the side of the pot while the sugar solution cooks. The syrup may begin to color in one section of the pot first. Swirl the pot to distribute the heat evenly. Boil until the caramel is amber-colored. (Check for desired color by placing a small amount on something white.)

Remove from the heat and pour in the heavy cream all at once. (The mixture will foam, climbing up the sides of the pot. It may appear that the mixture will overflow, but it won't.) Stir the mixture with a wooden spoon to distribute the heat and blend the ingredients together. Set aside to cool for only 10 minutes; then pour the cream into the baked tart shell, spreading it evenly with a rubber spatula.

Classic Praline

CLASSIC Praline adds flavor and texture to several dessert creams, chocolate and even mousses.

MAKES 8 OUNCES

Cooking Equipment: 5-cup copper sugar pot or a 1½-quart heavy-bottomed saucepan or a 10-inch skillet, baking sheet

2	ounces (⅓ cup) blanched almonds
2	ounces (⅓ cup) hazelnuts
2	teaspoons vegetable oil
50	small (100 grams) sugar cubes

Ingredient preparations: Roast the almonds and hazelnuts in a preheated 325-degree oven on a baking sheet for 10 to 15 minutes, or until lightly colored.

Pan preparation: Lightly grease a baking sheet with 2 teaspoons vegetable oil; set aside.

Cooking the sugar syrup: Place the sugar in the 5-cup copper sugar pot or the 1½-quart heavy-bottomed saucepan or a 10-inch skillet. Place over low heat until the sugar dissolves; swirl to distribute the heat evenly if necessary. When the sugar has dissolved, raise the heat to medium-high until the melted sugar reaches an amber color (about 8 to 10 minutes). If the syrup begins to color in one spot first, swirl the pot to distribute the heat evenly.

When the color is amber, pour in the roasted nuts. Remove from heat and swirl; then pour out onto the baking sheet. Set aside to cool and firm for about 1 hour.

Storing the praline: If you are not using the praline immediately, store in an airtight metal container for 7 to 10 days at room temperature.

Baker's Notes

☞ You can use only one type of nut instead of the traditional combination of almonds and hazelnuts.

☞ Roasting the nuts adds flavor. Removing the hazelnut's brown skin also takes away its bitter flavor.

☞ If you don't have small sugar cubes, substitute ½ cup (100 grams) granulated sugar.

☞ Praline should be made ahead of time so it can cool and firm.

Praline Powder

GREAT for flavoring buttercream or pastry cream or for decorating cakes.

MAKES 1 ¼ CUPS CRUMBS

Prepare Classic Praline as directed on page 308. Set aside to cool and firm.

To make Praline Powder, break the cool, firm praline into small pieces and place them in the bowl of a food processor fitted with a steel blade (or blender). Process with short on/off bursts until the praline has the consistency of crumbs. Pour the crumbs through a sieve over a bowl to strain out any larger lumps. If not using immediately, store no more than 2 days in an airtight metal container at room temperature.

Praline Paste

PRALINE Paste is the opposite of Classic Praline (page 308). Its consistency is that of a paste, similar to peanut butter. It may be added to buttercreams or whipped cream as a flavoring.

MAKES ½ CUP

Prepare Classic Praline as directed on page 308. Set aside to cool and firm.

Break up the praline and process it in the food processor beyond the stage of forming crumbs, as for Praline Powder (above), for a total of 5 to 6 minutes, or until it has the consistency of peanut butter. If not using right away, store in a covered container at room temperature up to 1 week.

Classic Nougatine

THIS NUT brittle of caramelized sugar and lots of finely chopped nuts may be shaped into forms for filling with ice cream, sherbet, sorbet or fruit, or rolled thin and cut into shapes for decorating desserts.

MAKES 9 OUNCES

Cooking Equipment: 5-cup copper sugar pot or a comparable-size heavy-bottomed saucepan, ½-inch (#6) round decorating tip, hammer

4	ounces (⅔ cup) toasted blanched almonds
⅓	cup corn syrup
½	cup plus 2 tablespoons (125 grams) granulated sugar

Preparations: Lightly oil a clean plastic cutting board or marble slab; rub about 2 to 3 teaspoons of vegetable oil on your rolling pin. Lightly oil a pastry scraper, and if you plan to cut out shapes from the nougatine, dip the cutter's surface in oil, too.

Chop the almonds with a chef's knife on a cutting board until they are small dice, about ¾ cup. (For a clearer, shinier nougatine, place the chopped nuts into a sieve and shake it to remove the fine nut powder; you will have about ⅔ cup chopped nuts now. Either amount of nuts is fine.)

Preheat oven to 140 degrees. Pour the chopped almonds into a small bowl and warm them while you cook the sugar syrup.

Cooking the syrup: Heat the corn syrup in the 5-cup copper sugar pot or a comparable-size heavy-bottomed saucepan just to warm it. Then pour in the sugar and stir to combine. Over low heat, dissolve the sugar in the corn syrup (about 5 to 7 minutes). Raise the heat and cook the syrup, swirling the pan occasionally to distribute the heat, until amber-colored (about 2 to 2½ minutes). Remove from the heat and stir in the nuts. (As the different temperatures blend together, the mixture foams up briefly.) Pour onto the oiled work surface. Let the mixture cool for 45 to 60 seconds to make rolling easier.

Rolling the nougatine: After cooling the nougatine briefly, lift the outside portions five or six times toward the center with the oiled pastry scraper to cool it evenly. Then roll over it while it is warm and flexible until it is close to ⅛ inch thick. (If you roll it too soon, the syrup will stick to the rolling pin because it is too hot. On the other hand, if the syrup is too cool, it will not be flexible enough to move.)

Shaping nougatine circles: While the nougatine is warm and flexible, not cold and brittle, hammer an inverted ½-inch pastry tip into it to form circles, then lift them out.

Shaping a nougatine bowl: Lift the warm, flexible nougatine over the outside of an inverted oiled mixing bowl, and press it to form the bowl's shape. Then turn the nougatine-covered bowl right side up. While the nougatine is warm, cut the excess nougatine around the bowl's rim with oiled scissors. Invert the bowl again with the nougatine on top. When it is cool and firm, remove it from the mixing bowl.

Storing the nougatine: Store in airtight metal containers for up to 2 or 3 days at room temperature.

Macadamia Nut Brittle

A DELICIOUS candy to give as a gift in a decorative tin.

Macadamia Nut Brittle is used in Macadamia Cream Pie (page 335).
MAKES 1 CUP

Cooking Equipment: 5-cup copper sugar pot or a 1½-quart heavy-bottomed saucepan, mercury candy thermometer

3	ounces unsalted macadamia nuts
¼	teaspoon baking soda
¼	cup (2 ounces) water
½	cup (100 grams) granulated sugar
1	ounce (2 tablespoons) unsalted butter
1	tablespoon butter

Preparations: Using a paper towel, spread a thin film of unflavored vegetable oil on a baking sheet; set aside.

Pour the nuts into a food processor fitted with a steel blade, and process with on/off bursts until you have ¾ cup coarsely chopped nuts. (Or chop into coarse pieces on a cutting board with a chef's knife.) Pour into a small bowl, sprinkle with the baking soda, and toss briefly just to combine.

Cooking the syrup: Pour the water, then the sugar into the 5-cup copper sugar pot or the 1½-quart heavy-bottomed saucepan, and place over low heat; swirl to moisten the sugar. Heat until the sugar dissolves. Add the butter, raise heat to medium and boil the mixture until it registers 280 degrees on the mercury candy thermometer (about 5 to 7 minutes).

Finishing and storing the brittle: Remove from heat, immediately add nuts and stir briefly just to combine. The mixture will foam because the heat activates the soda, which lightens the brittle's texture. (Too much stirring will deflate the brittle.) Pour the mixture onto the baking sheet; set aside to cool and harden.

When the brittle is completely cool, store it in an airtight metal container for up to 1 month at room temperature.

Baker's Notes

☞ Cashews or even unblanched almonds may be substituted for the macadamia nuts.

☞ Unsalted macadamia nuts may be found at health food stores.

☞ If only salted nuts are available, toss and roll them first in a dry towel, then in a damp towel; spread them in a thin layer on a baking sheet to air-dry for a few hours.

Understanding Pastrymaking

~

Introduction

MENTION PASTRY and visions of light, thin, golden crusts filled with fresh fruits, satiny creams and nut-studded mixtures come to mind. In a sense, pastrymaking is the art of making containers for different fillings: The type of dough you make will depend on the texture of the container you want.

Pastry doughs, which bakers also call pastes, can be either stiff or soft. They are classified according to the proportion of liquid to flour they contain. Doughs are higher in fat and lower in liquid than a cake batter. All pastry doughs have three common ingredients: flour, fat and liquid.

The types of fat, liquid and flour, as well as their proportion to one another, contribute to a large variety of textures in pastrymaking. These same factors also influence the method you choose to make different doughs. Although these ingredients may be similar in different recipes, the techniques employed for forming the dough will determine its texture. So, too, will proper gluten development.

THE INGREDIENTS AND THEIR ROLE

FLOUR

FLOUR is a complex, varied ingredient essential to all baking—but nowhere are its capabilities more important than in pastrymaking because it is always a major ingredient in the recipe.

The type of flour most commonly used to make pastry dough is wheat flour, milled from the wheat kernel. Its primary components are starch and protein. It also contains fat, ash, minerals, enzymes and moisture in smaller amounts.

The wheat kernel consists of three principal parts: the endosperm, the bran and the germ. Whole-wheat and graham flours are achieved by milling the whole kernel; white flour is produced by removing the bran and germ and milling only the endosperm.

I use white flour for cake and pastrymaking because of its fine texture, mild flavor and its ability to form gluten. When you add liquid to flour and manipulate the dough, the protein in the flour develops into gluten, which allows the dough to stretch and expand in the oven and gives shape and structure to baked goods. The dough's ability to form an elastic network is what ranks white flour over all other grains in making dessert pastries.

There are many different varieties of white flour, which vary in flavor and their ability to develop gluten. Unfortunately, there is no hard and fast rule about selecting white flour for pastry other than the wisdom you acquire from personal experience. The process of developing a keen understanding of flour is complicated by the fact that the same brand can vary from year to year, depending upon the wheat crop and the market to which the miller wants to cater.

In addition, when you choose white flour for a recipe, you must consider a number of factors: the other ingredients you are adding to the dough; the amount of fat; whether you will be rolling the dough a lot; whether the batter must withstand the effects of chemical leavening without collapsing and whether the ingredients need merely to bind together.

The quality of the protein in wheat flour, which in turn affects the formation of gluten, depends on the region in which the wheat was grown, the condition of the soil and the time of year it grew. Hard wheat is planted in the spring and harvested in the fall; it is grown in climates that have short, hot summers. Hard wheat produces a flour that is low in starch and high in protein, ensuring good gluten development. Such flours are known as strong flours or bread flours. Durum is a special variety of hard wheat used for producing semolina, a high-gluten flour used in pasta making.

Soft wheat is planted in the winter and harvested the following summer; it is usually grown in southern climates, where there is a long growing season. Soft-wheat flours are lower in protein (about 6 to 9 percent) and higher in starch. They are also known as weak flours and include cake and pastry flours. They are used for cakes, biscuits and some pastry doughs, such as piecrusts.

The main component of all white flour is starch (70 to 75 percent). When mixed with water and exposed to heat, the starch granules swell, producing bulk and contributing to the texture. As the starch is heated, the granules burst, losing their original shape and forming a paste, sucking up moisture. Starch, however, does not absorb as much liquid as protein.

Between 6 to 20 percent of white flour is protein, the single most important element. (Not all the protein in the flour will develop into gluten, however.) Protein is what a baker looks for when selecting the proper flour for a cake or pastry. It has a great capacity to absorb moisture, so the higher the protein content, the more liquid it can absorb.

Flour contains two enzymes: diastase and protease. Diastase acts upon some of the starch in the flour, converting it into malt sugar. Protease changes some of the insoluble proteins in the dough to a soluble form: It mellows and softens the gluten, making it more extendable during rolling. This is why pastry dough is easier to roll after it has been rested.

TYPES OF WHITE FLOUR

ALTHOUGH there are basically four types of white-wheat flour: hard-wheat flour, all-purpose flour (a mixture of hard- and soft-wheat flour) and the two soft-wheat flours pastry flour and cake flour, there are innumerable brands of each available.

HARD-WHEAT FLOUR

CREAMY colored and granular in texture, milled from hard winter wheat, the high-protein content (12 to 14 percent) of this flour assures the good gluten development necessary for bread, strudel dough and some puff pastry recipes.

ALL-PURPOSE FLOUR

CREATED by blending both hard- and soft-wheat flours, all-purpose flour is a medium-strength flour with a protein content that ranges from 10 to 11 percent. Professional bakers, however, do not use all-purpose flours, preferring to use one particular type depending on what they are making. Don't be misled and think all-purpose flour is best for almost everything you bake. Since each miller may blend his all-purpose flour with different amounts of protein and starch, the flour you buy can vary from brand to brand. Check the protein content listed on the nutritional label for a close indication. The same brand of flour may even contain a different amount of protein when packed in smaller bags, according to Shirley Corriher, a fellow baker. This practice is allegedly based upon the miller's assumption that small bags of flour will be used for pastry creams, gravies and sauces, whereas the larger bags will be used primarily for bread making.

Bleached all-purpose flour has usually been bleached of any pigmentation and contains a dough conditioner as well. This makes the flour slightly more acidic and the gluten more extensible when rolling doughs. When I need all-purpose flour for cakes, cookies or doughs, this is the type I most often use.

Some bakers feel unbleached flour has more flavor than bleached flour and is healthier. The only difference I find is that doughs made with unbleached flour turn gray after being stored a day or two in the refrigerator. The graying doesn't affect baking results.

Most of the major brands of all-purpose flour declare on the package that the flour has been presifted at the mill to make it more free flowing. After you get the bag of flour home after shopping, however, it is essentially unsifted flour. For accurate measurement, sifting will be necessary before baking (unless you weigh your ingredients).

Self-rising all-purpose flour refers to a flour that has had baking powder and salt added at the mill. It is used for biscuits and sometimes cakes and pastries.

PASTRY FLOUR

MILLED from soft winter wheat, pastry flour contains about 8 to 9 percent protein. Its texture is soft, and it is ivory in color. It is usually found in specialty shops such as health-food stores. It is wonderful for pie, galette or tart doughs.

CAKE FLOUR

THIS FLOUR is also milled from soft winter wheat and contains only about 6 to 8 percent protein; it is smooth and velvety in texture, packing together easily when pressed in the hand. Low-protein flours are best for chemically leavened baked goods, such as cakes and muffins.

Flour Power

Flour	Wheat	Approx. Protein Content	Strength	Uses
All-purpose, bleached	soft & hard	10.5 %	medium	all-purpose: cakes, cookies, bread, pastries
Cake, bleached	soft	6 to 8 %	weak	cakes & cookies
Pastry	soft	9 %	weak	pies, galettes, cookies
Bread	hard	12 to 13 %	strong	breads & some pastries

LIQUIDS

WATER and milk are the most commonly used liquids in pastrymaking. But orange juice, lemon juice, heavy cream, even sour cream are fine for certain recipes. It is only after liquid has been added, hydrating the protein in the flour particles, that gluten can begin to develop in a dough. Thus the amount of liquid absorbed can affect a dough's toughness or tenderness. A small amount of liquid is added to a pie dough where little gluten development is needed. During the baking process, liquids change to steam, contributing to the leavening of your pastry. Milk products add color and richness and prolong the freshness of baked goods.

FATS

WHEN MAKING pastries, you want the flavor of fat not of flour to predominate. Besides adding richness, tenderness and flavor, fat (shortening) has a physical effect: It interrupts the formation of a strong gluten network by literally shortening the gluten strands and coating some of the flour particles. This coating prevents the liquid from penetrating all the protein in the flour and activating it.

Thus fat lubricates and tenderizes pastries and improves their eating quality. Other ingredients such as milk or sugar are absorbed into the dough, but fat always remains separate. It may seem to disappear, but the texture will reveal that the fat did not actually unite with the other ingredients.

Besides tenderizing, fat contributes flakiness and assists in leavening doughs. The method you use to disperse the fat (creaming, cutting it in, melting it or rolling it in), the amount, the type of fat, its temperature, how you manipulate it and for how long all influence the pastry.

The various fats used in pastrymaking differ in flavor and in their physical abilities:

BUTTER

BUTTER is 80 to 84 percent milk fat; I use it for its flavor, even though it has a low melting point. Unsalted (sweet) butter is the best choice, for it has a natural, delicate flavor. If you use salted butter, you never know how much salt it contains, so it is difficult to control the taste of your pastry. The effects of this unknown quantity of salt may not combine favorably with the protein in your flour. (Salt fortifies the protein, which could provide more gluten development than you want.) Unsalted butter freezes well, but freezing does modify its flavor slightly.

MARGARINE

MARGARINE is made with vegetable or animal fats and churned with milk or cream, though some margarines are 100 percent vegetable fat. It has a higher melting point than butter but does not contribute the same texture or taste.

If you must use margarine, shop for the unsalted variety usually found in the freezer section at the supermarket.

SOLID VEGETABLE SHORTENING

THIS shortening is 100 percent fat, making for tender pastries, because its plastic (malleable) consistency and lack of liquid give it more shortening power than butter. I use solid all-vegetable shortening when I want a very high, tender, flaky-textured pastry, such as a piecrust.

LARD

LARD is rendered from pig fat, and although it is excellent for some types of pastry such as savory meat pies, I do not use it for desserts because of its flavor. It, too, is 100 percent fat, but not as plastic as vegetable shortening.

EGGS

WE ARE accustomed to egg yolks in cakes and cookies, but are less familiar with them in puff pastry. Egg yolks are an additional source of fat and lubricate the gluten strands and contribute tenderness.

VEGETABLE OIL

ADDING vegetable oil together with solid fat helps coat the flour particles and reduces the strength of the protein, making the gluten less likely to develop a strong, continuous network. Any type of melted or liquid fat will contribute tenderness, but not the flakiness that a firm, solid fat does.

SALT AND SUGAR

SALT strengthens the gluten and enhances the flavor of the other ingredients. I use very little salt in recipes for sweet desserts.

Sugar caramelizes during the baking process, adding color to the dough.

ACID

AN ENZYME in flour called protease converts some of the insoluble proteins in the flour into a soluble form, mellowing and softening the gluten strands and making the dough easier to roll. This requires time and involves a long rest period.

Adding acid performs a similar function to the natural enzyme in the flour, but it does so more quickly. Some bakers add 1 teaspoon of lemon juice or vinegar to the liquid when forming the dough package for puff pastry. Cream of tartar is an acid, but I prefer the flavor of a liquid acid in my doughs; its liquid form also makes it easier to distribute in the dough. Sour cream, crème fraîche or the milky residue from clarified butter are wonderful liquid additions to doughs, making them more supple to work with.

TIPS FOR DEVELOPING GLUTEN PROPERLY

GLUTEN development is necessary in all baked goods. We want our cakes tender with little gluten development and our butter-rich puff pastry to be flaky, with full expansion, which requires more gluten development. The ingredients and their proportions, even the techniques we use, can affect gluten development.

☞ Always use the specific flour your recipe suggests. Use quality flour; it is impossible to upgrade an inferior brand. Strong flours are not always an asset. Do not substitute a hard-wheat flour that is strong (has a high protein content) for a cake flour that is weak (low protein content). Remember, you need a medium or strong flour for strength and elasticity for flaky puff pastry and a weak flour for light, fine-grained cakes.

If I feel my flour is too high or too low in protein, I make my own by combining 5 parts all-purpose flour with 1 part cake flour for a pie dough or puff pastry.

☞ If I don't have any cake flour on hand, I create my own mixture by stirring together 3 parts all-purpose flour with 1 part cornstarch or potato starch. Too much cornstarch or potato starch will affect the cake's structure as well as the flavor.

☞ Fat curtails gluten development. Some recipes, such as butter cakes and puff pastry, use vegetable oil in conjunction with a solid fat to help coat the flour and reduce the protein's strength or chance of overdeveloping. The vegetable oil surrounds the gluten strands, making it less likely to form a continuous network.

Such a combination contributes tenderness rather than flakiness.

☞ The first step in gluten development is moistening the protein in the flour. Especially in doughs, it is important to add just enough liquid to form a cohesive mixture. Too little, and the dough will fall apart; too much, and more gluten than desired can develop.

☞ Without some form of manipulation, gluten cannot develop. A minimum of handling is necessary when adding flour to a cake, when adding water to form pie dough or when rolling the dough in order to avoid toughness after baking. The more manipulation, whether stirring, kneading or rolling, the more gluten is developed.

☞ Did you rest your puff pastry when it showed signs of resistance to rolling? (I have rolled out some puff pastries using all my strength because they did not move easily. But after I rested the dough, they baked flaky and tender.) After rolling or stretching, the gluten strands become elastic and tend to shorten like a rubber band. The rest allows them to adjust to their new dimension and the enzymes in the flour to mellow the protein so the dough is ready for rolling again.

☞ The temperature of the liquid you add to your flour mixtures, the temperature of your rolling surface, as well as the temperature at which you rest your dough can be allies in controlling gluten development. Cold temperatures retard gluten development; heat promotes it.

Recipes for Pies and Galettes

Pies and Galettes:
Unsweetened Short Pastry

~

A HIGH proportion of fat (shortening) and a low proportion of liquid in relation to the flour in pastries provide a tender, slightly crisp, somewhat flaky result. This is because the fat coats the gluten strands in the dough, shortening them and preventing them from forming a strong bond or network. (That is why fat is called shortening.) Short is a common reference for these pastries, which break easily and cleanly when cut with a knife or fork.

Short pastry is divided into two groups: unsweetened (pie and galette doughs) and sweetened (tart doughs).

Whereas a pie is an unsweetened short pastry with a filling baked in a pie pan, a galette is a flat, rustic French pastry that is not formed in a pan. The unsweetened short pastry, usually filled with fruit, is shaped by hand, free-form pizza style.

Galette doughs are firmer after chilling than pie doughs because they are made entirely with butter. (Doughs made with a portion of solid shortening or lard are softer and not as firm.) Therefore, it is easier to construct shapes free-form on baking sheets with galette doughs than with pie doughs. Galette doughs are also baked longer than pie doughs since their texture and flavor are best when crisp.

Piecrusts, on the other hand, should be tender, flaky and golden brown, with a rough, blistered surface texture. When baked with a filling, the bottom crust should be golden brown and crisp, not soggy. Pies may include a top crust, lattice work or cut-outs.

THE INGREDIENTS AND THEIR ROLE

FLOUR

A LL-PURPOSE flour is fine for short pastry. I love the results when I use pastry flour too. Pastry flour, though milled from soft wheat, is not milled as finely as cake flour. Therefore, it will not become pasty when you add liquid. Little gluten development is necessary. The ingredients should bind together just enough so they don't fall apart.

FAT

Each type of fat has its own characteristics that will bear on your results. I always use some butter in my unsweetened short doughs and all butter in my galette doughs. When I use solid shortening with the butter, it contributes to the dough's flakiness and tenderness, whereas the butter is for flavor. If you are inexperienced in making unsweetened short doughs, working with the two fats first is easier and ensures good results.

LIQUID

Whatever liquid (water, milk, orange juice) you add to the flour and fat mixture, its temperature should always be cold to keep gluten development to a minimum.

SALT

When the dough is to be used for desserts, I use less salt than for savory pastries.

Factors Affecting Texture

Short pastries can be either flaky or mealy. Each type can have the same ingredients and proportions, but varying the fat's temperature and the way in which you blend it into the flour determines the texture. Flaky dough is achieved by blending the fat into the flour until the fragments are roughly the size of peas, then adding just enough liquid to make the mixture cohesive. The portion of flour not coated with fat absorbs the liquid and, through mixing, develops some gluten. Rolling flattens the dough and elongates the nuggets of fat, producing random layers of fat and moistened flour; this gives the crust a flaky texture after baking. This type of dough is recommended for prebaked pie shells or pies with top crust or lattice treatment. Fillings may be pastry cream, chiffon or Bavarian cream.

For mealy dough, the fat is blended more intimately into the flour until the mixture resembles coarse meal. This type of dough will require less water (as there is less flour left uncoated with fat) to make it cohesive. Because of the effect of the shortening upon the gluten network, less gluten is developed. This ensures a tender, crisp, less fragile pastry—perfect for soft or juicy fillings such as custards and fresh fruit, since the fat is dispersed throughout the dough; therefore it absorbs moisture more slowly and resists sogginess longer.

This type of dough is perfect for galettes, which are usually made with juicy fruits. Since their doughs are classically made with all butter, they are stronger, more resilient to the fruit's juice, but still tender and flaky.

Flakiness and Tenderness

Both flakiness and tenderness are desirable in a crust, but one does not necessarily follow the other. Flaky crusts are tender, but tender crusts are not always flaky.

Whether your pastry is primarily flaky or tender depends on what method you use to disperse the fat.

A flaky dough has random nuggets of firm, cold fat interspersed throughout the mixture; rolling creates different concentrations of fat in layers. In the oven, the liquid in the dough converts to steam and pushes upward, creating air pockets and accentuating the layered effect. When completely baked, this dough will have a flaky texture.

The more intimate the blending of fat and flour, the smoother and more homogenous the dough, and the "shorter" and more tender the result.

The techniques in the following recipes provide pastries that are both flaky and tender.

TIPS FOR MAKING PERFECT UNSWEETENED SHORT PASTRY

↪ For optimum control, prepare unsweetened doughs by hand rather than by machine. Your hands can feel what is happening to the dough as it takes shape. Unsweetened doughs should not be overworked.

↪ Use a bowl, such as stainless steel, that contrasts in color with the flour and fat to provide more precise visibility and allow you to see the progress of the dough more clearly.

↪ Use a pastry blender with rigid blades rather than one with flexible wires for quick, efficient integration of cold fat and flour.

↪ The fat should be cold and firm, not pasty or oily. Even solid shortening should be chilled so it will be more plastic and coat the flour evenly. Your goal is to coat the flour, not have the flour absorb the fat, which can happen with a warmer, softer fat.

↪ Cold liquids keep the fat firm and reduce gluten development. Too much gluten development makes the dough more elastic and therefore more difficult to manipulate and roll.

↪ Add the liquid slowly, tossing the mixture with a fork. Remember to maintain the cold fragments of fat, rather than smearing them into a paste. You want only enough liquid to make the mixture cohesive; examine it with your fingers to see if the dough is ready to come together as a unit.

↪ Rest the dough *at least* an hour after forming; this gives the flour time to completely absorb any liquid and the gluten time to mellow. The dough will be more manageable, easier to roll and less susceptible to shrinkage during baking.

↪ For the best crust possible, don't roll the dough out a second time.

Classic Piecrust

Besides being flaky and tasting delicious, this dough handles beautifully for both the novice and experienced pie maker. Another name for it is pâte brisée.

This is the crust for Flag-Raising Apple Pie (page 329) and for Macadamia Cream Pie (page 335).

MAKES ONE 9-INCH PIE CRUST (11 OUNCES)

Baking Equipment: 9-inch Pyrex pie pan

1	cup (140 grams) unsifted all-purpose flour
⅛	teaspoon salt
1 ½	ounces (2 ½ tablespoons) unsalted butter, chilled
⅓	cup (2 ounces) solid vegetable shortening, chilled
3 to 4	tablespoons ice water

Making the dough: Pour the flour and salt into a 3-quart stainless steel mixing bowl and stir with a pastry blender to disperse the salt. Divide the cold butter into 6 to 8 pieces for a single crust and scatter them over the flour. With the blender, cut in the butter until the largest pieces remaining are the size of peas.

Divide the shortening into 6 to 8 pieces and scatter them over the butter-flour mixture; cut in with a pastry blender until the pieces range in size from bread crumbs to small lima beans. Clean off the blender as you work, keeping pieces of fat from adhering to the blades. Lift the flour from the bottom of the bowl with the pastry blender from time to time.

If the fats seem soft or oily at this time, refrigerate them for 15 minutes to resolidify before adding liquid.

Pour the ice water into a liquid cup measure. Sprinkle 1 tablespoon evenly over the flour mixture, using a fork to distribute the moisture but not mixing the ingredients together. (Move the fork in circles, scraping the bottom of the bowl and then moving it upward, lightly tossing the flour.)

Repeat the procedure, removing excess dough from the fork as it accumulates, adding 3 tablespoons liquid for a single crust or 6 tablespoons for a double crust. With your fingertips, test to determine if the mixture is moist enough to stick together. If it appears dry and crumbly, and reluctant to stick together, or if loose flour particles remain in the bottom of the bowl, add water, 1 tablespoon at a time, until the dough can be shaped into a single unit. If the mixture feels sticky, dust it with a little flour.

With your hands, gather the moistened particles together, using the side of the bowl to help shape it. Transfer it onto a sheet of plastic wrap, and form the dough into a package, using the 4 corner flaps: Alternating between opposing sets of flaps of the plastic, gently manipulate the dough into a round, flat circle. (The plastic keeps the warmth of your hands away from the dough and provides a loose mold to help shape it.)

Once the dough is wrapped, gently massage its surface into a cohesive round, flat disk (or a flat square, according to the shape you will be rolling later). The disk should measure about 4½ inches across. If you plan to divide the double recipe for two separate crusts or

Baker's Notes

☞ Butter is incorporated before the shortening because it's the firmer of the two fats and does not blend into the flour easily. If both fats were cut in simultaneously, the softer fat would be overworked into the flour, resulting in a mealier, shorter dough.

☞ After incorporation, the fat pieces should be a variety of sizes. If all the particles are small, less water will be required to form the dough and a crumbly, short crust will result. If the particles are large, more water will be needed and a crisper, flakier crust will result.

☞ If, while rolling out the dough, you notice that the particles of fat are too large, ranging from that of large peas to lima beans, the crust will not be as flaky and tender as it should be. Correct this by folding the dough in half and resting it for 15 to 30 minutes in the refrigerator, then rolling it to the dimensions the recipe directs.

☞ For rolling the dough, a cool, smooth surface work area standing at about hip level provides the best leverage for rolling the dough. To roll a circular shape, begin with a flat disk, not a square or rectangular piece of dough.

portions, do it now; form two disks, each 4½ inches across, using the plastic-wrap method as above.

Storing the dough: Refrigerate for at least 2 hours. The dough may be refrigerated for up to 3 days at this stage, or it may be wrapped in aluminum foil and frozen for up to 1 month. Label the contents and date.

Rolling the piecrust: Dust the work surface with all-purpose flour in the following manner: Holding the flour lightly in your hand, sling it onto the rolling surface, crossing in front of your body from right to left (for a right-handed person) as if sowing grain or feeding chickens. This efficiently coats the surface with the least amount of flour.

Using a paper towel or your fingers, apply a very light film of solid vegetable shortening to the bottom of the pan, but not on the sides or rim (greasing the sides encourages your dough to slip while baking).

Roll a circle of dough with even thickness. Sprinkle the chilled disk of dough with just enough flour to keep it from feeling sticky. Redust the work surface lightly and coat the rolling pin with flour. (Since Classic Piecrust is higher in fat than most pie doughs, you can use extra flour in rolling to make it more manageable if necessary. With experience, you will need less, but either way, the crust will be flaky.)

Beginning in the center of the disk, push the rolling pin away from you in one stroke, using enough pressure to extend the dough gradually. Do not extend more than 2 inches at a time in any one direction and avoid rolling over the edges; this method helps eliminate cracking or creating too thin an edge. If some cracking occurs when you begin rolling, simply pinch the edges together. Coax the dough to become larger, always keeping its shape in mind.

Lift and rotate the dough a one-eighth turn clockwise (one-eighth turns keep the dough circular, one-fourth turns make it square), and repeat rolling procedures, pushing away from the center in one stroke. Continue to lift, rotate and roll, dusting with additional flour as needed to prevent sticking to the rolling surface. Never turn your dough over and roll on the other side. If the dough sticks to the work surface, carefully slide a metal spatula under the stuck portion, then lift and dust it with a little flour. Rub off any pieces of dough adhering to the rolling pin; they could puncture the dough.

Roll until the circle of dough measures around 12 to 13 inches and ⅛ inch thick for a 9-inch pan. A good rule of thumb is that the edge is approximately 2½ inches larger than the base of the pie pan.

Lining the pie pan: To maintain the shape of the dough and avoid stretching it, lay your rolling pin on the top third section of the dough. Lift the edge of that section and fold it toward you, draping it over the pin. Roll the pin toward you, wrapping the remaining dough loosely around it. (The ends of the rolling pin remain exposed.) Lift the rolling pin, and suspend it about 1 inch above the farthest edge of the prepared pan. Allowing for an 1-inch overhang, unroll the dough away from you, easing it into the pan's contour. When completely unrolled, it should be perfectly centered; if not, carefully adjust its position.

Fit the dough into the pan by pressing it lightly with your fingertips, molding it into the creases. If it doesn't seem to fit snugly in some places, lift it gently without stretching it

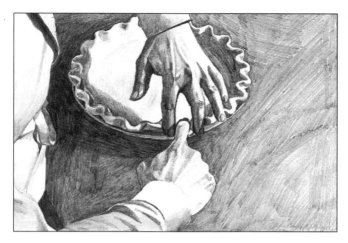

Crimping the dough's edges.

and lower it into pan. Careful fitting against the pan prevents air bubbles from forming under the dough. Should a tear occur while you are draping or fitting, patch it by overlapping the edges slightly and pressing them together.

Fluting the edges: Fluting forms a decorative ledge, making it difficult for juicy fillings to boil over and out. If necessary, trim the dough with kitchen scissors until you have a uniform overhang that measures ¾ to 1 inch. (You can use any scraps from trimming to patch a skimpy overhang.)

With the pie pan in front of you, work along a section of dough that is farthest away from you; tuck half the overhang under to form two layers of pastry as if you were preparing to hem an article of clothing. Rotate the pan slightly and tuck another section. Continue working in the same position, rotating the pan, until the circle has been completed.

Dip your fingertips in flour if the pastry begins to feel sticky. Crimp the edges around the pan to seal them together. To flute, spread the index and middle fingers of your left hand about 2 inches apart and place them against the outer edge of the crust. Insert the index finger of your right hand into the 2-inch gap, and rest on the crust. Using the tips of your fingers at a 90-degree angle, push the fingers of your right hand against the folded overhang until you reach the edge of the pan. At the same time, pull gently outward with the index finger of your left hand. This will create the fluted effect (see illustration).

Refrigerate the pastry-lined pan until it's time for filling and baking. If you are partially or completely baking the pastry, place it in the freezer for 30 minutes just to firm it before you line it with foil. (For this length of time, you need not wrap the dough.)

Baking the piecrust: For fillings that do not require baking with the piecrust, bake your piecrust completely and separately. This requires baking the crust "blind" at the beginning to hold the dough in place until it is set enough to maintain its shape on its own. (The term "baking blind" applies because the crust is not visible while it is weighted.)

To blind-bake, position rack in lower third of oven and preheat oven to 450 degrees at least 15 minutes before baking. Remove the partially chilled unbaked crust from the freezer, and line it with a 13-inch sheet of aluminum foil, fitted into the shape of the dough. (Firming the dough prevents the foil from making impressions in it.) Fill to the top with dried small beans (about 3 cups), spreading and pressing them in the foil to rest snugly into the creases of the sides of the dough. Fold the top of the foil over the beans, away from your fluted edge, to expose it to the heat better. (The beans prevent the dough from shrinking while baking.)

Bake at 450 degrees for 10 minutes; then reduce oven temperature to 375 degrees for 5 minutes longer, or until the edge of the crust no longer appears shiny or raw and its shape appears to be setting. Lift the bean-filled foil from the pastry carefully and slowly in case a portion of the dough is sticking to it. Prick the bottom of the crust with a skewer in three or four places to allow steam to escape. Return it to the oven for 15 minutes longer, pricking it again if necessary; reduce the temperature to 325 degrees and bake for 10 more minutes, or until light golden brown. Remove to a cooling rack.

Butter Pastry

THIS ALL-BUTTER crust is flaky and crisp rather than mealy and short. It prevents fruit juice from soaking completely through while baking.

This is the crust for Fresh Pineapple Galette (page 332).

MAKES ONE GALETTE CRUST

Baking Equipment: 12-x-15½-x-½-inch baking sheet or 12-inch pizza pan

1 ½	cups (210 grams) unsifted all-purpose flour
¼	teaspoon salt
6	ounces (1 ½ sticks) unsalted butter, chilled
5 to 7	tablespoons ice water

Making the dough: Prepare Butter Pastry following the directions for Classic Piecrust (page 325) with the following difference:

Increase the amount of butter as indicated, eliminating solid shortening completely. Cut the butter into the flour mixture until butter fragments range in size from that of bread crumbs to that of small peas.

Rolling the dough: Wrap in plastic, shape dough into a disk and refrigerate for at least 2 hours.

Baking the dough: See page 334 for rolling and shaping a galette; see pages 326 to 328 for rolling and baking a piecrust.

Milk Pastry

MILK substitutes for water in this dough. The result is a wonderfully flaky, tender and flavorful pastry.

This is the crust for Country Pear Galette (page 334).

MAKES ONE 10-INCH GALETTE (1 POUND 4 OUNCES)

Baker's Note

☞ The dough of this tart can be fitted into a 12-inch pizza pan or be shaped free-form on a baking sheet.

Baking Equipment: 10-x-15-x-1-inch jelly roll baking pan, 12-x-15½-x-½-inch baking sheet

 2 cups (280 grams) unsifted all-purpose flour
 ½ teaspoon salt
 3 ounces (6 tablespoons) unsalted butter, chilled
 ⅔ cup (4 ounces) solid vegetable shortening, chilled
 6 to 8 tablespoons cold milk

Making the dough: Prepare Milk Pastry following the directions for Classic Piecrust (page 325) with the following differences:
 Divide the butter into 9 to 10 pieces.
 Divide the shortening into 9 to 10 pieces.
 Substitute the 6 to 8 tablespoons milk for the water.

Rolling the dough: If making Country Pear Galette, divide the dough into two portions: 12 ounces (two-thirds of the dough) and 8 ounces (one-third of the dough). If making two 9-inch piecrusts or one double-crusted pie, divide the dough in half. Shape dough portions into round disks, wrap in plastic and refrigerate for at least 2 hours.
 To roll out and bake, see Country Pear Galette (page 334) or Classic Piecrust (page 325).

Flag-Raising Apple Pie

The taste of lightly spiced tart apples, crisp streusel and flaky pastry is a guaranteed winner.

MAKES ONE 9-INCH PIE

Baking Equipment: 9-inch Pyrex pie pan

Baker's Notes

☞ You can shape the pastry free-form on a baking sheet into any size or shape galette you want.

☞ You need a bit more salt than in Classic Piecrust to bring out the pastry's flavor.

☞ You can use this dough for either two 9-inch piecrusts or one double-crusted pie.

        1   9-inch Classic Piecrust (page 325)
        1   recipe Streusel (page 272)

Filling
     1 ½   ounces (3 tablespoons) unsalted butter
       ¼   cup (50 grams) dark brown sugar, packed
       ¼   cup (50 grams) granulated sugar
     3 ½   tablespoons unsifted all-purpose flour
       ½   teaspoon cinnamon
       ¼   teaspoon nutmeg
        3   pounds (about 7) Pippin or Granny Smith apples
        1   tablespoon fresh lemon juice

Advance preparations: Prepare Classic Piecrust as directed on page 325. Refrigerate it for at least 2 hours before rolling.

Prepare Streusel as directed on page 272. Store in a sturdy container in the refrigerator for 1 week or freeze it for up to 1 month. Remove from container and spread it on a baking sheet about 1 hour before it is to be used. This removes some of the chill, allows you to break the large chunks into smaller pieces and makes it easier to handle.

Rolling the dough: Follow the instructions on page 326 for rolling the piecrust dough and for lining a 9-inch pie pan. Refrigerate after fluting while you make the apple filling.

Baking preparations: Position rack in lower third of oven; preheat oven to 450 degrees.

Making the filling and applying the streusel: When you're ready to bake the pie, melt the butter in a small saucepan; set aside.

Mix the sugars, flour and spices in a small bowl.

Peel the apples with a vegetable peeler, cut them into halves and core them with a melon baller. Cut ⅛-inch slices on a cutting board with a chef's knife, or slice apple halves using a food processor with a ⅛-inch slicing blade. You need 9 cups sliced thin. Pour into a large mixing bowl, sprinkle with the dry mixture and toss gently and briefly with a rubber spatula. Sprinkle with the lemon juice and melted butter, tossing again just to combine.

Remove the pastry-lined pan from the refrigerator. Spoon the filling into the pan, spreading the apple slices evenly. (They will mound higher in the center.) Pat out the streusel to form a thin topping over the apples.

Baking the pie: Bake for 10 minutes. Reduce the temperature to 350 degrees and bake for 30 to 40 minutes longer, or until the bottom crust is golden.

Cooling and serving the pie: Remove from oven to a cooling rack. Serve lukewarm or at room temperature with vanilla ice cream or Classic Crème Anglaise (page 247) as an accompaniment.

Baker's Notes

☞ A food processor with a slicing disk considerably speeds the task of preparing the apples.

☞ When the pie cools, the fruit contracts, absorbing the juice. The warmer the fruit pie, the more difficult it is to cut neatly. Serving it slightly warm or at room temperature is best.

Buttery Apple Tarts

Imagine juicy, thin slices of apples, lightly flavored with a lemon-butter sauce on a golden, crisp pastry. This recipe is adapted from Jacques Pépin's apple galette.

Makes 12 to 14 servings

Baking Equipment: 10-x-15-x-1-inch jelly roll pan

Butter Pastry
2	cups (280 grams) unsifted all-purpose flour
¼	teaspoon salt
8	ounces (2 sticks) unsalted butter, chilled
8 to 10	tablespoons ice water

Butter Glaze
3	ounces (6 tablespoons) unsalted butter, room temperature
⅓	cup (65 grams) granulated sugar
1	tablespoon honey
1	tablespoon fresh lemon juice

Filling
2	pounds (about 3) Golden Delicious apples
1	cup (100 grams) unsifted powdered sugar, optional

Advance preparations: Prepare Butter Pastry following the recipe for Classic Piecrust as directed on page 325 but with these differences:

Increase the butter to 8 ounces and eliminate the shortening. Cut in the butter until the fragments range in size from bread crumbs to small peas. Wrap dough in plastic, shape into a 6-inch square and refrigerate for at least 2 hours.

Prepare the butter glaze. Place the butter in a 1½-quart mixing bowl. Mix until soft and fluffy with an electric hand mixer; then add the sugar in a steady stream, and continue to whip until light and fluffy. When the mixture is quite soft, continue to whip as you dribble the honey over it and incorporate it. Then pour in the lemon juice, teaspoon by teaspoon, until combined. Set aside at room temperature until it is time to glaze the assembled tart.

Baking preparations: Position rack in lower third of oven; preheat oven to 450 degrees.

Grease only the bottom of the jelly roll pan with a very light film (1 teaspoon) of solid shortening to ensure the pastry's release after baking.

Rolling the dough: Roll out the dough on a lightly floured surface to an 18-x-15½-inch rectangle less than ⅛ inch thick. Trim the dough to 18 x 12½ inches with a pastry

Baker's Notes

☞ The only fat in this pastry is butter. It bakes crisper than a dough made with a combination of butter and solid shortening. This pastry is ideal for baking fruits that exude juice, since it is more resistant to sogginess than other kinds. The juice from apple slices soaks into the upper part of the pastry and provides a splendid contrast to the crispness underneath.

☞ For the optional decoration of the tarts, you must turn each one upside down. The apple slices will not fall out of the pastry.

☞ They are best served the day they are made.

Branding pastry with a hot metal skewer for decoration.

wheel, and with the aid of the rolling pin, transfer it to line the jelly roll pan. Set aside while preparing the apples.

Making the filling: Peel the apples with a vegetable peeler, cut them in half and core with a melon baller. Cut the halves into ⅛-inch slices. Arrange the slices in rows (like a tile arrangement), overlapping them slightly on the pastry-lined pan. Fold the overhanging pastry around the edges of the pan (it should be about 1 inch) over the apple slices.

Brush the apple slices with the butter glaze, using a pastry brush. Hold the slices in place with the fingers of one hand while you "paint" with the other hand. (The glaze is creamy, not liquid.) Reserve at least 1 tablespoon.

Baking, cooling and glazing the tarts: Bake for 45 to 50 minutes, or until the crust is golden and sounds and feels crisp when pierced with a metal skewer. Remove the pastry from the oven to a cooling rack. While it is warm, brush the apples with the reserved butter glaze.

Decorating the tarts: When the pastry is lukewarm or at room temperature, cut it into individual servings, each about 3x5 inches, with a pastry wheel. If desired, invert, pastry side up, onto a baking sheet and dust generously with the powdered sugar.

If desired, heat a metal skewer on a hot stove element for 3 to 5 minutes; then brand each pastry with an X (see illustration). Reheat the skewer each time you use it. Remove each tart to a serving plate. Serve the same day.

Fresh Pineapple Galette

WHAT could be better and more refreshing than juicy, fresh, sweet slices of pineapple and flaky, crisp pastry?

MAKES ONE 12-INCH GALETTE, 8 TO 12 SERVINGS

Baking Equipment: 12-x-15½-x-½-inch baking sheet or 12-inch pizza pan

1 cup Streusel (page 272)
1 recipe Butter Pastry (page 328)
1 medium (3- to 3 ½-pound) ripe pineapple
¼ cup strained warm apricot jam

Advance preparations: Prepare Streusel as directed on page 272. Store in a sturdy container in the refrigerator for up to 1 week or freeze for up to 1 month. Prepare Butter Pastry as directed on page 328.

Baking preparations: Position rack in lower third of oven; preheat oven to 400 degrees.

Preparing the pineapple: One hour before baking the galette, peel the pineapple. Cut it into ¼-inch-thick slices; then cut slices into halves or quarters and remove core. Place on paper towels to absorb some of the juice.

Rolling, filling and shaping the galette: Roll out the pastry as directed on page 334 to a 15- to 16-inch circle ⅛ inch thick. Trim it even with a pastry wheel (or sharp-edged chef's knife), forming a 14½- to 15-inch circle. Roll it loosely onto the rolling pin and transfer to the ungreased baking sheet or a 12-inch pizza pan.

Arrange the pineapple slices over the pastry in concentric circles, overlapping them slightly, leaving a 1-inch border around the edge. When you are finished, lift the pastry border and fold it over the edges of the pineapple slices all around the galette. Sprinkle the streusel over the top.

Baking and glazing the galette: Bake for 40 to 45 minutes, or until the crust is golden brown and sounds and feels crisp when pierced with a metal skewer in several places. When the galette is finished baking, remove it from oven and brush the warm apricot glaze over the pineapple slices.

Serve lukewarm or at room temperature the same day.

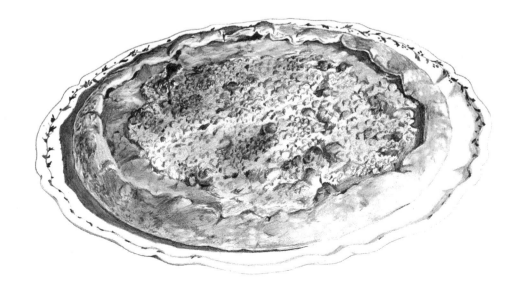

Understanding Pastrymaking

Country Pear Galette

ACHARMING, rustic, free-form pastry, filled with delicately flavored pear chunks, perfect for any time of the day. **(See photograph, page 160.)**

MAKES ONE 10-INCH GALETTE, 8 TO 10 SERVINGS

(See photograph, page 160.)

1	recipe Milk Pastry (page 328)

Filling

2	pounds (4 medium) firm, ripe pears
1	tablespoon fresh lemon juice
¼	cup (50 grams) granulated sugar
3	tablespoons unsalted butter
1	recipe Translucent Sugar Glaze (page 268)

Advance preparations: Prepare Milk Pastry as directed on page 328.

Position rack in lower third of oven; preheat oven to 400 degrees.

Prepare the filling. Peel the pears with a vegetable peeler and halve them lengthwise. With the point of the peeler, remove the flower end and the core of each pear, including the long, stringy section that continues to the stem. Cut each half into four strips; then cut these strips crosswise into four sections. You should have 5½ to 6 cups coarse chunks. Spread them in the jelly roll pan and sprinkle with the lemon juice and sugar; cut the butter into thin pieces and scatter over the pear pieces.

Bake, uncovered, tossing occasionally to ensure even baking and to mix with the thickening juices (18 to 20 minutes). The pears will be only slightly tender, offering some resistance when pierced with tip of paring knife. (Partially baking the pears evaporates some of the juice, concentrating their flavor.) Remove from the oven and cool until no longer steaming. Then place in a bowl, cover with plastic wrap and refrigerate until cold. You will have about 2 cups pear pieces after baking.

Baking preparations for the galette: At least 20 minutes before baking, position rack in lower third of oven; preheat oven to 450 degrees.

Line the baking sheet with parchment paper; set aside.

Shaping the galette: Roll out the larger portion of dough to a 13- to 14-inch circle ⅛ inch thick. (The most important factor is the ⅛-inch thickness. If the diameter is larger, cut to the size indicated.) Roll the pastry loosely onto rolling pin and transfer it to the parchment-lined baking sheet.

Scoop the cold pear filling with a slotted spoon to drain any juice and pile it in a 9-inch diameter on center of the pastry. Roll out the smaller portion of the dough to a 12-inch circle ⅛ inch thick (less dough is used because only a thin layer is required to cover the pear pieces). Roll up onto the rolling pin, suspending it about 1 inch over the filling. Unroll it to center the pastry over the filling. With a pastry wheel or scissors, trim the bottom layer ½ to 1 inch larger than the edge of the top layer of the pastry. Then press the top and bot-

Baker's Notes

☞ I prefer bosc or comice pears for this dessert.

☞ This galette may be prepared over a 2-day period.
First day: Prepare Milk Pastry and pear filling.
Second day: Assemble galette, bake and serve.

☞ Baking the galette on parchment paper enables you to lift it with its parchment paper to a cooling rack without breaking it, since pastries are fragile when warm.

☞ It is best served the day it is baked.

Sealing and rolling the two layers of dough together.

tom layers gently where the two meet.

With the galette in front of you, begin on a section closest to you, sealing the layers together, forming a border (see illustration). Lift the extended bottom layer and roll it up about 1 inch toward the center, incorporating the top crust to seal the two layers together until you reach the edge of the filling. Repeat the procedure on an adjacent section, rotating the pan until the galette is completely sealed. Make 5 to 6 small slits with the tip of a knife near the center of the pastry to allow steam to escape during baking.

Baking the galette: Bake for 10 minutes in the preheated 450-degree oven, then reduce temperature to 400 degrees and bake for 20 to 25 minutes more, or until golden brown.

Ten minutes before the galette is finished baking, prepare Translucent Sugar Glaze as directed on page 268.

Glazing and cooling the galette: Remove galette from oven to a cooling rack. Immediately apply the glaze, brushing it over the entire surface (the glaze hardens like an icing as it cools, adding a sparkle). Cool on the rack for about 30 minutes. Then gently lift the galette with its parchment paper liner off the baking sheet and put it back on the cooling rack to cool completely. Slip a wide metal spatula under the galette and transfer it (without the paper) to a serving platter. Serve the same day.

Macadamia Cream Pie

THIS PIE, with its Bavarian cream filling dotted with nut brittle, is a perfect ending to a simple meal.
MAKES 6 TO 8 SERVINGS

Baking Equipment: 9-inch Pyrex pie pan

¾   cup coarsely chopped Macadamia Nut Brittle (page 310)
1   recipe Classic Piecrust (page 325)

Filling
3   large eggs
1   tablespoon rum
½   teaspoon gelatin
1   cup (8 ounces) milk
2   tablespoons (25 grams) *plus* 2 tablespoons
   (25 grams) granulated sugar
1   tablespoon cornstarch
1   ounce (2 tablespoons) unsalted butter
¾   cup (6 ounces) heavy cream
1   tablespoon granulated sugar
1   teaspoon vanilla
1   tablespoon granulated sugar

½   cup (4 ounces) heavy cream

Baker's Notes

☞ Make the filling 1 to 2 hours before serving, but for best texture and flavor, don't fill the crust until shortly before baking.

☞ This pie may be prepared over a 2-day period.
First day: Prepare pastry and Macadamia Nut Brittle.
Second day: Bake crust, prepare filling and decorate pie.

☞ For a note on uncooked egg whites, see page 31.

Advance preparations: Prepare Macadamia Nut Brittle as directed on page 310. Store at room temperature in an airtight metal container until ready to use.

Prepare and bake Classic Piecrust as directed on page 325. Cool completely before filling.

Making the filling: At least 1 to 2 hours before serving the pie, separate the eggs, placing whites in a deep 1½-quart bowl and yolks in a small bowl. Pour the rum into a small bowl, sprinkle the gelatin over it and set it aside until it is softened.

Pour the milk and 2 tablespoons of sugar into a 1½-quart saucepan and heat over medium heat just until it comes to a boil. While it heats, whisk yolks to combine, then add the additional 2 tablespoons of sugar, and whisk again; add the cornstarch and whisk until combined. When the milk boils, remove it from heat and pour about half of it into the yolk mixture, whisking to combine completely.

Pour this mixture into the milk in the saucepan. Return to medium heat and cook, stirring constantly with the whisk as mixture begins to thicken. Then whisk rapidly until the mixture is smooth and very thick; remove from heat. Scrape the softened gelatin into the hot mixture with a rubber spatula, and stir until dissolved. Add the butter and whisk until melted.

Pour the mixture into a 1½-quart mixing bowl; place plastic wrap on top of the filling to prevent a film from forming as it cools. Using the tip of a paring knife, poke 4 or 5 slits in the plastic to allow steam to escape. Set aside until it is no longer steaming. Then refrigerate until it is room temperature (70 degrees) or cooler.

Chop Macadamia Nut Brittle into coarse pieces by putting it in a plastic bag and tapping it with a rolling pin or by chopping it in a food processor fitted with a steel blade. You should have about 1 cup. Reserve ¼ cup for decoration.

Whip the ¾ cup heavy cream with the 1 tablespoon granulated sugar and the 1 teaspoon vanilla in a deep 1-quart mixing bowl with an electric hand mixer on medium-high speed until the cream clings softly to the beaters and is thick enough to create swirls in the bowl but liquid enough to move when the bowl is tilted (Chantilly stage, page 240). Refrigerate it until you are ready to fold it into cooled filling.

When the filling has cooled, fold in the nut brittle with a rubber spatula.

Whip the egg whites on low speed (#3) of an electric hand mixer until small bubbles appear and the surface is frothy (about 30 to 45 seconds). Then increase the speed to high (#10), add the 1 tablespoon sugar and continue whipping until stiffer, shiny white peaks form.

Fold about ¼ cup egg whites into the cream mixture with a rubber spatula to lighten it; then fold in half the softly whipped cream. Add the remaining whites, folding to combine; then fold in remaining whipped cream.

Pour the macadamia cream into the cooled baked crust and refrigerate it for at least 1 hour until firm. Cover with plastic wrap.

Decorating the pie: Whip the ½ cup heavy cream in a deep 1-quart mixing bowl until soft peaks form. Spread it smoothly over the filling. Sprinkle the sides near the fluted edge with the reserved Macadamia Brittle and sprinkle a few pieces in the center.

Recipes for Tarts

INDICATES ❁ EASY RECIPE

Tarts:
Sweetened Short Pastry

~

THESE shallow crusts are more portable than piecrusts because they can be removed from their baking pans before serving. This dough is related to a butter-rich cookie dough, though it is not as sweet. It is high in fat and low in moisture with some part of an egg being used as liquid. Sugar is added, and the fat is intimately blended into the dry ingredients. All these factors yield a short, crisp and tender crust. The perfect tart crust has both body and tenderness, good color and a rich, well-balanced taste to complement the filling.

Sugar and egg make the dough stickier, which can be tricky during rolling. The sugar curtails gluten development, however, reducing the risk of shrinkage or toughness. Unlike pie dough, tart dough may be rolled out again or pressed into a baking pan.

THE INGREDIENTS AND THEIR ROLE

- I use all-purpose flour for tart doughs.

- As in all pastries, unsalted butter provides the best taste.

- Some part of an egg is used as liquid.

- Granulated or powdered sugar may be called for. Powdered sugar has 3 percent cornstarch added to prevent its lumping, and besides affecting texture, it can affect flavor. Granulated sugar is generally used in doughs with more moisture.

The doughs in the recipes that follow may be used interchangeably.

TIPS FOR MAKING PERFECT SWEETENED SHORT PASTRY

☞ Be sure to roll the dough so that it is no thicker than ⅛ inch; otherwise, it may not bake all the way through and may become soggy.

☞ To roll sweetened dough evenly: Cut and glue strips of cardboard to form a ⅛-inch thickness. Place the dough between these strips and roll out until the dough is level with the top surface of the cardboard strips.

☞ Fillings are thickened primarily to reduce sogginess. Cornstarch, tapioca and flour are the most commonly used

thickeners. To reduce the possibility of sogginess, cook and store as the recipe directs. Acidity in the filling can break down thickeners, as can freezing.

☞ To further reduce sogginess, brush a thin film of very soft unsalted butter or melted semisweet or bittersweet chocolate on the baked crust before adding juicy or thin fillings that don't require baking, such as pastry cream, lemon curd or raw fruit. The butter or chocolate will not dissolve as would an apricot glaze or a washing of egg white.

Classic Sweet Pastry

I've tried many recipes for sweetened pastry over the years, but this one still tastes and handles the best. It is also known as pâte sucrée. The addition of egg and sugar makes the pastry shell richer and sweeter yet less flaky than an ordinary piecrust.

Makes three 8-inch tart crusts (1 ½ pounds dough)

Baking Equipment: 8-inch quiche pan with removable bottom

8	ounces (2 sticks) unsalted butter
2 ½	cups (350 grams) unsifted all-purpose flour
⅛	teaspoon salt
½	cup (100 grams) granulated sugar
1	large egg
1	teaspoon vanilla

HAND METHOD

Ingredient preparations: Remove the butter from the refrigerator about 30 to 45 minutes before preparing the pastry, and test it for correct consistency by sticking a finger in it to feel if it is pliable and close to room temperature (about 65 to 70 degrees).

Pour the dry ingredients onto a smooth work surface. If it's a very warm day, a cold work surface, such as a marble slab or a chilled plastic cutting board, is helpful. With the side and fingers of your hand, clear an 8-inch circle out of the center of the dry ingredients, creating a moat into which you will place the other ingredients.

Mix the egg and vanilla in a small bowl just to combine.

Making the dough: Using the tips of your thumb and first two fingers, rub the butter, egg and vanilla together until a thick paste is formed.

Still using your fingertips, gradually pull in the wall of flour by drawing it into the center and mixing with the paste. The mixture will be sticky to begin with, but as more flour is added, it will become malleable and uniform. Continue adding the dry ingredients until a dough is formed.

Then, with the heel of your hand, smear a small amount of the dough (the size of an egg) on your work surface by pushing it away from you. (See illustration, page 343.) Repeat with small amounts of the remaining dough. When you've worked all the dough in this manner, give it a couple more strokes to bring it together.

HEAVY-DUTY MIXER METHOD

Ingredient preparations: Remove the butter from the refrigerator about 1 hour before preparing the pastry. When it is at room temperature and malleable, cut it into ½-inch pieces.

Pour the dry ingredients into the bowl of a heavy-duty mixer, and with the flat (paddle) attachment, briefly mix them on the lowest speed (#1).

Mix the egg and vanilla in a small bowl just to combine.

Making the dough: Scatter pieces of butter over the surface of the dry ingredients. Mix on the lowest speed (#1) until the mixture resembles cornmeal (about 2 minutes). Maintaining the same speed, pour the egg mixture on the ingredients in the bowl in a steady stream until dough just comes together (about 35 to 40 seconds).

Remove the dough from the bowl and place it on a clean, dry work surface. Then, with the heel of your hand, smear a small amount of the dough on your work surface by pushing it away from you. Repeat with small amounts of the remaining dough. When you've worked all the dough in this manner, give it a couple more strokes to bring it together into a smooth, homogeneous mass

FOOD PROCESSOR METHOD

Ingredient preparations: Place the dry ingredients into the bowl of a food processor fitted with a steel blade and process with 2 or 3 short on/off bursts to blend.

Mix the egg and vanilla in a small bowl just to combine.

Making the dough: Cut the chilled, firm butter into 12 to 16 pieces and scatter them over the dry ingredients. Process the butter and dry ingredients until the mixture resembles bread crumbs (about 15 to 20 seconds).

Then, with processor running, pour the egg mixture down the feed tube in a steady stream and continue to process just until the ingredients come together.

Remove the dough from the bowl and place it on a clean, dry work surface. Then, with the heel of your hand, smear a small amount on your work surface by pushing it away from you. Repeat with small amounts of the remaining dough. When you've worked all the dough in this manner, give it a couple more strokes to bring it together into a smooth, homogeneous unit.

Baker's Notes

☞ A 9-ounce disk, measuring 1 cup dough, is enough to fit into a 9-inch quiche pan.
A 13-ounce disk, measuring a scant 1½ cups, is enough to fit into an 11-x-8-x-1-inch rectangular quiche pan.
A 12-ounce disk, measuring 1⅓ cups, is enough to fit into a 12-x-4-x-1-inch rectangular flan form.

☞ In pastrymaking, it's best to work with your hands to keep in contact with the ingredients and to give you a sense of what is happening (Is the butter too soft, the dough too moist?) Then, after you become accustomed to the feel of making the dough, you can use a machine.

☞ Correct butter temperature is the key to making sweetened pastry by hand successfully. It shouldn't be too firm (cold) or too soft (warm); the best description is cool and malleable.

☞ Kneading the dough by smearing it with the heel of your hand is called *fraisage*. It not only forms the dough into a smooth, cohesive unit, but it develops just enough structure so that the dough is less likely to tear or crack while being rolled and lifted.

Forming Sweet Pastry Dough by hand.

Chilling the dough: At this point, you may divide the dough into thirds (8 ounces each, a scant 1 cup). Flatten each third into a round disk 4 to 5 inches each and wrap each in plastic. Or, if you prefer, you may shape all the dough into a long cylinder; this makes it easy to slice off a portion later and requires less time to soften.

Refrigerate for at least 1 hour, or until the dough is chilled and slightly firm. (Chilling reduces the strength of the gluten in the flour when the dough is rolled. It also makes it easier to roll without sticking.)

Rolling the dough: If the dough is cold and firm, remove it from the refrigerator to room temperature for 1 hour, or until it is still cool (room temperature, 70 degrees) and feels malleable, though it may crack at the edges slightly when pinched.

These doughs may be pressed with the fingertips into pans, rather than rolled. However, rolling is faster, gives a more even thickness and requires less manipulation than pressing.

Dust the work surface lightly with flour. Position the rolling pin across the center of the disk and push the pin away from you in one stroke; use just enough pressure to extend the dough about 2 inches. Let up on the pressure as you near the edge. If any tearing or cracking occurs as you roll, press the edges together, sprinkle with a little flour and continue to roll. (If the dough cracks too much, it is too cold; if it is soft and sticky, it is too warm. Should it crumble into pieces as you begin to roll, repeat the kneading process; this will not overwork it.)

Gently lift the dough and rotate it a one-eighth turn in one direction. Repeat rolling procedure, working from the center out, always rotating dough a one-eighth turn in the same direction. Lightly flour the surface when necessary to prevent sticking. If the dough does stick, carefully slide a metal spatula under that portion, lift and dust with flour. Rub off any particles adhering to the rolling pin; they could puncture the dough.

Continue rolling and rotating until the circle of dough is ⅛ inch thick and measures the diameter you need. The most important guideline for lining the pans is an ⅛-inch thickness; any thicker, and it will not serve as a container for the filling.

Fitting the dough into the pan: Lay the rolling pin across the upper third of the circle of dough. Lift the edge of that section and fold it toward you, draping it over the pin. (The ends of the rolling pin will remain exposed.) Roll the pin toward you, wrapping the remaining dough loosely around the pin.

☞ If you refrigerate the tart dough, return it to room temperature 40 to 60 minutes before you roll it. Since it is high in butter, you must wait until it is softer and more workable.

☞ Unlike pie dough, scraps of this dough may be saved and reused.

Understanding Pastrymaking

Lift the rolling pin, and suspend it 1 inch above the farthest edge of the tart pan. Allowing for a 1-inch overhang, unroll the dough toward you, easing it into the pan's contours as you go. (Unrolling the dough toward you, rather than away from you, is best since you can see the pan and guide the dough precisely.) When the dough is completely unrolled, mold it into the pan's crevices, pressing down slightly with fingertips until it fits snugly against the sides and bottom. If it tears, patching is easy: press the two torn edges together.

Rest the rolling pin on top of the pan, and roll across with enough pressure to cut off the overhang on all sides. (The overhang can be as much as 1 ounce for an 8-inch quiche pan, but that is preferable to not having enough dough to fill the pan evenly and efficiently.)

Storing the dough: At this point you may bake the unfilled shell or cover the dough's surface with plastic wrap and refrigerate it for up to 2 days or freeze it for up to 1 month by covering the plastic-wrapped package with foil. Don't forget to label it with the contents and the date.

Baking the tart shell: At least 15 minutes before baking, position rack in lower third of oven; preheat oven to 350 degrees.

Bake in preheated oven for 17 to 22 minutes, or until the shell appears golden, looks done and contracts from the side. After the initial 5 to 7 minutes in the oven, the shell may blister; if so, prick the bottom in 3 or 4 places with a metal skewer, allowing the steam to escape so that the dough will fit snugly in the pan again. It is important to prick it before it bakes too long and sets its shape.

Cooling the tart shell: Remove from oven to cooling rack. After 5 minutes, place on top of a can smaller than the baking pan, releasing the pan's metal rim from the baked crust.

Fill and serve the day it is baked.

Classic Sweet Almond Pastry

This sweet crust can resist moisture from a filling longer than other sweet crusts.

This is the foundation for Melon and Lime Curd Tart (page 348).
MAKES TWO 8-x-⅞-INCH OR 9-x-⅞-INCH TART CRUSTS AND ONE 11-x-8-x-1-INCH TART CRUST (2 POUNDS DOUGH)

Baking Equipment: Two 8- or 9-inch quiche pans or one 11-x-8-x-1-inch rectangular quiche pan, with removable bottoms

7	ounces (1 ¾ sticks) unsalted butter
5	ounces (1 scant cup) unblanched almonds
2 ½	cups (350 grams) unsifted all-purpose flour
⅛	teaspoon salt
1 ¼	cups (125 grams) unsifted powdered sugar
1	large egg

Baker's Note

☞ Since this dough is made with ground nuts, I prefer making it by hand or in a heavy-duty mixer. If you make it in a food processor, take care not to overprocess it or the nuts will become oily.

1   egg yolk
1   teaspoon vanilla
½   teaspoon almond extract

Making the dough: Prepare as for Classic Sweet Pastry according to the directions on page 341, using the hand or heavy-duty mixer methods with the following difference:

Ingredient preparation: Add the almond extract to the egg with the vanilla. Grind the nuts in a nut grinder or other rotary-type grater until they have the consistency of cornmeal and make 2 cups ground. Blend the nuts with the flour and sugar.

Rolling and baking the dough: Chill, roll and bake as directed on pages 343 to 344.

Cranberry Pecan Tart

A MOIST, rich filling of pecans, jeweled with bright, tangy cranberries on a tender pastry crust.

MAKES 6 TO 8 SERVINGS

Baking Equipment: 9-inch quiche pan with removable bottom

1   cup (9 ounces) Classic Sweet Pastry (page 341)

Filling
¼   cup water
½   cup dark corn syrup
½   cup (100 grams) granulated sugar
1 ½   cups (6 ounces) fresh cranberries, washed and picked over
2   ounces (4 tablespoons) unsalted butter
2   large eggs
½   cup (2 ounces) whole pecans
1   teaspoon orange zest

2   tablespoons unsifted powdered sugar
1   raw cranberry

Advance preparation: Prepare Classic Sweet Pastry as directed on page 341; wrap and refrigerate for at least 1 hour.

Baking preparations: Position rack in lower third of oven; preheat oven to 375 degrees.

Rolling the dough: You may want to review rolling sweet doughs on page 343.

Roll the dough to a circle 11 to 11 ½ inches and ⅛ inch thick. Fit into the pan and trim the overhang by rolling the rolling pin across the top rim of the pan.

Baker's Notes

☞ The tart shell is partially baked before being filled and baked again.

☞ You will need only a part of the recipe for Classic Sweet Pastry for this tart; make the entire portion, use 1 cup and freeze the remainder for future use.

Save the excess dough for pastry leaves or petals. (If desired, roll the leftover dough out again ⅛ inch thick and cut leaf or petal shapes with a knife or a cutter. Bake the leaf cookies on a parchment-lined baking sheet for 5 to 6 minutes in the preheated oven with the tart shell.)

Bake the tart shell in the preheated oven for about 10 to 12 minutes, or until the surface of the dough is no longer shiny and the dough appears set and ivory-colored. Check after 5 to 6 minutes for signs of blistering; if necessary, prick dough in 4 or 5 places to release steam so the dough fits the pan snugly.

Remove from the oven to a cooling rack while you prepare the filling.

Making the filling: Pour the water, corn syrup, sugar and cranberries in that order into a 1½-quart heavy-bottomed saucepan. Place over medium heat and swirl the pan occasionally until the sugar dissolves completely (about 1 minute). Increase heat to high, bring to a boil and cook, stirring occasionally, until the cranberries pop (about 3 minutes). If the mixture begins to rise in saucepan, reduce heat slightly, but maintain a boil.

Remove from heat and stir in the butter until melted. Set aside to cool to 100 degrees (close to body temperature); this will take about 30 minutes.

Whisk the eggs in a mixing bowl briefly to combine yolks and whites. Stir into the cooled cranberry mixture with a rubber spatula; then add the pecans and zest.

Baking the tart: Pour the filling into the partially baked tart shell. Return the shell to the 375-degree oven for 30 to 35 minutes, or until the crust's edge is golden and the filling appears thicker and set when the side of the tart is tapped. (The filling bubbles around the edges during baking, but at the end, the entire surface bubbles.) Remove to a cooling rack and cool for 10 minutes. Then, with the tip of a knife, gently poke any area of crust that appears stuck to the tin. Remove the outer rim and return the tart to the cooling rack until it reaches room temperature.

Decorating and serving the tart: Pour powdered sugar into a sieve and tap it to sprinkle sugar over top of tart. Place pastry petals and 1 cranberry on top.

Serve at room temperature.

Lemon Tart With Blueberries

THE FRESH flavors of lemon and blueberry are at their best in this easily assembled, elegant tart. (See photograph, page 69.)

MAKES 6 TO 8 SERVINGS

(See photograph, page 69.)

Baking Equipment: 9-inch quiche pan with removable bottom

1	cup (9 ounces) Classic Sweet Pastry (page 341)

Filling

2	large eggs
¾	cup (150 grams) granulated sugar
6	tablespoons fresh lemon juice, strained
2	ounces (4 tablespoons) unsalted butter, melted
2	teaspoons lemon zest

Fruit

3	tablespoons strained apricot jam
2	cups (1 pint) fresh blueberries

Advance preparation: Prepare Classic Sweet Pastry as directed on page 341. Wrap and refrigerate it for at least 1 hour.

Baking preparations: At least 15 minutes before baking, position rack in lower third of oven; preheat oven to 375 degrees.

Rolling the dough: Roll the dough into an 11- to 11½-inch circle ⅛ inch thick as directed on page 343. Fit the dough into the pan; trim the overhang by rolling the pin across its rim.

Bake in preheated oven for 10 to 12 minutes, or until the surface of dough no longer looks raw or shiny but appears set and ivory-colored. (Check after 5 to 6 minutes in the oven for signs of the crust's blistering; if necessary, prick it in 4 to 5 places to release steam so that the dough fits the pan snugly.)

Remove from the oven to a cooling rack while you prepare the filling.

Making the filling: Place eggs in a small bowl and whisk just to combine. Pour in the sugar and whisk. Add the lemon juice, again whisking to combine. Add the cooled melted butter and lemon zest and blend.

Baking the tart: Pour the filling into the partially baked pastry shell.

Return to 375-degree oven and bake for 16 to 18 minutes longer, or until the crust is golden and the filling is set. (The filling bubbles toward the end of baking.) Remove and cool on a rack for 10 minutes.

Set the pan on a narrower elevated surface (such as a tin can), so the bottom of the pan

Baker's Notes

☞ This tart is best served the day it is baked.

☞ You will need only a part of the recipe for Classic Sweet Pastry for this tart; make the entire portion, use 1 cup and freeze the remainder for future use.

Understanding Pastrymaking

is released as the metal rim slips down. Cool to room temperature.

Preparing the fruit: Heat the apricot jam just until melted but not bubbly hot. Pour into a 2-quart mixing bowl. Pour the blueberries next to the warm preserves and toss gently with a rubber spatula briefly to coat most of them. Spread over the tart, leaving a 3-inch center portion of lemon filling uncovered. Serve the same day for best flavor.

Melon and Lime Curd Tart

The sweet piquancy of lime curd filling marries superbly with the fresh, mellow flavors of cantaloupe and honeydew.
MAKES 10 TO 12 SERVINGS

Baking Equipment: 8-x-11-x-1-inch fluted pan with removable bottom

1	recipe Lime Curd (page 258)
1 ½	scant cups (13 ounces) Classic Sweet Almond Pastry (page 344)
1	egg yolk
11	ounces honeydew melon, peeled and sliced $1/16$ inch thin
11	ounces cantaloupe melon, peeled and sliced $1/16$ inch thin
	Peppermint or strawberry leaves

Advance preparations: Prepare Lime Curd as directed on page 258. Refrigerate until 1 hour before filling the tart shell.

Prepare Classic Sweet Almond Pastry as directed on page 344. Wrap and refrigerate it for at least 1 hour.

Baking preparations: Position rack in lower third of oven; preheat oven to 350 degrees.

Rolling and baking the dough: On the day of serving, pat the dough into a 4-x-6-

☞ You may substitute Classic Sweet Pastry (page 341).

☞ Placing the melon slices on top of a thick filling prevents the pastry from becoming soggy.

☞ You will need only a part of the recipe for Classic Sweet Pastry for this tart; make the entire portion, use 1½ scant cups and freeze the remainder for future use.

☞ This tart is best served the day it is baked.

inch rectangle. Roll it on a lightly floured surface to prevent its sticking. (Avoid using too much flour or a dry pastry will result.) Roll it into a 13-x-10-inch rectangle, ⅛ inch thick. Roll it onto the pin to transfer into pan. Trim off any overhang by rolling the pin across the top rim of the pan.

Bake in preheated oven for about 15 minutes, or until dough appears set, the surface no longer appears wet or shiny, the crust is pulling away from the pan and its edges are light golden. (After the initial 5 to 7 minutes in the oven, check for blistering; if necessary, prick the dough in 4 or 5 places to release steam so that the dough will fit the pan snugly.)

Remove from oven and set on a cooling rack for 10 minutes.

Filling and baking the tart: Mix the egg yolk with Lime Curd. Spread it evenly over the tart shell with a rubber spatula. Return to 350-degree oven for about 10 minutes more, or until the filling is set. Remove to a cooling rack until the tart is at room temperature.

Decorating the tart: Place the tart on a serving plate. Arrange overlapping slices of melon diagonally, alternating layers of cantaloupe and honeydew. Decorate with peppermint or strawberry leaves. Serve the same day for best flavor.

Banana Caramel Tart

IN THIS delicious alternative to banana cream pie, banana slices are arranged on a thin caramel cream layer and topped with a light pastry cream.
MAKES 10 TO 12 SERVINGS

Baking Equipment: 12-x-15½-x-½-inch baking sheet, 12-x-4-x-1-inch flan form

12	ounces (scant 1 ⅓ cups) **Classic Sweet Pastry (page 341)**
1	recipe **Diplomat Cream (page 248)**

Filling
1	recipe **Classic Caramel Cream (page 307)**
1	large **banana**
1	ounce (¼ cup) **sliced almonds**
2	tablespoons unsifted **powdered sugar**

Advance preparations: Prepare Classic Sweet Pastry as directed on page 341. Wrap and refrigerate it for at least 1 hour.

Prepare Classic Pastry Cream in the Diplomat Cream recipe as directed on page 248. Cover with plastic wrap and refrigerate until ready to use.

Baking preparations: Line the baking sheet with parchment paper and place the flan form on top of it.

Position rack in lower third of oven; preheat oven to 350 degrees.

☞ This tart may be prepared over a 2-day period.
First day: Prepare and bake tart shell; prepare Classic Pastry Cream (page 248).
Second day: Prepare Caramel Cream, finish Diplomat Cream; assemble dessert.

☞ You will need only a part of the recipe for Classic Sweet Pastry for this tart; make the entire portion, use 1⅓ scant cups and freeze the remainder for future use.

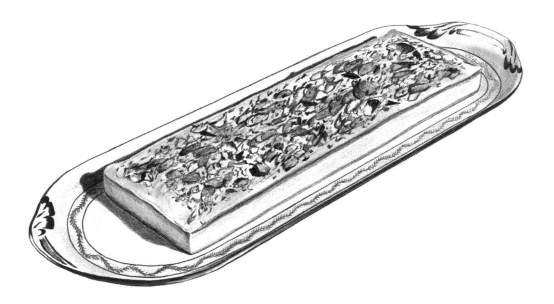

Rolling the dough: Before proceeding, you may want to refer to page 343 for more information on rolling sweet doughs.

Shape the dough into a square; then roll it on a lightly floured surface into a rectangle about 6 x 16 inches and ⅛ inch thick. Transfer and ease it into the flan form, fitting it to the flan's contour with fingertips. Trim the pastry edges by rolling the pin over the rim.

Baking the pastry shell: Bake in the preheated oven. Check the dough after 7 to 10 minutes of baking for any blistering; if necessary, prick the bottom of the crust in 4 or 5 places to release steam so that the pastry will fit snugly to the pan's form again. After baking for 15 minutes, the dough no longer appears raw or shiny (it will sink slightly into the form). Reduce oven temperature to 325 degrees and bake for 12 to 15 minutes longer, or until the crust is light golden brown.

Cooling the pastry shell: Remove from oven and set the baking sheet on a rack to cool for at least 10 minutes. Then remove the flan form, leaving the baked pastry on the baking sheet.

Making the filling: Prepare Classic Caramel Cream as directed on page 307. Set aside to cool for 10 minutes; then pour into baked tart shell, spreading evenly with a rubber spatula. Cool in the pastry for at least 15 minutes before assembling the tart.

Assembling and serving the tart: Position oven rack 6 to 7 inches from boiler element; preheat boiler.

Just before you are ready to top with Diplomat Cream, slice the banana ⅛ inch thick, and arrange slices on cooled Caramel Cream.

Pour the ¼ cup heavy cream in the recipe for Diplomat Cream into a medium-size bowl and whip it by hand (or electric mixer) until soft peaks form. Stir the pastry cream briefly until smooth; then fold in the whipped cream with a rubber spatula.

Scoop Diplomat Cream over the banana slices in the tart. Using a flexible metal icing spatula, spread it over the bananas until the surface is smooth. It will come up to (or just slightly above) the top rim of the tart.

Sprinkle with the almonds. Pour the powdered sugar into a sieve and tap it to coat the tart lightly.

Place under broiler for a few seconds, or just until lightly browned. Remove and cool it for at least 30 minutes.

Transfer to a serving plate with the aid of two large spatulas. Serve at room temperature.

Vendôme Caramel Tart

A RICH, creamy caramel, honeycombed with pecans and encased in a shortbread-type of pastry, is one of my favorite desserts. I tasted something like this in a bakery in Los Angeles, and since they could not share the recipe, the challenge began. After three years, my reward is this tart.

MAKES 10 TO 12 SERVINGS

Baking Equipment: One 8-x-2-inch heavy-gauge straight-sided round cake pan

2	scant cups (1 pound) Classic Sweet Pastry (page 341)

Filling

2	ounces (4 tablespoons) unsalted butter
1 ½	cups (12 ounces) heavy cream
¼	cup water
⅓	cup light corn syrup
1 ½	cups (300 grams) granulated sugar
¼	teaspoon salt
2 ½	cups (9 ounces) whole pecans

Glaze

1	large egg

Advance preparations: Prepare Classic Sweet Pastry as directed on page 341. Divide it into three 8-ounce portions, and wrap and refrigerate it for at least 1 hour. Freeze one of the 8-ounce portions of pastry dough; only two portions are needed for this tart.

Rolling the dough: Before proceeding, you may want to refer to page 343 for more information on rolling sweet doughs.

Roll one portion of dough into an 11-inch circle less than ⅛ inch thick. Roll it up onto the rolling pin, and suspend it about 1 inch over the cake pan. Aligning the edge of the dough with the rim of the pan, unroll it toward you. Then fit the dough into the pan, easing it gently into its contour with your fingertips. The pastry should extend 1 ½ inches up the sides of the pan. If it tears, patch it by overlapping torn edges and pressing them together. Set aside while preparing the filling.

Baking preparations: Position rack in lower third of oven; preheat oven to 375 degrees. Remove the second portion of dough from the refrigerator so it will be malleable enough to roll when you finish making the filling.

Making the filling: Have the butter at hand. Pour the cream into a 1-quart saucepan; warm it over low heat. Pour the water into a 4½-quart heavy-bottomed saucepan; then add the corn syrup and sugar. Place over low heat, and stir with a wooden spoon occasionally until the sugar dissolves completely (about 3 minutes).

Increase the heat to medium-high and boil the sugar syrup, swirling the pan occasionally to distribute the heat evenly, until it is *amber-colored* and the mercury candy thermometer registers 310 to 320 degrees (about 5 minutes). Then remove from the heat briefly, and add the butter (the mixture will bubble). Immediately return the pan to the heat, and stir to combine most of the butter. Before it is completely melted, pour in the warm cream in a steady stream. (Careful: At first it will bubble up and steam.) Add the salt. Continue to boil the mixture, stirring often to prevent scorching, and cook it until the thermometer registers 232 degrees (about 5 minutes). Immediately remove from the heat, and stir in the nuts briefly, but leave the thermometer in this caramel-nut mixture. Set aside until the caramel's temperature cools to 180 degrees (about 5 minutes).

While the filling is cooling, prepare the egg glaze. Whisk the egg in a small bowl to combine the yolk and white. Set aside.

Filling the tart: When the caramel filling cools to 180 degrees, pour it into the pastry-lined pan. Gently fold the excess dough along the sides of the pan over the filling.

With a pastry brush, lightly coat the overlapping edge of dough (approximately 1 inch) with the egg glaze.

Roll the other portion of dough to a 10-inch circle ⅛ inch thick. Roll it onto the rolling pin. Suspend it about 1 inch over the edge of the pan farthest from you. Unroll the dough toward you, centering it over the filling. Press the dough gently against the lower crust to seal the two doughs. Trim the excess dough on top, being careful not to disturb the seal.

Baking the tart: Coat the top of the tart with the egg glaze, using the pastry brush. Cut a V in the crust's surface with the tip of a sharp knife. It serves a dual purpose as a vent and a decorative touch.

Baker's Notes

↪ You can substitute 2½ cups whole walnuts for the pecans.

↪ Preparing the filling is not difficult, but it does require attention. Its preparation is made easier with an accurate mercury candy thermometer. A gas stove provides a larger area of heat to your saucepan than an electric stove so the filling will cook faster.

↪ You will need only part of the recipe for Classic Sweet Pastry for this tart, so make the entire portion, use 2 cups, and freeze the remainder for future use.

↪ Wrapped in foil, this tart remains fresh for a week. Store it at room temperature.

Bake in the preheated oven for 30 to 35 minutes, or until top crust is light golden brown. Remove from oven to a cooling rack for about 35 to 40 minutes. Run a small metal spatula or the thin blade of a table knife between the tart's outer edge and the metal rim, freeing the sides and allowing air to get under it. Place another rack on top and invert the tart onto it; then lift the baking pan. Place the original rack on the tart and invert again, right side up.

Cool for at least 2 hours or overnight before serving.

Milano Rice Tart

R ICE HAS its place in pastrymaking, especially in Italian desserts. This tart has a simple creamy filling, reminiscent of one I tasted in Italy.

MAKES 6 SERVINGS

Baking and Decorating Equipment: 8-inch quiche pan with removable bottom, 16-inch pastry bag, #127 decorating tip

1	**scant cup (8 ounces) Classic Sweet Pastry (page 341)**

Filling

1	**large egg**
1	**egg yolk**
3	**tablespoons (35 grams) granulated sugar**
1 ½	**cups (12 ounces) milk**
1	**cup (8 ounces) heavy cream**
¼	**teaspoon salt**
⅓	**cup uncooked long-grain rice**
2	**teaspoons vanilla**

½	**recipe Swiss Meringue (page 264)**

Baker's Notes

☞ You will need only part of the recipe for Classic Sweet Pastry for this tart, so make the entire portion, use 1 scant cup and freeze the remainder for future use.

☞ The pastry is partially baked, then filled and baked until completely done.

☞ Serve the tart the same day you bake it.

☞ The #127 decorating tip used to pipe the meringue and decorate the tart is best known for piping buttercream rose petals.

Advance preparations: Prepare Classic Sweet Pastry as directed on page 341. Wrap and refrigerate it for at least 1 hour.

Baking preparations: Position rack in lower third of oven; preheat oven to 350 degrees.

Rolling and baking the dough: On a lightly floured surface, roll the dough as directed on page 343 into a 10-inch circle ⅛ inch thick. Roll it onto the rolling pin and transfer it to the pan. Fit the dough into the pan by pushing some of the overhang down the sides. Then roll the pin across the metal rim, cutting off the excess dough.

Bake for about 12 to 15 minutes, or until crust's surface is no longer shiny and is lightly colored (darker than ivory) and the dough appears set. Check after initial 5 to 7 minutes of baking for signs of blistering; if necessary, prick dough in 4 to 5 places to release steam so that the dough will fit snugly in the pan again.

Remove from oven to cooling rack while preparing filling. Maintain the same oven temperature.

Making the filling: Whisk the whole egg, egg yolk and sugar in a 1-quart mixing bowl briefly to combine. Set aside.

Combine the milk, cream and salt in a 1½-quart saucepan. Bring to a boil, add the rice and stir to blend. When the mixture returns to a boil, reduce heat to medium and simmer, uncovered. Continue to simmer, stirring occasionally, for 18 to 20 minutes, or until the rice is tender. (The mixture reduces during this time, and though it is thicker, it still appears liquid.)

Pour about ½ cup of the hot rice mixture into the egg mixture, stirring to combine. Then return egg-rice mixture to remaining hot rice and stir until blended. Stir in the vanilla.

Baking the tart: Spoon the rice filling into the partially baked pastry shell, spreading it level with a rubber spatula. Return to the 350-degree oven for 12 to 15 minutes longer, or until filling is set and the pastry is light golden near the rim of the pan.

Remove from oven and set aside to cool on a rack.

Decorating and serving the tart: Position the oven rack 6 to 7 inches from the broiler, and preheat it. Fit the pastry bag with the decorating tip.

Prepare Swiss Meringue as directed on page 264. Scoop it into the pastry bag and pipe petals around the cooled tart. (Begin along the edge of the tart and work toward the center, leaving the center portion of the filling uncovered.)

Place on a baking sheet and put under the broiler just long enough to shade some of the meringue light golden to highlight the raised areas of the petals.

Serve at room temperature the same day.

Recipes for Puff Pastry

FOUNDATION PUFF PASTRIES

PUFF PASTRY DESSERTS

Puff Pastry

~

PUFF PASTRY, the most elegant and sophisticated product in the baking repertoire, is often used for its dramatic effect as well as for its flavor and texture. But it can also be the most intimidating pastry to make.

My first attempt at puff pastry was not too bad, even though it lacked expert handling and knowledge. The thin layer of puff pastry began to rise magically in the hot oven, expanding from the top, working downward. Delicate, tender and multilayered, it was heaven to taste and eat. The experience encouraged me to learn more about the principles behind puff pastry.

A recipe for puff pastry reads like a recipe for pie dough because the same ingredients are used. The fat is high in ratio to the flour, but how the fat is handled is the key to producing the multilayered structure. The technique of making the layers is called lamination.

By manipulating the dough in such a way as to form horizontal layers of lean dough, separated by thin films of fat, lamination can expand, aerate and leaven pastry. Without layering, the baked result would merely be a high-fat, flaky, tender piecrust.

The methods used to roll the fat into the dough range from traditional to more modern adaptations patterned to fit our busy lives. The different methods provide a variety of textures: their flakiness can vary from brittle to tender.

One technique calls for rolling a butter block into a lean dough package, then rolling and folding the dough (called turns) to complete the formation of layers. Another way is to form a dough similar to a piecrust, then roll and fold it to form a layered structure. Each method forms a layering, one with more structure than the other. But the goal is always the same: to distribute the fat evenly.

As the pastry is exposed to the oven's heat, the moisture in the lean-dough layers converts to steam and in its attempt to escape, expands its layers upward. The gluten strands have enough tension so they extend with this pressure, but at the same time hold tight in an attempt to contain the steam. But the pressure is too great and expansion continues until the gluten strands are coagulated (set) by the heat.

Simultaneously, the fat melts between these layers, lubricating and separating them from one another. By maintaining its identity and not dissolving into the dough, the fat aids in the layering, creating puff pastry's distinctive texture.

THE INGREDIENTS AND THEIR ROLE

FLOUR

To sustain and retain the rich layered structure, the flour must support the high proportion of fat and withstand extensive rolling.

Generally, I use all-purpose flour or a blend of all-purpose and cake flour for my puff pastry recipes. If you find resistance while rolling any puff pastry recipe, remember that flours vary not only in each region, but each season too. Therefore, the fault may not be in the recipe; it could be in the flour. If the pastry is stubborn during the rolling and folding process, too much gluten is being developed. If you are having trouble, consider reducing the protein content of your flour, which develops into gluten, rather than changing recipes. You might begin by sifting together all-purpose flour with cake flour, which is lower in protein, in a 5 to 1 ratio (by weight), in place of pure all-purpose flour.

FAT

Fat in the dough package lubricates the dough, giving it flexibility and making it easier to roll. Butter's melting point is close to body temperature, so any pastry made with it will melt in your mouth. I use unsalted butter.

LIQUID AND SALT

Most recipes use water, though milk or cream is sometimes called for to add richness and flavor. The liquid must be cold enough to keep the gluten development to a minimum. Later it converts to steam in the oven. Obviously, the more moisture in a puff pastry dough, the more steam will be produced, making it possible to get greater lift. On the other hand, you should add no more liquid than is necessary to form a cohesive dough or too much gluten will be developed during the rolling process.

Salt flavors puff pastry. Many pastry chefs feel it is imperative for tightening and stabilizing the gluten.

ACID

The addition of lemon juice or a mild vinegar to the ice water in the puff pastry recipe lowers the pH (increases the acidity) of the dough. Though it has no effect on the leavening or flakiness of the pastry, it relaxes or conditions the gluten strands quicker than would the dough's natural acidity. Therefore, its addition can make the dough easier to roll in a shorter period of time. But good-quality puff pastry may be manufactured without it.

When acid is added, the dough will appear to soften. Actually, acid has an astringent effect that strengthens the gluten strands. Such elasticity reduces the danger of butter breaking through the layers of dough, which would result in unsatisfactory lift.

Puff pastry made with acid may not be refrigerated as long as one made without or it will not have the proper lift.

TIPS FOR MAKING PERFECT PUFF PASTRY

☞ For best baking results, make puff pastry the day before shaping and baking it.

☞ Weigh the flour. This is your best chance for duplicating the recipe successfully since the balance of flour to water is important. If weighing is impossible for you, accurate volume measurements are given in each recipe.

☞ Regardless of the method, prepare the dough package at least 12 hours before rolling in the butter. This initial rest relaxes and mellows the dough, making it easier to withstand the repeated rollings.

☞ Butter temperature and consistency are two of the most important elements in making successful puff pastry. It should be cold but not so firm that it is brittle so it will film between the dough layers smoothly. Pound the cold, firm butter with the end of a rolling pin until it is malleable enough so that it can be folded on top of itself without breaking. The process should take only about 30 seconds so the butter remains cold. Even a temperature change of 10 to 15 degrees will change its consistency drastically. Too firm, and it will form broken fragments while rolling between the layers; too soft, and it will integrate with the dough layers, making it impossible to build structure. (Butter that is softer than the dough is the worst.)

☞ Every brand of butter contains some liquid. How much depends on the quality. The liquid can weep during the rolling process, mix with the thin layers of dough, overdevelop the gluten and toughen the pastry. To get rid of the excess, wash the butter, or pound it on a towel, or add flour to it before rolling it into the dough package.

☞ Finish making the puff pastry after forming the butter block, since the consistency of the butter is just right at that point.

☞ The dough package and butter block, though separate, should be at similar consistencies for successful rolling and layering. If the butter block breaks through the dough, lightly flour to patch, forming a sort of Band-Aid over the area; then brush away the excess flour. No matter what happens, continue rolling and layering. You will be surprised at your success, even if the butter does not behave perfectly.

☞ Always roll the dough on a smooth surface that provides comfortable leverage. Roll from the center of the dough, stopping just short of the edge; if you roll over the edges, you could squeeze butter from between the layers. The goal is to extend not stretch the dough, never applying too much pressure on the rolling pin. Lightly flouring the dough and work surface as necessary makes rolling and layering the dough efficient.

Unlike most puff pastry recipes, the dough in my recipes is rectangular in shape, from the beginning when the butter block is incorporated, to its finish, making it easier to keep corners square and the butter evenly distributed.

☞ When rolling the dough to create more layers, it's easier to extend the width of the rectangle before rolling its length. While layering the puff pastry, roll in alternating directions, lengthwise and widthwise. As you extend the dough, you create tension on that side. Then, when the alternate side is rolled, it will give more easily.

☞ Rest the dough between turns to resolidify the butter layers and relax the dough, giving the gluten strands time to adjust to their new dimension. The rest is important, but if refrigerated too long, the butter may become so cold that it is brittle.

☞ Some puff pastry recipes are more difficult to extend than others. This does not mean the puff pastry will not be perfect. Don't force the pastry if it resists rolling, no matter what the recipe directs. Rest the dough in the refrigerator for a while, then proceed to roll as you can. (If it continues to be impossible, then consider changing the protein content of the dough next time.)

Classic Puff Pastry

After baking, this puff pastry rises three or four times its original thickness and becomes crisp and brittle.

Makes 2 ½ pounds

Dough Package

3	cups plus 2 tablespoons (375 grams) sifted all-purpose flour
¾	cup (75 grams) sifted cake flour
2	ounces (4 tablespoons) unsalted butter, chilled
¾	teaspoon salt
1	cup (8 ounces) ice water

Butter Block

14	ounces (3 ½ sticks) unsalted butter, chilled
2	tablespoons reserved flour

Egg Wash, optional

1	egg

Advance preparation: At least 12 hours before making the puff pastry, prepare the dough package either by hand or machine as directed below.

HAND METHOD

Making the dough package: Pour the flours into a triple sifter and sift into a mound on work surface. *Reserve 2 tablespoons for the butter package.*

Cut the 2 ounces butter into ½-inch cubes and scatter them over the flour mixture. With a pastry blender, cut in the butter until it is the size of small peas. (Don't take longer than 2 minutes so the butter stays cold and firm.)

Roll the rolling pin once or twice over the powdery mixture to flatten the particles of butter; then gather the mixture together in a mound again. Now cut in the butter with pastry blender just until mixture still appears powdery with some oatmeal-shaped flakes of fat throughout (about 1 minute).

With your hand, form an 11-inch well in the center of the flour mixture. Add the salt to center, pour in the ice water and with a fingertip, rub the salt until it is dissolved in the water. Slowly push the flour over the water, covering it. If a stream of water flows out, breaking through the flour moat, just keep gathering flour and water together until combined. (A pastry scraper is helpful here.) To disperse the moisture further, pick up large pieces of dough, and gently pull them apart with your fingertips for about 30 to 45 seconds. This disperses the moisture. Then gather the loose pieces into a mass.

Fold the dough on top of itself gently seven to eleven times with the aid of your hand. Shape into a 6-inch square. Don't worry if the dough is cohesive but not smooth. Score its surface with the tip of a sharp knife in a grid pattern. Wrap it in plastic, and refrigerate it for at least 12 hours or overnight. (The dough mellows because the flour absorbs the moisture, blending the ingredients together, making it smoother and easier to roll.) You can

☞ I can be sure my puff pastry is flaky, crisp and tender when I make my own. However, if in a pinch you need to buy puff pastry, check to see that the only fat used is butter. Contact a good local bakery; some sell unbaked puff pastry dough by the pound.

☞ Wrap the dough package in plastic wrap. It holds in the moisture so the dough mellows during its rest in the refrigerator.

☞ The dough is rested in the refrigerator after each turn. At that time I wrap it in aluminum foil rather than waxed paper or plastic. With waxed paper, the surface dries and crusts; plastic wrap causes moisture to condense on the surface. Aluminum foil attracts the refrigerator's chill. You can use the same piece of aluminum foil throughout the entire process.

Understanding Pastrymaking

freeze the dough for up to 1 week; cover the plastic-wrapped package with foil.

Making the butter block: Prepare the butter block just before it is to be enclosed into the dough package. Unwrap the butter and place it on a surface dusted with the reserved 2 tablespoons of flour. Pound the butter with the end of the rolling pin until it is one malleable unit, though still cold. Don't hesitate to use your palms and fingertips to help shape the butter block. You may lightly flour your hands with some of the reserved flour. Work quickly to keep the butter cold. Place the butter on a piece of waxed paper, place another piece of waxed paper on top, and roll a rectangle close to 9 x 5 ½ inches and ½ inch thick. Refrigerate the waxed paper-covered butter block, remove any tiny particles of butter from your rolling pin and rolling surface, and proceed to roll the dough package to enclose the butter. (If you didn't use all the reserved flour, that's fine.)

Enclosing the butter block in the dough package: Dust the work surface lightly with unsifted all-purpose flour; then place the dough package on it. At this time, do not flour the dough's surface so that it will seal well when it encloses the block of butter (dough sticks to dough firmly when it is not floured). Beginning in the center of the dough, roll it out, using firm, evenly pressured strokes and stopping short of the edges, until the dough is ½ inch thick and measures 11 inches square.

Place the butter block on half the dough, leaving a ½-inch border of uncovered dough. You may have to fit the butter onto the half. Lift other half of the dough over the butter package until the two edges of dough meet. Press edges together with fingers, enclosing the butter.

Creating the layers: Rotate the dough package 90 degrees to the left, and lightly dust the work surface under the dough with flour. Beginning in the center, roll out, using the same firm, evenly pressured strokes and stopping short of the edge. Return the rolling pin to the center, and roll other section of dough similarly, again stopping short of the edge.

Roll the package into a rectangle 7 x 16 inches and less than ½ inch thick. Square the corners by rolling carefully over the thicker edges. Push the rolling pin up against its sides to keep the edges straight if necessary. Should the butter break through the dough at any time during the layering process, sprinkle the opening with flour, pat gently with fingers, brush away excess flour with pastry brush and continue to layer the dough.

Turns 1 and 2: At this point, a short end of the dough is closest to you. Brush away any excess flour with a brush so that the dough sticks to dough more firmly. Then fold the bottom third up over the center; next fold the top third down over the bottom until it resembles a business letter. This fold is called a single fold. You have just completed the first turn.

Rotate the dough 90 degrees counterclockwise (its position now on your surface resembles the pages in a book), and lightly dust the work surface and dough with flour. Roll out as before until dough is ½ inch thick and measures 7 x 16 inches. (You will notice the dough is not extending as easily as the preceding time. This is a clue that a rest period is needed to relax the dough's protein network.) Brush off any excess flour and square the edges and straighten the sides with the rolling pin. Now make another single fold. This is the sec-

☞ The reason for rest periods in the refrigerator is twofold: The gluten strands relax, and the butter is chilled, maintaining the layering. Remember, the resting period is approximate; if at any time the dough resists rolling or the butter becomes too soft, a longer refrigeration period may be needed.

☞ My dessert puff pastry recipes call for less salt than do recipes for savories.

☞ A common problem with puff pastry is underbaking. Many times this accounts for toughness and has nothing to do with techniques of making the dough.

☞ If you don't want to make the dough package by hand, you can also form the dough package in the food processor by following the instructions in Food Processor Puff Pastry (page 363).

ond turn. (To keep track of the turns, record the time of each one on a piece of paper as it is completed.) Wrap dough in foil and refrigerate for 45 minutes (ideal refrigerator temperature is 40 degrees).

Turn 3: Lightly dust the work surface with flour and place the refrigerated dough so that the last fold is perpendicular to you and the flap on top opens like a book.

Roll again until dough is ½ inch thick and measures 7 x 16 inches; then brush off any excess flour and make a single fold again, business-letter style. If at any time the dough along the sides cracks or threatens to open slightly, it will not affect the final puff pastry. Rewrap the dough in the foil and return it to the refrigerator for 45 minutes.

Turn 4: Position the dough so that the last fold is perpendicular to you and the top flap opens like a book. Repeat the rolling and folding as directed for Turn 3. Each turn makes the butter thinner and creates more layers. If after any 45-minute rest period, the dough resists rolling, coax it to extend. Most puff pastries don't roll as easily or freely as pie or tart doughs. Rewrap the dough and refrigerate for 45 to 60 minutes before proceeding to the next step.

Turn 5: Position the dough so that the last fold is perpendicular to you and the top flap opens like a book. Repeat the rolling and folding as directed for Turn 3, but refrigerate the dough for 1 hour instead to give the butter longer to chill.

If at any time the butter breaks through the surface, merely dust the area with flour and brush off the excess before continuing.

Turn 6: Position the dough so that the last fold is perpendicular to you and the top flap opens like a book. Repeat the rolling and folding as directed for Turn 3. Rewrap in the foil, and return the dough to refrigerator to rest for 30 to 60 minutes before shaping for future use.

Rolling the puff pastry: After completing the turns and refrigerating the puff pastry for 30 to 60 minutes, roll it into a larger rectangle ½ inch thick (and about 8 x 11 inches). This is a more manageable shape for future convenience. Our goal is to reduce the puff pastry's thickness gradually. This is best accomplished in two to three stages so that the process of rolling the pastry thinner is easier and maintains the layering without overworking the dough.

Now wrap the puff pastry in plastic, and refrigerate it for at least 4 to 6 hours before rolling and baking it. This is ideal for firming the layers and again relaxing the gluten. You may refrigerate it for up to 2 days. Or cover the plastic-wrapped package with foil, and freeze for up to 3 months; mark the contents and date.

Unlike the layering process, in which you alternate directions of rolling, once you have rolled the puff pastry package for future use, it may be rolled in any direction when you form sheets.

Rolling the puff pastry sheets: If the puff pastry is frozen, remove it from the freezer to the refrigerator 24 hours before you attempt to roll it.

Cut off the amount you need for your recipe and return the remainder to the refrigerator. (Even if you plan to use the remainder shortly, it should be kept in the refrigerator until you are ready to roll it. Otherwise, the puff pastry will begin to get warm and soften so the layers crush together during rolling.)

When cutting off a portion from the puff pastry package, use a sharp knife, and press and lift the blade in a guillotine fashion (straight down) rather than pulling the knife across the dough. This gives a clean cut.

When the dough is ready to roll, it should be cold, firm and pliable, not stiff or rigid. Therefore, some puff pastries may need to sit at room temperature until they are more pliable (about 10 minutes). If you roll the pastry before it's ready to cooperate, you run the risk of overworking it.

When rolling puff pastry, use as little flour as possible to keep the rolling pin from sticking and the pastry freely sliding along the work surface. If the pastry sticks to the rolling surface, the layers could be crushed. To avoid flouring the pastry sheet too much, never flip it over while rolling.

No matter which direction you roll it, always begin in the center and stop short of the edges. This ensures that even pressure will be applied over the entire surface of the puff pastry sheet (even pressure yields uniform thickness). If the original shape of the puff pastry is rectangular, roll for width first; it is easier to widen the pastry in the beginning than later.

Roll it equally in each direction, alternating between length and width to enlarge the dough and to ensure it will bake evenly. As the piece of puff pastry increases in size, lift it when you want to change rolling directions with the aid of your pin. If the edges become uneven as you roll, you are applying uneven pressure on the rolling pin. This is not serious; they may be trimmed straight later with a ruler and pastry wheel.

Resting the sheets: After the dough has been rolled to the desired dimension, transfer it to a bare baking sheet and cover its surface with plastic wrap. (Don't line the baking sheet with parchment paper because it will absorb some of the pastry's moisture, which provides the steam that lifts the pastry.)

The longer puff pastry sheets rest, the better. A minimum of 30 minutes is acceptable, but a rest of up to 24 hours provides a firm, relaxed pastry sheet. The firmer the pastry, the easier it is to make clean cuts when shaping it and the less shrinkage there is during baking.

Shaping the puff pastry: After the puff pastry sheet has rested, you are ready to shape it as the recipe directs. If your time is limited and you can rest the puff pastry sheet for only 30 to 45 minutes, freezing it before cutting just until it is firm, not frozen, is helpful.

When cutting the puff pastry sheet, use a sharp knife, such as a chef's knife, a Chinese cleaver or a sharpened pizza cutting wheel. Cut straight down without drawing the blade across the dough, which pulls the cut edges and the puff pastry out of shape. Clean edges ensure an even rise in the oven.

Even when the puff pastry is cut carefully, the pressure from the knife blade rounds the cut edge slightly. When it is possible, turn the puff pastry over where the edge is not pinched.

After the puff pastry has been shaped into a form or individual forms, rest it in the refrigerator for at least 30 minutes to refirm the layers and give the gluten time to relax.

Baking the puff pastry: Position rack in the lower third of the oven and preheat the oven to 425 degrees. Line the baking sheets with parchment paper to insulate the bottom of the puff pastry from frying onto the pan while baking.

If desired, make the egg wash by beating the egg in a small bowl with a fork and brush it on the pastry. Two applications are best, one after shaping and the second just before baking. Don't let the egg wash touch the edges; it might inhibit the pastry's lift.

To control puff pastry's lift when flakiness, not volume, is desired, you must prick the dough. Pricking allows steam to escape instead of remaining in the pastry. How much you prick it depends upon how much you want to control its lift. (The more prick marks the less lift.)

Place the pastry in the hot oven. The major lift occurs in the first 15 minutes in the oven. Watch it carefully between the first 7 and 20 minutes of baking, especially if its shape is important, such as in Free-Form Puff Pastry Strip (page 368) and Round Puff Pastry Tart Shell (page 366). During this time, if it is rising too much, additional pricking may be required to maintain the desired shape.

The hot oven is usually necessary for only the first 10 minutes. Reduce the heat to 375 degrees and bake for another 10 minutes to sustain the steam but allow the interior to bake through. After the initial 20 minutes, reduce the temperature to 300 or 325 degrees and bake the pastry until a skewer or toothpick inserted into it meets with no resistance and the dough feels and sounds crisp; this last baking time can be anywhere from 10 to 30 minutes more. (Smaller puff pastry shapes expand and are done sooner.)

Using leftover puff pastry: Don't throw away scraps, no matter the size. Match leftover scraps of puff pastry together like pieces in a puzzle, wrap them and refrigerate them to rest before rolling for another use.

Food Processor Puff Pastry

T HIS puff pastry's texture is shorter than that of Classic Puff Pastry (page 359) with a more tender flake and a lift that is almost equally high. This puff pastry is similar to both Jack Lirio's and the late Jean Troisgros' recipes. M. Troisgros called his Warm-Weather Puff Pastry because he assembled both the dough and the butter package by hand, using very soft butter (about 75 degrees). It worked perfectly.

MAKES 2 ½ POUNDS

Dough Package

2 ¾	cups (330 grams) sifted all-purpose flour
3	ounces (6 tablespoons) unsalted butter, chilled
½	cup plus 2 tablespoons (5 ounces) ice water
¾	teaspoon salt
1	egg yolk

Butter Block

1	cup (120 grams) sifted all-purpose flour
13	ounces (3 ¼ sticks) unsalted butter, chilled

Advance preparations: At least 12 hours before making puff pastry, prepare the dough package. Pour 2¾ cups (330 grams) flour into the bowl of a food processor fitted with a steel blade. Cut the 3 ounces chilled butter into ½-inch cubes and scatter them over the flour. Process with on/off bursts until the mixture resembles cornmeal (about 10 seconds).

Combine the ice water and salt in a liquid cup measure; stir briefly to dissolve. Add the egg yolk and stir until blended. Turn on the processor and pour the liquid ingredients down the side of the feed tube in a steady stream. Process just until mixture begins to come together but not completely (about 20 to 25 seconds).

Shaping the dough package: Pour the mixture onto a sheet of plastic wrap and after enclosing it, manipulate the dough with fingertips into a 6-inch square. Refrigerate for at least 12 hours or overnight. (Since the ingredients are more finely dispersed together, this dough package will appear smoother than one made by hand.) After refrigeration it will be firmer than when you wrapped it in the plastic wrap.

Making the butter block: Pour the 1 cup (120 grams) flour into the bowl of food processor fitted with the steel blade. Cut the 13 ounces of chilled butter into ½-inch-thick slices on a baking sheet, and place in the freezer for 10 minutes. Then scatter the slices over the flour in the food processor bowl. Process with on/off bursts just until mixture appears crumbly like a streusel (about 17 to 20 seconds); it will look like small pieces of gravel stuck together. Do not allow mixture to form a ball, or the butter will be too soft and a pastelike dough will form. (Should this happen, wrap and refrigerate it for 30 minutes.)

With the aid of a rubber spatula, scrape the mixture out onto a sheet of plastic wrap, and pull edges together to enclose the butter. Work the butter through the plastic wrap with your fingertips into a 7-x-6-inch shape. (Working the dough through the plastic rather than directly by hand reduces the chance of warming and softening the butter; plastic wrap also restricts the dough and aids in forming the exact shape specified.) Refrigerate *briefly* while rolling the dough package.

Enclosing the butter block in the dough package: Dust the work surface lightly with flour; then place the dough package on it. Beginning in the center of the dough package, roll it out, using firm, evenly pressured strokes and stopping short of the edges, until the dough is less than ½ inch thick and measures 10 inches square.

Unwrap the butter package and place it on half of the dough; you may have to move some of the butter so it covers only half of the dough package. Then lift the other half of dough over the butter package until the edges meet. Press them together with fingertips, enclosing the butter completely.

Creating the layers: Rotate the package 90 degrees counterclockwise, and lightly dust the work surface under dough with flour. Beginning in the center, roll out, using the same firm, evenly pressured strokes and stopping short of the edge. Return the rolling pin to the center, and roll the other section of dough similarly, again stopping short of the edge.

Roll into a rectangle 7 x 16 inches and less than ½ inch thick. Square the corners by rolling carefully over the thicker edges, and push the rolling pin up against its sides to keep edges straight. Should the butter break through the dough at any time, sprinkle the area with flour, pat gently with fingers, brush away excess flour with pastry brush and continue layering the dough.

Turns 1 and 2: At this point, a short end of the dough is closest to you. Fold the bottom third up over the center; then fold the top third down over the bottom until it resembles an envelope. This fold is called a single fold. You have just completed the first turn. To complete both turns will take only 2 to 3 minutes.

Rotate the dough 90 degrees counterclockwise (its position on your surface now resembles pages in a book). Lightly dust the work surface and dough with flour if necessary. Roll out as before until dough is less than ½ inch thick and measures 7 x 16 inches. Brush off any excess flour and square the edges and straighten the sides with rolling pin.

With the short end closest to you, fold it into the center of the rectangle. Fold the other short end so that the two shorter ends meet in the center. Now fold dough in half again, forming a double fold consisting of four layers. This is the second turn.

Wrap the dough in foil, and refrigerate for 45 minutes.

Turn 3: Lightly dust the work surface with flour and position the refrigerated dough so that the last fold is perpendicular to you, its top flap opening like a book.

Roll as previously directed until dough measures 7 x 16 inches. (You will notice it rolls beautifully and easily.) Brush off any excess flour; then, with the short end closest to you, fold it into the center of the rectangle. Fold the other short end so that the two shorter ends meet in the center. Now fold dough in half again, forming a double fold, consisting of four layers. Rewrap in the foil and return to refrigerator for 30 minutes.

Turn 4: Position the dough so that the double fold is perpendicular to you and opens like a book. Repeat the rolling and double folding technique as directed in Turn 3. Refrigerate the dough for 1 hour.

Shaping the pastry: Roll the dough to a 6-x-11-inch rectangle for future convenience. Now you may wrap the puff pastry in plastic and refrigerate it for up to 2 days. Or cover the plastic-wrapped package with foil and freeze it for up to 2 months; label the package, indicating the contents and date.

Rolling and baking puff pastry: See pages 361 to 363.

Round Puff Pastry Tart Shell

W HEN YOU cut a portion from a batch of puff pastry, you get a square or a rectangle. The technique in this recipe demonstrates how to transform a square piece of dough into a circle.

This is the pastry for Windsor Tart (page 374).

MAKES ONE 8-INCH ROUND TART SHELL

Baking Equipment: 8-x-2-inch heavy-gauge cake pan

4-x-4-x-½-inch thick (5 to 6 ounces) square of puff pastry (page 359 or page 363)

Baking preparations: To prevent the dough from sticking to the metal during baking, grease the outside of the pan with solid shortening, using a paper towel. Then dust the sides of the pan with flour. Place an 8-inch circle of parchment paper on top of the pan (the parchment aids in releasing the pan after baking; otherwise, the pastry has a tendency to bake to the pan).

Rolling the dough: At least 1 hour before baking, place the square of puff pastry on your rolling surface. Cut each corner from the square, about ½ inch in, leaving an octagonal piece of dough. Put these four corners on the center of the dough. Press them lightly into the center so that they stick to it. (See illustration, page 367.)

Lightly flour the rolling surface under the puff pastry and roll a circle ⅛ inch thick and about 10 inches in diameter (the pastry should not be thicker than ⅛ inch). If the circle is larger than 10 inches, trim it with a pastry wheel.

Forming the tart shell: Roll the pastry onto the rolling pin to maintain its shape without stretching it, and transfer it to the inverted prepared pan. The pastry will drape over the pan and form pleats like a piece of material. Don't be concerned that it does not hug the sides of the pan; it will correct itself during baking. Prick close together all along the sides and top of the pastry with the tines of a fork. (Pricking the dough thoroughly helps to conform its shape to the pan during baking.)

Place the pan with its pastry in the freezer for 15 to 30 minutes. (This hastens the chilling period, firming the layers of fat; since it cannot freeze in that length of time, the dough also rests.)

Baking the tart shell: At least 20 minutes before baking, position rack in lower third of oven; preheat oven to 425 degrees.

Remove the pan with the pastry from the freezer and place it on a baking sheet. Make a few slits along the sides and top with the tip of a small paring knife. (The pricking and the slits control the pastry's expansion in the oven.) Place in the oven. As the pastry begins to bake, it will appear to melt down the sides, completely conforming to the pan with no creases. As the steam forms in the puff pastry, the sides and the center lift and expand. After 10 minutes, reduce temperature to 375 degrees.

Check the pastry the first 15 to 20 minutes of baking to see if additional pricking is nec-

☞ This pastry shell is intentionally deep for drama as well as for providing each serving with additional bites of flaky pastry; *do not fill it to the rim.* It can be used for many fillings, sweet or savory. I enjoy filling it with ratatouille and heating it to serve as a first course. Or fill it with your favorite soufflé, bake and serve.

☞ Baking the pastry on the outside of an inverted cake pan allows the pastry to puff and expand fully. If it were baked inside a container, it would have to be weighted initially during baking, which would inhibit expansion as well as thorough baking.

☞ I prefer to use Food Processor Puff Pastry (page 363).

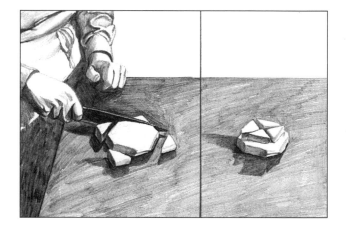

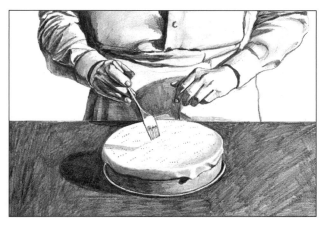

Clockwise from top left:
Cutting corners from square piece of puff pastry. Placing triangular-shaped corners on top of the dough. Rolling corners and dough together to form a circle. Pricking dough well.

essary. If the tart shell is puffing unevenly or wildly, prick it with a skewer. Prick firmly through the pastry, but be careful not to tear it since you will be filling it later.

After the shell has baked about 20 minutes and appears set, remove the baking sheet from the oven. Gently lift the baked shell from the pan, turn it right side up and put it back on the baking sheet. Remove the parchment liner (the pastry will look raw on the bottom), and return the shell to the oven. Reduce the oven temperature to 325 degrees, checking as it bakes to see if pricking the bottom is necessary. Continue to bake for about 10 to 15 minutes more, or until the pastry is light golden and the bottom is done; the pastry bottom should sound and feel crisp when tested with a skewer. Remove to rack to cool before filling.

Storing the tart shell: If the shell is not being served the same day, wrap it in aluminum foil when it is completely cool and freeze it for up to 1 week. Remove it from freezer to a preheated 325-degree oven to freshen and recrisp it; leave in oven until warm to the touch. Fill it as you wish.

Free-Form Puff Pastry Strip
With Fruit

A TREASURE chest of dazzling glazed fresh fruits could adorn the center of your table elegantly—until it's time for dessert. (**See photograph, page 159.**)

MAKES ONE STRIP, 6 TO 8 SERVINGS

Baking Equipment: Two 12-x-15½-x-½-inch baking sheets

12	ounces (approximately ⅓ recipe) puff pastry (page 359 or 363)
1	large egg

Filling

6	cups fresh fruit
⅓	cup cherry jelly
	Peppermint leaves

Advance preparation: Prepare the puff pastry as directed on page 359 or 363. Refrigerate it for up to 2 days before using.

Rolling the puff pastry: At least 1 hour before baking, roll the puff pastry into an 8-x-15-inch, ⅛-inch-thick rectangle on a lightly floured surface.

Roll the dough up loosely on a rolling pin and transfer it to a baking sheet. Cover surface completely with plastic wrap. Refrigerate it for at least 30 minutes before shaping.

Shaping the puff pastry: Line a baking sheet with baking parchment.

Prepare an egg wash glaze by beating the egg in a small bowl briefly with a fork just to combine the yolk and white.

Remove chilled puff pastry sheet from refrigerator and trim ¹⁄₁₆-inch from the two long edges with a ruler and pastry wheel. Lift and transfer the trimmed rectangle of dough to the parchment-lined pan.

With the ruler as a guide and using a sharp knife or pastry wheel, cut off two ¾-inch-wide strips from length of pastry. Lightly brush each long side of pastry rectangle with the egg wash (avoid using too much, or instead of sticking, the dough will slip). Turn one of the strips upside down and place it on top of an egg-washed area, setting it ¹⁄₁₆ inch in from the edge. Press in the strip gently with your fingertips so that it will adhere to the pastry base. Repeat with the other strip. Avoid stretching the strips when you put them on the base; otherwise, they will shrink shorter than the base during baking. (You turn each strip upside down before positioning because the pressure from the knife or pastry wheel compresses each strip's edge, affecting its even rise in the oven.)

Using the dull side of a paring knife, press slanted lines along the sides of the two pieces of puff pastry at ⅛-inch intervals. This creates a fringelike effect that unifies the strip to the base along the two long sides of the tart. Brush the top of each strip with a thin coat of egg wash (not down the sides) and refrigerate it for at least 30 minutes before baking.

Baker's Notes

☞ Since this pastry is constructed free-form, you may tailor it to fit any serving plate—square or rectangular.

☞ For the fresh fruit filling, I recommend blueberries, pitted bing cherries, raspberries, boysenberries, small seedless green grapes and strawberries.

☞ This puff pastry shell is marvelous for savory fillings too.

☞ Any puff pastry recipe (Classic [page 359] or Food Processor [page 363]) is fine for this dessert.

Joining the pastry strip to its base.

Baking the puff pastry strips: At least 20 minutes before baking, position rack in lower third of oven; preheat oven to 425 degrees.

Remove the free-form strip from the refrigerator. Trim each short end even. Prick close together over the entire surface of the strip's base, using a pastry docker or the tines of a fork. (Pricking in this instance keeps the base from puffing too much, causing the strips to be kicked off.) Apply a second coat of egg wash to the strips; then poke the tip of the paring knife straight down into each strip in three or four places. These slits serve the same purpose as pricking.

Place in the preheated oven and bake 10 minutes. Reduce temperature to 375 degrees, and bake for 10 minutes longer. Especially during the initial 15 to 20 minutes of baking, check the strip's lift. If necessary, prick the area with a skewer to release any trapped air.

Reduce temperature to 325 degrees and bake for 10 to 15 minutes longer, or until the pastry is golden brown and sounds and feels crisp when pierced in two or three places with a skewer, signifying it is baked through. Remove from oven; lift parchment with the pastry to a rack to cool completely.

Filling the puff pastry strip and serving: Pour the jelly into a 3-quart mixing bowl. Add the fresh fruit and toss. (The jelly holds the fruit together in the baked shell as well as providing gloss.) Fill the strip with the fruit. Decorate with peppermint leaves.

Serve the day assembled, cutting the entire pastry into 2- to 3-inch-wide strips.

Fruit Puff Pastry Palettes

Shaped like an artist's palette, these chocolate-glazed puff pastry masterpieces are decorated with fresh fruit like dabs of paint.

MAKES 6 SERVINGS

Baking Equipment: Two 14-x-17-x-½-inch baking sheets

1	**pound (about ½ recipe) puff pastry (page 359 or page 363)**
1	**recipe Classic Crème Anglaise (page 247)**
½	**recipe Chocolate-Butter Glaze (page 289)**
36	**blueberries**
1	**kiwifruit**
18	**raspberries**
6	**strawberries**

Advance preparations: Prepare the puff pastry as directed on page 359 or page 363. Refrigerate until ready to use.

Prepare Classic Crème Anglaise as directed on page 247. Refrigerate for up to 2 days before serving.

Prepare ½ recipe Chocolate-Butter Glaze as directed on page 289. Refrigerate for up to 1 week before using.

Draw a painter's palette, measuring approximately 5 x 4 inches across, onto stiff cardboard. Cut out to make a stencil.

Rolling the puff pastry: At least 1 hour before baking the puff pastry, cut the puff pastry in half, wrap one portion and return it to the refrigerator for another use. (When you cut, it's important to use a sharp knife and cut straight down, lifting the blade each time to preserve the layers rather than pulling it across the dough and smashing them.)

Dust the work surface lightly with flour and place the pastry on it. Beginning with one side, roll from the center up; lift the rolling pin and roll from the center down, using firm, even-pressured strokes and stopping short of the edges. Reverse the dough and roll to extend in the other direction, repeating procedure. When the dough is ⅛ inch thick, measuring approximately 14 inches square, roll it up loosely on your rolling pin and transfer it to a baking sheet. Cover completely with plastic wrap and rub your fingers over the surface to press the plastic directly onto the dough. Refrigerate for at least 30 minutes before baking.

Baking the pastry: At least 15 minutes before baking, position rack in lower third of oven; preheat oven to 425 degrees.

Line the other baking sheet with parchment paper. Carefully transfer the chilled pastry from the refrigerator to the parchment-lined pan by lifting the entire puff pastry sheet with both hands. (Additional chilling firms it enough to do this so that its shape won't be disturbed yet it will be flexible enough to maneuver.) Trim about 1/16 inch from each edge, using a sharp knife or pastry wheel and a ruler to encourage an even, uninhibited rise in the oven. The pastry will measure approximately 14 x 14 inches.

Prick the pastry with a pastry docker or with tines of a fork, covering the entire surface. Pricking reduces the amount of lift. Though some lift will occur anyhow, the pricking aids in making it more even. Without some leavening, the puff pastry would not bake through completely.

Bake for 7 to 10 minutes before opening the oven. During this time the steam forms to lift the layers. Reduce temperature to 375 degrees and bake for 10 minutes longer. After the initial 10 to 15 minutes of baking, check occasionally to see if the pastry is puffing unevenly. If so, prick the area with a skewer to release the trapped air. This must be done before the outer portion of the pastry sets. A lot of lift is not important in this recipe, so if the entire pastry sheet has lifted, place another baking sheet on top to weight it. Bake it this way for 1 minute; then remove the baking sheet from the puff pastry.

Now reduce oven temperature to 325 degrees and bake for 12 to 17 minutes longer, or until the pastry is golden brown, and sounds and feels crisp when pierced in four or five places with a skewer. Remove from oven and set aside on rack to cool completely.

Cutting the pastries: Holding the baked sheet of pastry in place with one hand, carefully trace and cut six palettes with the tip of a small paring knife. Cut slowly in an up-and-down sawing motion while resting the knife against the cardboard stencil as the shape is traced.

Glazing the pastries: Reheat the chocolate glaze over a large container half filled with hot tap water. (If the glaze is cold and firm, you may place the makeshift double boiler over very low heat to maintain the water's temperature until it is smooth and liquid.) When the glaze is ready, brush the surface of each palette. Set palettes aside at room temperature while preparing the fruits.

Decorating the pastries: No more than 3 hours before serving, arrange the fruits on top of the chocolate-glazed palettes. Spoon the crème anglaise on each dessert plate and place a fruit-studded palette in the center of each.

Baker's Notes

☞ Puff pastry tends to shrink during baking, affecting the final dimensions, so I prefer to cut shapes such as palettes or rectangles from a baked puff pastry sheet.

☞ Don't roll puff pastry if it's too firm from the refrigerator; forcing it might disturb its layering, overwork it and make it elastic. Let it sit on the work surface for 5 to 10 minutes to lose some of its chill.

☞ Never work with too much dough at a time, or you may overwork it and cause it to shrink and toughen.

☞ If you prefer, instead of cutting the pastry in the shape of a palette, cut it into squares, rectangles or circles.

Soufflé Feuilleté

FEUILLETÉ is a flaky French pastry dough rolled out and folded on itself several times so that it puffs during baking.

A first course in the restaurant Taillevent in Paris inspired this dessert. The flaky puff pastry and the airy vanilla soufflé hide a layer of apple filling.

MAKES 6 SERVINGS

Baking Equipment: 12-x-15½-x-½-inch baking sheet

½   recipe (1 pound) **Classic Puff Pastry (page 359)**

Apple Filling

1   **pound (about 2) Golden Delicious apples**
1   **ounce (2 tablespoons) unsalted butter**
¼   **cup (50 grams) granulated sugar**

1   **recipe Vanilla Soufflé (page 249)**

Egg Wash

1   **large egg**

Advance preparations: Prepare Classic Puff Pastry as directed on page 359. Store in refrigerator up to 2 days.

Prepare the apple filling: Peel, halve and core each apple. Slice each half into three pieces; then slice these sections across into thirds. Melt the butter in a 10-inch skillet over medium heat, add the sugar and mix. Add the apple pieces and allow the mixture to cook and bubble for about 15 minutes over medium heat, stirring occasionally. (The sugar dissolves in the apples' juice and caramelizes during the slow cooking.) Remove from the heat and cool for about 5 minutes. Then dice the larger apple pieces with a rubber spatula so they are still chunky but not pureed like an applesauce; this yields about 1 cup. Store in refrigerator for up to 2 days. Remove from refrigerator 1 hour before needed.

Prepare the cream base in the recipe for Vanilla Soufflé on page 249 up to 2 hours before completing the soufflé. Set it aside at room temperature. Place the egg whites from the same recipe in a deep 1½-quart mixing bowl and set the 1 teaspoon sugar nearby.

Rolling the puff pastry: At least 1 hour before baking, roll the puff pastry on a lightly floured surface until it is ¼ inch thick and measures close to 10 x 11 inches. Transfer it to the baking sheet; cover it completely with plastic wrap, rubbing over the surface to press the plastic directly onto the puff pastry. Refrigerate it for at least 45 minutes before you cut it into individual cases and bake it. (Since this sheet of pastry is thicker than the other recipes' pastry sheets, it is best to let it chill longer. If you're in a hurry, you can hasten the chilling by placing it on the baking sheet in the freezer for about 30 minutes.)

Forming the pastries: At least 20 minutes before baking, position rack in lower third of oven; preheat oven to 425 degrees.

Transfer the chilled pastry from the refrigerator to the work surface. Trim the edges and cut six 3-x-5-inch rectangles, using a ruler and a sharp knife.

Brush the entire baking sheet lightly with water, using a pastry brush. Transfer the pastry rectangles by inverting them onto the baking sheet, spacing them 1 inch apart.

Trace a line with the tip of a sharp paring knife ½ inch from the edge and ⅛ inch deep around the perimeter of each rectangle (see illustration). Do not cut completely through the dough. (This ½-inch border separates from the base as it bakes.)

Using the tip of the knife, cut a small, gridlike design to decorate the center portion just on the surface of each dough rectangle.

Make an egg wash by mixing the egg to combine the yolk and white. Lightly coat only the pastry borders with the egg wash. Be careful that it doesn't touch the sides, or it could inhibit the pastry's expansion.

Baking the pastry: Place in the preheated oven and bake for 10 minutes without opening oven door, allowing the moisture from the wet baking pan to create steam to help lift the layers of pastry to their maximum height.

Reduce oven temperature to 375 degrees and bake for 10 minutes. Check to see if the pastries are lifting evenly, and if necessary, prick the raised area with a skewer to release any trapped air.

Reduce oven temperature to 325 degrees and bake for 10 to 15 minutes longer, or until pastries are golden brown and sound and feel crisp when pierced in one or two places with a skewer. Remove from oven and set aside on a rack to cool for 5 minutes. Gently remove the pastry lids, using the tines of a fork to lift them off. Set the lids aside for decoration later. Then, using the fork, remove any uncooked puff pastry and discard. Set the rest aside on a rack to cool completely. (You roll the puff pastry ¼ inch thick to create a high rise for a deep container. However, it's difficult to bake the interiors completely without overbaking the exteriors.)

Assembling, baking, and serving the pastry: At least 15 minutes before baking, preheat the oven to 375 degrees with the rack in the lower third.

Tracing a line with a knife tip to create a ½-inch border.

Baker's Notes

☞ A substantial lift is important for a dramatic presentation, so use Classic (page 359) or Food Processor Puff Pastry (page 363).

☞ This is an easy method for forming individual puff pastry cases.

☞ You can bake the cases, cool them completely, then place them on a baking sheet, wrap foil around the sheet and freeze for up to 3 days. On the day of serving, remove the cases from the freezer 2 hours before filling.

☞ These puff pastry cases are useful for a savory first course as well as for dessert.

☞ Even though you cut them straight down with a sharp knife, the pressure of the incision compresses the first few layers so that inverting the trimmed, unbaked puff pastry forms on the baking sheet provides a more even lift in the oven.

Understanding Pastrymaking

Place the baked shells, now at room temperature, on a baking sheet lined with parchment paper. Spoon 1½ to 2 tablespoons of the apple filling, also at room temperature, into each shell just to cover each base.

Whip the reserved egg whites for Vanilla Soufflé on low speed until small bubbles appear and the surface is frothy. Increase speed to medium, add the 1 teaspoon sugar from that recipe and whip until soft peaks form. Fold about ½ cup of the whipped whites into the pastry cream to lighten it; then fold in the remaining whites. Spoon 3 to 4 tablespoons over the apple filling. (You can pipe the soufflé into each shell if you wish.)

Bake for 20 to 22 minutes, or until the soufflé is puffy, golden brown and creamy-soft inside. Serve while hot on warm plates, resting the lid next to each Soufflé Feuilleté.

Windsor Tart

HEAVY CREAM and sugar combine to create a silky filling, the flavor of which is somewhere between rich vanilla and delicate butterscotch. A blanket of fresh juicy raspberries complements this tart perfectly.

MAKES 6 TO 8 SERVINGS

1   **Round Puff Pastry Tart Shell (page 366)**

Filling
1   **cup (8 ounces) heavy cream**
½   **cup (100 grams) granulated sugar**
1   **cup fresh raspberries**

Advance preparation: Prepare Round Puff Pastry Tart Shell as directed on page 366. Fill when it is completely cool.

Making the filling: On the day of serving, mix the cream and sugar in a 1½-quart heavy-bottomed saucepan. Allow mixture to stand until the sugar has dissolved, producing a syrupy consistency.

Baker's Note

☞ Fresh red currants or huckleberries are wonderful alternatives to the raspberries.

Over medium heat, bring mixture to a continuous boil, stirring occasionally to prevent scorching. If it begins to boil over, reduce the heat and continue to bubble it lightly until it is thicker and has a very pale butterscotch color (about 12 to 15 minutes). Stir and watch the cream toward the end of the cooking time since it scorches easily. Pour it into the baked shell. Let the cream cool completely at room temperature before you arrange fresh fruit on top.

Decorating and serving the tart: Arrange the fresh raspberries over the cooled Windsor cream. (If you prefer glazed raspberries, toss in 2 tablespoons raspberry jam before arranging over the filling. See glazing blueberries, page 348.)

Serve at room temperature.

Millefeuille Royale

THIS IS a cousin to the classic Napoleon, but with a different, easier shape. Literally translated from the French, Millefeuille means "a thousand leaves," an appropriate description of the flaky layers of this pastry.

MAKES 8 TO 12 SERVINGS

Baking Equipment: 14-x-17-x-½-inch baking sheet

½	recipe (20 ounces) **Food Processor Puff Pastry (page 363)**
1	recipe **Diplomat Cream (page 248)**
1	recipe **Classic Royal Icing (page 269)**
2	tablespoons chopped nuts

Advance preparations: Prepare Food Processor Puff Pastry as directed on page 363. Refrigerate until ready to use.

Prepare Classic Pastry Cream in the recipe for Diplomat Cream as directed on page 248. Refrigerate for up to 2 days before serving.

Rolling the pastry: At least 2 hours before baking, begin to roll the pastry. To achieve the dimensions for this sheet without overworking it, roll it in several stages. First roll it on a lightly floured surface into a rectangle about 12 x 15x⅛ inches thick. With the aid of the rolling pin, transfer it to a 14-x-17-inch baking sheet and cover it with plastic wrap to rest (at least 30 minutes).

After this rest, return the pastry sheet to the lightly floured surface, and roll to extend it about ½ inch more in both length and width. Return it to the baking sheet, prick the surface with a pastry docker or the tines of a fork, cover it with the plastic wrap and place it in the freezer to firm for about 45 minutes. (The main purpose for firming the pastry at this time is to provide a firm base to spread the stiff royal icing in a thin layer.)

Baking preparations: At least 20 minutes before baking, position rack in lower third of oven; preheat oven to 425 degrees.

Line the baking sheet with baking parchment to fit.

Baker's Notes

☞ The key to this dessert's success is the thorough baking of the puff pastry so that the combination of flaky puff pastry and pastry cream are shown to their best advantage.

☞ You can use another puff pastry recipe than the suggested Food Processor (page 363) one; however, don't forget that different recipes produce different degrees of lift, so you may have to prick the pastry's surface more or less to control its rise in the oven properly. Classic Puff Pastry (page 359) rises the most.

☞ Royal Icing bakes crisp and doesn't taste too sweet.

☞ You can assemble this dessert 2 hours before serving.

Understanding Pastrymaking

Glazing and baking the pastry: On the day of serving, prepare Classic Royal Icing as directed on page 269.

Transfer the chilled sheet of puff pastry from the freezer to the parchment-lined baking sheet. Trim the edges even with a ruler and pastry wheel or chef's knife. Spread Royal Icing with a small metal icing spatula, such as a 3½-inch inverted metal spatula, in a thin, even film over half the pastry. As you spread, stop ⅛ inch short of each edge since any icing touching an edge will inhibit the puff pastry's lift.

Bake for 10 minutes. Reduce temperature to 375 degrees and bake for 10 minutes more. (The unglazed side may lift unevenly; if so, prick it with a skewer.) Reduce temperature to 325 degrees and bake for 12 to 17 minutes longer, or until the pastry is golden brown, and the unglazed portion sounds and feels crisp when pierced in three or four places with a skewer. Remove from the oven to a rack to cool.

Assembling and serving the dessert: When the pastry is completely cool, cut it in half. Place the unglazed portion, baked side up, on a baking sheet.

Whip the heavy cream in the recipe for the Diplomat Cream in a deep 1-quart bowl until soft peaks form. Remove the pastry cream from the refrigerator and stir it until smooth; then fold in the whipped cream. Spread evenly over the unglazed pastry layer; then top with the glazed layer. With the flexible metal icing spatula, smooth the cream around the sides, giving the dessert a finished look. Sprinkle chopped nuts on each corner and in the center.

Serve at room temperature.

Papillon

THIS PASTRY, made in the shape of a butterfly and spread with ground almonds, is not too rich or sweet and so is ideal to serve at brunch. It is the same as the classic Pithiviers. The inspiration for its dramatic shape came from Switzerland at the Richemont Professional School.

MAKES 8 SERVINGS

Baking Equipment: Two 14-x-17-x-½-inch baking sheets, ½-inch pastry tip

1	recipe Classic Puff Pastry (page 359)
½	recipe (3/4 cup) Ground Almond Frangipane (page 270)
1	large egg

Advance preparations: Prepare Classic Puff Pastry as directed on page 359. Refrigerate it until ready to use.

Prepare Ground Almond Frangipane as directed on page 270. Refrigerate it until firm (at least 4 hours).

Rolling the pastry: At least 2 hours before baking, cut the puff pastry in half; return one half to the refrigerator until needed. Roll the first half on a lightly floured surface into a 14-inch square ⅜ inch thick. Transfer it with the aid of the rolling pin to a 14-x-17-inch baking sheet. Cover with plastic wrap and refrigerate. Repeat with the other portion of puff pastry. Transfer it to top of the first sheet of puff pastry, cover with plastic wrap and refrigerate it for at least 1 hour.

Assembling the pastry: At least 1 hour before baking, make an egg wash by mixing the egg in a small bowl.

Remove Ground Almond Frangipane from the refrigerator.

Remove the chilled puff pastry sheets from the refrigerator and transfer the top sheet to your work surface nearby. Using a pastry brush and the egg wash, paint a 1-inch-wide outline of a butterfly on the puff pastry sheet on the baking sheet. About a 1- to 1½-inch border of puff pastry will remain on the other side of the egg outline. (See illustration, page 378.)

Spoon the cold filling to form an X with a 2½-inch bridge in the middle. Each leg of the X is about 10 inches long. (The filling cannot come too close to the edge of the puff pastry, or it will leak out during baking.) Roll the second puff pastry sheet lightly on the rolling pin, and lift and center it over the filling and the bottom layer of pastry. Press the pastry sheets together so that the top layer sticks to the bottom layer where you painted the butterfly outline.

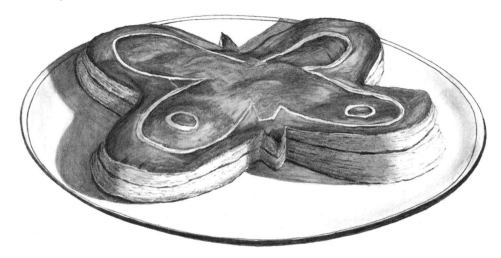

☞ Classic Puff Pastry (page 359) is best for this recipe because it has a precise layered structure that rises high and evenly.

☞ Since this is a large quantity of puff pastry with a filling, you must give it time to bake through or the form will deflate during cooling. Color is an indicator of doneness; testing with a skewer to see if the pastry is crisp may spoil its appearance. It will be perfectly done if you use the recommended length of baking time.

☞ If you don't want to bake the Papillon after shaping and glazing it, return the glazed butterfly, uncovered, to the refrigerator. (The egg glaze seals in the puff pastry's moisture.) At baking time, remove the Papillon from the refrigerator, apply another coat of egg wash and then make the decorative markings. Bake as directed.

☞ Use puff pastry trimmings from this recipe to make Round Puff Pastry Tart Shell (page 366) or Free-Form Puff Pastry Strip (page 368).

Understanding Pastrymaking

Applying the filling.

Creating a butterfly shape.

Cover the pastry with plastic wrap, and place it in the freezer for about 45 to 60 minutes, or until the layers are firm, not frozen.

Baking preparations: At least 20 minutes before baking, position rack in lower third of oven; preheat oven to 425 degrees.

Line another 14-x-17-inch baking sheet with parchment paper to fit.

Shaping the pastry: Remove the chilled pastry from the freezer, and with a sharp small paring knife, cut a butterfly shape, duplicating as closely as you can the shape and dimensions you made previously with the egg wash. (If it's easier for you, paint another egg wash outline on top of the pastry to use as a guide for cutting the butterfly shape. Then cut around the outer edge of the marking.) When you measure diagonally from the upper left wing to the lower right wing, the diameter of the butterfly should be 14 inches. The consistency of the chilled pastry while cutting should be similar to that of muenster cheese or fudge.

Glazing and baking the pastry: Remove the trimmings (see Baker's Notes, page 377 for leftover trimming information). Lift the butterfly shape onto the parchment-lined baking sheet. Coat the surface with egg wash, using a pastry brush. Then lightly trace decorative markings on the butterfly, with the tip of the sharp paring knife and the wide end of a ½-inch pastry tip, penetrating just a few of the top layers of pastry. With the tip of the knife, cut small vents within the circular shapes created by the pastry tip; this placement doesn't mar the design, and it allows steam to escape during baking.

Place in the preheated oven and bake for 12 to 15 minutes. Reduce temperature to 375 degrees and bake for 10 minutes more. (During this time the Papillon bakes and rises from the exterior first; the center interior section lifts last.) Reduce temperature to 325 degrees and bake for about 20 to 25 minutes more, or until golden brown. Remove from the oven; lift off the baking sheet with the parchment paper to a cooling rack.

Serve at room temperature on the same day.

Recipes for Cream Puff Pastry

Cream Puff Pastry

FASTER and easier to make than puff pastry, cream puff pastry, which is also called *pâte à choux*, has similarly magical qualities. Its name in French means "cabbage paste" because the small shapes resemble cabbages.

Although their names are similar, cream puff paste and puff pastry are totally different from one another. Two steps are required to make cream puff paste. The first involves cooking the ingredients to partially swell the flour's starch, hasten some gluten development and distribute the fat throughout the paste. Cooking the flour forms a thick, smooth, glossy emulsion; without cooking, it would remain a sticky mass incapable of puffing in the oven. The second step involves adding the eggs to stabilize the stiff mixture. Eggs are the paste's main source of leavening and moisture, so they should not be added when the mixture is too hot or too cold.

Large pastry forms are bulkier, so the mixture for them should be thicker and drier; small forms bake faster, so the mixture for them may be slacker and moister. Thus Paris-Brest (page 384), a heavier pastry form, has a thicker paste, while Chocolate Éclairs (page 382) are smaller and made from a moister mixture.

Leavening occurs when you place the cream puff paste in a very hot oven to convert the moisture to steam quickly. The paste should take form from the inside out, pushing up and out to produce a center cavity. As it bakes, the shell around this cavity sets. When the paste is finished baking, the pressure of any steam has subsided. Small holes are then poked into the baked form and it is returned to the oven to dry any moisture in the interior. (If this is not done, the trapped moisture could make the baked form soggy.) Your goal is to produce fine expansion with a good cavity.

THE INGREDIENTS AND THEIR ROLE

FLOUR

A MEDIUM to strong flour is needed for sufficient structure in baking cream puff paste. I have success with all-purpose flour, though some bakers prefer hard-wheat flour.

LIQUID

WATER is usually the liquid, though I like some milk for richness and color. Milk also makes a thinner shell.

FAT

I PREFER unsalted butter for its flavor, though vegetable oil is sometimes used since it creates an emulsion easily.

EGGS

EGGS emulsify and hold the fat in the paste during baking. They supply most of the moisture for leavening and, along with the flour, form the structure. The number of eggs determines the volume of your cream puff paste. More eggs will thin the paste, creating a delicate, lighter cream puff pastry with less defined shape. Without egg, there will be no increase in volume, and the result will be a compact, firm cream puff pastry.

TIPS FOR MAKING PERFECT CREAM PUFF PASTRY

☞ Measure your ingredients carefully.

☞ Bring the fat and liquid just to a rolling boil, remove from heat, then add the flour. Too much evaporation of the liquid can alter the ingredients' proportions and affect your results.

☞ Avoid overcooking the flour-fat-liquid mixture when drying it on low heat in the saucepan, or the fat will separate from it. After the eggs are added, the fat will then ooze from the paste during baking.

☞ Add the eggs slowly to the paste for a smooth emulsion, which is necessary for good expansion in the oven.

☞ Be certain to bake the paste until completely done so it doesn't collapse when it is removed from the oven.

Chocolate Éclairs

(CLASSIC CREAM PUFF PASTRY)

A TRADITIONAL favorite: elongated cream puffs filled with pastry cream and glazed with chocolate. Don't confuse this with puff pastry. The only factor the two have in common is that both are leavened by steam.

(See photograph, page 157.)

MAKES FOUR DOZEN 3-INCH-LONG CHOCOLATE ÉCLAIRS

Baking and Decorating Equipment: 16-inch pastry bag, ½-inch (#6) round decorating tip, 14-x-17-inch baking sheet, #2 open star decorating tip, ¼-inch (#2) round decorating tip

Double recipe Diplomat Cream (page 248)

Paste

1	cup (140 grams) unsifted all-purpose flour
1	cup (about 5 large) eggs
¼	cup (2 ounces) milk
¾	cup (6 ounces) water
½	teaspoon salt
3	ounces (6 tablespoons) unsalted butter

1	large egg for egg wash
1	recipe Glossy Cocoa Glaze (page 289)

Advance preparations: Prepare a double recipe of Classic Pastry Cream in the recipe for Diplomat Cream as directed on page 248. Cover its surface with plastic wrap, and poke 4 to 5 slits in it to allow steam to escape. Refrigerate until time to fill the éclairs.

Baking preparations: Fit the pastry bag with the ½-inch (#6) round decorating tip.

Using a paper towel, lightly grease the baking sheet with solid shortening. Dust *very lightly* with all-purpose flour and tap to remove excess. Marking a baking sheet for piping éclairs is similar to the procedure for shaping ladyfingers shown on page 170. A toothpick serves as a pencil to trace rows of parallel lines on the baking sheet, so the paste may be piped in strips, their edges touching the guidelines.

Draw four sets of parallel lines, each set measuring 3 inches wide, along the entire length of the baking sheet. Leave 1 inch between each set to allow for expansion and air flow.

Position rack in lower third of oven; preheat oven to 400 degrees for at least 20 minutes before baking. At the same time, pour about 2 cups hot tap water (120 degrees) into a shallow stainless steel bowl and place it on the floor of the oven. (The water produces a humid environment, which aids in leavening the paste, since it prevents the exterior from setting its shape too quickly.)

Ingredient preparations: Pour the flour into a triple sifter; sift it onto a sheet of waxed paper to remove any lumps, and set aside.

Crack the eggs into a liquid cup measure until you have 1 cup. Whisk briefly just to combine yolks and whites and set aside.

Making the cream puff paste: Pour the milk, water and salt into a heavy-bottomed 1½-quart saucepan. Slice the butter into ½-inch pieces, drop them into the saucepan and bring the mixture to a rolling boil over medium heat. Immediately remove from heat.

Stir the mixture with a wooden spoon to combine the liquid and melted butter. Add the sifted flour all at once, stirring vigorously and scraping the sides of the pan, until a stiff paste forms and comes together in a ball. Return to medium heat, stirring quickly for about 10 seconds to eliminate extra moisture. Remove from heat immediately. The paste should be smooth, thick and glossy. The entire mass can be lifted on a spoon, and the saucepan will appear almost unused. Transfer the thick paste to the bowl of a heavy-duty mixer.

Separate the mass into 7 or 8 pieces and cool them for 10 minutes, or until the paste registers 150 degrees on an instant bi-therm thermometer. (The temperature of the paste is important because of its effect on the eggs. Too hot, and they will set and the paste will not puff sufficiently in the oven; too cool and it will be difficult to incorporate the eggs, and the paste will be lumpy, interfering with expansion in the oven.)

Attach the bowl to the mixer, and with the paddle attachment, mix the paste on lowest speed (#1) while slowly adding 2 to 3 tablespoons of egg. (Adding small amounts slowly gives smoother results.) As the paste absorbs the egg, increase the speed to medium-low (#2 to #3) and mix just until the mixture is homogeneous and resembles the consistency of a thick pastry cream. Further increase the mixer's speed only if the mixture appears curdled. (Fast and lengthy mixing when adding the eggs whips more air into the paste and produces puffier, blossoming shapes.)

Reduce the speed to low (#1), and repeat the procedure three or four more times, adding 2 to 3 tablespoons of egg each time and increasing the speed when they are partially absorbed. The entire sequence should not take more than 3 minutes.

Remove the bowl from the mixer; detach the paddle, and mix the batter vigorously with a rubber spatula for about 10 seconds to incorporate the ingredients completely. The batter should be very smooth, shiny, glossy and stiff, yet fall slowly in a ribboning effect when dropped from the spatula.

Forming the éclairs: Scoop all the cream puff paste into the pastry bag fitted with the decorating tip.

Place the baking sheet in front of you. Pipe a strip of cream puff paste 3 inches long and as thick as the tip's opening, using the lines as an indicator of where to begin and end each éclair. Keep the tip at a 45-degree angle suspended about ½ inch above the pan, and lift it up slightly when you finish an éclair to cut off the flow of paste. Space the éclairs ½ inch apart to allow for expansion and air flow.

When all rows are filled, you may glaze each éclair with an egg wash to create shiny surfaces, but the glaze can seal the surface and cause cracking as the éclair puffs and releases steam.

If you prefer not to seal the paste, lightly brush each éclair with water (or milk) rather

☞ Variation: Fill the baked éclairs with softened vanilla ice cream, as if you were filling with Diplomat Cream as directed below; freeze them until firm, then glaze them as directed below and return them to the freezer until serving time.

☞ Merely greasing the baking sheet is not enough; during baking, the paste will not grip and the cream puffs' base will be hollow. Lining the baking pan with parchment paper is not desirable since the paste will expand faster when it is in direct contact with the metal baking sheet. A nonstick pan is fine to use if its coating is in good condition. Before piping the paste on it, you may sprinkle it with cold water to provide additional steam during baking.

☞ If you want a more perfectly shaped, less puffy éclair, do not pipe and bake immediately after making the paste. Cover the paste's surface in the bowl with plastic wrap; leave it at room temperature for 1 hour; then pipe and bake.

Understanding Pastrymaking

than with an egg glaze. The paste absorbs these liquids like a sponge, and the brush helps shape each form neatly and smoothly.

Baking the éclairs: Place in preheated 400-degree oven and bake for 18 to 20 minutes. Remove one éclair from the oven to check if the baking is finished. The baked éclair should be golden brown, its sides rigid enough so they will not collapse when removed from the oven, and the crust should be tender on the outside and hollow inside.

When the baking is finished, remove the baking sheet from oven. Using the point of a #2 open-star decorating tip, poke a hole in an end of each éclair. Return baking sheet to oven for 3 to 5 minutes to allow the éclairs' interiors to dry.

Remove from the oven, and transfer the éclairs to a rack to cool completely. (Do not place close together, or the steam may soften the éclairs and make them soggy.)

Baked cream puff paste stales quickly, so after baking and cooling, freeze the éclairs for up to 5 days in sturdy containers to avoid crushing them in the freezer. (You cannot freeze them for too long because they are susceptible to odors, which become trapped in their cavities.)

Filling the éclairs: Two hours before serving, stir the pastry cream until smooth. Then whip the heavy cream in the recipe for Diplomat Cream on page 248. Fold it into the pastry cream. Scoop into a pastry bag fitted with the ¼-inch round decorating tip. Insert the tip into the hole in the end of each éclair and fill the interior. Repeat for remaining éclairs.

Glazing the éclairs: Prepare Glossy Cocoa Glaze as directed on page 289. Turn an éclair upside down, dip its top into the glaze, lift it up slowly and shake it back and forth, removing the excess. Turn it right side up and place it on a rack to allow glaze to dry. Repeat for remaining éclairs.

Paris-Brest

THIS CLASSIC cream puff paste dessert, a French specialty, is one of my favorites. After baking, its ring shape is split and filled with the rich flavors of caramelized sugar, nuts, coffee and cream.

MAKES 6 TO 8 SERVINGS

Baking and Decorating Equipment: 14-x-17-x-½-inch baking sheet, ½-inch (#6) round decorating tip, #9 open star decorating tip, 16-inch pastry bag

    1   recipe Praline Paste (page 309)

Paris-Brest Paste
    1   cup (140 grams) unsifted all-purpose flour
    ¾   cup (about 4 large) eggs
    ¼   cup (2 ounces) milk
    ¾   cup (6 ounces) water

☞ After shaping, bake the paste right away to produce the maximum volume.

☞ Small cream puffs bake at a lower temperature (400 degrees) than large ones (425 degrees).

½   teaspoon salt
3   ounces (6 tablespoons) unsalted butter

Egg Wash
1   large egg

Decoration
1   ounce (¼ cup) sliced almonds

Filling
1   cup (8 ounces) heavy cream
2   teaspoons Coffee Essence (page 269)
2   tablespoons unsifted powdered sugar

Advance preparations: Prepare Praline Paste as directed on page 309. When it is cool and hard, store it in an airtight container if you are not using it right away.

Baking preparations: Using a paper towel, lightly grease the baking sheet with solid shortening. Dust *lightly* with all-purpose flour; tap to remove excess. Using a toothpick as a pencil, trace two 8-inch circles on the prepared baking sheet; this is your guide for piping the paste.

Position rack in lower third of oven; preheat oven to 425 degrees at least 20 minutes before baking. At the same time, pour 2 cups hot tap water (120 degrees) into a shallow stainless steel mixing bowl, and place it directly on the floor of the oven.

Making the cream puff paste: Prepare Paris-Brest Paste following the recipe for Classic Cream Puff Paste as directed on page 382 with the following difference:

Decrease the amount of egg from 1 cup (about 5 large) to ¾ cup (about 4 large).

Scoop all the paste into the pastry bag fitted with the ½-inch round decorating tip. Pipe the paste along a circular marking until a ring is formed. Keep the tip at a 45-degree angle,

☞ This paste makes two 8-inch rings. I freeze one for another time.

☞ While piping, keep a steady pressure on the pastry bag to maintain a string of paste that is about 2 inches between the pastry tip and the baking sheet. This allows you to see your work as you form a circle.

☞ This is a drier, thicker paste than Classic Cream Puff Paste because it requires more body to maintain its structure.

suspending the paste about 1 to 2 inches above the pan as you pipe. Twist the tip as you lift up slightly when you are finished in order to cut off the flow of paste. Pipe a second ring inside this circle, allowing the edges to touch. Finally, pipe a third ring of paste on top of these two in such a way that it straddles the bottom rings.

Repeat this procedure for the second circle.

Glazing, baking and storing the pastry: Whisk the egg in a small bowl to make the egg wash. Brush each circle of paste lightly with the egg wash, using a pastry brush.

Sprinkle with the sliced almonds.

Bake for 20 minutes. Then reduce temperature to 375 degrees and bake for 10 to 15 minutes more, or until sides are golden brown and they feel rigid.

Remove from oven to a cooling rack, slice off the top third of each circle with a small serrated knife, and remove any raw paste with a spoon. Return the 4 pieces to the oven for 3 to 5 minutes to dry.

If you are not using the circles on the day baked, place each in a sturdy container and freeze for up to 5 days.

Making the filling: Up to 1 hour before serving, place the bottom half of one of the Paris-Brests on your work surface.

Fit the pastry bag with the #9 open star decorating tip.

Place Praline Paste in a bowl of a food processor fitted with the steel blade and process until it forms a paste like peanut butter (about 5 to 6 minutes). Transfer to a 3-quart mixing bowl.

Whip the cream with Coffee Essence until slightly thicker than the decorating stage, page 240. Fold it into the paste until smooth, using a rubber spatula.

Assembling and serving the dessert: Scoop the praline cream into the pastry bag. Pipe it into the Paris-Brest base; then retrace, piping exaggerated swirls that extend beyond the bottom edges.

Replace the top, pressing down just until it adheres to the cream filling.

Pour the powdered sugar into a sieve, and gently tap the sides to sprinkle it over the top.

Transfer to a serving plate, using two flexible metal icing spatulas. To serve, cut the top portion of the Paris-Brest with scissors into individual portions. Finish cutting each portion with a knife.

Resources

BAKER'S SHOPPING SOURCES

If the equipment, utensils or chocolate you need are not available in your area,
contact the following stores:

Albert Uster Imports, Inc.
9211 Gaither Road
Gaithersburg, MD 20877
(800) 231-8154

Bridge Kitchenware
Corporation
214 East 52nd Street
New York, NY 10022
(212) 838-6746

Dean & Deluca
560 Broadway
New York, NY 10012
(212) 431-1691

Istanbul Express
2434 Durant Avenue
Berkeley, CA 94704
(510) 848-3723
(chocolate only)

La Cuisine
323 Cameron Street
Alexandria, VA 22314
(800) 521-1176

Lindco Associates
P.O. Box 1375
Martinez, CA 94553
(510) 356-3999

Louise's Pantry
859 Santa Cruz Avenue
Menlo Park, CA 94025
(415) 325-1712

Maid of Scandinavia
3244 Raleigh Avenue
Minneapolis, MN 55416
(800) 328-6722

Paprikas Weiss Importer
1572 Second Avenue
New York, NY 10028
(212) 288-6117

Prévin Incorporated
2044 Rittenhouse Square
Philadelphia, PA 19103
(215) 985-1996

Sugar 'n Spice
3200 Balboa
San Francisco, CA 94121
(415) 387-1722

Sur La Table
84 Pine Street
Seattle, WA 98101
(206) 448-2244

Williams-Sonoma
Mail Order Department
P.O. Box 7456
San Francisco, CA
94120-7456
(415) 421-4242

Conversion Table for Weights

MY SCALE is marked both in ounces and grams, but if yours is only ounces or grams, this conversion table will prove invaluable to you. Though the ounce's true value is 28.35 grams (to convert ounces to grams, you multiply the number of ounces by 28.35), for the sake of simplification, I will make it equivalent to 30 grams. This will not affect your baking results because the balance of the ingredients will be consistent.

Ounces	*Grams*
1 ounce	30 grams
0.882 ounces	25 grams
1 ¾ ounces	50 grams
2 ¾ ounces	75 grams
3 ½ ounces	100 grams
5 ¼ ounces	150 grams
7 ounces	200 grams
8 ¾ ounces	250 grams
16 ounces (1 pound)	454 grams

BAKER'S MEASURE AND WEIGHT EQUIVALENTS

ALL-PURPOSE FLOUR	Sifted		Unsifted	
	ounces	*grams*	*ounces*	*grams*
¼ cup	1	30	1 ¼	35
⅓ cup	1 ⅓	40	1 ½	45
½ cup	2 ¼	60	2 ½	70
1 cup	4 ½	120	5	140
2 cups	8 ½	240	10	280

CAKE FLOUR	Sifted		Unsifted	
	ounces	*grams*	*ounces*	*grams*
¼ cup	¾	25	1	30
⅓ cup	1 ¼	35	1 ⅓	40
½ cup	1 ¾	50	2 ¼	60
1 cup	3 ½	100	4 ½	120
2 cups	7	200	8 ½	240

GRANULATED SUGAR

	ounces	grams
1 tablespoon	-	12
¼ cup	1 ¾	50
⅓ cup	2 ¼	65
½ cup	3 ½	100
1 cup	7	200
2 cups	14	400
2 ¼ cups	16 (1 pound)	454

BUTTER

	grams	tablespoons	sticks	cups
½ ounce	15	1	⅛	-
1 ounce	30	2	¼	-
2 ounces	60	4	½	¼
4 ounces	113	8	1	½
8 ounces	217	16	2	1
16 ounces	454	32	4	2

Bibliography

The books in this list aided me in many ways, whether it was researching ingredients, crystallizing my own techniques, suggesting presentations or just baking through them for pleasure. I recommend these publications and am grateful to their authors.

Amendola, Joseph, *The Baker's Manual.* New Jersey: Hayden Book Company, 1972.

L'Art Culinaire Française. Paris: Ernest Flammarion, 1950 and 1976.

Beard, Glaser, Wolf Ltd. *The Cook's Catalogue.* New York: Harper & Row, 1975.

Berman, Matthew. *The How and Why of Candy Making.* Chicago: Emmet Boyles, 1925.

Campbell, Susan. *Cook's Tools.* New York: William Morrow and Company, Inc., 1980.

Casella, Dolores. *A World of Baking.* New York: David White, 1968.

Cook, L. Russell. *Chocolate Production and Use,* rev. Dr. E. H. Meursing. New York: Harcourt Brace Jovanovich, 1982.

Daniel, Albert R. *Bakery Materials and Methods.* London: Maclaren and Sons, 1947.

—. *Bakery Questions Answered.* London: Applied Sciences Publishers, 1972.

—. *Up-to-Date Confectionery.* London: Applied Sciences Publishers, 1978.

D'Ermo, Dominique. *The Modern Pastry Chef's Guide to Professional Baking.* New York: Harper & Row, 1962.

Fance, Wilfred J., ed. *The New International Confectioner.* Lugano-Castagnola, Switzerland: René Kramer, 1973.

—. *The Students' Technology of Breadmaking and Flour Confectionery.* London: Routledge and Kegan Paul, 1976.

Floris, Maria. *The Wine and Food Society's Guide to Bakery.* Cleveland: World Publishing Company, 1968.

Foods of the World, series. New York: Time-Life Inc.

Good Cook/Techniques and Recipes. New York: Time-Life, Inc.

Halliday, Evelyn G., and Isabel T. Noble. *Hows and Whys of Cooking.* Chicago: University of Chicago Press, 1933.

Hanneman, L. J., *Patisserie.* London: Heinemann, 1971.

Heatter, Maida. *Book of Great Desserts.* New York: Alfred A. Knopf, 1974.

Hopkins, Dennis M. *Simple but Effective Cake Decorating.* Chicago: Clissold Publishing Company, 1952.

Hughes, Osee. *Introductory Foods.* New York: Macmillan Company, 1950.

Kollist, E. J. *The Complete Patissier.* London: Maclaren and Sons.

Lenôtre, Gaston. *Lenôtre's Desserts and Pastries.* New York: Barron's, 1977.

—. *Lenôtre's Ice Cream and Candies.* New York: Barron's, 1979.

Lowe, Belle. *Experimental Cookery.* New York: John Wiley and Sons, 1943.

Mayer, Edward. *Wiener Süss-speisen.* Linz, Austria: Rudolf Trauner Verlag, 1968.

Minifie, Bernard W. *Chocolate, Cocoa and Confectionery.* Westport, Conn.: AVI Publishing Company, 1980.

Moller, Carl, Leo Madsen, and Helmut Rosenthal. *Danish Cakes.* London: Maclaren and Sons.

Morton, Marcia Colman. *The Art of Viennese Pastry.* New York: Doubleday 1969.

Pasquet, Ernest. *La Pâtisserie Familiale.* Paris: Flammarion, 1974.

Paul, Pauline C., and Helen H. Palmer. *Food Theory and Applications.* New York: John Wiley and Sons, 1972.

Peck, Paula. *The Art of Fine Baking.* New York: Simon & Schuster, 1961.

Pellaprat, Henri Pierre. *Les Desserts.* Paris: Jacques Kramer, 1937.

—. *Modern French Culinary Art.* Cleveland and New York: The World Publishing Co., 1966. Adapted for American kitchens by Avanelle Day.

Phillips, Bert J. *The Pastry Chef.* New York: A. S. Barnes, 1965.

Pomeranz, Yeshajahu, and J. A. Shellenberger. *Bread Science and Technology.* Westport, Conn.: AVI Publishing Company, 1971.

Pope, Antoinette. *The New Antoinette Pope School Cookbook.* New York: Macmillan Company, 1973.

Reich, Lilly Joss. *The Viennese Pastry Cookbook.* New York: Macmillan Company, 1970.

Storer, E. *The Complete Book of Marzipan.* London: Maclaren and Sons, 1969.

Sultan, William J. *Practical Baking.* Westport, Conn.: AVI Publishing Company, 1969.

Thuries, Yves. *Le Livre de Recettes d'un Compagnon du Tour de France.* Paris: Société Editor Cordes, 1983.

Ward, Artemas. *The Encyclopedia of Food.* New York: Peter Smith, 1941.

Wihlfahrt, J. E. *A Treatise on Baking.* New York: Fleischmann Company, 1928.

Index